D0212486

THE GREEKS ON PLEASURE

THE GREEKS ON PLEASURE

J. C. B. GOSLING

and

C. C. W. TAYLOR

CLARENDON PRESS · OXFORD
1982

JEROME LIBRARY–BOWLING GREEN STATE UNIVERSITY

Oxford University Press, Walton Street, Oxford OX2 6DP
London Glasgow New York Toronto
Delhi Bombay Calcutta Madras Karachi
Kuala Lumpur Singapore Hong Kong Tokyo
Nairobi Dar es Salaam Cape Town
Melbourne Auckland
and associates in
Beirut Berlin Ibadan Mexico City Nicosia

Published in the United States by
Oxford University Press, New York

© J. C. B. Gosling and C. C. W. Taylor 1982

All rights reserved. No part of this publication may be reproduced,
stored in a retrieval system, or transmitted, in any form or by any means,
electronic, mechanical, photocopying, recording, or otherwise, without
the prior permission of Oxford University Press

British Library Cataloguing in Publication Data
Gosling, J.C.B.
The Greeks on pleasure.
1. Philosophy, Ancient — History
2. Pleasure
I. Title   II. Taylor, C.C.W.
180'.938   B171
ISBN 0-19-824666-8

Library of Congress Cataloging in Publication Data
Gosling, J.C.B. (Justin Cyril Bertrand)
The Greeks on pleasure.
Bibliography: p.
Includes indexes.
1. Pleasure.   2. Philosophy, Ancient.   I. Taylor,
C.C.W. (Christopher Charles Whiston), 1936–
II. Title.
BJ1481.G636 1982   128   82-7940
ISBN 0-19-824666-8   AACR2

Typeset by Hope Services, Abingdon,
Printed in Great Britain,
at the University Press, Oxford
by Eric Buckley
Printer to the University

Preface

This work aims to provide a critical and analytical history of ancient Greek theories of the nature of pleasure and of its value and role in human life, from the earliest times down to the period of Epicurus and the early Stoics. While there have been many valuable studies of particular aspects of the topic, and several surveys of the treatment of pleasure by individual ancient writers (notably the monographs of Tenkku and Voigtländer on Plato, and Lieberg and Ricken on Aristotle), this is to our knowledge the first attempt at a comprehensive review of the contribution of the ancient Greeks to the theoretical understanding of pleasure. In view both of the central position which the major thinkers of the period accorded to the topic and of the inter-connectedness of many of their theories, it seemed to us that the lack of such a study was a lacuna in the literature which we should attempt to fill.

A co-operative work of philosophy is a bird of sufficient rarity to give a certain curiosity value to a brief account of its genesis. The work may be said to have had its long-distant beginnings in Taylor's B. Phil. thesis on Plato's treatment of pleasure, written in 1961–2 and extensively commented on by Gosling, who had already published on pleasure in the *Philebus*. Of that juvenile essay nothing survives in the present work beyond the author's interest in the topic. Subsequently both of us worked independently on pleasure as a philosophical topic in its own right and on various aspects of its treatment in ancient thought, and each contributed to the Clarendon Plato series a volume on a dialogue concerned with pleasure, of which traces will be discernible in the corresponding sections of this book. Community of interest and geographical proximity eventually suggested that collaboration was a rational procedure; the value of that suggestion must be subject to the verdict of our readers. While each chapter was originally drafted by one author, all were worked over, in some cases exhaustively, by both; consequently every part of the book is our joint responsibility.

Preliminary studies and drafts of various chapters have been read to meetings of the Southern Association for Ancient Philosophy and to seminars and colloquia in Oxford and elsewhere. A shortened version of chapter 17 was presented at the Seventh Congress of the International Federation of the Societies of Classical Studies in Budapest in 1979 and will, no doubt, one day appear in the proceedings of that congress. We are grateful to the participants in those discussions, whose criticisms have brought about many improvements. We owe especial acknowledgements to the editors of the Oxford University Press, who have combined tact with amiable persistence in forwarding the work and have done much to smooth the path of authorship. We are also indebted to the Press's reader for his helpful suggestions.

We assume that our readers will have a general familiarity with the works (particularly those of Plato and Aristotle) which we discuss, but have tried to make our detailed discussions of passages dealing with pleasure self-sufficient. No knowledge of Greek is assumed.

Reference to ancient authors are by abbreviated titles (see Abbreviations) or by fragments (see Collections of Fragments). In citing passages relating to Epicurus we generally give the number of the quotation in Usener as well as the ancient source. Evidence for the Stoics is cited by volume and quotation number in *SVF* as well as by the ancient source. Modern works are cited by author's surname alone, different works by the same author being distinguished by the addition of a numeral in parentheses; full references are given in the bibliography. This includes all works cited in the text, together with a few not cited, but nonetheless significant for anyone interested in the subject.

Oxford,					J. C. B. G.
October 1981					C. C. W. T.

Contents

Contents

Abbreviations

A. Ancient works

Aristotle

De An.	*De Anima*
EE	*Eudemian Ethics*
EN	*Nicomachean Ethics*
GA	*De Generatione Animalium*
GC	*De Generatione et Corruptione*
Met.	*Metaphysics*
Phys.	*Physics*
Rhet.	*Rhetoric*

Cic.	Cicero
Acad.	*Academica*
Fin.	*De Finibus*
Tusc.	*Tusculan Disputations*

DL	Diogenes Laertius

Epicurus

PD	*Principal Doctrines* (*Kuriai Doxai*)
VS	*Vatican Sentences*

Eusebius

PE	*Praeparatio Evangelica*

Plato

Apol.	*Apology*
Euthyd.	*Euthydemus*
Hp. Ma.	*Hippias Major*
Lach.	*Laches*
Ph.	*Phaedo*
Phil.	*Philebus*
Pol.	*Politicus*
Prot.	*Protagoras*
Rep.	*Republic*
Soph.	*Sophist*
Tht.	*Theaetetus*
Tim.	*Timaeus*

Plut.	Plutarch
Col.	*Against Colotes*

Non Posse	*That Epicurus Actually Makes A Pleasant Life Impossible* (*Non Posse Suaviter Vivi Secundum Epicurum*)

SE ·	Sextus Empiricus
M	*Against the Mathematicians*
P	*Outlines of Pyrrhonism*

| Stob. | Stobaeus (Cited by volume, page, and line of Wachsmuth's edition, Berlin, 1884) |

| | Theophrastus |
| *De sens.* | *On the Senses* |

| | Xenophon |
| *Mem.* | *Memorabilia* |

B. Modern Works

AGPh	*Archiv für Geschichte der Philosophie*
AJP	*American Journal of Philosophy*
APQ	*American Philosophical Quarterly*
CQ	*Classical Quarterly*
DK	H. Diels and W. Kranz eds., *Die Fragmente der Vorsokratiker*, 7th and subsequent eds., Berlin, 1954–
JHP	*Journal of the History of Philosophy*
JHS	*Journal of Hellenic Studies*
PAS	*Proceedings of the Aristotelian Society*
PASS	*Proceedings of the Aristotelian Society*, Supplementary Volume
Phron.	*Phronesis*
PQ	*Philosophical Quarterly*
PR	*Philosophical Review*
SVF	H. von Arnim ed., *Stoicorum Veterum Fragmenta*, 4 vols., Leipzig 1903–24, reprinted Stuttgart, 1964
U	H. Usener ed., *Epicurea*, Leipzig, 1887

Collections of Fragments

Fragments of ancient authors are cited from the following collections:

Antisthenes	Caizzi, F. D., *Antisthenis Fragmenta*, Varese — Milano, 1966
Aristippus	Mannebach, E., *Aristippi et Cyrenaicorum Fragmenta*, Leiden and Cologne, 1961
Aristotle	Ross, W. D., *Aristotelis Fragmenta Selecta*, Oxford, 1955
Damoxenus	Kock, T., *Comicorum Atticorum Fragmenta*, 3 vols., Leipzig, 1880–8
Democritus	DK
Empedocles	DK
Epicurus	Bailey, C., *Epicurus, The Extant Remains*, Oxford, 1926, reprinted Hildesheim and New York, 1970
Heracleides Ponticus	Wehrli, F., *Die Schule des Aristoteles* VII, Basel, 1953
Simonides	Page, D. L., *Poetae Melici Graeci*, Oxford, 1962
Solon	Diehl, E., *Anthologia Lyrica Graeca*, 3rd ed., Leipzig, 1949
Speusippus	Lang, P., *De Speusippi Academici Scriptis*, Frankfurt, 1964 (reprint)
Theophrastus	Wimmer, F., *Theophrasti Opera*, 3 vols., Leipzig, 1854–62

Introduction

0.0.1. On the face of it, if a course of action leads to distress for the agent it seems that the onus is on its proponent to give some good reason why one should do it. In many cases it is easy to show that apparently unpleasant courses of action lead to pleasure in the long term, and this has tempted philosophers at many periods to claim that one's pleasure is the only worthwhile goal or even the only goal that one has in life. The classical Greek period from Democritus to Epicurus and the early Stoics was no exception. In what follows we propose to examine the development of philosophical views on the nature of pleasure and the importance it does or should have in human life during this period. As philosophical doctrines the various forms that such hedonism might take did not come in for careful consideration before the time of Plato. Plato did not, however, invent the doctrines. Not all people are attracted to traditional moral ideals and some form of hedonism is liable to be an attractive alternative. There is evidence of this in pre-Platonic Greece and of reactions to it by early moralists. The material is not extensive, and, as one would expect of early positions, there are confusions and uncertainties which make sharp attributions of stance impossible. Confused though they may be, however, these positions set the scene for Plato's explorations, and influence his development. There were those who made the pleasures of the Life of Pleasure their goal in life, and those who thought some overall balance of pleasure over distress in life should be pursued. There were those who insisted on a contrast between a life of virtue and one of pleasure, and those who thought that a life of virtue was pleasanter than a life without it. There is also some evidence of the influence of a picture of pleasure derived from physiological theory, which saw pleasure as the restoration of a natural balance. Since some physiological views saw the body as having a

natural nisus towards its proper balance, towards its own
good in other words, this picture could be used to support an
equation of pleasure with the good. Further, there was an
attractive moral, or anti-moral, view which claimed that the
ideal was to be in a position to do what one wanted. A being's
nature was displayed in the direction in which it tended, and
so man's nature by man's desires. Their satisfaction is the
good towards which man tends, their thwarting by legal and
moral conventions a violation of nature. We would all prefer
to be free of these restrictions, if possible, free to satisfy our
desires. But desires are readily pictured as forms of distress,
seen on the physiological model as perceptions of disharmony
or imbalance in our nature, or even identified with that disharmony or imbalance itself. What they are directed to is the
restoration of balance. But that, of course, is pleasure. So this
ideal of being in a position to do what one wants can get
tangled with the physiological model so as to seem to lead to
hedonistic conclusions. Further, it is a view which leads one to
look upon law and morality as unnatural. Such a position relies
upon an attractive ideal that is not overtly hedonistic, and
can appeal to many to whom a life of pleasure as usually construed might seem effeminate; indeed it will now be the life of
virtue which seems weak. Consequently its support of hedonism would have added importance to that doctrine in the eyes
of someone who, like Plato, viewed the erosion of law and
as an evil, and one of the greatest dangers of his day.

0.0.2. Clearly, if this sketch is right, Plato was faced with
a mixed bag of positions on the relation of pleasure to virtue,
which should receive separate treatment and different reactions. Even if we confine ourselves to positions hostile to the
cultivation of such virtues as justice and self-control, there
are various promising lines to explore. One might, for instance,
avail oneself of the argument to hand, that really the life of
virtue is pleasanter than any alternative. Or one might contrast
reason, which is divine, with the irrationality of desire and
pleasure; then, since virtue sets its face against irrationality
it sets its face against pleasure. Or again, one might argue
that pleasure cannot be used in any intelligible way as a
criterion to decide between courses of action or ways of life;

consequently the opposition programme with its vaunted claims to intelligence must be a delusion.

0.0.3. Variations on all these themes will be found in Plato, and examination of them used to trace the developments in his views. It is a sad fact that our major source for the period during which Plato wrote, from the beginning of the fourth century until his death in 347 BC, is Plato himself, and that it largely concerns his own views. While there is strong evidence that many philosophers concerned themselves with questions of hedonism, evidence for the details of their views is tantalizingly slight. Plato himself, however, is a rewarding field of study. Like so many Greek philosophers he did not make a sharp division between purely academic and useful enquiries. His concern with hedonism, and indeed philosophy generally, arose from his analysis of the ills of society in his time and his view of the sources of those ills in human nature. The result was, undoubtedly, an increasing pessimism leading to views which had little hope of acceptance by his contemporaries. His own reactions were sharpened by the impact made on him by Socrates. This is clear in the early dialogues, and perhaps especially in the great dramatic middle dialogues, the *Phaedo* and *Symposium*. His admiration for Socrates and the trauma of Socrates' trial and execution have to be borne in mind in attempting to understand Plato's development, as also the social and political situation in Greece as they might strike someone of his aristocratic background. In addition one has to remember his experience of failure in making any political impact either in his home city of Athens, or in Syracuse where he was called to advise. All these factors are important for understanding Plato's philosophical development, and this latter is, of course, important for understanding his changing views on hedonism. It is part of our thesis that he started at the very least attracted to a form of hedonism which could be used to defend the traditional virtues. This, we argue, would seem to him true, in so far as it shows the life of virtue to be pleasanter than any other, to be polemically satisfying, in that it turns the tables neatly on some of his most formidable opponents, and would be in itself a plausible view to try. As time went on Plato acquired an increasingly dualistic thesis about the tension between the soul and the body, which led to a suspicion of the body and its pleasures, and made him unwilling to allow the pleasures of the body on the plus side in the same calculation with those of reason. In addition he changed his views on the role of reason and knowledge, and their importance, in ways which affected his approach to pleasure. At first, in the *Gorgias* and *Phaedo* he was left not knowing quite what to make of his earlier hedonistic views: as yet unwilling to drop their attractive aspects, he had no theory of pleasure which would enable him to keep them while giving way to his new-found distaste for the body. The *Republic* is a classic Platonic *tour de force*: a theory of pleasure is devised which promises to fit all the desirable facets of the early hedonism into the new pessimism. Both internal difficulties, however, and developments on the general philosophical front led to the abandonment of the theory of the *Republic* and the greater sophistication of the *Philebus*.

0.0.4. While the social/economic background and Plato's general philosophical development are, in the ways indicated, important for a full understanding of his changing views on pleasure, we have tried, so far as possible, to confine ourselves to problems arising from that topic itself. Anyone who reflects on the size of the book will, we hope, sympathize, if, indeed, they are not relieved. The wider context should, however, be borne in mind, and we are aware that at various points our thesis relies on assumptions about it which might well not be granted.

0.0.5. To resume the sketch of our theme: we argue that Plato was early on much influenced by a physiological model of pleasure of the sort already mentioned, and that this restricted his treatment of the subject up to and including the *Republic*. Some time after that, possibly under the impact of Eudoxus' hedonistic views, there seems to have been an up-surge of controversy on the subject, to which the *Philebus* is probably a reaction. At this stage Plato is laying great stress on the variety of pleasures, a point which he seems to consider important against hedonism, and is also both treating a wider range of examples and supplying more detailed analyses.

0.0.6. The general picture is one of a move from an early hedonism, through a stage where he hoped to show that although the good life is not good because pleasant, still it is possible to show that the pleasantest life and the best are identical, to a final stage where the criterion of pleasantness cannot be used to determine any life as pleasantest. This final position is probably part of a reaction to Eudoxus, and is reached through a thesis that pleasures differ from each other radically in kind, some kinds even being opposed to others. Plato seems to have thought that this would show that we need a criterion for the choice of the right combination of pleasures and that there will be no notion of greatest pleasure to play this role.

0.0.7. This opposition of Plato and Eudoxus sets the stage for Aristotle. For the period down to Aristotle's death in 322 the main source is Aristotle himself who, like Plato, tells us comparatively little about the treatment of pleasure by other philosophers. The literature on Aristotle's *Ethics* does, indeed, commonly suggest that we can also learn a good deal about Plato's successor Speusippus, but we hope to reduce enthusiasm for that view. The early evidence on Aristotle suggests someone struggling away from Plato. Book X of the *Nicomachean Ethics* can be seen as a brilliant attempt to retain a Eudoxan thesis while taking account of Platonic criticisms. So far as we can see there is no difference of philosophical position between Books X and VII, though there is a considerable difference of opponents. Consideration of these differences, and the not too reliable evidence about developments in the Academy and elsewhere, suggests that it is at least as likely that Book VII is the later treatment as that it is the earlier.

0.0.8. Both Plato and Aristotle try in different ways to secure the conclusion that only the good man experiences the pleasantest life because his activities are pleasantest. Not only are these interesting manoeuvres in themselves, but they bring out how unconvincing both were likely to be to their contemporaries. Aristotle's ecstatic language about the delights of philosophizing is not likely to arouse an answering echo among many practitioners, let alone among non-philosophers. Plato's and Aristotle's intellectual feats can only win one's admiration, but a cool look at the results enables one to understand how Epicurus might have seemed more in contact with the subject. For if we are right, Epicurus was not advocating the pursuit of some passionless state which could only be called one of pleasure in order to defend a paradox. Rather he was advocating a life where pain is excluded and we are left with familiar physical pleasures. The resultant life may be simple, but it is straightforwardly pleasant.

0.0.9. Throughout the period it is notable that, among those philosophers who have survived, flirtation with hedonism, or more, seems to have been the fashion. So far as we can make out, most attacks on hedonism are directed at advocates of bodily pleasure. It is not until the time of the later Plato and of Aristotle that we start getting evidence of views of pleasure as something bad in itself. Even the Stoics, who are popularly regarded as a very severe school, were surprisingly tolerant. They regarded pleasure, properly so called, not as bad, but as indifferent, and distinguished from it the rational joy of the good in their virtuous activity, accounting the latter an element, admittedly subsidiary, in the good life. Generally, a tolerant attitude to the more respectable pleasures predominates.

0.0.10. Also running through the period is a tendency to relate views on pleasure, its nature as well as its value, to views about the human and/or animal organism. This leads to interesting obscurities as to whether pleasure or good states are playing the role of determinant of value.

0.0.11. Historically there is no doubt that the philosophers of this period, especially Plato and Aristotle, have been very influential on developments in the philosophical treatment of pleasure by Anglo-Saxon philosophers over the past thirty years. This influence, philosophically fruitful though it has undoubtedly been, contains an element of misinterpretation, in that it has suggested that the aims of the ancient writers were closer to those of modern analytic philosophers than in fact they were. The ancient philosophers were not interested primarily in conceptual analysis, nor in how words work. So far as pleasure is concerned, their predominant aim was to isolate those conditions of the organism necessary and sufficient for the occurrence of (real) pleasure. One of the interests of studying them is to see how different is their view of their enterprise and so how different their practice.

0.0.12. So much for the general picture. Now for the details.

Chapter 1

The Background

1.0.1. With the possible exception of Democritus, no Greek writer before Plato seems to have made pleasure a central topic for discussion. In so far as earlier writers dealt with it incidentally, their thought is dominated by two main traditions. On the one hand there is the didactic tradition represented by e.g. Hesiod, Theognis, and the accumulated folk wisdom associated with the Seven Sages, a tradition which was developed, rather than radically transformed, by the fifth-century sophists. Writers in this tradition are concerned with moral and practical exhortation, in isolation from any theoretical interest. Hence their treatment of pleasure is, broadly, restricted to fairly unsystematic reflections on the value of pleasure in human life, together with direct moral exhortation on how to act with respect to pleasure, without any attempt to derive those maxims and reflections from any comprehensive theory of human life, or any theory of the nature of pleasure. On the other hand we have the scientific tradition of the pre-Socratic philosophers, in whose work pleasure is seen, in common with all other aspects of human life, primarily as a phenomenon to be incorporated in a comprehensive proto-scientific theory, and specifically as a subject for physiological explanation. While the didactic writers were concerned almost exclusively with questions like 'Are any pleasures to be avoided?', the meagre evidence for the scientific writers gives no hint of any moral or practical concern, or even of interest in the part which pleasure plays in the explanation of action. As far as our evidence goes, they confined themselves to the question 'What is pleasure?', i.e. to the investigation (or rather postulation) of physiological processes assumed to account for pleasure in the same way as similar processes were supposed to account for e.g. respiration or perception. (Questions as to whether pleasure is literally identical with any such process, or is rather a purely psychological state or entity produced by a distinct physical cause, were not raised at this stage; some of these problems will be discussed in connection with various passages in Plato and Aristotle.) Diverse though these traditions were in their origins and their focus of interest, we can find evidence in Plato not merely of the influence of both, but also of the integration of elements of both within a single theory. Medical theory seems to have played a significant part in thus linking the two traditions. The outline thus sketched must now be filled in.

1. The didactic tradition

1.1.1. The use of the term 'tradition' is not intended to suggest total or even virtual unanimity on the part of Greek didactic writers in their attitudes to pleasure. Rather the term conveys the accumulation, via the activity of generations of authoritative figures, poets, sages, and lawgivers, of an accepted stock of practical wisdom, whose content, though dominated indeed by a particular outlook, which had specific implications for pleasure, nevertheless admitted considerable diversity. Thus some passages of Theognis advocate whole-hearted enjoyment of the pleasures of the moment; a striking expression of this mood is given in lines 983–5

Let us give our mind up to merry-making, while it can yet endure the lovely deeds of joy: for splendid youth is over as quick as thought. (Cf. 877–8, 1047–8, 1063–8).

Similarly, the widely-respected Simonides can say (fr. 79, Page) that not even the life of the gods is worth living without pleasure. (It is likely that the poet has in mind not the rarified pleasures of an Aristotelian deity absorbed in self-contemplation, but the robust pleasures of sex, feasting, etc. which the Homeric gods enjoy.) In these passages, then, we have the expression of the view that pleasures, and in particular the bodily pleasures of feasting and sex, are worth having in themselves, and perhaps even what make life as a whole worth living. Yet this uncritical hedonism is not by any means the dominant theme in the didactic tradition. It is indeed true that expressions of extreme asceticism, which condemns, if not all pleasure, at least bodily pleasures as totally bad, are even rarer. Indeed that extreme view hardly belongs to the main stream of the tradition at all, since the evidence for it is virtually confined to Iamblichus' account of the teaching of the Pythagoreans, who founded an ascetic way of life on the assumption that the real self was a discarnate soul, condemned to a succession of reincarnations to atone for the sins of a previous existence and ever struggling to escape from its bodily fetters (DK 58 C 4, §85; 58 D 8, §204). While this picture of the soul, with its accompanying image of bodily pleasure as a fetter shackling the soul to its bodily prison, was an important influence on at least one stage of Plato's thought (see Chapter 5), its wholesale condemnation of bodily pleasures finds comparatively few echoes in other writers. Perhaps the best-known was Antisthenes, a pupil of Socrates, who was celebrated for saying that he would rather go mad than feel pleasure (frs. 108 A–F, 109 B), and that if he could get hold of Aphrodite he would shoot her full of arrows for all the harm she had done (frs. 109 A–B). Yet even this violent hostility seems to have been directed against bodily pleasure not as such but on the traditional ground that such pleasure causes distress (frs. 110, 112-16), while he seems to have been prepared to recommend or at least to accept the pleasures of the simple life (frs. 113, 117).[1] While neither of these extreme positions was without its influence on subsequent thought (e.g. the positions of Callicles and Philebus show some signs of unreflective hedonism), nevertheless the prevailing attitude to pleasure in the didactic tradition was an intermediate one.

1.1.2. This attitude was a reflection of a generally accepted picture of how a man should live, a picture which integrated elements of diverse origin into a fairly coherent ideal. In Homeric times excellence (*aretē*), i.e. those qualities which made a man outstanding, consisted primarily of qualities characteristic of aristocratic birth, namely prowess in warfare, practical shrewdness, and personal splendour. While this ideal was considerably civilized in the sixth and fifth centuries by a

[1] Cf. Lieberg p.61.

greater emphasis on the co-operative virtues of fair-dealing, truthfulness and self-restraint, it or its descendant continued to exert some influence. Thus it is clear from the *Protagoras* (e.g. 316b–c) that the ideal of the man who gets to the top in the city-state through his outstanding qualities of intellect and personality had strong attractions for ambitious young men. Yet while Protagoras claims to be able to impart those qualities by instruction, the details of his programme put much more stress on fair-dealing and right-mindedness (*sōphrosunē*, a word originally meaning 'soundness of mind', which has strong connotations of self-restraint and respect for others), and he accepts without question a specification of total human excellence as consisting in intellectual merit (*sophia*), piety or religion, courage, right-mindedness, and fairness. In so far as this ideal of the all-round man represents an amalgamation of the best qualities of the aristocratic hero and the dutiful, selfless citizen, courage or manliness (*andreia*, usually rendered 'courage' is literally 'manliness') is essential to either aspect. The Homeric hero must obviously be tough and courageous; but equally the good citizen must be prepared to stand fast in the hoplite ranks. So when Thucydides in his Funeral Speech (II. 37–40) portrays Pericles as offering an ideal of the well-rounded Athenian, he takes care to claim that the true democrat will be as brave as a Spartan innured to war and hardship from youth, and that though he loves wisdom, he loves it without unmanliness.

1.1.3. In this context, pleasure, which we have already seen to be commonly exemplified by bodily pleasures such as those of feasting, sex, soft clothes, and in general ease, is likely to be viewed with suspicion as something soft and unmanly, a distraction from the arduous path of virtue. Thus in Xenophon's *Memorabilia* (II. i. 21–34) we find a fable attributed to the sophist Prodicus (later fifth century BC), in which Heracles, the epitome of the manly hero, is approached successively by Wickedness (*kakia*) and Virtue (*aretē*), each offering him a kind of life. Wickedness offers a life of pleasure, i.e. of luxury, which is distinguished from the life of excellence or virtue by its softness and unwillingness to undergo hardship.

1.1.4. But the notion of the arduousness of the life of excellence, and the consequent suspicion of the easy choice of pleasures, had wider application than merely to physical courage and endurance. In the earliest expression of this idea, Hesiod says (*Works and Days* 287-92) that wickedness lives near at hand, and the way to it is smooth, but excellence dwells far away up a rough, steep path, and the gods make a man sweat before he achieves it. The context suggests that the poet may have in mind either of two thoughts, not totally unrelated: firstly, that a man must work hard to achieve prosperity and status, and secondly, that it requires effort to avoid the many temptations to unrighteousness. The two thoughts are connected, in that the prosperous man is not tempted to cheat and steal in order to keep alive (cf. Theognis 373-92). The fragility of human excellence, and the consequent necessity of strenuous efforts to keep to the strait and narrow path, especially by the avoidance of excess either in self-assertion or self-indulgence, is a recurrent theme in didactic poetry (e.g. Solon fr. 4 Diehl, lines 6-10; Theognis 497-8, 605-6, 693-4), and is one of the keynotes of the collection of *Maxims of the Seven Sages* preserved by the fourth-century writer Demetrius of Phaleron (DK 10,3). (Since Plato refers to the existence of such collections (*Prot.* 343a-b), quoting some maxims which actually appear in Demetrius' collection, it is likely that it reflects the tradition with reasonable fidelity.) In this context pleasure is treated with, to say the least, some reserve; the three maxims which mention it directly run 'Control pleasure', 'Avoid pleasure which brings distress', and 'Pleasures are mortal, but virtues are immortal'. Here the emphasis is on pleasure as transitory, and therefore less worth having than virtue, with which it is contrasted, as producing unpleasant consequences and as a force which needs to be controlled. Pleasure (still thought of primarily as bodily pleasure) is subject, if not to outright condemnation, at least to grave suspicion.

1.1.5. We must, however, guard against overemphasis. Firstly, the scarcity of direct references to pleasure, whether in the didactic poets or in the *Maxims*, suggests that it was not a central focus of interest. Secondly, to set against the mainly

negative picture which we have so far sketched, there are
some indications that the fourth and fifth-century moralistic
writers were developing greater awareness both of the complexity and of the value of pleasure. One of the maxims just
quoted, 'Avoid pleasure which brings distress' (attributed to
Solon) may be taken as showing the first stage of this development. For it conveys a recognition that there are different
kinds of pleasures, some indeed to be avoided because of
their unpleasant consequences, which implies that others,
which do not have those consequences, need not be avoided.
Further, a formulation like this naturally provokes the
question (which need not have occurred to its author)
whether there are any other reasons for avoiding pleasures
than the fact that some pleasures have unpleasant consequences. Some of these developments are indicated, rather
than explicitly stated, in Prodicus' story of Heracles, mentioned above. After Vice has attempted to allure Heracles
with offers of bodily pleasures, Virtue replies that no matter
what one wants, be it wealth, friendship, victory in war, or
whatever, one has to work hard for it. When Vice repeats that
this way is difficult, whereas hers is easy and pleasant, Virtue
replies that ultimately her way of life is pleasanter, since it
not only allows real enjoyment of bodily pleasures, but also
produces the pleasures of good reputation and friendship,
whereas vice stores up all kinds of unpleasantness for itself.
Two points in particular stand out. Firstly the distinction
between the immediate pleasantness of something (e.g.
having a drink) and its long-term consequences is of central
importance. Secondly, the long-term consequences of the
virtuous life are recommended primarily on the grounds that
they are pleasanter than their competitors. It is not indeed
explicitly stated nor clearly implied that the virtuous life is
better than the luxurious life *because* it is in the long run
pleasanter. The fable does not presuppose any developed
theory of the nature of goodness or of the relation between
goodness and pleasure. But firstly it plainly contains the
statement that the conventionally virtuous life is pleasanter
than the life of luxury, and secondly it presupposes that the
best, if not necessarily the only way to show the virtuous life
to be *desirable* is to show that it is pleasanter. We need only

the further assumptions that something can be shown to be desirable only by specifying what makes it desirable, and that what makes it desirable is identical with what makes it good, to arrive at a version of evaluative hedonism, viz., that what makes a given kind of life better than another is that it is in the long run pleasanter. That view, with the implication that what makes a particular action or experience better than another is that it contributes more to a life that is in the long run pleasanter, is certainly presented by Socrates in the *Protagoras* as one which the man in the street can be induced to accept. We may accept Plato's evidence (a) that hedonistic theories of value had in fact been formulated by his time and (b) that it was not obviously implausible to represent these as acceptable to the ordinary man. If this is correct, then we may take the proto-hedonism of the fable as illustrating — first by its formulation by a sophist and then by its transmission by a writer of conventional views — the process by which untheoretical hedonism became part of the general climate of opinion.

1.1.6. There are important differences between this and the unreflective hedonism mentioned earlier. While the latter tends to restrict pleasure to bodily pleasure and to assume that it is the pleasure of the moment which makes an action worthwhile, the message of the fable of Heracles is firstly that there are pleasures, such as those of having a good reputation, which are at least as significant as bodily pleasures, and more importantly, that what is valuable is not the pleasure of the moment but the long-term pleasantness of one's life. Hence while unreflective pursuit of pleasure undermines the control of life by reason, the 'hedonism' advocated by Prodicus and Xenophon must emphasize the rational direction of life, since it requires the weighing up of long-term effects with a view to the best organization of one's life as a whole. Again, since it requires the modification and in some cases total renunciation of immediate satisfactions in favour of long-term pleasure, it can incorporate the traditional wisdom on the necessity for moderation, which is rejected by unreflective hedonism. Immediate pleasure can still be seen as a dangerous attraction, leading one to ignore or put aside considerations of long-term welfare.

1.1.7. By the early fourth century, then, Greek didactic thought had incorporated some elements favourable to hedonism. This was not especially revolutionary, since these elements allowed or even required insistence on the traditional virtues of practical wisdom, courage and moderation. Nor did that aspect of didactic thought itself depend on any explicit theory. But since it is not likely that in a speculative and critical age moral thought should develop entirely independently of theory, we have now to consider the development of the theoretical treatment of pleasure prior to Plato.

2. The physiological tradition

1.2.1. Theories of the nature of pleasure are attributed to three major figures in fifth-century thought: Empedocles, Anaxagoras, and Diogenes of Apollonia. In each case our main source is Theophrastus' *On the Senses*, where Theoprastus appends a brief note on their treatment of pleasure to his more extended account of their theories of perception. (In fact, the Greek term *aisthēsis*, which is the classificatory term used by Theophrastus, conveys no clear distinction between perception and sensation; see below.) This arrangement of subject-matter reflects Theophrastus' view of the content of the theories in question; he states that both Empedocles and Anaxagoras regard pleasure and pain as either kinds of *aisthēsis* or as always associated with *aisthēsis* (*De sens.* 16; DK 31 A 86 §16). The classification of pleasure and pain as kinds of *aisthēsis* is found also in Plato (*Tht.* 156b, and perhaps also *Tim.* 64a–65b). It is however unclear just what it means to classify pleasure as a kind of *aisthēsis*. In the passages from Theophrastus and Plato just cited pleasure is listed along with sight, hearing, etc., which are plainly sorts of perception, i.e. ways of acquiring information about the external world via the impact of external things on various bodily organs. Now while in fact it seems impossible to regard enjoyment as literally a form of perception (e.g. enjoying doing mental arithmetic cannot be thought of as a kind of perception of the external world), it might be suggested that early thinkers were led into this mistake by concentration on certain simple and obvious examples; thus one might think of enjoying one's food as perceiving a special quality of one's food (its niceness, so to speak), on the analogy of taste or smell. So despite the philosophical inadequacy of an account of pleasure as a sort of perception, Theoprastus might have intended just that as his account of the views of Empedocles and Anaxagoras on pleasure.

1.2.2. In order to be justified in rendering *aisthēsis* in these contexts as 'perception', with its modern connotation of 'source of knowledge of what is external to the perceiver', we should have to find evidence that writers using the word do so in and only in contexts which fit, or which they may plausibly be supposed to have thought to fit, that connotation. That evidence is lacking. Thus in the context which contains the *Theaetetus* passage already mentioned, not merely pleasures, pains, desires, and fears, but also dreams are classed as *aisthēseis*. Further, some uses of '*aisthēsis*' should apparently be rendered 'feeling' (depending on context, in the sense either of 'emotion' or of 'bodily sensation') rather than 'perception': thus Orestes in Euripides' *Electra* (ll. 290–1) says that *aisthēsis* from other men's woes gnaws at mortals, i.e. one feels the pain of others' woes. Again, at *Tht.* 167b–c Protagoras says that, when plants are unhealthy, the farmer tries to get rid of their bad *aisthēseis* and give them healthy ones instead; the analogy with the doctor in this passage makes it plain that the plants are thought of as feeling ill, and being made to feel better.[2] Thus it appears that *aisthēsis* should be taken as having an undifferentiated use, covering both 'perception' and 'internal impression', similar to 'perception' in eighteenth-century English.[3] The thesis that Empedocles and Anaxagoras regarded pleasure as a kind of *aisthēsis*, or alternatively as something always accompanying *aisthēsis*, will then be undifferentiated between the thesis that they regarded it as a kind of perception and the thesis that they regarded it as a kind of internal impression,

[2] The statement in Ch. 9 of the Hippocratic treatise *On Ancient Medicine* that the doctor has no more precise measure of the correctness of his treatment than *tou sōmatos tēn aisthēsin* appears ambiguous between 'he has nothing to go on but the patient's bodily feelings' and 'he has nothing to go on but his perception of the patient's bodily condition'. See also *Aphorisms* II.6
[3] Cf. Hamlyn, Ch. I.

as something 'perceived' rather than a perceiving of something.

1.2.3. We should here note one peculiarity of Greek idiom which might tend to facilitate the treatment of pleasure as an object of perception. This is the use of *hēdonē*, the normal prose word for 'pleasure' in the sense of 'taste' and 'smell', found for example in fragment 67 of Heraclitus (DK 22 B 67) '. . . fire, when it is mingled with incenses, is named according to the smell of each' (*kath hēdonēn hekastou*) and fragment 4 of Anaxagoras (DK 59 B 4), '. . . seeds of all things, with all kinds of shapes and colours and *hēdonas*' where the context appears indifferent between 'flavours' and 'smells'. It is possible that this usage reflects a view of particular tastes and smells as modes of pleasantness and unpleasantness. This connection is clearly seen in a passage from the Hippocratic treatise *On Regimen* (I 23), where pleasantness and unpleasantness are listed as the objects of taste on a parallel with sounds as the objects of hearing and smells as the objects of the sense of smell. We should not, however, be led by this idiomatic feature to suppose that the fifth-century thinkers regarded pleasure as an object of perception *rather than* as a kind of perception; rather, these facts are adduced to show that, given an undifferentiated concept of *aisthēsis*, that aspect of the concept corresponding to our 'object of perception' should not be overlooked.[4]

1.2.4. The question whether the fifth-century thinkers thought of pleasure as something mental or something physical is another question which admits of no definite answer. Firstly, the physical/non-physical dichotomy was not sharply formulated in that period. Secondly, we lack sufficient detailed evidence of their views on pleasure to allow us to apply the modern concepts 'mental', 'physical', and 'non-physical' to them. The fact that they explained pleasure in physical terms does not settle the matter, for that raises the

[4] Note that we possess no evidence of the use of the term *aisthēsis* by Empedocles, Anaxagoras, or Diogenes themselves. It is argued here that since the use of the word in the fifth and fourth centuries indicates that it expresses an undifferentiated concept, it is likely that those writers thought of perception and related topics in terms of that concept, whether or not they expressed it by the word *aisthēsis*.

further questions of just how they conceived the relation between *explanans* and *explanandum*. The fact that Theophrastus, who read their works at first hand, was unable to decide whether pleasure was described as literally identical with various physical processes or as something over and above them is sufficient evidence that the relation between *explanans* and *explanandum* was not clearly set out.

1.2.5. We shall confine detailed consideration to the view of Empedocles, since the evidence for Anaxagoras and Diogenes is too meagre to allow any worthwhile conclusions to be drawn. For Empedocles the fundamental physiological process was the action on particles of the four elements composing the body (earth, air, fire, and water) of particles of the same elements composing the external world (earth acting on earth etc.). This process, which was a special instance of one of Empedocles' fundamental cosmological principles, that like acts on like, was posited to account alike for thought, perception, and pleasure (DK 31 B 106-9); it is this common pattern of explanation which leads Aristotle (*De an.* 427a21-9) to cite Empedocles as an example of the tendency of early theorists to identify thought and perception. But according to Theophrastus (*De sens.* 2; DK 31 A 86, §2), Empedocles, unlike other early thinkers, did not rest content with a general formula like 'Perception is caused by like acting on like', but made some attempt to fill in the details of the workings of the particular senses. One particular feature of his account of vision, mentioned in passing by Theophrastus (*De sens.* 8), may have some significance in relation to his view of pleasure. While some details of text and interpretation are obscure (see Guthrie II, pp. 234-8), the main outline of the theory is plain: vision occurs when particles of fire and water, shot out from the eye like the light from a lantern, join up with similar particles emitted from the objects round about to form physical images which are then transmitted back to the eye, where they are physically 'picked up' by fitting into pores or channels leading from the eye to the organ of sensation, which Empedocles thought was the blood round the heart. It was essential to this process that the amounts of the elements emitted by the eye and the object seen should be properly proportioned to one another; one can see neither if the object sends out too much water and not enough fire (for then there will be too much shadow or darkness and not enough illumination), nor if it sends out too much fire and not enough water (for then the light will be dazzling). Here Empedocles is appealing to another fundamental cosmological principle, viz. that the existence and functioning of organic substances requires a mixture of elements in proper proportion, the proportion differing for each kind of stuff (DK 31 B 96 and 98; cf. Guthrie II, pp.211–16). According to this principle, perception occurs when the amounts of the elements emitted by the eye and object complement each other, so as to produce the right amount of each element, i.e. each may be said to make up the deficiency in the other. This, according to Theophrastus, is how Empedocles explained why some animals see better by day and others better in the dark; those that have less fire in the eye see better by day, when the smaller amount of fire emitted from the eye is made up to the right amount by the greater quantity of fire emitted by objects, and those who have less water in the eye see better by night, 'for they too have the deficiency made up' (*epanaplērousthai kai toutois to endees*). The relevance of this to pleasure is that this passage provides clear evidence from Theophrastus that Empedocles treated at least one form of *aisthēsis* as involving the making up of a deficiency, and thus strengthens the evidence, otherwise somewhat weak (see below), that he described pleasure itself, which, as we have seen, he closely associated with *aisthēsis*, in the same terms.

1.2.6. Theophrastus himself says merely (*De sens.* 9) that Empedocles held that pleasure occurs when like elements act on like, according to the constitution of the different parts of the percipient, and distress when unlike elements interact. If this were indeed all we had to go on we should have to agree with Theophrastus that on Empedocles' theory it is quite obscure why not all acts of perception are pleasant, a point which might be generalized to raise the question why, on that view, not all organic functioning is pleasant. What is needed is some more specific account of pleasure, which will explain why, out of the range of organic functions which involve the action of like on like, pleasure is associated with some rather than others. We find at least a hint of this in two notes on Empedocles' view of pleasure, one in the writer of the fifth century AD John Stobaeus, the other in a summary of earlier views attributed to Plutarch; both are based on a compilation of the second century AD, itself derived indirectly from Theophrastus (DK 31 A 95; for further details see Kirk and Raven, pp. 1–7). The first passage runs 'Empedocles says that pleasures occur by [or perhaps 'to'] likes from likes, and according to what is deficient with a view to the filling up, so that that which is deficient (has) the desire for the like'. The point is put rather more straightforwardly in the second passage: 'Empedocles says that desires arise in living things from their deficiencies in the elements which make each other complete, and pleasures from what is appropriate, according to the mixtures of things which are like and of like natures, and pains and sufferings from what is inappropriate'.[5] The picture here presented is that of a normal (in the evaluative sense) or complete state of the organism, consisting of a balance of the four elements composing it. When this balance is disturbed, producing a deficiency of one element, there is a natural impulse to rectify it by assimilating more of the deficient element, and this process of making up the deficiency is pleasant. This model has many attractive features. Firstly, it lends itself to very simple observational confirmation: e.g. when there is a deficiency of the moist element in the body the lack is felt as a desire to rectify the balance by drinking, and the process of drinking is itself pleasant. Secondly, it goes some way to providing the necessary differentiation of pleasure from other physiological processes such as perception; one might argue that pleasure is associated, not with every instance of like acting on like, but specifically where like acts on like in accordance with the natural impulse of the organism to seek its own state of well-being or completion. Thirdly, in emphasizing this differentiating feature of pleasure it gives at least a rudimentary account of its action-influencing role, a feature which is neglected in the

[5] The above translates H. Diels' restoration of a severely corrupt text. The manuscripts do, however, preserve uncorrupted 'Empedocles . . . complete'.

simple treatment of pleasure as a kind of *aisthēsis*. Someone who is puzzled why, if pleasure is merely one among a number of essentially similar physiological processes, it is such a particularly potent stimulus to action, can now be told that the urge towards pleasure is in fact the natural instinct of the organism to seek its own best state, an explanation which fits the broadly teleological cast of Empedocles' cosmological theory. This kind of view is of obvious interest to those who are concerned with pleasure in its relation to conduct. Thus on the one hand it could be argued that, if pleasure is the process by which the organism attains its best state, the right way to live is to try for as much pleasure as possible. On the other hand, one could appeal to the same theory to argue that, since pleasure requires that the best state, i.e. the state of balance, has been lost and must be regained, the best life consists in the preservation of that state of balance as far as possible, i.e. ideally in a life which eliminates the necessity of both desire and pleasure. As we shall see, this controversy was of central interest to Plato. Hence if these passages do express Empedocles' actual thought they show that he represents a significant stage both in the merging of the physiological and didactic traditions and in the development of the controversies on pleasure with which we shall be chiefly concerned.

1.2.7. The qualification is necessary, since the testimony cited is not altogether immune from suspicion. Firstly, it is disquieting that we have no direct testimony from Theophrastus for Empedocles' having described pleasure in terms of the filling up of a deficiency. In view of this silence, the very coincidence with Platonic discussions noted above must arouse suspicion that a later writer may have been influenced by his memory of those discussions to fill in a gap in Theophrastus' account with a little theorizing as to what Empedocles might have said. But Theophrastus does not undertake detailed discussion of any early theory of pleasure; such discussion would be irrelevant to his main theme, which leads him to mention pleasure at all only to the extent to which early thinkers treated pleasure as an adjunct to their theories of perception. Secondly, we have already seen that Empedocles applied the deficiency-replenishment analysis to one case of perception and that that analysis fits naturally into the structure of his general theory. Thirdly, there is independent evidence that this model of organic functioning was developed in the fifth century and had attained considerable influence by the time of Plato. So even if we were doubtful about attributing such a view to Empedocles, we should have to attribute it to someone or other in the fifth century. But, for the reasons just given, the attribution of the view to Empedocles seems reasonably secure. It is neither necessary nor possible to determine whether he originated it.

1.2.8. Apart from Empedocles, the earliest thinker said to have held this kind of view is Alcmaeon of Croton, whose date is disputed, but who is most safely treated as a contemporary, perhaps slightly older, of Empedocles. A summary of his physiological theory, which may preserve some of his own words (DK 24 B 4), runs as follows: health is preserved by equilibrium (*isonomia*, literally equality before the law, or political equality) of the 'powers' in the body, hot, cold, wet, dry, bitter, sweet etc., and disease is produced by the predominance (*monarchia*, literally monarchy) of any of them. We have here a summary of the physiological theory which is presupposed in many of the writings ascribed to the Hippocratic school of medicine, which attained pre-eminence in the later fifth and fourth centuries. Health consists in a balance of elements making up the body; there is dispute over what and how many these are, and whether they are identical with observable constituents such as blood and bile, but the general theory is unchallenged. Disease occurs when the balance is upset, producing an excess or a deficiency of one or more elements; hence treatment characteristically takes the form of an attempt to restore the balance, either by making up a deficiency by special diet, or by getting rid of an excess by some form of purge. (For representative texts see e.g. *On the Nature of Man*, esp. Ch. 2–4 and 9; *On Breaths*, Ch. 1; *On Regimen*, I.2; *On Ancient Medicine*, Ch. 16; further examples cited by Lloyd.) While there is much dispute over the dating of particular Hippocratic texts, it is generally agreed that some at least belong to the fifth century (see Lloyd), and we can see from the speech of Eryximachus in Plato's *Symposium* (esp. 186a–e and 188a–b) that the central idea of the theory was expected to be familiar to the ordinary reader;[6] we are, therefore, entitled to accept this picture of man as forming part of the accepted background to Plato's thought.

1.2.9. Now while the medical writers have very little to say about pleasure as such (naturally enough, since pleasure, unlike pain, is not in general a clinically significant symptom), we have already seen how this model of human functioning can have implications for theories about the nature and value of pleasure. Firstly, since pain and in general distress arise from an imbalance of elements, it is natural to regard pleasure, which seems intuitively to be in some sense opposite to distress, as arising from the restoration of the correct balance, especially when that association receives empirical confirmation from such everyday cases as that of slaking one's thirst. (In fact there are other observations, equally obvious, which fail to confirm the theory; thus if pleasure is, or is caused by the process of getting rid of, an unpleasant state of imbalance, the theory would lead one to expect that processes of evacuation would be just as pleasant as those of eating and drinking. But vomiting for example is not normally pleasant. It is, however, not uncharacteristic of theories to concentrate on favourable examples to the exclusion of unfavourable ones.) Secondly, bodily appetites, such as hunger, which in terms of the theory either are or are caused by states of imbalance, are sometimes assimilated to diseased states, since 'imbalance of bodily elements' is the theory's general account of disease (*On Breaths* Ch. 1). This assimilation provides powerful ammunition for attacks on bodily desires and their associated pleasures, as we see from Plato's discussions in *Gorgias*, *Republic*, and *Philebus*. On the other hand, a teleologically-slanted theory would naturally interpret pleasure as a sign that the organism was working properly, in so far as it was satisfying its natural impulse to

---

[6] Note in particular that love is seen as a physical impulse causing the bodily elements to unite.

seek its own best state. Though the medical writings themselves contain few evaluative pronouncements, we have seen
some hints of this position in Empedocles, and it certainly
could be used to support the view that man, and living
creatures generally, are naturally directed towards pleasure.
(In fact we see from the *Philebus* (e.g. 11b) that some
hedonists attached great importance to the universal impulse
towards pleasure, though there is no evidence that they
supported that thesis by arguments from medical theory.)
Finally, the lack of a clear distinction between a bodily
deficiency, e.g. lack of food, and the corresponding desire,
i.e. desire for food (an association facilitated by the use of
terms such as 'hunger', 'thirst' and their Greek equivalents,
which straddle the two concepts), leads to a view of pleasure
as consisting indifferently in the satisfaction of either, and
as being indifferently the end towards which the organism
tends and its intentionally pursued objective.

1.2.10. By the time of Plato, then, the tradition of physiological theorizing about human nature, itself for the most
part evaluatively neutral, had led to the development of a
widely accepted picture of pleasure, relating it closely, in the
context of a theory of human functioning, to lack and desire.
Different aspects of that picture could be, and apparently
were, used to support opposite positions on the value of
pleasure. In order to complete our survey of the background
to Plato's treatment of the topic, we should now look at the
evidence for the development in the pre-Platonic period of
explicitly evaluative theories concerning pleasure. This will
involve firstly consideration of the views of Democritus, and
secondly an attempt to discover what can be known about
the position of Socrates. As Plato's early dialogues, especially
the *Protagoras*, are among our main sources for the latter,
this investigation will lead directly into our main topic.

Chapter 2

Evaluative Theories

1. Democritus

2.1.1. Democritus is, of course, best known as the chief proponent, though not the originator, of atomism, which attempted to give a comprehensive account of the universe as a structure composed of innumerable physical corpuscles moving ceaselessly in an infinite void. The ancient scholarly tradition, beginning with Aristotle, preserves a substantial amount of information on this cosmology, including the theory of the nature of man which it comprised, but says little about Democritus' ethical views. For the latter we are largely dependent on a collection of ethical maxims, purporting to be by Democritus, preserved by two late sources; this collection, in turn, contains nothing which is directly concerned with the physical theory. Since, therefore, we are not able to confirm the authenticity of the fragments by observing that their subject-matter coincides with what we know from good sources in the doxographical tradition, we must raise the question of how far we are justified in accepting the former as evidence for the actual views of Democritus.

2.1.2. The two main sources of the ethical maxims are the anthology of Stobaeus, and a collection entitled *The golden sayings of Democrates the Philosopher*, first published from a single manuscript in the seventeenth century, whose date of compilation is apparently unknown. Since many of the maxims from the latter collection also occur in Stobaeus, ascribed to Democritus, it is clear that the two collections have a common source. Further, one or two of the maxims cited by Stobaeus are independently ascribed to Democritus by good sources, among them one of the key fragments, no. 188, ascribed to Democritus by Clement of Alexandria (second to third centuries AD) (DK 68 B 4 and 188). It seems, then, reasonable to accept that the source for Stobaeus and

'Democrates' was a collection containing some undoubtedly genuine quotations, and passing as a whole for the work of Democritus, and that 'Democrates' is a scribe's error for 'Democritus'. Any answer to the further question whether the collection as a whole *is* genuine must be conjectural. At least one can say with confidence that some reasons that have been adduced to show that it is spurious are not good reasons. Thus the fact that many of the maxims are 'extremely commonplace and banal' (Guthrie II, p. 409) is plainly irrelevant; such writing belongs to the established didactic tradition of the Seven Sages, many of whose maxims are hardly less banal. Again, suspicion has been aroused by the fact that some of the maxims recall Socratic and Platonic doctrines, notably fr. 45 'The man who does wrong is more unfortunate than he who is wronged' (for other examples see Guthrie loc. cit.) But Democritus, born about 460, was a contemporary of Socrates, and travelled widely, including a visit to Athens (DK 68 B 116), where, according to one source, he knew Socrates but was not known by him, i.e. heard him talk but was not one of his intimates (DK 68 A 1, §36). He came from the same town as Protagoras, and is known to have written in criticism of him (DK 68 B 156). That is to say, he is likely to have had first-hand knowledge of the kind of discussion of ethical topics which is reflected in Plato's early dialogues. Finally, if the accounts of his very long life are to be accepted, he did not die till Plato was nearly seventy, and thus may well have been familiar with much of Plato's writing. The Socratic and Platonic echoes may cast doubt on the originality of some of the sayings, but hardly on their authenticity. It is worth noting that the list of titles of Democritus' works preserved by Diogenes Laertius (IX. 45-9; DK 68 A 33) includes in the section on ethics the title *Ethical Notes*, which would be an appropriate title for a collection (or collections, as there were apparently several books under this title) of maxims. In what follows it will be assumed that the fragments are genuine. While this is avowedly conjectural, it is not unreasonable, at least in so far as no compelling reason has been adduced for concluding that they are not genuine. The sceptically minded reader should therefore prefix to every statement of the following section the qualification 'Assuming that the fragment in question is genuine'.

2.1.3. The main interest of Democritus' ethical writings, and their particular importance for an enquiry into ancient theories of pleasure, lies not so much in the content of the didactic sayings themselves, as in the fact that he attempted to ground his moralizing in a systematic ethical theory. He may in fact have been the first philosopher to do so; we neither can nor need establish that beyond doubt. What is significant is firstly that he had what can reasonably be called an ethical theory, and secondly that pleasure was not only examined from the standpoint of that theory but also given a central place in it.

2.1.4. The attribution of an ethical theory to Democritus comes to this: he explicitly laid down a test or criterion to be applied in deciding questions of conduct, that criterion being fixed by consideration of an ultimate aim or purpose in human life. The achievement of that aim was the supreme good, and human conduct and things which human beings use were to be judged good or bad in so far as they tended to help or hinder the achievement of it. The doxographical tradition gives some information on these fundamentals; the ultimate aim of human life was the attainment of a state of well-being, for which various writers record a number of quasi-technical terms (DK 68 A 1, §45; 166-9). While the achievement of a fully satisfactory life was universally agreed to be what everyone wants, and thus unquestionably good, Democritus seems to have made two significant innovations in his treatment of this familiar ideal. Firstly, he seems to have given deliberate emphaiss to the assertion that, contrary to popular thought, what makes one's life really worth-while is not one's possessions or any externals, but one's state of mind. This seems to be the message of two fragments, 170, 'Good and ill fortune reside in the self', and 171 'Good fortune is not found in herds or in gold; the self is the dwelling-place of one's guardian spirit'. ('Good fortune' renders *eudaimonia*, lit. 'having a good spirit looking after one', i.e. having a fully satisfactory life. Fragment 171

therefore plays on the word *daimōn* to convey the sense that
one's overall good depends not on externals but on the state
of one's essential self (*psuchē*).) This may be the point of his
having chosen to express his conception of the ultimate aim
of life by the term *euthumia*, a word current in the sense of
'gladness' or 'joy', whose basic sense is 'having one's
emotional and appetitive self (*thumos*) in a good state'. One
of Democritus' ethical works, according to Diogenes Laertius,
was entitled *On Euthumia* (DK 68 A 33, §46), and his use of
the term is also attested by Plutarch (DK 68 B 3) and
Clement (DK 68 B 4), as well as by one of the quotations
from Stobaeus (DK 68 B 191). *Euthumia* was more appropriate than the somewhat more common *eudaimonia*, since
the latter frequently conveys those overtones of prosperity
and external well-being which Democritus seems to have
sought explicitly to reject. Secondly, he is reported as having
given a more precise specification of *euthumia*, as consisting
primarily in tranquility of mind. The fullest report is that by
Diogenes Laertius (IX, 45: DK 68 A 1, §45):

He said that the end is *euthumia*, which is not the same as pleasure, as
some have mistakenly reported, but is that state in which the soul
remains in calm and stability, not shaken by any fear or superstition or
any other emotion.

Similar summaries are given by other writers (DK 68 A
166-9), who also report that he called the final end *ataraxia*
(lit. 'freedom from disturbance') and *athambia* (lit. 'freedom
from wonder or alarm') as well as *euthumia* and *euestō* (lit.
'well-being'). *Ataraxia*, which was the standard Epicurean
term for the ideal state of soul, does not occur in the fragments, nor was it in common use prior to Epicurus; it is
possible that its use (by Stobaeus) reflects a specifically
Epicurean tradition about their great predecessor rather than
Democritus' actual terminology. But *athambia* and its
cognate adjective occur in two fragments (215 and 216), and
in addition this general picture receives some support from
the fragments. Fragment 174 contrasts the state of the
euthumos who enjoys health and peace of mind in consequence of his just actions with that of the wicked man who

is continually tormented by remorse and fear, while fragment 3 advises the man who wants to be *euthumos* not to busy himself with many things either in private or in public life, nor ever to attempt more than he can manage, but always to be on guard against a sudden reverse. A number of fragments (e.g. 71, 191, 233) give the traditional exhortation to moderation, especially in the pursuit of pleasures, with particular emphasis on the unpleasant and disturbing consequences of the wrong choice of pleasures. But while the evidence, both of the fragments and of the doxographers, thus indicates unambiguously that Democritus saw the aim of life as the achievement of a state of tranquillity rather than as a life of pleasure as it would commonly be recognized, and thus anticipated the central doctrine of Epicurean ethics, it would be a misreading of the evidence to conclude that Democritus conceived of tranquillity as something independent of pleasure, or still less as something opposed to it. It is clear that he thought at least that the life of tranquillity is the pleasantest life; more problematic is the question whether he went as far as to say what makes it the most desirable of all lives is just that it is the pleasantest life.

2.1.5. One piece of doxographical evidence confirms the close association between *euthumia* and pleasure: Stobaeus (DK 68 A 167) reports Democritus as holding that *euthumia* consists in the distinction and discrimination of pleasures, which is the finest and most beneficial (*sumphorōtaton*) thing for men. This is supported by evidence from the fragments both of discrimination between pleasures and of its connection with the concept of what is beneficial. Fragment 74 gives the advice 'Accept nothing pleasant, unless it is beneficial' (*sumpherēi*); clearly, the ultimate test of something's being beneficial is whether or not it promotes *euthumia*, and we can see this general advice being given more specific content in the fragments already cited on the necessity of moderation and forethought in the choice of pleasures. But Democritus also tells us (fr. 188, cited also by Clement, fr. 4) that 'the distinguishing mark of things beneficial and harmful is pleasure and unpleasantness'. Two features of this dictum need explanation; firstly, why is the distinguishing mark of what is beneficial said to be pleasure, rather than some aspect of *euthumia*? Secondly, how can Democritus say both that pleasures are to be discriminated according to their usefulness, and that what distinguishes useful things is pleasure? In fact the two explanations coincide. Fragment 74 is naturally read as a rule for the choice of particular pleasures; a particular pleasant thing, e.g. going to a party, is to be rejected if it is not advantageous in the long run. Fragment 188, on the other hand, tells us what marks off what is advantageous from what is disadvantageous; this is pleasure, not, obviously, the pleasure of the moment, but something which can sensibly be appealed to as a test for the long-run outcome of actions. It must, then, be pleasure seen as characterizing, not any particular action, but one's life as a whole, the sort of state which someone expresses when he says that he has an enjoyable life. When we recall that that is very close to the standard sense of *euthumia*, viz. joy, gladness, or cheerfulness, it is clear that fragment 188 does not differentiate useful from harmful things by reference to some feature extraneous to *euthumia*, but rather by reference to *euthumia* itself, or at least to an intrinsic feature of it. It is at least a universal feature of *euthumia* that the *euthumos* enjoys his life (cf. fr. 174).

2.1.6. Whether we can go further, and say that Democritus' view is that the life of *euthumia* is worth having *because* it is the pleasantest life, depends in part on how we understand the word in fragment 188 which has so far been rendered 'distinguishing mark'. The word is *horos*, literally 'boundary mark', which can also mean 'standard' and 'measure'. If pleasure were said to be the standard of usefulness and harmfulness, then we should be justified in taking that as saying that what *makes* something useful is that it promotes the enjoyment of life, in which case the enjoyment of life would be the desired end-state, i.e. *euthumia*. If, on the other hand, pleasure is merely a distinguishing mark of what is useful, then one might indeed tell whether something is useful by observing whether it promotes the enjoyment of life, though what makes it useful is not directly its promotion of the enjoyment of life, but its promotion of a desired end-state

which is invariably accompanied by enjoyment. The difficulty
is not merely that, lacking a context, we cannot tell in which
of these senses *horos* is used in fragment 188. There is also
the deeper problem that we have no justification for attributing to Democritus the very distinction which we are making
here, viz. that between a sign that a state obtains and a
feature constitutive of that state. The lack of this distinction
comes in at two levels: firstly, we have no sign of the distinction between

(1a) You can tell if something is useful by seeing whether it
promotes the enjoyment of life, and,

(1b) Something is constituted as useful if it promotes the
enjoyment of life,

and secondly, we have no sign of the distinction between

(2a) You can tell if someone has the best sort of life by
seeing whether he enjoys it, and,

(2b) Someone's life is constituted as the best sort of life by
the fact that he enjoys it.

It is virtually certain that our inability to detect these distic-
tions in our extant texts reflects not merely the fragmentary
state of the evidence, but the absence of these distinctions
from Democritus' thought. We must, then, have recourse
once again to undifferentiated concepts, and ascribe to
Democritus a position indeterminate between (a) the most
desirable life, i.e. the life of untroubled calm, is the pleasantest life, and (b) the life of untroubled calm is the most
desirable life because it is the pleasantest life.

2.1.7. Despite the vagueness of this conclusion, it has the
merit of making good sense of a number of fragments which
are anomalous on any view which makes a sharp distinction
between *euthumia* and pleasure, since they stress the role of
pleasure in a worthwhile life. So fragment 200 says 'Fools
live without enjoying life', fragment 201 'Fools desire long
life though they do not enjoy long life', and, most striking of
all, fragment 230 'A life without celebrations is a long road
without an inn', which implies that the feasting and

merrymaking associated with religious festivals have a place in the good life. Other fragments which appeal to pleasure as a positively worthwhile goal are 207, 211, and 232.

2.1.8. Two objections have now to be considered. The first, a comparatively minor one, consists in pointing out that Diogenes Laertius expressly differentiates Democritus' *euthumia* from pleasure, and says that some writers have made a mistake in identifying the two. Without the texts it is difficult to be sure quite what the issue is. One possibility is that what Diogenes (or rather, his source) is concerned to deny is that Democritus identified *euthumia* with pleasure as commonly understood, i.e. with sybaritic luxury, or with the pleasure of the moment. The writers on the other side may have pointed out (correctly if what has been said above is right) that Democritus' *euthumia* was no more independent of pleasure than Epicurus' *ataraxia* and Diogenes may have confused these two views, which are not only quite compatible, but are both true. In any event, this passage cannot outweigh the evidence which we have found in the other doxographers and in the fragments. The more substantial objection comes from one of the fragments, no. 69, which runs: 'For all men the same thing is good and true, but pleasant is different for different men'. Here the point is that the same thing can be pleasant to one man and unpleasant to another, unlike goodness and truth, which are independent of the particular state of any observer, and thus objective features of reality, the same for everyone. (Pleasantness is thus classified as an observer-dependent quality, in the same class as sweetness, redness etc., in terms of the famous contrast between 'reality' and 'convention': 'By convention sweet, by convention bitter, by convention hot, by convention cold, by convention colour, but in reality atoms and void' (DK 68 B 9 and 125).) How, then, can the supreme good for man, that in which a desirable life consists, be identical or even closely connected with pleasure? It is worth remarking that the Greek for 'pleasant' in fragment 69 is *hēdu*, while overall enjoyment of life is referred to in fragment 188 by the word *terpsis*. Thus it is *terpsis* which is the distinguishing mark of what is useful and harmful, while fragment 74 tells one not to accept anything *hēdu*, i.e. any particular pleasant thing, which is not useful. Though Democritus does not preserve a strict contrast between *terpsis* on the one hand and *hēdonē* and its cognates on the other (see e.g. frs. 211 and 235), the fragments do not provide any clear case of *hēdu* or *to hēdu* used in the sense of 'pleasure', as opposed to its basic sense 'something pleasant'. Moreover, the context of fragment 69 cleary requires that basic sense, since the point is that *what is pleasant* to one man (on one occasion, in one circumstance, etc.) is different from what is pleasant to another. That is plainly compatible with the view that there is one ultimate good for all men, viz. a state of untroubled enjoyment of life. Moreover, the conservative tone of the fragments strongly suggests that Democritus held, not merely that all men have the same supreme good, viz. *euthumia*, but that a certain specific style of life, viz. the life of moderation, is necessary in order to achieve it. Fragment 69 does not, then, constitute any objection to this interpretation; the characterization of pleasure which it contains is not inconsistent with recognition of untroubled enjoyment of life as man's supreme good, and our evidence indicates that Democritus not merely made that identification but probably that he regarded it as requiring the adoption of a particular kind of life.

2.1.9. The substantive moral views revealed in the fragments are, then, fairly conventional, though the quietism of fragment 3 suggests that Democritus did not attach much importance to the 'success' conception of *aretē*. The interest of his ethical work lies in the underlying theory, specifically in his having made explicit the thesis that things are ultimately to be evaluated by reference to a supreme good or goal of life, and in his having assigned to pleasure an essential place in that supreme good or goal. The phrase 'good or goal' is deliberately vague, to indicate the fact that we have no information on whether he distinguished the thesis that *euthumia* is everyone's goal, i.e. what everyone does in fact want or aim at, from the thesis that *euthumia* is everyone's supreme good, i.e. that which is for everyone the most worth having of all things, and which everyone therefore should aim at, if he is to be rational. Comparison with discussions in

Plato and Aristotle, e.g. the argument with the many in the *Protagoras*, and *EN* I, suggests that he is unlikely to have done so. He may well have taken the alleged fact (assumed or argued for) that everyone desires *euthumia* as showing that it is the supreme good, as Eudoxus later argued that the fact that all living creatures desire pleasure shows it to be the supreme good (*EN* 1172b9-11). Lack of information about the chronology of Democritus' writings and about the extent to which they were known makes it impossible to make any useful pronouncements about his priority or his influence as an ethical theorist. While it was argued above that it was quite likely, on general grounds, that Democritus was familiar with the context of Socratic and sophistic debate which forms the background to Plato's early ethical dialogues, and perhaps even with some of those dialogues themselves, there is no definite evidence that Plato was familiar with the works of Democritus, at least in his early period. Whereas Aristotle knew Democritus' works in detail, and devoted a complete work to an attack on them, Plato never mentions Democritus by name, and does not clearly refer to any work of his earlier than an apparent reference in the *Sophist* (246a ff.). Democritus himself said that when he came to Athens nobody knew him (fr. 116), which suggests that he was an obscure figure at the time. The most that we can say with confidence (and even that is subject to the qualifications about the authenticity of the ethical fragments made above) is that at some time in the late fifth century or in the first half of the fourth he developed an explicit theory of value which is suitable to provide theoretical support to the kind of moderate hedonism which is exemplified by the fable of Heracles, and which is very close to the view ascribed to the many in the *Protagoras*.

2.1.10. In the foregoing discussion Democritus has been treated purely as a theorist of value, and no attempt has been made to relate his treatment of pleasure to the physiological tradition. This is in accordance with the doxographical evidence. The very full treatment of his theory of perception by Theophrastus (*De sens.* 49-83; DK 68 A 135) does not mention pleasure, while there is no direct evidence that he associated pleasure with any particular physical process, e.g. with the filling up of a deficiency on the lines of Empedocles' theory. Some modern scholars have, however, endeavoured to demonstrate connections between Democritus' ethics and his physical theory, on the basis of such indirect evidence as certain resemblances between terminology occurring in the fragments and technical terms of the physical theory mentioned by the doxographers. The conclusions of this line of enquiry have been at best speculative, and in particular have included nothing which is both firmly established and relevant to Democritus' treatment of pleasure. For details see Vlastos (1), Taylor (2), Guthrie II, pp. 496-7.

2. Socrates

2.2.1. In trying to assess the contribution of Socrates to the background of Plato's treatment of pleasure, we face the opposite problem from that which we encountered in dealing with Democritus. In the case of the latter we know, or can at least reasonably conjecture, the main outline of his view on pleasure, but have no evidence that it actually influenced Plato. Socrates, on the other hand, is known to have been a major influence on Plato; the problem here is that it is very difficult to find evidence sufficient to justify the attribution to the historical Socrates of any particular philosophical doctrine. As is well known, the main source of the problem is threefold: firstly Socrates wrote nothing himself; secondly most of the surviving ancient works in which specific views are ascribed to him are by Plato; and thirdly it is clear both from internal and external evidence that a great deal of what is put into the mouth of Socrates in Plato's dialogues represents Plato's own views. The situation with respect to Socrates' views on pleasure reflects this general situation. While Aristotle occasionally refers to Socrates' ethical views, he does not mention his views on pleasure, and in any case his evidence on this topic is, in general, not clearly independent of Plato and, in some cases at least (e.g. *EN* 1145b23-4) plainly derived from him. The question of how far any of the views of the Platonic Socrates on pleasure may be taken to represent the position of the historical Socrates will arise in our discussion of those passages, in particular of the

Protagoras. This leaves us with the other main non-Platonic source, Xenophon, whose *Memorabilia of Socrates* contain a number of passages dealing with pleasure. It should be emphasized that Xenophon's Socrates is no more to be taken as a historically accurate portrait than is Plato's. Each author presents an idealized picture appropriate to his general purpose, which in Xenophon's case was to show the injustice of Socrates' conviction for impiety and corruption of youth by presenting him as an ideal exemplar of conventional morality. Thus the things that Xenophon's Socrates says about pleasure are direct evidence not of what Socrates actually believed, but of what Xenophon thought it proper that his reader should think he believed. Their evidential value is indirect, in that if Xenophon's defence was to carry any conviction it could not present a picture of the opinions and personality of Socrates which was at total variance either with what people remembered of the man or with the picture of him as presented by other writers. Thus had the actual Socrates been an out-and-out anti-hedonist such as Antisthenes was, it is hardly plausible that Xenophon could have represented his views on pleasure as he did (see below). The work does, of course, also provide some evidence of the general climate of opinion with regard to pleasure, in that it shows the sort of view of pleasure which would be accept-able to a basically decent and conventionally-minded Athenian of the first half of the fourth century.

2.2.2. On the whole, Xenophon's Socrates stands for a moderate hedonism. Of course he despises the life of sybaritic luxury, and one of the main themes of the work is his mastery of bodily appetite; but one of the grounds for preferring the simple life is .that it is pleasanter than the luxurious one (e.g. I.vi.4 ff., esp. 8–9 and IV.v.9 ff.). Once again, the fable of Heracles is a key text. This is put into the mouth of Socrates at the end of a set-piece debate with Aristippus, the representative of the sybaritic life (see 2.3). So what we have described as the proto-hedonism of the fable is presented by Xenophon as the genuinely Socratic view, in conscious opposition to the distortion purveyed by the erring disciple, Aristippus. At I.vi.8–9 and again at the end of the work (IV.viii.6) Socrates says that he has had the pleasantest of all lives, since pleasure arises from the consciousness of doing well whatever one is doing, and he is conscious of success in his task of becoming better himself and making others better. Strictly speaking, that implies that what actually makes a man a good man, or his life a good life, is something independent of his having had a predominantly pleasant life, since pleasure is something consequent upon the consciousness of doing well and causing others to do well. But, firstly, we have at least the unqualified and emphatic assertion that the best life is the pleasantest life, and, secondly, these passages are not supported by any explicit theory of goodness as something independent of pleasure. In fact, the very little that Xenophon has to say about Socrates' views on the nature of goodness at least allows, though it admittedly does not require, a hedonistic account. Thus at IV.vi.8 Socrates is said to have defined the good as the useful, and while no further analysis is given of the latter, it is clearly susceptible of analysis in terms of long-term pleasantness, as we saw from our examination of Democritus. Again, at IV.ii.34 ff. we have an argument that the test of genuine goods is their long-term effects; hence, even such acknowledged constituents of *eudaimonia* as good looks, strength, and wealth are good only on condition that they do not bring about long-term disadvantages. While those advantages are admittedly not described in terms of pleasure and distress, the whole passage is reminiscent of the more explicitly hedonistic message of the fable, and of *Prot.* 353c–354e, where Socrates secures the agreement of the ordinary man that good and bad things are to be recognized as such on account of their long-term results, measured in terms of pleasure and pain. Xenophon's Socrates is not, then, an explicit hedonist. Some of the things he says suggest, rather than strictly imply, that what makes things good is, ultimately, their long-term pleasantness, while other things strictly imply that what makes things good must be something else. But he is favourable to pleasure, at least to the extent of insisting on the superiority of the virtuous life in terms of its pleasantness. Moreover, his most extended treatment of pleasure, the fable, is one of the passages which favours the hedonistic interpretation.

2.2.3. Xenophon's evidence, then, suggests that it is unlikely that the historical Socrates was a declared opponent of pleasure as such, or even of bodily pleasure. Any more positive conclusion must await the investigation of the Platonic evidence.

3. Aristippus

2.3.1. Plato was not the only one of the immediate associates of Socrates to take an interest in pleasure. We have already mentioned the extreme anti-hedonism of Antisthenes. At the opposite extreme stands the interesting but somewhat shadowy figure of Aristippus, whom Xenophon represents as the champion of the sybaritic life. As that was clearly a position which Plato took very seriously, we shall conclude this chapter with some brief remarks on what can be known about Aristippus' views.

2.3.2. The attempt to determine those views is highly problematic, for very similar reasons to those which apply in the case of Socrates. Among the schools of philosophy which grew up in the fourth and third centuries BC was the Cyrenaic school (named after Aristippus' native city of Cyrene in North Africa) which claimed to derive its doctrines from Aristippus and was actually founded by his grandson of the same name. As all our evidence ascribing specific doctrines to Aristippus dates from long after the establishment of the school, it is systematically impossible to determine which doctrines are actually his and which were developed subsequently by the school. There is, however, a great deal of anecdote in the sources (especially the life by Diogenes Laertius, II.65–104) about his luxurious manner of life, and it is in general plausible to suppose that this, in a follower of Socrates, reflected a theoretical position. Moreover, as we saw, Xenophon thought him sufficiently important to make him the spokesman for the sybaritic life. Finally, it is unlikely that the later doctrines of the school did not at least develop from a basic position of his. In describing the Cyrenaic view of pleasure, then, we shall take it that at least its outlines reflect the position of Aristippus himself.

2.3.3. The basic position is radical hedonism: the supreme good is pleasure (frs. 155–62); specifically the pleasure of the moment, which the Cyrenaics explicitly distinguished from and held to be more valuable than the overall enjoyment of life (DL II.87–8), and especially bodily pleasure (frs. 181A–183D) though they did recognize the value of non-bodily pleasures, e.g. those of the arts (DL II.89), and also held that no pleasure was pleasanter than any other (DL II.87). They supported the claim of pleasure to be the supreme good by the argument that all living things pursue pleasure and shun pain (frs. 176–80). They seem to have given some quasi-physiological account of the nature of pleasure; reporting what is clearly a piece of technical terminology, Diogenes and other writers report (frs. 191–8) that they said that pleasure is a smooth motion (or 'a smooth process of change') and pain a rough one. We have insufficient evidence of just what sort of process they had in mind, though the words of Sextus Empiricus (*P* I.215; fr. 198) 'the smooth motion of the flesh' indicate that it was a physical process. The fact that the difference between pleasure and pain lies in the manner in which the process occurs, rather than in its direction, so to speak, suggests that the model of deficiency and repletion cannot have been the dominant one. They apparently argued for the supreme value of the pleasure of the moment on epistemological grounds: the past no longer exists, hence memory of past pleasure does not give us anything real; the future is uncertain; hence the only thing with which the wise man will concern himself is pleasure here and now (frs. 207–9). This reflected a generally sceptical stance in epistemology, according to which they held that it was impossible to know anything beyond one's immediate sensations, among which, of course, pleasure and pain were prominent (frs. 210–18). Though the details of this position probably reflect later developments, when arguments of this kind had been codified by the sceptical school, it is at least not impossible that Aristippus himself put forward some ideas of this kind under the influence of the kind of Protagorean position which Plato discusses in the *Theaetetus*. Interestingly, one of the sources (fr. 208, from Aelian (first to second centuries AD)) relates the supremacy of the pleasure of the moment to the ideal of *euthumia*; Aristippus, he says, said that it is the mark of the cheerful mind to be content with the present, and not to trouble itself with the past or the future. Of course the use of this particular word by Aelian is no evidence that it was used by Aristippus, still less that it was used with any reference to Democritus, but the passage is interesting in that it shows how a sybaritic hedonist, especially of a sceptical turn of mind, could turn the tables on the conventional long-term hedonist by appeal to his own ideal of untroubled enjoyment of life. If the future is wholly uncertain and the past unreal, then how can the attempt to plan one's life with a view to getting the pleasantest life in the long run ever be free from the anxiety that one's calculations will turn out to be baseless? The untroubled enjoyment of life will then reduce to the untroubled enjoyment of all that we have available to us, i.e. the present moment.

2.3.4. As we have said, we cannot be sure how much of this was actually maintained by Aristippus. But we know from Plato that sybaritic hedonism, as well as rational long-term hedonism, was in the air in the fourth century, and it is at least not unlikely that as well as untheoretical adherents, it had theoretical supporters. If that is so, then it is reasonable to associate Aristippus with that position.

2.3.5. On the assumption, then, that the ethical discussions of Socrates were one of the major influences on Plato, we should expect the latter to treat pleasure as a topic of central interest. We have evidence of the development within the Socratic circle itself of theoretical support for radical hedonism, which could be used to give intellectual respectability to a life of self-indulgence. Socrates, on the other hand, is represented by Xenophon as defending the traditional ideals of toughness and self-mastery by the argument that it is there, rather than in luxury and effeminacy, that true pleasure is to be found. This appeal to enlightened hedonism, assuming it actually to have been made by Socrates, may or may not have been supported by an explicit theory of the relation of pleasure to the supreme good. A theory of that kind was, it appears, proposed by Democritus, but we do not know whether Plato knew of it. We must now try to see from the dialogues how Plato reacted to the interplay of moderate and sybaritic hedonism which our evidence has so far suggested.

Chapter 3

Protagoras

3.0.1. Given his concern to defend such fundamental ideals as rationality, justice, and self-control, Plato might be expected to have reacted in one or more of a number of different ways to the varieties of hedonism he was faced with. Against sybaritic hedonism he might contrast the stable tranquillity of virtue with the restless turbulence of the body and its pleasures, or contrast reason with the anti-rational tendency of pleasure, or contrast the craven comforts of the body with the manliness of virtue. Or he might take advantage of the sort of enlightened hedonism proposed by Democritus to turn the tables on the hedonist, either by accepting that pleasure is the supreme good and arguing that it can be attained only by a life of virtue, or, while denying that it is the supreme good, by arguing that the life of virtue is in fact the pleasantest, so that on his own premises a hedonist ought to pursue virtue. Alternatively, he might argue that while appeal to pleasure cannot be used to determine that any particular kind of life is the pleasantest, nevertheless the virtuous life is in fact the pleasantest among serious candidates for the title of the best life.

3.0.2. There are signs of all these reactions in Plato. Thus in the *Gorgias* (493d–e) and *Phaedo* (65a–67b) we get the contrast of stability and turbulence; in these and the *Republic* (580d–587a) the contrast of reason and bodily pleasure; and in the *Republic* (439e–440b) the spirited element that flowers into manliness is at odds with the demands of the body. In the *Protagoras*, by contrast, Plato seems to maintain the stronger version of Democritean hedonism (see Ch. 3), while *Republic* IX perhaps expresses the weaker (see Ch. 6). By the *Philebus* it looks as though Plato does not think that any one style of life is the pleasantest (see Ch. 7).

3.0.3. A special problem arises from the fact that of these

dialogues the *Protagoras* is the only one where Plato appears to defend a whole-heartedly hedonistic position. If we leave this dialogue aside we seem to have a plausible picture of a gradual shift from outright hostility towards pleasure to a qualified benevolence towards it. In the *Gorgias* and *Phaedo* there is outright opposition. By the *Republic* it is given a place in the good life, except that bodily pleasure gets a bad press. In the *Philebus* even some bodily pleasures are admitted as elements that add value to the good life. If we take the *Protagoras* seriously, on the other hand, we seem to have to posit an inexplicable period of euphoria. It does not matter very much whether we put the *Protagoras* earlier or later than the *Gorgias*. If the latter, then there seems to be a wild vacillation from *Gorgias* to *Protagoras* and back to *Phaedo*, without any acknowledgement of change. But even if we put the *Protagoras* early, its position on hedonism might well appear quite out of keeping with the rest of Plato, and nowhere does he explain why it was abandoned. But again, if we are not to take it seriously we need some persuasive account of how we are to take it.

3.0.4. It is, therefore, apparent that if we are to have an intelligible picture of the development of Plato's views on pleasure we must answer a number of questions which centre on the *Protagoras*. There are four main questions:

(i) What view on the relation of pleasure to goodness is maintained by Socrates in the *Protagoras*?

(ii) May that view be supposed to have been that of Plato himself at the time of writing the dialogue?

(iii) Is that view consistent with views expressed by Plato in other dialogues?

(iv) In so far as any inconsistency exists, how is it to be accounted for?

(In the above 'view' should be read as 'view or views' since we wish at this stage to leave open the question whether Socrates has one view or more on the relation of pleasure to goodness.) In our subsequent discussion it will be assumed that, unless there are indications to the contrary, the views attributed to the main speaker in each dialogue (i.e. Socrates, in the dialogues with which we shall be concerned) are the views of Plato. Some of the indications which show that this general thesis does not hold of some particular passages will be discussed in connection with question (ii) (see 3.2.2).

1. Socrates' thesis

3.1.1. When considering the first question it is worth recalling that the discussion of pleasure is confined to the concluding pages of the *Protagoras* (351b–360e), where Socrates is trying to show that courage is a kind of knowledge or wisdom. His strategy is to argue that in order to act rightly in the face of danger (and indeed in any situation) it is necessary and sufficient that one have knowledge of which of the available courses of action will produce the best outcome, assessed in terms of pleasure and distress. While Socrates does indeed argue that the ordinary man can be brought to accept that hedonistic scheme of evaluation, it is not introduced as a view which the ordinary man initially holds. Rather, Socrates introduces at 351b–c a thesis or theses on the relation of pleasure to goodness which he himself maintains as true against the initial opposition of the ordinary man (351c); the latter's views come in for detailed examination from 352d onwards only to refute an objection which they bring against the thesis of the sufficiency of knowledge for right conduct, a thesis which Socrates apparently derives from his hedonistic premiss (see 3.1.5–9). Our first task is to see what the initial premiss is. It is introduced at 351c4–5 in the words 'With respect to that in which they (i.e. pleasant things) are pleasant, are they not with respect to that good, leaving their other consequences out of account?' and restated at e2 as 'In so far as they are pleasant, are they not good?' (the interrogative form is clearly rhetorical, see 3.1.4). Those formulations allow two interpretations: (i) 'in respect of their being pleasant, they are good', i.e. their being pleasant is an aspect in which they manifest goodness, or in other (and less elegant) words a 'good-making' characteristic; (ii) 'to the extent to which anything is pleasant, it is to that extent good', i.e. the extent to which the predicate 'good' is

applicable to anything is determined (wholly or at least predominantly) by the extent to which the predicate 'pleasant'
is applicable to that thing. On the former view A might be
pleasanter than B, yet B be good and A be bad, the goodness
of B and badness of A being attributable to characteristics
totally independent of pleasure, e.g. B's being honourable
and A's being dishonourable. On the latter, if A is pleasanter
than B it is *ipso facto* better than B; on the stronger reading
of this view, no other factors could count at all towards the
assessment of A and B either severally or relative to one
another, while on the weaker, though other factors might
indeed count, no other factor or set of factors could outweigh pleasantness in the final determination. These two
interpretations give rise in turn to different interpretations of
the qualification 'leaving their other consequences out of
account' (c5). Given the first, the phrase should be taken as
'leaving out of account any features other than pleasantness
and unpleasantness'; the emphasis is wholly on 'other', while
'consequences' has to be taken loosely. Given the second,
the emphasis is on 'consequences'; considering A and B in
isolation from their consequences, if A is pleasanter than B,
then A is better than B, but if we consider their consequences A may yet be worse than B (i.e. if the consequences
of A are less pleasant than those of B, cf. 353c ff.). The
occurence of 'other' would on this view be explained perhaps
as expressing the thought that the immediate pleasantness
or unpleasantness of A and B are themselves effects 'resulting
from' the experiencing or performance of A and B, or
perhaps as referring to consequences other than pleasant
consequences, i.e. (in context) unpleasant consequences. If
interpretation (i) is correct, there is no disagreement between
Socrates on the one hand and Protagoras and the ordinary
man on the other. In order to defend their view that there are
some bad pleasures all that the latter need to do is make clear
that such pleasures are bad not *because* they are pleasant, but
for some other reason. Socrates, however, clearly thinks that
his position is incompatible with that view (351c2-3). Hence
if interpretation (i) is correct Socrates is confused on a
central point, whereas if (ii) is correct he is free of that confusion, which favours the latter interpretation.

3.1.2. There is, however, a third possible interpretation which must be considered. Since this interpretation contains an ambiguity or indeterminateness, it presents a set of alternatives rather than a single alternative. At 351e2–3 Socrates follows his restatement 'In so far as they are pleasant, are they not good?' with the words 'I'm asking whether pleasure itself is not good'. These words could be taken as 'I'm asking whether pleasure itself is not something good', which would favour interpretation (i) viz. that something's being pleasant is something good about it. But they may equally well be taken as 'I'm asking whether pleasure is not (the) good'. And the expression 'pleasure is the good' is itself capable of at least two interpretations, (a) 'Pleasure is the only thing which is (underivatively) good' and (b) 'Pleasure (= pleasantness) is the same thing as goodness'. Protagoras appears to understand Socrates as proposing this stronger thesis, understood in sense (b), for he proposes (e3–7) to examine the question, 'and if your thesis appears reasonable and the pleasant and good are the same, we shall agree'. If we could be sure that Plato represents Protagoras as correctly understanding Socrates we should be able to decide in favour of this third interpretation, but there is always the possibility that Plato means to represent him as *mis*understanding (cf. Vlastos (2) n. 24, pp. 77–8).

3.1.3. Interpretations (a) and (b) of 'Pleasure is the good' might well seem totally distinct in meaning: after all, (a) is a value judgement to the effect that a certain mental state is the only thing worth having, while (b) is naturally taken as an analytic statement to the effect that two expressions have the same meaning. Moreover, the two expressions in question are 'good' and 'pleasant' with the result that in the material mode the analytic statement is about pleasantness, a characteristic of objects, whereas the evaluative statement is about pleasure, a mental state. Given those assumptions, we have a clear choice of interpretations of this third version of Socrates' thesis. In fact this appearance of clear alternatives is illusory. For firstly, it is improbable that Plato intends to make any distinction between pleasure and pleasantness; cf. 355a–b, where the thesis that the good is nothing other than *pleasure* is held to license the treatment of the adjectives 'good' and *'pleasant'* as interchangeable. The expression *to hēdu*, which is used interchangeably with *hēdonē* at 351e, may in context designate either pleasure or pleasantness, and is frequently used in contexts which suggest no differentiation (a good example is 356a, where *to parachrēma hēdu* might equally well be rendered 'immediate pleasure', 'immediate pleasantness' or 'something immediately pleasant'). Secondly, we see no reason for imputing to Plato any thesis about the meaning of terms, as distinct from entities which those terms stand for. But if we take him as saying that 'pleasantness' (= 'pleasure') is the name of the same entity that 'goodness' names, and allow that he takes it for granted that it is the goodness in anything which alone makes it worth pursuing, then it follows that it is the pleasantness in anything which alone makes it worth pursuing. And that is not an analytic statement, but is also evaluative, and at any rate very close in meaning to 'Pleasure is the only thing underivatively good'. We suggest, then, that the third possible interpretation of Socrates' thesis is that it is the undifferentiated thesis that pleasure is the only underivatively good thing and that 'pleasant' and 'good' are different names for one and the same characteristic. Understood as we suggest, that undifferentiated thesis at least avoids the charge of gross confusion of different kinds of statement.

3.1.4. While 351b–e does not allow us to identify Socrates' thesis, it does make it clear that he has one, and is not merely raising questions or finding out what Protagoras or the ordinary man thinks. For it is quite clear from 351c that he thinks that Protagoras and the ordinary man are wrong to think that there are bad pleasures, i.e. he is committed at least to the view that everything pleasant is good. Secondly, Protagoras says at 351e that if Socrates' view proves to be supported by the arguments, they will agree, but if not they will carry on arguing. Plato might perhaps make Protagoras misidentify Socrates' thesis; he would hardly represent him as mistakenly believing that Socrates *has* a thesis.[1]

---

[1] Zeyl, who argues that in this passage Socrates is represented merely as

3.1.5. Since we cannot identify Socrates' thesis from 351b-e alone, if we are to have any chance of doing so we must consider the rest of the section to 360e. This invites the objection that in that section of the dialogue Socrates is not advancing any thesis of his own, but merely pointing out that the hedonistic scheme of evaluation accepted by the ordinary man and (ultimately) by the sophists commits both to the truth of the Socratic thesis that it is impossible to act against one's knowledge of what is the best thing to do. In this whole section, it is claimed, Socrates is careful to emphasize that the hedonistic views under examination are not his own, but those of the ordinary man (especially 354a-e). Against this view, we interpret Socrates as obliging the ordinary man (and subsequently the sophists) to admit that they can see no alternative to accepting the view of the relation of pleasure to goodness which Socrates is proposing *as true*, and from which it follows that it is impossible to act against one's knowledge. Given that interpretation, it will clearly be the simplest hypothesis that the thesis which Socrates obliges the ordinary man to accept is identical with the one he introduces at 351b-e. We shall now try to justify this interpretation.

3.1.6. Firstly, some general considerations of the structure of the dialogue. The whole section from 351b to 360e is intended to support the conclusion that courage is identical with knowledge of what it is best to do, an identification which Socrates says also holds for all the other virtues (361b1-3); hence this section provides a programme for the demonstration of Socrates' thesis that the specific virtues are

---

forcing Protagoras to elucidate his own position, takes no account of this second point. Translation of e3-5 is crucial. At e1-3 Socrates poses the question 'In so far as things are pleasant are they not good? I'm asking whether pleasure itself is not good'. Protagoras replies that they must examine that (*skopōmetha auto*), 'and if the *skemma* seems reasonable (*pros logon*) and pleasant and good turn out to be the same we shall agree'. Zeyl renders the first half of the protasis as 'if our examination appears reasonable' (p. 251). But *skemma* has the sense, not of 'examination' but 'thing examined': it is used in three passages in Plato of a question to be gone into (*Crito* 48c; *Rep.* 435c, 445a). Here while the topic is indeed introduced by a question, the thing under examination is Socrates' thesis, viz. that pleasure itself is (the) good, which, if it appears reasonable, will be agreed on by both parties. (See Adam and Adam, p. 177) If that thesis does not seem reasonable, the parties will dispute: it takes two to make an argument.

all one and the same. It is not, we take it, disputed that at the time of writing the dialogue Plato believed that account of courage and the other virtues to be true; and *prima facie*, at least, this section looks like a serious effort to show it to be true. Contrast this section with the immediately preceding section (349e–351b), where Socrates gives an argument for the same conclusion, Protagoras points out a flaw in it, and it is immediately abandoned in favour of the argument we are at present considering. Leaving aside the question of whether Protagoras is right in his detailed diagnosis of the fault in the argument, it is quite clear that by leaving him with the upper hand Plato means to point out to the reader that that particular argument is inadequate, while the development from that section to the next shows that he sees the inadequacy as consisting at least in part in a wrong conception of knowledge. As at *Lach.* 193, technical expertise is not the sort of knowledge which makes a brave man brave; and as in that dialogue, we have to think instead of the knowledge of what is good and bad in one's life as a whole. As soon as this shift is begun at 351b Socrates takes over as a much more authoritative figure than hitherto. Protagoras is not allowed to claim that there are any flaws in Socrates' arguments, and indeed from 351e he ceases to play any substantial part in the discussion at all, with the result that the rest of the dialogue consists virtually of continuous exposition by Socrates. There are no textual indications (as at 332a) that the ostensible conclusions are to be given less than their full weight. There is of course Socrates' aporetic conclusion at 361a–d, but that looks more like irony than qualification, since Plato has already indicated how the apparent contradiction in Socrates' position is to be resolved; when he denied that *aretē* could be taught he meant *aretē* as conceived by Protagoras, i.e. practical skills and habits of socially desirable conduct. Lacking any basis in knowledge, such traits cannot be taught in a scientific way, but merely passed on by the hit-or-miss process of habituation; when and only when right conduct is seen as produced by knowledge of the right way to live can it be taught. So the apparent volte-face indicates neither confusion nor uncertainty, but the conscious rejection of an incorrect conception of *aretē* in favour of the correct one.

3.1.7. Granted, then, that this section contains a serious attempt to establish Socrates' account of courage and the virtues generally as true, it is more readily intelligible on the assumption that he is obliging the ordinary man to accept his (Socrates') account of the nature of goodness than on the assumption that he is merely showing that the common man's assumptions, irrespective of their truth, commit him to Socrates' position on courage. For the only reason for discussing the common man's view at all is that the common man points to a phenomenon which apparently refutes Socrates' thesis that knowledge is a necessary and sufficient condition of courageous and generally right conduct, viz. the apparent fact that people often do what they know to be wrong, a fact which the common man explains as follows, that the agent acts in that way because he is overcome by pleasure or other appetitive forces. Socrates has therefore to show that the alleged phenomenon does not in fact occur, which he attempts to do by an argument designed to show that if the goodness of an action is identical with its long-term pleasantness then (a) the description of the phenomenon given by the ordinary man is incoherent, (b) the correct description of that phenomenon is that the agent acts as he does through incorrect estimation of the pleasures and pains anticipated from his action. But of course this actually removes the objection only if the thesis identifying goodness and pleasantness is *true*. Failing that assumption, the most that the argument could show is that the ordinary man is inconsistent; but even if he is, that of itself in no way weakens the force of his objection to Socrates' thesis about knowledge and right conduct. Further, demonstration of inconsistency between *p* and *q* does not of itself show which of those propositions is false; there is then the further question which is to be rejected. Socrates shows himself well aware of this methodological principle at 333a; but there is no suggestion that the common man has the viable option of resolving the contradiction in his position by abandoning the identification of goodness with long-term pleasantness while sticking to his thesis that action against knowledge does occur. (The possibility of his abandoning the account of goodness is indeed raised by Socrates at 354e8–355a2, only to be dismissed immediately without discussion.) Further, on the interpretation proposed the argument with the common man secures both the removal of an objection to Socrates' central thesis and a positive argument in its favour, since the argument purports to show both that that thesis follows from a true principle about goodness and pleasantness and that the objection depends on the misdescription of a phenomenon which is correctly described in the light of that principle and the conclusion which follows from it. But if Socrates is not proposing the principle as true, then the section of the dialogue down to 357e contains no argument in support of his main thesis. In that case we must ask (a) How does Socrates attempt to support his main thesis? and (b) What is the point of the episode involving the common man?

3.1.8. A possible answer to (a) is that the positive support for the main thesis is given for the first time at 358c, where Socrates states independently of hedonism the principle that it is not in human nature to act contrary to one's knowledge or belief of what is the best thing to do. The positive argument for the identification of courage with knowledge can be seen as relying solely on that principle, without any reference to the earlier discussion. Someone who took this line might then suggest in answer to (b) that the argument with the common man aims not at the direct refutation of his objection, but is rather a softening-up operation, designed to discredit his objection by showing it inconsistent with principles which he inclines to accept, prior to the enunciation of the principle whose application shows his objection actually to be false.[2]

3.1.9. There are the following objections to this suggestion. Firstly, since the principle stated at 358c itself contains the necessary materials for the required redescription of the phenomenon of action against one's better judgement, viz. that it is action arising from misestimation of the consequences of one's action, it is quite obscure on this view why Socrates should not use it (as in *Meno* 77b–78b, *Gorg.*

---

[2] So e.g. Manuwald. Despite the acuity of many of his detailed observations we find it impossible to accept his account of the argumentative structure of this part of the dialogue, for the reasons given in the next paragraph.

466a–470a and *Euthyd.* 278e–281e) to construct a direct refutation of the ordinary man's objection, instead of proceeding to a lengthy and unnecessary formulation of the point in hedonistic terms. One might add that the final identification of courage with knowledge would be more convincing if it were not dependent on hedonistic assumptions: it is quite plausible to suggest that the courageous man (e.g. the man who sacrifices his life to save his comrades) knows how to achieve the good in situations of danger, but very implausible to suggest that what he knows is how to achieve the best possible balance of pleasure over pain in his life as a whole. Secondly, this suggestion ignores the fact that Socrates is already committed to a fair measure of hedonism before the objection rears its ugly head at all (see above 3.1.3). Thirdly, it is quite clear from 358a–d that Socrates presents the argument which is to follow as relying on the conclusions of the argument with the many. Further, in the application of the conclusions of that argument to the question of courage, no distinction is drawn between what Socrates has asserted (which the sophists explicitly agree to be true (358a 3–5) and what the common man has accepted; thus at 360a Protagoras reluctantly accepts the inference from '*x* is good' to '*x* is pleasant' on the grounds that it has been agreed, where the reference must be to the common man's acceptance of this inference at 354b–c. The sophists, then, clearly understand Socrates as obliging the common man and themselves to accept his own view of the relation between pleasantness and goodness as the ground of his thesis that courage is a sort of knowledge. And since Plato gives the reader no indication of any other ground for that thesis, nor any indication that the sophists are incorrect in their belief as to what Socrates' ground is, the most plausible assumption is that Plato intends the reader to have the same belief. We have so far argued for this conclusion from the text of the *Protagoras*: arguments external to the dialogue, purporting to show that our conclusion conflicts with independently established Socratic or Platonic theses, will be considered below (3.2.4–9).

3.1.10. From this point, then, we shall take it as established that the view of the relation between pleasantness and goodness which the common man accepts is in fact Socrates' own view. According to this view, something is good iff it promotes a life in which pleasure predominates over pain (354a–355a), and further the terms 'good' and 'pleasant' (understood as 'promoting a life in which pleasure predominates over pain') are names of one and the same thing, i.e. the goodness of an action or experience is identified with its contribution to an overall pleasant life. Central to the understanding of this position is the fact that goodness is identified, not with the pleasantness of an action or experience in isolation from its consequences, but with its contribution to a life in which pleasure predominates. This identification, which is made explicitly at 355a, licenses an extended use of the subjective 'pleasant' as equivalent to 'promoting a life in which pleasure predominates over pain', which we find employed at 360a in the argument that since going to war (or perhaps 'going into battle') is better and finer than running away, it is therefore also pleasanter. The emergence of this account of goodness and the related extension in the sense of 'pleasure' and 'pleasant' in the course of the argument with the common man may represent a development on the position originally taken by Socrates in 351b–e, but there are two grounds for caution on this point. (*a*) When at d7–e1 Socrates gets Protagoras to agree that he calls 'pleasant' things which either 'share in pleasure or produce pleasure', one way of understanding him is as securing agreement to the use of 'pleasant' as either 'characterized by pleasantness' (standard use) or 'productive of pleasantness' (extended use). The extension of the sense of 'pleasant' may, then, be part of Socrates' original position. (*b*) In the course of the argument with the common man, the distinction between the standard and the extended uses of 'pleasant' is not strictly observed; for the argument against the common man's substitution of 'pleasant' for 'good' depends on a failure to observe the distinction. The common man equates goodness with contribution to long-term pleasure, and his account of the weak-willed man is that the latter is overcome by short-term pleasure; yet the argument turns on the description of the weak-willed man as 'overcome by the good'. It seems that while Socrates' intention is to identify goodness with contribution to long-term pleasure, he may not have distinguished that concept from the concept of immediate pleasure as clearly as we might wish.

3.1.11. The thesis that pleasure is the good, as identified above, is of course an evaluative thesis, viz. the thesis that pleasure, understood (with the qualifications made in the previous paragraph) as a life in which pleasure predominates over distress, is the only thing ultimately worth seeking, with its corollary that it is the contribution to such a life which makes any particular thing worth seeking or having. But it is anachronistic to read into the dialogue the sharp distinction between evaluative and psychological theses which is taken for granted by most modern ethical theory. The ordinary man readily agrees (354c) that he pursues pleasure as good and avoids distress as bad (probably to be understood, in the context, as 'as *the* good' and 'as evil' (i.e. as *the* bad), since he has just agreed that he has no other ground for calling things good or bad than their production of pleasure or distress). It is plausible to suppose that both he and Socrates are represented as accepting that pleasure is the good (in the sense of 'worth seeking') because they take it for granted that pleasure is everyone's actual aim. The Socratic thesis that no-one does of his own free will what he takes to be the wrong thing to do appears to depend on the assumption that every action is directed towards the achievement of some ultimate end conceived as such by the agent, whether it be pleasure as in this dialogue, a worthwhile life (*eudaimonia*) as in the *Meno* (78a-b), or simply the good as in the *Gorgias* (468b-c). The identification of pleasure with what is aimed at gives particular point to the argument (352d-356b) that it is impossible for anyone to be led astray by pleasure, for the attractions of the ultimate aim cannot deflect one from the pursuit of that very aim; hence the explanation of the error must lie, not in the fact that the agent was overcome by pleasure as if by a force leading him away from his true aim, but in his mistaken estimation of where true pleasure is to be found. Of course, the opponent of the Socratic thesis can find his answer in the *Protagoras* itself; he has only to deny the assumption that the agent is uniformly motivated by the desire for a single ultimate aim, and point out that while his ultimate aim is the best balance of pleasure over pain, he is led astray by the desire for immediate pleasure, irrespective of long-term effects. It is ironical that the distinction between long-term and immediate pleasure, which is central to the hedonism of the *Protagoras*, should undermine the principal argument for the very thesis which hedonism is used to support, viz. that knowledge of what it is best to do is both necessary and sufficient for doing the right thing.

3.1.12. We have, then, to understand the thesis that pleasure is the good not only as the evaluative thesis stated in the previous paragraph, but also as the psychological thesis that 'long-term' pleasure is the goal which everyone in fact aims at. There is nothing to suggest that Plato saw these as separate theses.

2. Did Plato hold that thesis?

3.2.1. Having thus identified the view of the relation between pleasure and goodness which Socrates maintains in the *Protagoras*, we turn to the second of our four questions, whether that view may be supposed to have been that of Plato himself at the time of writing the dialogue. In accordance with our assumption (3.0.4) that the views of Socrates are to be taken to be those of Plato unless there is particular evidence to the contrary, we shall ask whether there is any such evidence in this case. We shall first examine features of the dialogue itself, which have sometimes been thought to show that Socrates is being ironical, is arguing *ad hominem*, is parodying sophistic method, or is being otherwise non-serious in maintaining his position on the relation of pleasure to goodness. Secondly we shall consider whether any external considerations might indicate non-seriousness even in default of internal evidence. This second question involves some consideration of the views of the historical Socrates and of the relative dating of the *Protagoras* and other dialogues.

3.2.2. As regards the internal evidence, most of the points of significance have already been touched on. Up to 351b, the *Protagoras* itself provides fairly clear examples of various kinds of non-seriousness. To take the most notorious example, the fact that Socrates' interpretation of Simonides' poem is a parody of sophistic method is made clear first internally by the transparently outrageous character of much of the exegesis and then externally by Socrates' explicit diagnosis of the unsoundness of such methods at 347b–e. Then we have at two points in the text a clear indication that Plato intends the reader to see that Socrates' argument is less than fully cogent, an indication given by the device of allowing Protagoras to voice an objection which meets with no adequate reply from Socrates. The more striking instance is the treatment of the first argument about courage (349e–351b; see above, 3.1.6), and the argument on holiness and justice (329d–331b) ends similarly. Protagoras' riposte (331d–e), though not so crushing as in the later instance, still draws attention to a weak point in Socrates' argument, viz. the fluidity of the crucial notion of likeness, while Socrates, instead of securing the definitive assent of his opponent which his dialectic requires (see 360a) explicitly leaves the argument unfinished and passes to another. By contrast, as we have already seen (3.1.6) from 351b the argument proceeds, not indeed directly, but none the less surely, towards its conclusion, with Socrates in full control at every stage. We have already seen sufficient grounds for rejecting the view of the argument as a whole as *ad hominem*, and there is no indication of any element of parody. The admission of self-contradiction at 361a–b is indeed ironical, but the function of the irony seems rather to emphasize the change in the conception of *aretē* which the Socratic conception of knowledge has produced than to cast any doubt on that conception itself. Finally, the assertion (361c–d) that the subject needs further examination is best understood as referring to the inadequacies in the arguments of the first part of the dialogue.[4]

---

[4] An extreme version of the view that Socrates' apparent espousal of hedonism is ironical is upheld by Dyson. According to him, Socrates, in purporting to derive the conclusion that *aretē* is knowledge from the premiss that pleasure is the good is actually trying to refute the premiss by showing that it both entails and is inconsistent with that conclusion, and hence that it is internally inconsistent. He states his central argument succinctly (p. 43): 'For knowledge to be possible . . . there must be something to know, facts or entities which can be known and used

3.2.3. There is, then, no substantial internal evidence to suggest that the hedonist thesis of the *Protagoras* is not intended seriously. But it is still possible that this could be established by external evidence alone, if it could be shown either that it was widely accepted that the historical Socrates was strongly opposed to hedonism, or that he had regularly been portrayed as such by Plato in dialogues earlier than the *Protagoras*. Similarly, were a modern writer to write a dialogue in which Bertrand Russell is represented as arguing with total conviction for the existence of God, he could rely on his readers' general knowledge of Russell to alert them to the fact that the piece was not intended to be taken seriously, not merely as a historical record, but even as a piece of philosophy. Was there, then, an established picture of an anti-hedonist Socrates?

3.2.4. Our brief account in the previous chapter of the evidence on Socrates' views on pleasure shows that no such picture is presented by the non-Platonic sources. Discounting the caricature in Aristophanes' *Clouds*, which would certainly (and rightly) not have been considered by Plato's readers as

---

in action . . . But in the case of hedonism there is nothing which can count except the amounts of pain and pleasure attendant upon the outcome of an action, and these are not, from the view-point of an agent, capable of being apprehended by knowledge, since they do not yet exist. Hedonism, then, is analysed to reveal a contradiction in what it implies, for it both requires right actions to be founded on knowledge, and at the same time shows its nature to be inaccessible to knowledge.' For this interpretation to have any plausibility, Dyson must provide some reason to believe that both premisses of the above argument were accepted by Plato, and that they were regarded by him as so uncontroversial that he could rely on his reader's using them to detect the real intention behind Socrates' purported derivation of his conclusion from his hedonistic premiss. He fails to satisfy this requirement. This may be allowable as regards the first premiss, but is certainly not so with respect to the second. While the theses that there can be no knowledge either in general of the future, or in general of what is hypothetical, or in particular of the outcomes of various possible courses of action, are all *defensible*, we see no reason to suppose that Plato took any of these for granted in writing the *Protagoras*, and still less (if there can be less than none) to suppose that he assumed that he could rely on his reader's acceptance of any. It is hard to see how anyone could find this interpretation plausible who was not already convinced that Plato could not have wished to represent Socrates as espousing any variety of hedonism.

For another defence of the thesis that one of Plato's aims in the *Protagoras* is the refutation of hedonism, see Duncan. His implied claim that Plato is relying on the reader's recognition of the incompatibility of hedonism with the description of courage as a virtue is open to the objections made above. See further 3.2.4–9.

giving an accurate picture of Socrates' views on anything, and in any case says nothing about pleasure, we have to consider only Xenophon and Aristotle, of whom only the former gives any substantial information. As we saw, he presents Socrates as firmly opposed to sybaritic hedonism, but not to pleasure as such, and puts into his mouth arguments which are quite close to the enlightened hedonism of the *Protagoras*. Even if it were accepted that Xenophon's Socrates reproduces the picture of Socrates generally accepted when Plato wrote the *Protagoras*, and that is something which we have not the slightest reason to accept, there is nothing in Xenophon's picture which would lead the reader to reject, or even suspect the hedonism of the *Protagoras*. The established picture would therefore have to be painted by Plato himself in other, and *ex hypothesi* earlier dialogues.

3.2.5. This hypothesis requires that some dialogue or dialogues earlier than the *Protagoras* represent Socrates as holding views clearly opposed to the hedonism attributed to him in the *Protagoras*. If we confine ourselves to dialogues where pleasure is discussed, the only one which can be suggested for this role with any plausibility is the *Gorgias*; we take it as established that the *Phaedo*, the only other dialogue earlier than the *Republic* to mention pleasure at all, is later than both *Protagoras* and *Gorgias*. The question of disagreement between the latter two will be considered in the next chapter; as far as the relative chronology goes, the evidence strongly indicates that the *Gorgias* is the later. It shares with the *Phaedo* an emphasis on soul-body dualism, with a corresponding interest in eschatology, which is wholly lacking from the *Protagoras*, and which it is customary, and reasonable, to ascribe to Pythagorean influence, perhaps acquired during Plato's first visit to Sicily about 387 BC. It shares with the *Republic* a psychology in which the virtues arise from the proper organization of the elements of the personality, specifically the proper ordering of the bodily desires (503d–508c). This, too, is best seen as a development from the *Protagoras*, which contains no account of the nature of the soul, nor any distinction of kinds of desires. Then, despite the importance of pleasure in the dialogue, the *Protagoras* contains no theory of its nature, while the *Gorgias* introduces the theory of pleasure as consisting in the filling-up of a deficiency, which remains for some time, with modifications, Plato's dominant model. Finally, at 454c–d Socrates draws the distinction between knowledge and belief with such care as to suggest that Plato does not expect that it is already familiar. In the *Protagoras*, by contrast, the distinction is not drawn at all, though it would have clarified the argument. Thus we find Socrates, having argued to 357e that it is impossible to act against knowledge of what is best, maintaining at 358b–c, apparently on the basis of the preceding argument, that it is impossible to act against one's knowledge or belief about what is best, and defining *amathia* accordingly as false belief. Yet at 360c–d the opposite of *amathia* is not true belief but *sophia*, which is generally equivalent to *epistēmē*. In all these instances we find present in the *Gorgias*, but lacking from the *Protagoras*, concepts which are central to Plato's thought throughout various phases of its development. The conclusion is irresistible that the *Gorgias* is the later.

3.2.6. The thesis of the establishement, prior to the *Protagoras*, of a Platonic picture of an anti-hedonist Socrates thus gains no support from the dialogues dealing with pleasure. But assuming, as we shall accept, that the *Apology* and *Crito* are among the earliest Platonic writings, and in particular that both were written before the *Protagoras*, it might with some force be urged that precisely that picture is established in those works. For in both Plato depicts a Socrates who holds it better to die than to act unjustly (see especially *Apol.* 28b, 28d, 32b–d; *Crito* 49a–b). Yet, notoriously, hedonism is unable to explain why courage in the face of death is virtuous; if the good is the maximization of pleasure, it cannot be achieved by ending one's life, and with it the possibility of any future pleasures.[5] If this argument is to be conclusive, it is not enough to establish the philosophical thesis that in fact hedonism cannot allow that courageous acceptance of death is a virtuous act; it must also be shown,

[5] This argument has been urged in private conversation by Professor Charles H. Kahn. It is used by Zeyl, p. 263.

or made plausible, that that was so clear to Plato's readers that they would have been at least likely to reject the explicit hedonism of the *Protagoras* on the strength of the picture of Socrates which they had derived from the *Apology* and *Crito*. We are sceptical on this point, partly on the ground that the philosophical issue itself is not as clear-cut as this argument requires. Firstly, a hedonist who believes in an afterlife and in posthumous rewards and punishments need have no trouble in explaining on hedonistic grounds why one ought to endure death rather than do things which will attract punishment after death. (It is, admittedly, doubtful if hedonism can account for the alleged fact that the gods punish such acts as cowardice; but that is a question of what is ultimately defensible, not of what is immediately obvious.) Socrates is, indeed, agnostic in the *Apology* as to whether there is an afterlife in which the soul is conscious (40c–e); but in the *Crito* (54b–d) the laws of Athens threaten him with an unfriendly reception by their brothers in Hades, without any suggestion of hesitation as to the reality of the afterlife. So the anti-hedonist picture would have to be presented, not in both *Apology* and *Crito*, but solely in the former, if at all. Further, leaving the afterlife aside, the stock hedonistic reply is that a courageous death is preferable, on hedonistic grounds, to a subsequent life of shame, disgrace, slavery, etc. Once again, this is certainly open to philosophical objections, but it is far from being so obviously absurd that it is apparent that no-one who recommends courage in the face of death can possibly be thought to accept hedonism. Moreover, even in the *Crito* Socrates is portrayed as thinking along similar lines; at 47d–48a he calls injustice a sickness of the soul, and argues that, just as it is not worth living with a sick and disordered body, even more it is not worth living with a sick and corrupt soul. There is indeed no mention of pleasure or pain in this passage, but it would be perfectly consistent with what is said if Socrates were understood as taking it for granted that bodily sickness is undesirable because it is painful and because it destroys the pleasure of life, and as assuming that the same must be true of the far worse sickness of the soul. A final hedonistic justification of courage is that one needs to acquire a courageous disposition in order to free oneself from the distress of fear during life, and that once acquired that disposition will lead to the choice of death in preference to dishonour or injustice, irrespective of the hedonistic consequences of the act itself. Here too a hostile critic might press for a distinction between a hedonistic justification for acquiring a disposition and a hedonistic justification for acting in accordance with a disposition once acquired; for us it is sufficient to show that it is possible for hedonism to underly an ethic which allows for or even prescribes the acceptance of death.[6]

3.2.7. It is, further, worth noting that in the *Gorgias* Plato criticizes the view that pleasure is the good, claiming that it is not consistent with Callicles' position that courage is a virtue. He does not, however, seize upon the supposedly obvious objection that the highest courage will lead to the cessation of all pleasure, and so if pleasure is good cowardice is often to be recommended. Instead he takes the weaker position that a courageous man does not experience any more pleasure than a coward in dangerous situations (see Ch. 4).

3.2.8. The example of sacrificing one's life is only an obvious objection to an egoistic hedonist. It is commonly

---

[6] For an actual example see J. S. Mill's justification of self-sacrifice in *Utilitarianism*, ch. II (Everyman ed. p.15): ' . . . the conscious ability to do without happiness gives the best prospect of realising such happiness as is attainable. For nothing except that consciousness can raise a person above the chances of life, by making him feel that, let fate and fortune do their worst, they have not power to subdue him: which, once felt, frees him from excess of anxiety concerning the evils of life, and enables him, like many a Stoic in the worst times of the Roman Empire, to cultivate in tranquillity the sources of satisfaction accessible to him, without concerning himself about the uncertainty of their duration, any more than about their inevitable end.'

The obligation to sacrifice one's life for some good end presents Aristotle with essentially the same problem as it poses for the hedonist. For the latter the problem is how pleasure, which presupposes life, can be maximized by the termination of life. For Aristotle the problem is how *eudaimonia*, which *is* excellent life, can be maximized by the termination of life. His answer, that excellence of life is maximized by the splendour of the action of sacrificing one's life, which is worth more than a lifetime of humdrum action (*EN* 1169a18-26), is indeed unsatisfactory (see Hardie pp. 329-31), but it is undeniable that he *thought* that his theory could accommodate self-sacrifice. Equally Plato may have *thought* that Socrates' commitment to justice at the cost of his life could be accommodated by hedonism.

felt to be obvious that no egoist can consistently advocate the pursuit of other-regarding virtues at the expense of diminution of one's welfare, and it is clear that Plato wishes to advocate the pursuit of justice. In the *Republic* (540b) he faces the difficulty of guardians who are living the best life possible having to be persuaded to undertake the uncongenial task of ruling the city. The evident weakness of the argument that it is only just to do so may be a sign of some discomfort on Plato's part, but he does not take incompatibility of achieving one's good and being just as so obvious as to force a critical choice. Indeed, it is unlikely that the implications of the egoistic strands in his position struck Plato as forcibly as they have later philosophers. In the early dialogues there is constant vacillation between describing what the agent wants as his own good, the possession of goods or to be good (cf. *Crito* 48b; *Euthyd.* 279 ff.; *Meno* 77–8). Plato is at the beginning of exploration of the relationships between these notions.

3.2.9. We find, then, that neither the dialogues which deal expressly with the topic of pleasure nor the *Apology* and *Crito* support the thesis that there was established, prior to the *Protagoras*, a Platonic picture of Socrates as someone committed to views incompatible with hedonism. Rather, Plato's earliest account of Socrates' views on pleasure represents him as an enlightened hedonist, while the pre-existing picture given by the *Apology* and *Crito* contains nothing obviously incompatible with hedonism and includes, in the allusion to sickness of the soul at *Crito* 47d–48a, at least a hint of a hedonistic outlook. In accordance with our assumption (3.0.4) we shall therefore take it that Plato's first position on pleasure was that of enlightened hedonism, and attempt to trace an intelligible development from that initial position to his later views.

3.2.10. The absence of any discussion of epistemology or psychology (including any account of pleasure) from the *Protagoras*, together with the absence of any hint of the theory of Forms, suggest that the dialogue is an early work, written before he had developed the metaphysical and epistemological doctrines which we regard as characteristically Platonic. This hypothesis, suggested to account for the negative evidence, coheres well with the positive content of the dialogue. In its main themes, the unity of the virtues and the necessity and sufficiency of knowledge for right conduct, the *Protagoras* forms a group with the *Laches* and the *Charmides*, both of which start from the examination of a single virtue and reach an aporetic conclusion, which yet conveys a strong hint that all the virtues are to be identified with knowledge of what is best. (The same view is perhaps also adumbrated in the *Euthyphro*.) Both dialogues, like the *Protagoras*, lack any substantial element of metaphysics, epistemology, or psychology. The *Protagoras* appears to represent a development over the other two in so far as it treats the virtues as a whole and offers an account of knowledge of what is best. At the same time the question of the teachability of *aretē* links the *Protagoras* with the *Meno*, where epistemology becomes a serious concern, the distinction between knowledge and belief is clearly drawn, and the doctrine of recollection requires the separation of soul and body and marks a first step on the road towards transcendent objects of knowledge.[7] We produce a plausible picture if we assume that the *Protagoras* belongs with the *Laches*, *Charmides*, and *Euthyphro* to an early stage of Plato's development where he was chiefly concerned to present discussions, Socratic in style, of the fairly restricted range of ethical topics which had actually interested Socrates, out of which his own metaphysical and epistemological interests gradually crystallized. We have seen that features of the content of the dialogues suggest that

[7] As in the case of the *Gorgias*, the predominance in the *Meno* of 'Platonic' themes absent from the *Protagoras* suggests that the *Meno* is the later. Cahn argues for the priority of the *Meno* on the ground that while both dialogues contain the argument that *aretē* must be unteachable because outstanding men fail to transmit it to their sons (*Prot.* 319e–320b; *Meno* 92e–94e), the *Protagoras* supplies the necessary rebuttal viz. that the pheomenon is explained not by the unteachability of *aretē* but by lack of aptitude on the part of those taught (326e–327e). In fact this topic too suggests rather that the *Protagoras* is the earlier since the explanation by lack of aptitude is expressly rejected at *Meno* 93d. Further the *Meno*'s distinction between knowledge and true belief provides the definitive statement of the position: *aretē* as ordinarily conceived cannot be taught if it arises from true but unsystematized belief. True *aretē*, consisting in knowledge of the good, can be taught by the genuine expert (99e–100a).

the *Protagoras* may be the latest of the group, a conclusion which is also strongly suggested by its dramatic sophistication, which is parallelled in the whole Platonic corpus only by that of the *Symposium*.

3.2.11. One particular feature of this group of dialogues gives some support to the suggestion that initially Plato kept fairly close to what he took to be actual Socratic topics and arguments. This is the fact that in the *Charmides* and *Protagoras sōphrosunē* is treated, not in the sense of 'mastery of appetite' which predominates in Plato's mature dialogues, e.g. *Gorgias* and *Republic*, but in its fundamental sense of 'soundness of mind', and is in the *Protagoras* identified with *sophia* (332a–333b), an identification which Xenophon reports Socrates as having made (*Mem*. III.ix.4). It is therefore quite likely that the treatment of *sōphrosunē* in the *Charmides* and *Protagoras* represents a specifically Socratic view.

3.2.12. We suggest, then, that we have sufficient evidence to render at least probable the hypothesis that in writing the *Protagoras* Plato presented what he took to be Socrates' actual view of the nature of goodness, viz. that goodness is identical with long-term pleasantness. This thesis embraces in undifferentiated form the three theses: (*a*) long-term pleasantness is the only thing that everyone ultimately aims at, (*b*) long-term pleasantness is the only thing ultimately worth having, (*c*) what makes those things we call 'goods' worth having is their contribution to a life in which pleasure predominates over distress. This hypothesis is consistent with the general character of the group of dialogues to which the *Protagoras* may confidently be assigned by reason of its content, and is not excluded by any other evidence available to us of the ethical views of the historical Socrates. If anything, it is supported by the evidence of Xenophon that Socrates both maintained that his life was the pleasantest of all and used against the sybaritic hedonism of Aristippus an argument which contains elements of long-term hedonism.

3.2.13. We have now concluded our treatment of the

second of our four questions (3.0.4). In the following chapters we shall consider the third and fourth, by examining the treatment of pleasure in other dialogues and its relation to that which we have discovered in the *Protagoras*. In so doing we shall test the hypothesis that in the *Protagoras* Plato presents a position on pleasure which, though no doubt accepted by Plato himself at the time of writing, was essentially what he took to be the Socratic view, out of which his independent view was gradually to develop.

Chapter 4

Gorgias

4.0.1. We shall consider the *Gorgias* first, both because it is, of the dialogues where pleasure is discussed, most probably the nearest in date to the *Protagoras*, and because it appears to contain an explicit rejection of the identification of pleasure with the good, which, we have argued, is maintained by Socrates in the latter dialogue. At 495a-d Callicles asserts 'that pleasure and good are the same', which reproduces word for word the formulation of Socrates' position given to Protagoras at 351e5-6, a formulation which we argued to be correct. Socrates then attacks that thesis of Callicles', and at 500d it is agreed that it has been refuted, and 'the good' is something distinct from 'the pleasant'. But the view that the treatment of pleasure in the *Gorgias* is directed towards the direct refutation of the hedonistic thesis of the *Protagoras* does not depend solely on the verbal reproduction of a key formula, but seems also to be supported by the opposition of doctrine which may be discerned throughout the two discussions. Thus at *Prot.* 351c Socrates suggests that the good life is one of pleasure, while it is Protagoras who holds that some pleasures are good and some bad. In the *Gorgias* (492c, 494c, 494e, 497a) it is Callicles who holds that the good life is one of unrestrained pleasure and who initially refuses to distinguish between good and bad pleasures. In the *Protagoras* pleasure is the *telos* which makes good things worthy of pursuit (354a-d), but in the *Gorgias* we are told firmly (506c-d) that pleasure is to be pursued for the sake of the good, not vice versa. Further, the whole attitude to pleasure in the *Gorgias* is extremely severe. Thus, to aim at the pleasure of others without consideration of their overall good is the merest sycophancy (501a-c), while pursuits (such as confectionery, cosmetics, and play-writing) which have that aim are mere knacks as opposed to genuine skills (462d-465d, 501a-505b). Real skill in any field is the knowledge of how to put the materials into proper order; in the highest form of skill, viz. knowledge of how to direct human life, whether in oneself or in others, the materials are the elements in the personality, and the proper order is that in which the desires are subordinated to the requirements of justice and temperance (503d–508e). That is to say, the highest virtue consists in the control of the appetite for pleasure.

4.0.2. All this does indeed suggest recantation of the hedonism of the *Protagoras*, or alternatively an attempt to make clear that that position was not after all to be read as representing Plato's own opinion. But in fact the situation is not so simple. For the position which Callicles defends is very far from the enlightened hedonism of the *Protagoras*, and the arguments by which Socrates attacks that position have no force against the thesis of that dialogue. So if the *Protagoras* is a target in the *Gorgias*, Plato is wide of the mark.

1. Callicles' position

4.1.1. Callicles does not set out to defend any version of hedonism, but is led to take up a hedonistic position by a suggestion of Socrates' that rulers should be able to rule themselves, being in control of their pleasures and desires (491d), and so being restrained. Callicles takes this as a description of someone not in complete control, for why should the man in complete control of things refrain from satisfying his desires? Now the desires and pleasures with which self-control (*sōphrosunē*) is associated form a sub-set of all human desires; they are all those bodily desires which a sybarite would espouse. The ideal man (429a) will have large desires and the ability to satisfy them, while the man who lacks desire is a lifeless stone. Socrates, for his part, reinforces this interpretation of 'desire' and 'pleasure' in his two images of the soul (493–4), which he presents to contrast his own position with that of Callicles. In the first of these people who seek to satisfy their bodily appetites are likened to damned souls condemned to carry water in sieves to fill a leaky jar; the second contrasts the temperate man, whose jars, once filled, remain so, so that he doesn't have to trouble about them any more, with the self-indulgent man, condemned to the endless task of filling his leaky jars. Callicles prefers the life of the latter, since the recurrence of unsatisfied desire provides the repeated opportunity of replenishment, i.e. of pleasure. This view is then developed with examples of the satisfaction of hunger and thirst to give a general account of pleasure, in which pleasure is treated as consisting in the satisfaction of desire, desire is treated as equivalent to lack or depletion (*endeia*) and all depletion is unpleasant (494a–497a, esp. 496d). It is an account which is most plausible when applied to certain bodily pleasures, e.g. those of satisfying hunger and thirst, and it is nowhere applied to any others. In short, Callicles is portrayed as advocating the cultivation of certain desires and their satisfaction; the desires in question are treated as bodily lacks, their satisfaction as the replenishment of those lacks. The life of pleasure which Callicles advocates, is, then, a life devoted to the satisfaction of short-term bodily appetite. There is no indication of what Socrates might say to someone who had other pleasures in mind. That he would have to say something else were he to attack the position upheld in the *Protagoras* is quite plain. For, confronted with the picture of the self-indulgent man, endlessly slaving to satisfy his insatiable desires, all that the Socrates of the *Protagoras* has to reply is that such a man has not assessed the prospects of pleasure and pain properly. Instead of working out the total consequences he is led astray by the attractions of each pleasure as it occurs, and so gives himself up to a self-frustrating way of life. The fault is not that he has the wrong aim, but that he goes the wrong way about achieving it. Nothing in the *Gorgias* constitutes an objection to that position.

2. Socrates' counter-arguments

4.2.1. The arguments which are actually employed in the *Gorgias* do not in fact tell against the hedonistic thesis of the *Protagoras*. We saw that in the *Protagoras* the formula 'the pleasant is the good' was ultimately to be read as 'goodness is identical with long-term pleasantness', or, even more explicitly 'goodness is identical with a contribution to a life in which pleasure predominates over distress'. But the arguments against Callicles depend on the identification of goodness not with long-term pleasantness but with immediate pleasantness. There are two main arguments. The first (495e–497d) runs as follows. It is impossible (a) to be benefited and harmed in the same respect at the same time, (b) to cease to be benefited and to cease to be harmed in the same respect at the same time. (E.g. it is impossible (a) to have good eyesight and bad eyesight at the same time and (b) to recover one's good eyesight and to lose it at the same time.) But all lack and desire is unpleasant. Hence those who experience the pleasure of satisfying bodily desire such as hunger and thirst experience pleasure and distress in the same respect at the same time. Therefore, those cases of feeling pleasure are not cases of being benefited, and those cases of feeling distress are not cases of being harmed. Further, the pleasure of satisfying a desire such as thirst ceases at the moment when the desire itself ceases. But by the second part (b) of the first premiss, it is impossible to cease to be benefited and to cease to be harmed in the same respect at the same time. Hence, once again we reach the conclusion that such cases of feeling pleasure are not cases of being benefited, nor such cases of feeling distress cases of being harmed. Hence good things are not the same as pleasant things, nor bad things the same as unpleasant things.

4.2.2. This argument is both difficult to interpret and, whatever interpretation is adopted, unconvincing. Firstly, it is unclear whether Socrates is to be thought of as assuming that every case of pleasure consists in the pleasure of satisfying some desire, and as arguing on that assumption that, since all desire is unpleasant, every case of pleasure involves the coincidence of pleasure and distress, from which, together with the first premiss, it would follow that no pleasure is a benefit, and no pain a harm. Alternatively, he might be represented as arguing that, since some pleasures (e.g. those of satisfying hunger and thirst) involve that coincidence, *those* pleasures are not benefits. The latter, weaker thesis is all that Socrates needs to refute the identification of goodness with pleasantness, since that identification, entailing as it does the universal thesis 'Whatever is immediately pleasant is good' can be refuted by the production of a single instance of something which is pleasant but not good. Moreover, the weaker thesis does not require the additional premiss which has to be understood on the stronger reading, viz. that all pleasure consists in satisfying some desire. On the other hand, the stronger thesis does require a step which *is* stated in the test, the generalization that all desire is unpleasant; this is unnecessary for the proof of the weaker thesis, which could be derived from any of the instances (e.g. hunger) which precede that generalization in the text. It is hard to see why Plato should put that step in unless he had the stronger thesis in some way or other in mind. Perhaps the correct answer to this problem is that Plato did not see the two versions of the argument as distinct. Concerned as he was with the refutation of the thesis that pleasure is the good as maintained by someone who conceives pleasure as the immediate pleasure of satisfying bodily desires, it is not implausible to suggest that he may have given no thought to the satisfaction of desires other than bodily desires. If he were concentrating exclusively on bodily desires, then the stronger and weaker versions of the argument would be extensionally equivalent. The main defect of the argument lies in the thesis that all lack and (bodily) desire is unpleasant. For, firstly, that formulation blurs the distinction between physiological deficiency, felt appetite and want (e.g. protein deficiency, hunger, and desire for food), which are all distinct from one another; thus hunger implies desire for food but not vice versa, and deficiency has no logical relations with the other two. Since the pleasures of *over*-indulgence are presumably high on Callicles' list, this point is crucial; the sybarite is, among other things, the sort of person who goes on eating when he is not hungry. Secondly, even when applied to felt appetite, where it is at its most plausible, the thesis is untrue. Not all cases of hunger, thirst, or sexual desire are unpleasant; one works up a nice appetite for lunch, and may find a state of sexual arousal itself something pleasant. Such appetites are unpleasant not as a general rule, but only when their satisfaction is impossible or excessively delayed.

4.2.3. But even if these objections were set aside, together with others which a full discussion would require, it is immediately clear that the most that the argument could show is that the immediate experience of pleasure in the satisfaction of some bodily desire is not necessarily beneficial to the person who experiences it. But the hedonistic thesis of the *Protagoras* explicitly allows that, since on that thesis the criterion of goodness (i.e. benefit) is not the immediate experience but the long-term effect. Nor can the argument of the *Gorgias* be turned against long-term pleasantness. For even if it were conceded that immediate bodily pleasure is always or even usually accompanied by a corresponding bodily distress, it would be impossible to maintain that the long-term pleasantness of such bodily satisfaction is always counter-balanced by some long-term unpleasantness. For that would be to maintain the self-contradictory thesis that a life in which pleasure predominates over distress is also, necessarily, a life in which distress predominates over pleasure.

4.2.4. The second argument (497d–499d) also leaves the hedonism of the *Protagoras* untouched. It runs as follows. Good men are good by the presence of good things. In certain situations, inferior sorts of person have at least as much pleasure as superior (e.g. cowards are at least as pleased as brave men when the enemy withdraws). Therefore, the pleasure which the inferior man feels is not something good (sc. for if it were, it would by its presence make the inferior man at least the equal of the superior). Again, we can leave aside the various questionable features of the argument and merely point out that, like the first, it is concerned exclusively with the immediate pleasantness or unpleasantness of such a situation as facing the enemy in battle. Someone who accepts the enlightened hedonism of the *Protagoras* would of course accept that in the immediate situation the coward will derive more pleasure (or, more plausibly, less distress) than the brave man; what he must insist on is that in the long run the coward will find his life predominantly unpleasant, while the brave man finds his predominantly pleasant. The weakness of that position is that there is no reason to believe that it must always be true that a brave man's life will be pleasanter than a coward's, and very hard to see, in some special circumstances (e.g. where the alternative to cowardice is death under torture) how it *could* be true, failing some very unplausible assumptions (e.g. that the coward will feel so ashamed that his subsequent life will be not only not worth living, but not worth preferring to death by torture). But these arguments, which have considerable force against the hedonistic thesis of the *Protagoras*, are distinct from Plato's actual argument, which has none.[1]

4.2.5. A similar result emerges from consideration of the contrast made in the *Gorgias* between the pursuit of pleasure, which is seen as a mere untheoretical knack, and genuine skills such as building and medicine. The arguments of 462–5 and 501–5 which contrast knacks and skills do not show that there could be no skill concerning pleasure, but just that those who claim skill in the production of pleasure do not in fact have any. Once the admission is extracted from Callicles (499b) that some pleasures are good, some bad, it is claimed (500a) that it will require skill to discriminate them. According to the thesis of the *Protagoras*, the necessary skill is the correct application of the hedonistic calculus; the *Gorgias* is silent as to the precise nature of the skill required, and while indeed the language does not sound as though Socrates is thinking along the same lines as in the *Protagoras*, the dialogue contains no argument to show that the account given in the *Protagoras* is to be rejected. Both dialogues in fact agree that some highly developed skill involving mathematical techniques is required to be a good man; they differ in that while the *Protagoras* tells us what is to be measured, viz. pleasure and distress, the *Gorgias* does not.

3. *Protagoras* and *Gorgias*

4.3.1. The outcome of all this is that Socrates' tirade against pleasure in the *Gorgias* contains no argument that

---

[1] Irwin (2), pp. 203–6 suggests that by the time of writing the *Gorgias* Plato may have accepted that the brave man is not a more efficient pleasure-seeker than the coward, and hence have rejected the enlightened hedonism of the *Protagoras*, which includes the identification of courage as knowledge of what is best (i.e. pleasantest) for the agent. There is, of course, room for difference of opinion as to how strong Plato may have felt the hedonistic counter-arguments to be. It is, however, quite clear that the arguments of the *Gorgias* do not *as they stand* require the supposition that in writing them Plato had abandoned the hedonism of the *Protagoras*.

refutes the enlightened hedonism which he maintains in the
Protagoras. Hence if the refutation of the hedonism of the
Protagoras is among Plato's aims in writing the *Gorgias* he is
totally confused, having altogether failed to grasp his own
distinction between long-term and immediate pleasantness,
and consequently failed to see the strength of the position
which he has assigned to Socrates in the *Protagoras*. Since we
saw that the argument against the common man at *Protagoras*
355b–d depended on blurring that distinction, this diagnosis
of what is going on in the *Gorgias*, though regrettable, is not
altogether impossible. We should not, however, attribute such
a degree of confusion to Plato unless the evidence for this
interpretation is virtually irresistible. There is thus a strong
presumption in favour of the alternative hypothesis that the
refutation of the hedonism of the *Protagoras* was not one of
Plato's aims in writing the *Gorgias*. That hypothesis has this
degree of independent support, that it gives a better fit with
the dialectical situation of the confrontation of Socrates and
Callicles. The latter is induced to present himself as the
advocate of a life of unrestrained satisfaction of desire,
especially bodily desire; the ideal is to keep the pleasure
flowing in as much as possible (494b2), and he accepts
Socrates' characterization of his view of the good as pleasure
of whatever sort (*to pantōs chairein*). Against this undiscrimi-
nating lust for pleasure, which threatens to overthrow every
standard of behaviour, it is clearly relevant to point out the
paradoxical consequences of maintaining that every immediate
pleasure is good, and the consequent necessity of a criterion
to distinguish good from harmful pleasures. Such a criterion
might, of course, be provided by a refined hedonism of the
type found in the *Protagoras*; but in the context of the
debate with Callicles the central issue is not *what* the criterion
is, but that a rationally acceptable life requires some criterion,
which is what Callicles sets out by denying. That is to say,
the situation of the argument with Callicles suggests that
Plato's dominant thought is not 'Pleasure, as conceived in the
Protagoras, cannot be the good', but 'Pleasure, as conceived
by Callicles, cannot be the good'.

4.3.2. It thus appears that the alleged inconsistency

between the *Protagoras* and the *Gorgias* is illusory. What is maintained in the former is not what is attacked in the latter, nor is Socrates' position on pleasure in the former inconsistent with the stance which he adopts in the latter. But in dissolving one problem we seem merely to have created another. For since, as we have seen, the hedonism of the *Protagoras* could itself have been used to *refute* Callicles, and since the style of argument would have been particularly telling against his hedonism (for it would show him to be an *incompetent* hedonist), we surely require some explanation of why Plato made no use of it in the *Gorgias*. And if we suggest that the reason is that by the time of writing the *Gorgias* he had ceased to believe it, we may reasonably ask why he nowhere indicates what defects he had discovered in it.

4.3.3. The point that Plato could be expected to use the hedonistic argument in the *Gorgias* is not, in fact, as powerful as at first sight it seems. It is, after all, an argument that is most easily and satisfyingly used against someone who is a committed hedonist. Then one can argue that he needs to be more serious about his pleasure estimates. Against someone who is not primarily a hedonist or not one at all it would be necessary to establish first the hedonistic premiss. Now Callicles is not primarily a hedonist. In his original outburst at 482c–486c he is not arguing that since pleasure is the good, Socrates must be wrong, but rather that philosophy is a pastime for children, that a man of the world will recognize that justice and law are not naturally acceptable, and that nature's law is to reward the stronger. Philosophy makes a man no man, without experience of human desires or pleasures, ignorant of the law and the ways of the state, unable to fend for himself and make his way in public life, and in general unfit to become a leading man with a well-deserved reputation. The general picture is that nature drives us to the acquisition of goods and power, to the position where restraint is no longer needed since there is no other power to fear, and it is the person who approximates to that position who wins our admiration, who is a real man, in contrast with the unmanly snivelling of philosophers.

4.3.4. The dominant theme here is the ideal of success in rising above the need to submit to laws. Of course, it will be natural to resist advocacy of temperance and self-restraint, but it is not putting forward pursuit of pleasure, and certainly not a life of effeminate indulgence, as the ideal. Socrates' strategy is to play on the opposition to self-restraint so that emphasis is put on the real man's ability to satisfy his desires. Also, as a real man he will not desire pusillanimously, but will be big in his desires as elsewhere. By interpreting this as a thesis in favour of developing and satisfying bodily desires, and developing a particular picture of bodily desires, Socrates aims to redraw Callicles' man as not manly but sycophantic, pandering to his body, not strong but weak, not a paragon of intelligence but a man lacking the intelligence to ask or answer what for his own purposes should be the important questions. Of course, someone who accepts Socrates' arguments still has a choice. He can either abandon the step that makes it a good thing to indulge desires, or he can go sybaritic and drop the manly picture. Plato is clearly relying on the manliness of success continuing its appeal. His diagnosis is that at least some advocacy of pleasure relies on this ideal of the successful man. Faced with a person in this position, it is obviously polemically more promising to argue that the sybaritic hedonism he half-espouses is a poor bedfellow for his aspirations to success and competence, than to argue that it is pleasure that is the good but its achievement will involve foregoing many bodily pleasures. So, even if Plato retained his belief in hedonism, as espoused in the *Protagoras*, it would not necessarily be appropriate for him to bring it out on each occasion, and in the case of Callicles one can see that the actual strategy has a good deal to be said for it.

4.3.5. There is, then, no need to postulate the abandonment of the hedonism of the *Protagoras* in order to explain its absence from the *Gorgias*. Nevertheless there are some differences between the two dialogues which make it likely that Plato was led, if not to abandon his original view, at least to consider how it should be modified to conform to the development of his thought. This process of reconsideration might then provide a partial explanation, if explanation is needed, of the absence of this view from the *Gorgias*.

4.3.6. Firstly, the *Gorgias* places considerable emphasis on dualism of body and soul (*psuchē*), a view of the person which is altogether absent from the *Protagoras*. Socrates does indeed insist in his opening discussion with Hippocrates (313a–314b) that the *psuchē* is much more important than the body, but the contrast there is between two aspects of the person, the physical on the one hand and the moral and intellectual on the other. There is no suggestion that the body and *psuchē* are separate entities, or that the individual can be identified with one rather than the other. Consistently with this unitary view of the person the dialogue assumes unitary motivation; all action is motivated by the desire for pleasure, and all pleasures have to be measured alike by the hedonistic calculus, being distinguished in point of value only by their contribution to the overall good. In the *Gorgias*, on the other hand, especially in the later sections of the dialogue, there is a strong suggestion that the individual is the *psuchē*, and that the body is rather a hindrance to its proper activity than an essential aspect of it. Socrates quotes with approval the suggestion of an unnamed (presumably Pythagorean) sage that the body is the tomb of the soul (493a), and the concluding myth presents a picture of the soul revealing its true nature when stripped of the body and achieving its final destiny, for good or ill, in separation from it. Since the pleasures and desires which are discussed are exclusively bodily pleasures and desires, which are seen as confusing and disturbing the *psuchē* (493a), as enslaving it (493e–494b) and as disfiguring it (525a), Plato might well have begun to think that such pleasures should not be given any positive value to be weighed against the distress which they produce in the long term. We should not exaggerate the extent of this dualism, since Socrates accepts that the bodily desires are 'in the soul' (493a). That is to say, he denies that desires are physiological events in the history of an entity linked only contingently with the essential self. On the other hand, this has to be set against the equation of desire with deficiency, and pleasure with the making up of deficiency (496d–e), which at least encourages, without strictly necessitating, the treatment of both as physical processes. While we must therefore recognize that we cannot clearly characterize the status of pleasure and desire in the *Gorgias* in terms of the mental-physical dichotomy (since Plato's text supplies no clear criteria for the application of those concepts), it is plain that bodily pleasure and desire are thought of on the whole as obstructing the attainment by the real self of its overall good. Yet at 499d bodily pleasures which promote health are good, so at least *some* bodily pleasures make *some* contribution to the overall good. The hedonism of the *Protagoras* would clearly require substantial modification if it were to fit this new picture of the self and its accompanying complications.

4.3.7. Secondly, where the *Protagoras* contains no account of the nature of pleasure, the *Gorgias* does give one, or at least an account of the nature of the pleasures which Callicles is interested in. This is the view of pleasure as the filling-up of a bodily deficiency, of which we found some evidence in Empedocles (1.2.6–7) and which may have come to interest Plato via the influence of Pythagoreanism, much of which is close to the thought of Empedocles. It is an analysis which is very attractive when applied to certain prominent bodily pleasures, and well suited to an outlook which combines dualism with hostility to the body. The availability of a plausible account of the nature of one large class of pleasures, with no obvious analysis of any others, would leave one in a position of not knowing what to say about non-bodily pleasures. In that event it would once more be clear that the hedonism of the *Protagoras* would have to be modified, but not clear just what form the modification should take.

4.3.8. A third development which might have led to re-assessment of the hedonism of the *Protagoras* is the interest in psychological structure which we find for the first time in the *Gorgias*. The view that right conduct depends on some state of the agent's personality is already present in the *Laches*, *Charmides*, and *Protagoras*, which are largely devoted to the attempt to identify the state or states which account for the various kinds of virtuous conduct. What is new in the *Gorgias* is the specification of the psychological basis of right conduct as an organizational state, in which different elements of the personality are arranged in the proper order. This is

presented as a special case of the general law that anything of
any kind, whether artefact or organic substance, is in its best
state when its parts or elements are arranged in the proper
order (503d ff., 506d). Rational order and proportion may
then naturally be seen as what makes things good, which is
to say that one might expect Plato to identify goodness with
order and proportion. In fact he does not do so explicitly in
the *Gorgias*, but the prominence which he assigns to those
concepts and their close association must at the very least
have suggested to him some questions about the identification
of pleasure with goodness which had seemed so unproblematic
when he wrote the *Protagoras*. Among such questions are
'What determines which order of elements in the soul is the
right order? Is the order in which the bodily desires are under
the control of reason the proper order *because* the man with
that order in his soul will live a life in which pleasure predominates over pain? Or is such a life the reward which
accrues to one who has in his soul the proper order, the rightness of which is, however, determined by some independent
principle? Or is the life of the rationally ordered soul worth
living for reasons which are totally independent of any
considerations of pleasure?' In the first case, the new psychology would slot neatly into the hedonism of the *Protagoras*.
In the third, hedonism would have no part in the thinking of
the virtuous man. In the second, while hedonism would no
longer provide an ultimate criterion of value, the application
of a hedonistic calculus in the manner of the *Protagoras*
might still be the best mode of deliberation. For instance, the
best way to keep one's bodily desires in the proper subordi-
nation to reason might be to subject them to the rule of
always following the course of action which seemed likely to
bring most pleasure in the long run. None of these questions
is raised in the *Gorgias* though some are considered in later
dialogues. Nor does the *Gorgias* suggest how Plato might
have answered them had they been put to him. It does, however, provide clear evidence of the emergence of ideas which
we may plausibly suppose to have led Plato to reconsider his
earliest thoughts on pleasure.

4.3.9. Strictly speaking, then, the answer to our third

original question (3.0.4) is that there is no inconsistency between the positions on pleasure upheld by Socrates in the *Protagoras* and the *Gorgias*. Hence the fourth question, how to account for inconsistency, does not arise. But this answer would be misleading in leaving out of account the probable development of Plato's thought from *Protagoras* to *Gorgias*. The latter appears to be a transitional dialogue, in which appear, in comparatively undeveloped form, themes which assume importance in Plato's later treatments of pleasure: we have mentioned dualism, accompanied by devaluation of the body and its appetites; the picture of the soul as a structured organism, in a context where order and proportion are emphasized as essential constituents of goodness; and finally a physiologically-slanted theory of pleasure, which is applied only to bodily pleasures and whose application to other kinds of pleasure is obscure. Consistently with our original hypothesis, we may thus see the *Gorgias* as showing the development towards a specifically Platonic view of pleasure from his original Socratic position. We must now consider whether the evidence of the *Phaedo* is consistent with this suggestion.

Chapter 5

Phaedo

1. Bodily pleasure in the *Phaedo*

5.1.1. There is much in common between the treatments of pleasure in the *Gorgias* and in the *Phaedo*. Both treat almost exclusively of bodily pleasures; both emphasize dualism of soul and body and rail against bodily pleasures as shackles which bind the soul in its bodily prison, preventing it from achieving its proper perfection apart from the body. The separation of soul and body is in fact the central theme of the *Phaedo*. Whereas in the *Gorgias* it is introduced incidentally to the main themes of the nature of human goodness and the form of education necessary to produce it, the central theme of the *Phaedo* is precisely the identification of a fully human life as the discarnate life of the soul, immersed in the contemplation of eternal reality, and the demonstration of the immortality of the soul which is presupposed by that conception. Accordingly the attack on bodily pleasures in the *Phaedo* is more sustained and vehement. The contrast between the proper life of the soul and the perverted life of attachment to the body is drawn in two main sections, 64c–69e and 80c–84b. The former describes the philosopher's preparation, while still in the body, for the true life which he will live after he is separated from the body by death. The very first point made (64d) is that the philosopher will pay no attention whatever to the 'so-called pleasures' of the body, instanced by the pleasures of food, drink, and sex; this is then generalized to the assertion that he frees himself as far as he can from cares about the body and concerns himself only with the things of the soul (64e–65a). Consequently, he will strike the ordinary man as someone with one foot in the grave, who doesn't deserve to be alive; here again, the main point picked out is that he does not like any of the things of the body nor go in for them (lit. 'nothing of such things is pleasant (*hēdu*) for him nor does he partake of them'), and that he cares nothing for the pleasures which come via the body. The distracting power of bodily pleasures is stressed again when Socrates turns to describe the activity of the philosopher (65c); the proper activity of the mind is thought, which is best exercised when it is free from any distraction from the senses, from pain or from any (sc. bodily) pleasure. The point is repeated with greater force and eloquence at 66c; the body 'fills us with lusts and desires and fears and fantasies of all kinds and a great deal of nonsense', so that it is impossible to think straight. Further, war and strife arise from the need to satisfy bodily desires; for all wars are caused by the desire for possessions, whose ultimate purpose is the satisfaction of bodily desires. This section leads into a contrast (68b–69c) between the genuine goodness of the philosopher and the spurious goodness of the lover of the body (*philosōmatos* as opposed to *philosophos* 68c1), who gives up some pleasures for the sake of others and faces up to some fearful things because he fears worse things. As this passage has seemed to some to contain an outright attack on the hedonistic calculus of the *Protagoras* it will be considered in more detail below (5.2); for the present it is sufficient to point out that it is set in the context of the opposition of the two lives, that dominated by the desires and pleasures of the body and that devoted to the proper activity of the soul.

5.1.2. In 80c–84b Socrates describes the goal for which the philosopher has been preparing himself, the life of the discarnate soul in communion with reality. Once again, the contrast between soul and body is starkly drawn. The soul will be in a blessed state if it has freed itself from 'confusion and stupidity and fears and wild lusts and the other evils of the human condition' (81a). By contrast, it cannot attain to the pure realm of the intellect if it lives a life of servitude to the body 'taken in by its tricks and those of its desires and its pleasures, so that it thinks nothing real except what is physical, the sort of thing you can touch and see and drink and eat and have sex with' (81b). The language is worth noting for its content as well as for its literary power. The word translated 'taken in by its tricks' (*goēteuomenē*) describes the state of someone who has been put under a spell or subjected to an illusion. A *goēs* is a magician, either a genuine sorcerer or, more frequently, and especially in Plato, a conjurer or illusionist (e.g. *Soph*. 235a; *Pol*. 291c, 303c; *Rep*. 598d), and *goēteuein* is the verb for what he does. The use of this verb strongly suggests that the desires and pleasures of the body make one take as real what is in some sense or other unreal; the victim of the illusion thinks that nothing is real (*alēthes*, which also means 'true') except what is physical and what gives bodily pleasure, whereas (it is implied) these things are not real at all, but mere illusion. The thought is continued at 83a–d. The enlightened man regards the senses as a source of deception and takes as true or real only what is grasped by the exercise of pure thought, while the desires, pleasures, and pains of the body nail the soul to the body, making it accept as true whatever the body says (d6). Though there is a striking linguistic resemblance between these passages and the contrast of real and illusory pleasure in *Republic* IX (expecially between *Ph*. 80b. and *Rep*. 548a), we must not impose on the *Phaedo*, purely on the strength of this resemblance, whatever doctrine of the unreality of bodily pleasures we find in the later passages. Rather, the interpretation of the *Phaedo* passages must be determined by their context, which is that of the contrast between soul and body, and between the levels of reality to which each belongs. The intelligible entities such as goodness and equality to which the soul is akin and which it grasps by pure thought are fully real in that they are what they are without qualification, whereas sensible things are what they are only in a qualified way, e.g. x may be equal to y but unequal to z, or beautiful by one standard but ugly by another. This suggests that the illusion brought about by pleasure may be seen as e.g. making one think that a certain experience is *really* good, when in fact it is good only to a limited extent, under certain conditions, etc., and thus only an inferior representation of the real thing. If this is approximately right, then the status of these pleasures themselves is obscure. If what one enjoys is, in the sense suggested above, unreal, does Plato think that one's enjoyment of them is therefore unreal? If so, does he think that one is mistaken when one thinks that one is enjoying e.g. food or sex? Or is his thought rather that since the objects of these pleasures are in one way or another less than fully real, the pleasures themselves are in one way or another less than fully satisfactory, perhaps because they are contaminated with pain (cf. 60b) or because they are evanescent? The text of the *Phaedo* does not suggest answers to these questions, and it is quite likely that at the time of writing the questions themselves had not been explicitly formulated. We must be content to say that Plato here represents for the first time, in a somewhat inchoate form, a picture of the bodily pleasures which associates them with illusion and unreality. One aspect of the development of Plato's thought on pleasure consists in the clarification of this picture, leading to the characterization of these pleasures themselves as in one way or another unreal (*Rep.* 584c–586d and *Phil.* 51a) and even of some of them as false (*Phil.* 36c–44a). As far as the comparison with the *Gorgias* goes, we can see this passage as further evidence for the devaluation of bodily pleasures; if they are seen not merely as hindering the soul on its journey to enlightenment but as actually productive of falsehood and illusion, then we have even stronger ground for refusing them any positive value in any assessment of pleasures.

5.1.3. Two incidental features of the treatment of pleasure in the *Phaedo* are worth noting, as indicating some divergence from the discussion in the *Gorgias*. The first passage, 60b, is not part of any theoretical discussion, but belongs to the dramatic introduction to the discussion; Socrates, whose fetters have just been taken off, rubs his leg and remarks on the strangeness of 'this thing which men call pleasure' (*hēdu*). It has, he says, a strange relation to what seems to be its opposite, distress (*lupēron*), in that they never occur together, but if you pursue and get the one you almost always have to get the other too. This is rather an obscure remark (on the problems of interpretation see Gallop, pp. 76–8), and in view of its untheoretical context it would be unwise to press it into a statement of a theoretical position. It is, however, worth noticing that Socrates seems to deny one of the premisses of the first argument against Callicles (495e–497d), viz. that pleasure and distress occur together. Rather, he suggests, the pursuit of pleasure (presumably, once again, it is bodily pleasure which Plato has in mind) will involve, even if successful, the experience of distress. He may be suggesting that bodily pleasure is generally followed by distress, as is suggested at *Rep.* 583e, or alternatively (or in addition) that it involves antecedent distress (*Rep.* 584a–c; *Phil.* 44c). There may also be a hint in the phrase 'what men call pleasure: that bodily pleasures are not *really* pleasant (see above). Secondly, intellectual pleasures and desires are at least mentioned in the *Phaedo*; there is an incidental mention at 59a of the pleasure of philosophical discussion, and at 66e the desire for intelligence or understanding (*phronēsis*) is contrasted with bodily desires. Perhaps the most significant passage is 114e, where Socrates gives at least a hint of the role of pleasure in the good life by his statement that the man who has ignored bodily pleasures and cultivated those of the intellect can face death with confidence. Bodily pleasures and generally the things of the body are 'alien' to the soul; by contrast intellectual pleasures and the practice of the virtues 'really belong to it'. This indicates, firstly, that the philosophic life will be pleasant, and it may be, if the hints about the unreality of bodily pleasures do point in the direction suggested, that it alone will be *really* pleasant. If so, it would be completely consistent for Plato to maintain that the application of a form of hedonistic calculus would lead one to the best kind of life.

2. The attack on hedonistic calculation

5.2.1. So far, then, the evidence suggests that the view of pleasure taken in the *Phaedo* bears much the same relation to the hedonism of the *Protagoras* as does the treatment in the *Gorgias*. In both dialogues Plato is interested in pleasure chiefly to the extent that he is concerned to attack bodily pleasures, the main difference being that in the *Phaedo* the attack is fiercer and introduces a new point in the connection of bodily pleasures with illusion and unreality. In neither dialogue is Plato's position inconsistent with enlightened hedonism, and indeed we have just seen how *Ph.* 114e suggests how the choice of the philosophic life could be defended on hedonistic grounds. But we have so far taken no account of the distinction made in 68b–69c between true and vulgar morality. The non-philosopher who observes conventional morality is described as brave from cowardice and self-controlled from self-indulgence, in that he faces fearful things because he is more afraid of the consequences of not facing them (like cowardly soldiers who hold their ground because they are more afraid of what their officers will do to them if they run away than they are of being killed by the enemy), and abstains from some pleasures the better to indulge in others. But, Socrates continues (69a), the right way to acquire goodness is not to exchange one pleasure, distress, or fear for another as if they were coins. The only true coin is understanding (*phronēsis*), and the right form of exchange is to exchange all one's pleasures, distresses, and fears for that. The buying and selling of all those things with and for understanding constitutes true goodness, whether or not accompanied by pleasure etc. The exchange of those things for one another without intelligence is a mere slavish counterfeit of goodness, with nothing sound or true in it, but true virtue consists in being purified from such things, and intelligence itself is a means of such purification.

5.2.2. This does undoubtedly suggest at first reading an all-out attack on the kind of hedonistic calculus which is defended in the *Protagoras*, but careful attention to the details of the passage and to its wider context suggests that that first impression should be modified. As already noted, the context of the passage is one of a sharp contrast between the philosopher and the lover of the body (*philosōmatos*). Anyone who is alarmed at the prospect of death must be a lover of the body, and consequently either a lover of money or a lover of honour. (The motivations of ambition on the one hand and bodily appetite on the other (leading to the desire for money as a means of satisfying those appetites), which Plato assigns in the *Republic* to separate parts of the non-rational soul, are here characterized without differentiation as manifesting 'love of the body'). The philosopher alone possesses true courage and self-control, whereas the *philosōmatos* manifests their spurious counterparts. It is plain that the crucial contrast is that between the objects of value which motivate the two kinds of life; the philosopher seeks what is really valuable, whereas the things that the *philosōmatos* seeks are not really valuable at all. Consequently, the method by which the latter decides what to do is mistaken; he aims to maximize bodily pleasure, but bodily pleasure is not worth having. That is to say, the *philosōmatos* goes wrong, not because he employs a hedonistic calculus, but because the units of his calculus are not actually units of value at all. This point becomes clear when we consider Plato's description of the spurious 'courage' of the *philosōmatos*; people of that sort face death for fear of greater evils, and so everyone except the philosopher is courageous 'through being afraid and through fear' and hence 'through cowardice' (68d). But given the definition of fear as expectation of evil, which is Plato's standard account (*Lach.* 198b; *Prot.* 358d; *Laws* 646e), together with the axiom that, given a choice of evils, everyone chooses the least (*Prot.* 358d), it follows that the philosopher too, like anyone else, must in a case where he shows courage by facing up to some evil, do so because he thinks any alternative is worse. Hence he too can be described as facing evils for fear of worse evils, and so being courageous through fear. This is of course precisely the account of courage given in the hedonistic argument of the *Protagoras*, but we cannot appeal to that discussion to support the interpretation of the present passage of the *Phaedo*, since the very point at issue is whether Plato's aim in this passage is to reject the account given in the *Protagoras*. It is, however, apposite to point out not only that the axiom itself is independent of hedonism, but also that Socrates is represented in the *Apology* as applying the axiom to explain his own willingness to face death rather than abandon his divinely-ordained mission to pursue philosophy. At 28d–29b he argues as follows. The majority of men would do anything to escape death, which they regard as the greatest of evils. Socrates, by contrast, does not know whether death is an evil at all, but does know that disobedience to the divine command would be something evil and shameful: 'so I shall never fear and flee from things which, for all I know, may even be good, rather than things which I know to be bad'. The implication is clear that Socrates does 'fear and flee from' genuine evils, of which the evil of acting unjustly is one, while the majority flee from things which are probably not evils at all. This is just the point which is made at *Phaedo* 68b–d. The contrast between real and illusory evils recurs at 83b–c; the philosopher abstains from bodily desires and pleasures as far as possible, on the ground that by indulging in them he will suffer the worst of evils, not the commonly recognized penalties of over-indulgence, but the false conception of reality to which those pleasures give rise. Here again the philosopher is motivated to avoid what appears to him as the greatest evil, and again his superiority over the common man lies in the fact that the philosopher alone knows what is in fact the greatest evil. Both will be 'courageous through fear', but the common man will be 'courageous through cowardice', i.e. through *error* as to what is to be feared (*Prot.* 360c: cf. *Lach.* 194e; *Rep.* 433c).

5.2.3. The attack on 'vulgar morality' at *Phaedo* 68 is not, then, an attack on the employment of a hedonistic calculus as a criterion of right action. It is an attack on those who take as things of supreme value pleasures in bodily appetite and the satisfaction of ambition, things which are not in fact of any value, and who regulate their conduct with the aim of maximizing those bogus goods. Such men may, of course, have developed an elaborate technique of assessing the long-term pleasure-value of particular pleasures, or they may simply have given priority to some set of pleasures and, under their domination, have given up others. The distinction is immaterial, since, no matter how rational they may be in calculation, they remain under the spell of the body, which makes them count as real what is spurious. Hence their very rationality would be a spurious rationality. So far, Plato has given no account of true rationality. In particular, no text which we have so far considered is inconsistent with the thesis that the right way to regulate one's conduct is to seek to maximize true pleasures, i.e. the pleasures of the intellect, and that the philosopher will have just that aim. We must now consider whether that interpretation is excluded by the second half of the passage, 69a–c.

5.2.4. First of all, it should be noted that this passage continues immediately from the one we have just examined. In 68d we have the description of the *philosōmatos* who is 'courageous through cowardice', and at 68e–69a the parallel account of those who are 'self-controlled through self-indulgence' (i.e. who abstain from some (sc. bodily) pleasures in order to maximize their enjoyment of others). Then in the next sentence (beginning at a6) Socrates introduces the contrast with true (i.e. philosophic) morality by pointing out that 'this isn't the right exchange for goodness, to exchange pleasures for pleasures and pains for pains and fear for fear, greater and less like coins'. While logically the 'this' could point either backwards, giving the sense 'this, viz. the one I have just described', or forwards, giving 'this, viz. an exchange of pleasures for pleasures etc.', it seems plain that in the context it points both ways, giving 'the sort of morality I have described, viz. an exchange of pleasures for pleasures etc., isn't the right kind of exchange'. Hence what is being contrasted with true morality is not the exchange of pleasures for pleasures etc. *as such*, but the sort of exchange of pleasures for pleasures etc. which we have just described. What sort of exchange was that? On the basis of our consideration of the earlier passage, we should expect Plato to emphasize above all that the items exchanged in the transactions conducted by the *philosōmatos* have no real value. And that is just what we find. The *philosōmatos* exchanges pleasures for pleasures like coins, but the only true coin, for which one ought to exchange all those things, is understanding (*phronēsis*) (a9–10). Hence, by implication, the coins (i.e. pleasures) which the *philosō-matos* receives in exchange for the pleasures which he trades in are false coins, i.e. they have no value. In its negative aspect, then, the commercial metaphor is both clear and well adapted to the context; the *philosōmatos* undertakes trans-actions on the assumption that the items which he exchanges have some value, while in fact they are worthless. But when we turn to the positive aspect of the metaphor, matters are not so straightforward.

5.2.5. At a9–b5 Socrates says the following things about *phronēsis*:

(i) *phronēsis* is the only true coin,
(ii) one ought to exchange all these things (i.e. pleasures etc.) for *phronēsis*,
(iii) when everything (i.e. presumably 'all these things' as in (ii)) is bought with this (i.e. *phronēsis*) and sold for this, it is really courage and self-control and justice, and, to sum up, true goodness (*aretē*) when accompanied with *phronēsis*, whether pleasures and fears and everything else of that kind are present or absent.

Proposition (iii) is presumably to be interpreted as follows: when one buys one's pleasures with intelligence and sells them for intelligence one possesses true goodness, of which intelligence is a necessary constituent (or perhaps accompaniment), while the presence or absence of pleasures, pains, etc. is irrelevant to it. But this still leaves us with the question of what Plato means when he writes of buying pleasures with intelligence and selling them for intelligence. The contrast with the predicament of the *philosōmatos*, in the context of which intelligence is described as the only true coin, would naturally suggest that, in contrast to the worthless pleasures of the *philosōmatos*, intelligence is the only thing intrinsically valuable, for which all pleasures should be exchanged. But that leaves out of account the fact that money is worth having, not for its intrinsic value, since it has none, but only for the sake of what you can buy with it; hence it is strictly speaking absurd to speak of some sort of currency as the only thing which is intrinsically valuable. It might, indeed, be suggested that Plato has simply overlooked this point, elementary though it is. But the text itself suggests that he has not overlooked it, or at least that he does not treat intelligence as the only thing with intrinsic value. For, firstly, he speaks of buying pleasure etc. with intelligence. The construction thus rendered (*meta* + noun in genitive case) is rarely if ever used of the means by which an action is performed, but commonly of the manner or circumstances; hence it is probable that 'buying pleasures with intelligence' means 'buying pleasures in an intelligent manner', and not 'buying pleasures in exchange for intelligence'. The latter interpretation commits us to reading Plato as saying that the philosopher in some circumstances reduces his supply of intelligence in order to acquire certain pleasures, which seems to make little sense (see Luce). But while we can avoid the difficulties of that interpretation, it is plain from the text that Plato regards the philosopher as buying certain pleasures, i.e. at least some pleasures have value for him too. We now have the further difficulty that in the same sentence 'pleasures, fears, and everything of that sort' are said to be irrelevant to true goodness; why, then, should the philosopher, who aims at true goodness, buy any pleasures whatever? The best explanation would seem to be that the pleasures, fears, etc. which are irrelevant to true goodness are the sort of pleasures, fears, etc. which dominate the mind of the *philosōmatos*, i.e. bodily pleasures etc., whereas the pleasures which the philosopher buys 'with intelligence' are the pleasures of the intellect. Hence the text gives strong indication that some pleasures are to be accorded intrinsic value.

5.2.6. Secondly, in the sentence already paraphrased (at a9–b5), true goodness is described as 'accompanied by intelligence'. The Greek is, once again, *meta phronēseōs*; the precise connotation of the phrase is unclear. It could be taken to indicate that intelligence accompanies goodness, or that it is a constituent of goodness, or even that it produces goodness. Whichever interpretation we adopt, or even if we settle for the compromise view that Plato did not differentiate between the alternatives, it is clear that *aretē* itself must be intrinsically worth having, whether co-ordinately with intelligence, or as the ultimate end to which intelligence is seen as the means. The next sentence (b5–c3) suggests the latter interpretation. It begins with a reference to the pleasures, fears, etc. which have just been mentioned: 'When they are exchanged for one another in isolation from intelligence, that sort of goodness is a kind of illusion (*skiagraphia tis*), fit for slaves, with nothing sound or true in it', and then contrasts that counterfeit with true goodness, described in terms of a new image derived from the mystery religions. 'But true self-control and justice and courage is really a purification (*katharsis*) from all that sort of thing, and intelligence itself is a kind of purificatory rite.' Here goodness is the final state of the initiate who has undertaken the rituals, the state of being purified from the sins etc. of the body, while intelligence is the means of achieving that state, viz. the ritual which the initiate must undergo (for the terminology see Luce and Gooch). If we take this literally, then intelligence can have at most instrumental value, since a purificatory rite is worth undertaking only for the sake of the end-state which, if successful, it produces. And if we read that interpretation back into the commercial metaphor of the earlier part of the passage, we find that the true coin of intelligence is ascribed, as it should be, instrumental rather than intrinsic value. One exchanges one's worthless bodily pleasures for something with real value, i.e. intelligence, but what gives intelligence its real value is what we can buy with it, viz. goodness and, perhaps, the pleasures of the philosophic life. At this point, of course, the metaphors break down; a buyer exchanges his money for a good, but one does not exchange one's intelligence for goodness or the pleasures of the intellectual life. The religous metaphor also breaks down at the same point; a purificatory rite leads on to a subsequent state of purification, but the perfectly good life is not preceded by an introductory process of the exercise of intelligence. Rather, moral goodness, the intellectual grasp of reality and the pleasure in that exercise are all mutually inseparable constituents of the completely good life. But, of course, the metaphors should not be pressed as would be appropriate if they were intended to express a rigorous argument. Their function is rather to present, in a cumulative and rhetorically vivid fashion, the contrast between, on the one hand, the futile activity of the *philosōmatos*, devoted to the pursuit of worthless and illusory objects, and on the other the pursuit by the philosopher of the one kind of life which is truly worth living. The precise delineations of the logical relations between the concepts of goodness, intelligence, and pleasure in the total description of that life, even had Plato been capable of such a task, would have been irrelevant to the context of this passage.

5.2.7. It does not, then, appear that 68b–69c is after all

directed against the sort of hedonistic calculus defended in the *Protagoras*. Rather, the target in this passage is the same as elsewhere in the *Phaedo* and in the *Gorgias*, viz. the man who makes his aim in life the satisfaction of bodily appetite (a conception here explicitly widened to include the 'spirited' motivations such as ambition). The pleasures arising from those satisfactions are worthless and illusory, and cannot therefore figure as items of value in the deliberation of the good man. But this very passage indicates that some pleasures have a significant role in the good life, though the passage contains no specific description of how the good man takes account of them, or how considerations of true pleasure relate to other considerations in his deliberation. In summing up Plato's attitude to pleasure in the *Phaedo*, therefore, we are not obliged to treat this passage as introducing any new doctrine, or even any new emphasis; his position is consistent in the various allusions to pleasure throughout the dialogue. That position can best be described as an extension of the process, begun in the *Gorgias*, of the development of Plato's own view of pleasure from its source in the Socratic hedonism portrayed in the *Protagoras*. The extension is threefold: firstly, in the association of bodily pleasures with illusion and unreality; secondly, in the extension of the notion of bodily pleasure to cover 'spirited' pleasure; and thirdly in the clearer recognition of intellectual pleasures, with at least a hint of their role in the perfectly good life. While in its dualism the *Phaedo* looks back to the *Gorgias*, these three themes also point forward to the *Republic*.

Chapter 6

Republic

1. Plato's Development to date

6.1.1. If we take the *Protagoras* as containing Plato's early approach to hedonism, then we get the following account of his development in the period up to the *Republic*. To begin with he takes a sophisticated hedonistic stance, which would enable him to reject the vulgar sybaritic hedonism and would lead to his viewing it as unsettled, in contrast with the wise man's tranquillity, and irrational, in the sense first that it is the pursuit of bad means to the preferred end, and secondly that it is conducted without benefit of the relevant developed skill. There is no inclination to view any pleasure as inherently hostile to reason. All pleasures have some value in virtue of being pleasures, though they may have to be avoided because of their long-term effects. With the *Gorgias* we see the beginning of Pythagorean influence and the first traces of a soul/body dualism. The view of the sybaritic life as unsettled and irrational in the senses just mentioned persists, but the picture of sybaritism is far darker. The sybarite is not simply blown hither and thither by varying appearances of pleasure, he is dragged at the wheels of insatiable desire. His life (cf. the images of the pitchers at 493–4) is seen as the fruitless attempt to satisfy the insatiable and to satisfy desires that come from the body, the tomb of the soul. In the *Phaedo* the picture is darker still. The body is in a state of constant change, whereas the soul has a natural kinship with the eternal and unchanging. Those desires which characterize not only the sybarite but the ordinary ambitious person drag the soul away from its natural concerns and concentrate its efforts on satisfying the interests of the body. A life governed by them is irrational, not only in that it fails to achieve man's good and is not lived under the direction of reason, but because the dominant force in it is a direct impediment to the exercise of reason and interest in the truth. The contrast of soul and body that is made in the *Phaedo* contrasts them not only in nature but in status. Since the sybarite's pleasures secure his attachment to the body, their tendency is deplorable in distracting a man from what is noble to what is base. So strong is this in the *Phaedo* as to make one feel that Plato could hardly at that period have admitted that every pleasure has value in virtue of being a pleasure. On the contrary, one gets the impression that the pleasurability of certain indulgences is what makes them deplorable, as it is the nail that secures the person to them; and whatever their fruitfulness in terms of further bodily pleasure it would all be regrettable fruitfulness in fixing the subject more firmly to base pursuits.

6.1.2. This development would make it hard to retain the form of hedonistic calculus proposed in the *Protagoras*. On the other hand, it is not likely that the view that the good life is really pleasanter would be abandoned overnight. It has too many attractions. Not only is it polemically satisfying, but it is likely to have struck Plato as true that in some sense Socrates' life was pleasanter than Aristippus'. But while he has acquired a theory of bodily pleasures, that very fact would draw attention to his lack of a general account of pleasure. If he was to preserve the view that the good life is the pleasantest while holding that bodily pleasures constitute a base attachment and should have a minus or at least a null value, then he would have to develop some general theory of the nature of pleasure that would both enable him to downgrade bodily pleasures as a class and show that the life of virtue was the pleasantest life. In the *Republic* Plato clearly thinks himself in a position to do just this. At least, he seems to be saying where he stands on the questions that it has been suggested remained problematic in the aftermath of growing Pythagoreanism. The problem is to see just where he stands.

2. The structure of the Book IX passage

6.2.1. The passage in question starts at 580c9. Socrates has just proved that the just man is 'happiest', the unjust least 'happy' (*eudaimōn*) by showing that considered as a whole the first succeeds, while the second most miserably fails, in satisfying his desires. He now proposes to give a second proof of this point by showing that the philosophic life is pleasanter. This proof, which occupies 580c9–583a11, takes the form of arguing that each part of the soul has its appropriate pleasure (580c9–581c6); that each type of person (philosopher, honour-lover, money-lover) would extol as pleasantest the pleasures appropriate to his dominant desires (581c7–e5); the proper tools for deciding which will be pleasantest are experience, wisdom, and reason, and since the philosopher, and he alone, has all three in the present case, his judgement is authoritative, and we must conclude that his life is pleasantest, the money-lover's the least pleasant (581e6–583a11). We then get a third, Olympic, victory with an argument, from 583b1–587e4, that the pleasures of the philosopher are the truest pleasures, those of the other lives charlatan ones, and, indeed, the just, philosophic life is 729 times as pleasant as the unjust, 'tyrannical' one.

6.2.2. This description suggests that the arguments that the philosophic life is pleasantest are intended as arguments that it is the most *eudaimōm*. This is certainly what seems to be said. At 580b–c Socrates gets agreement that the best and most just person is the most *eudaimōn*, and claims to have completed his first proof. He then (580c9–d1) says he is going to produce a second, and later (583b) a third. In the context these should be second and third proofs that the best and most just person is the most *eudaimōn*. There is no indication that it is a proof of a new conclusion, either that such a person also has the pleasantest life, or that that fact is an additional proof of some general superiority of the life of such a person over and above its *eudaimonia*. If Plato intended to separate his proofs of the greater pleasantness of the philosophic life from the proof of the greater *eudaimonia* of the just life, then he has certainly done his best to conceal that intention by his manner of introducing the second proof. Some commentators, however, have supposed that he does consider them as proofs of a different conclusion, and that he leaves obscure the relationship between the conclusion of these proofs and the conclusion of the first proof (cf. Murphy, Ch. X; White, p. 255 ff.; Cross and Woozley, Ch. 11). The argument can be supported by two passages. First, at 581e6, some way on in the second proof, Socrates says 'So when the pleasures and the life itself dispute about each kind (of pleasure), not with regard to living more nobly or basely, nor better or worse, but with regard to living precisely more pleasantly or more free of distress, how should we know which of them speaks most truly?' This, it is claimed, makes it clear that Socrates is not asking which life is best or most *eudaimōn*, but the different question, which is pleasantest. As a point about the question quoted, this is true. It has to be emphasized, however, that at this stage Socrates is developing an argument from authority. He wishes to bring out that proponents of the three lives will disagree about the pleasantness of the lives they advocate, so that it will seem a good question which of them is the most reliable judge. In order to do this he has to get it clear that the question is about pleasantness. But that merely shows what the question addressed to the proponents is. It does not show what the purpose is of the whole proof that the just life is pleasantest.

6.2.3. The second text to support the view that the second and third proofs are not aimed at showing that the philosopher's life is best or most *eudaimōn* is 588a. Here Socrates says, after completing the third proof, that if the just man has so large a victory in respect of pleasure, how much greater must it be in decorum and virtue. This might suggest that Plato has, and is clear that he has, introduced a new argument for a new conclusion. Having first shown that the just/philosophic life is most *eudaimōn*, he has then moved on to the different argument that it is also pleasantest. As Murphy acknowledges, this is a rather abrupt change, and no explanation is given as to why this point should be introduced or of what its relevance is to the main argument. One may speculate on motives for their intrusion, but the fact remains that the proofs that the best life is pleasantest just lie there as unexplained anomalies. An added strangeness is that we are only alerted to the fact that they are not intended as proofs that that life is most *eudainōm* after the proofs are over, and contrary to the clear implication of their mode of introduction.

6.2.4. What, then, are we to make of 588a? The first point

to note is that not only does this come after the end of the third proof, but it is tagged on at the end of the obviously non-serious calculation that the just life is 729 times pleasanter than the unjust. There are probably two thoughts in Plato's mind: first, that it will be easier to show that the unjust life falls short in decorum, nobility (beauty) and virtue, and secondly, that the difference in these respects will be greater than in the case of pleasure. It will be easier in that the very descriptions of the lives are in terms of the contrasts of decorum, beauty, and virtue (it is the virtuous life that the first proof proves to be most *eudaimōn*), and this is simply reinforced by the descriptions of the pleasures of the lives. The difference might be felt to be the greater, not because of any accurate measure, but just because whereas the unjust life had some pleasure (or at least some appearance of pleasure), it has no decorum, nobility or virtue: it is described as manifesting their antithesis. It is worth noting that Socrates does not say that if the just life excels to such a degree in pleasure how much more must it excel in *eudaimonia*.

6.2.5. We conclude, therefore that Plato nowhere denies that the purpose of the proofs that the just life is pleasantest is to show that the just life is most *eudaimōn*. Of course, his reason for trying to prove the conclusion this way might well have been that he wanted a proof that would bite with explicit and implicit hedonists, Thrasymachus possibly among them. There may be this much truth in Murphy's position. The fact remains that it is one thing to claim that he produces, and purports to produce, one proof that the just life is most *eudaimōn* and then two proofs of the different thesis that the just life is pleasantest, and quite another to claim that he purports to produce three proofs that the just life is most *eudaimōn*, two of them taking the form of showing it to be pleasantest. It seems to us clear that the second view is correct.

3. A return to hedonism?

6.3.1. If this description of the structure of the passage is right, it might look like a reversion to early hedonism. For at the beginning of Book II Socrates is challenged to show that the 'just' life is good in itself and better than an unjust life, even if it lacks the usual fringe benefits and these are added to the unjust life. By Book IX580 Socrates considers that the just life is best and the special sign of the gods' blessing, (*eudaimonestatos*), the unjust one worst. This is the conclusion of the argument in Book VIII and the earlier part of Book IX. He then says that he will produce a second proof (580c9–d1) and then a third (583b). These have to be proofs of the same point, that the just life is best. In other words, he must think that in showing it to be pleasantest he is showing it to be best. So he is not only purporting to show that the just life is pleasanter than the unjust one, nor only that if you wanted to live the pleasantest life possible you would live a just life, but that the just life is best because it is pleasantest. So either Plato has abandoned his Pythagorean hestitations, or he has developed a way of 'measuring' pleasure which enables him to retain his hedonism while being dismissive of bodily pleasures. In fact he takes the latter line, but developing a view about the relative reality of types of pleasure and matching degrees of pleasure to degrees of reality of pleasure. Bodily pleasures are less real and so as a class less pleasant than philosophical ones (585–6).

6.3.2. Whatever we are to make of these arguments, however, something must be wrong. For they surely rely on our ignoring entirely the central books of the *Republic*. In Book VI (508e–509a) we are told that while knowledge and truth are fine things, we should not call them good but only Good-like. The Form of the Good deserves more honour than either knowledge or truth, and these are to be honoured because of their relation to it. Now doubtless this kind of remark could be made by someone who thought pleasure was good. The difficulty is in equating pleasure with the Form of the Good. Nowhere does Plato talk in terms that suggest that the pleasures we pursue are Forms or a Form, and it is as well for plausibility. Pleasure is always spoken of as either some condition or the apprehension of some condition of a sentient being. The Forms are eternal unchanging objects beyond all sentient beings. Yet the doctrine of the central books, whatever in detail it amounts to, is clearly that anything is good only by its relation to the Form of the Good. This must go for the just life as for everything else. A proof that that is the best life must contain reference to the Form of the Good. So either Plato is in a complete muddle, or something has been missed.

4. The basic picture

6.4.1. The solution seems to be that when Socrates 'proves' that the just life is the best in Book IX he is answering the challenge as posed by Glaucon and Adeimantus. Now when they asked to be shown that the just life was best, and distinguished between things good in themselves, things good for their consequences and things good both in themselves and for their consequences, the question of goodness was treated as one about what answers to human desires. It is showing the good life to be best in these terms that Socrates purports to be doing in Book IX. It is clear from the central books, however, that to know that it was really best we should have to know that a life where desires are met is one that approximates to the Form of the Good. This is the most important thing to know which, at 505, we are said still not to know. Further, at 506d–e, Socrates declares his inability to give an account of the Form of the Good. He ducks the question and resorts to images. This is as clear a declaration as one could wish that one is not going to be presented with anything that would consitute a proper proof that anything is good (and cf. 611b9–d7).

6.4.2. Consequently, we must see the 'proof' of Book IX not as showing that the just life is best *tout court*, but as showing it best by the criteria set. Similarly, showing it to be best because pleasantest is showing that because it is pleasantest it must be best by those criteria. So Plato shows himself in the *Republic* unwilling any longer to hold that the good life is simply best because it is pleasantest. It may well be that he would hold that if we knew the Form of the Good it would become clear that it was best to construct beings so that the life that answered their desires coincided with how it was best for them to be. The proof, however, that this was how it was best for them to be would have to take the form of showing how this life approximated to the Form of the

Good, not of showing that it met their desires. Granted, however, that the best life for man and that alone will answer man's desires, then if we can show that a just life so answers them, it will follow that the just life is best. For completeness, however, the declared lacuna of the *Republic* would have to be filled.   .

6.4.3. If this is so, then the second and third proofs of Book IX must aim to show that the just life *best answers men's desires*, by showing that it is pleasantest. For this it is necessary to suppose that if X is pleasant X answers to a desire, and that if X is pleasanter than Y, X better answers to some desire than Y does to any desire. The second proof (580d–583a) claims that as only the philosopher has experience of the three main types of pleasure, the intelligence to judge between them and an account of their different natures, his judgement of preference for the philosophical life and its pleasures should be accepted. This will be discussed later in connexion with an argument of Aristotle's (see Ch. 17). The third proof (583b–586) supports this by arguing that philosophical activities really do answer the corresponding desires, whereas, e.g. sybaritic activities do not, and that a philosopher will choose the most adequate pleasures for each type of desire. This constitutes a decisive 'Olympic' victory, because it shows that not only does the just, philosophic life see that all desires are catered for (the point at 579e), nor only that it satisfies the desires preferred by intelligent men, but also that it satisfies the only really satisfiable desires and better satisfies each type of desire; in fact it alone contains real pleasures, since the pleasure of the other parts of the soul are bastard (587c1).

6.4.4. For present purposes it is the third proof that is important, since this purports to give some basis for assessing relative pleasantness in a general account of pleasure, and supply a theoretical backing for the post-*Phaedo* position. How, then, does the proof go? A first approximation might be the following: the context of the proof requires that pleasure be seen as what answers to desire. If a life can be pleasanter, but not answer to desire, then simply showing a life to be pleasanter would fail to show that it better answered our desires. If, on the other hand, a life can answer to desire but fail to be pleasant, the argument that philosophical activities really fill certain natural lacks will have no tendency to show them pleasanter. There may be a conflation of lack and desire (of which more later) but there seems to be an assumed account of pleasure such that X is pleasant if and only if X answers to a desire/lack. The argument of 585b-e seems to have the following structure: pleasure is the replenishment of a lack; the more genuine the replenishment, the more genuine the pleasure, that is, if X more truly/really replenishes lack A than Y does lack B, then X is more truly/really pleasant than Y. If X is more truly pleasant than Y, X is pleasanter than Y. But the desires of the body are insatiable, that is, they constitute or aim to meet a set of lacks such that no X really replenishes them; whereas the desires of the intellect are satisfiable, that is, intellectual lacks can be really replenished. Consequently, the class of bodily pleasures is a class of pleasures each member of which is less pleasant than any member of the class of intellectual pleasures. So a life predominantly taken up with intellectual pleasures will be pleasanter than one taken up with bodily ones. Further, the wise man will come as near as is possible to satisfying bodily lacks, so that even considered from the angle of bodily pleasure the episodes of bodily indulgence in his life will be pleasanter than those in the sybarite's.

6.4.5. This approximation suggests that Plato is trying to extend the physiologically inspired replenishment model of pleasure beyond the physiological sphere. This is done by looking upon the soul/person as a quasi-organism (see the analogy between virtue and health in Book IV 425-6, 444-5); by seeing any disproportion between the elements as a lack requiring replenishment; and by seeing the various desires as themselves lacks or felt lacks with their own replenishments. This gives him a general theory of pleasure. Further, the matching of degrees of pleasure to reality of pleasure enables him to grade intellectual and bodily pleasures on a scale of pleasantness, without having to allow that experience might show a life of bodily pleasure to be pleasanter. It thereby

relieves him from the intricate calculations required by the
Protagoras. For it emerges that whole classes of pleasure can
be downgraded on the pleasure-scale simply from an examination of their nature. They are, in fact, only dubiously
pleasures at all. On the other hand, the class in which the
philosopher indulges is a class of genuinely pleasant ones. So
the sybarite's pleasures do not ever have to be weighed equally
in the pleasure balance with philosophical ones.

6.4.6. This supplies Plato with an argument for one point
in the *Protagoras*, that the excellent life is pleasanter than
any going rivals. But also, granted this view of pleasure, he
might hope to be able to show that if you started your
enquiry by asking, as a hedonist should, 'What form would
the pleasantest life take?', then your answer should be 'A
philosophical form'. For an understanding of pleasure would
reveal that you were looking for a desire-filling life, and the
only satiable human desires are philosophical ones. So a
proper use of the hedonistic criterion would lead to the same
result as the use of the proper criterion, the Form of the
Good. At the same time, he no longer holds that the good life
is good because pleasantest. The Pythagorean influence would
make him want to say that what makes the good life a good
thing is its association with the divine and its development of
the intellect. He can now hold this, satisfying the *Phaedo/
Gorgias* desire to contrast bodily pleasure with good activities
and at the same time preserve the *Protagoras* thesis that the
good life and the pleasant life are identical.

6.4.7. In this way the approximation suggests that we can
see the *Republic* as settling the uncertainties that Plato could
be expected to have felt after the transition from *Protagoras*
to *Gorgias* and *Phaedo*. While this is basically right, however,
the development of the passage in *Republic* IX is not so clear
as this might suggest. As its obscurities are important for the
development of Plato's views, they will have to be gone into
at greater length.

5. Modifications of the basic picture

6.5.1. It is tempting, on first reading the passage

583b–586, to impose upon it the following structure: at 583b Socrates' declared aim is to show that only the wise man's pleasure is true pleasure, but he proceeds in two stages. In the first he shows only that most non-philosophic pleasures are less than true, and not until the second does he reach his main objective. The first stage starts by drawing attention to a common error of people in distress, that of mistaking a condition of being free of distress for one of pleasure (583c–584a). Then it is declared that most bodily pleasures arise from distress, and are releases from it (548b–c). At 584c9–11 the anticipations of these pleasures are said (obscurely) to be in like case. Then the situation of these pleasures is likened to positions on a vertical line which has a centre point (584d–585a). All these pleasures can be seen as movements from below centre up towards the centre point. They are upward movements, but not movements in the upper atmosphere. They are just movements from distress to its absence, mistakenly considered pleasure because further up, but *mistakenly* so considered because not in the upper area.

6.5.2. This all suggests that most bodily pleasures come with release from distress. But not all, for at 584b we are told that quite a number are not preceded by distress. The only examples are pleasures of smell, but we are assured that there are many others (584b5–6). These, presumably, not being releases from distress, are in the upper area. So this part of the discussion is only satisfactory in that as most of the sybarite's pleasures will be releases from distress, the important bodily pleasures will be disposed of. But it fails to establish what Socrates set out to show. So he now embarks on the second stage (585b–586a), where he contrasts all bodily pleasures with all intellectual ones in respect of the reality of replenishment involved. Only here is the promise of 583b fulfilled.

6.5.3. Unfortunately, when one gets down to the details of the passage it shows signs of confusion which makes one doubtful about this clear break. To begin with, one cannot get over the fact that the initial claim is that no pleasures apart from the wise man's (= intellectual ones) are really true (583b). We append some remarks at the end of the chapter on the term for 'true', but it may be as well to say something now about what Plato would think he had shown in showing something to be a real pleasure. When put into English this way of talking strongly suggests that if X is not a real pleasure/not really a pleasure, then it would be simply incorrect to describe it as pleasant or enjoyable: it would be on a par with $\sqrt{2}$. Plato, however, clearly thinks of unreal pleasures as having some relation to real ones. They are at least distorted representations of the real thing (586b7-8), and so it is understandable that one should take them for pleasures. Though not proper replenishments, bodily pleasures are quasi- or partial or attempted replenishments. Again, they may be related comparatively on the pleasure scale: they are not forms of distress and some may be pleasanter than others. In fact, Plato is not concerned with what native Greek speakers would agree to be correctly described as pleasure. At most, a native Greek speaker, in using the concept of pleasure, is showing some dim apprehension of reality; but an examination of that reality will reveal that he will never be satisfied by the phenomena which in his ignorance he deems satisfying. The ordinary person is mistaken, not about language, but reality. So when Plato says that bodily pleasures are not really pleasures he is not meaning that they are not in any ordinary sense pleasant, but that they do not measure up to criteria yielded by a (meta-)physical investigation into the nature of pleasure.

6.5.4. With this gloss, then, we repeat that the initial claim is that no pleasures apart from the wise man's are (really) true. Further, this is what Plato claims to have shown by 587b13 where Socrates says 'It seems there are three (types of) pleasure(s), one genuine, two bastard . . .'. This must refer back to 580d7-8, where there are said to be three pleasures corresponding to the three parts of the soul. Consequently the conclusion would seem to be that pursued from the beginning, that only one set of pleasures is true. So while Plato might allow that some of the bastard pleasures are truer than others, he ought not to be prepared to say that in any serious sense they are true. Nor, indeed, does he clearly do so. (For further reflections on this see 6.6.) The nearest he comes to it is at 584c1-2, when immediately after drawing attention to bodily pleasures not preceded by pains, he says, 'Let us not be persuaded, then, that escape from pain is (a) "pure" pleasure, nor escape from pleasure (a) pain.' At 583b (and cf. 585b12, 586a-b) 'purity' (*katharos*) is connected with truth. A natural way to interpret the notion therefore might seem to be in line with *Phil.* 53 where pleasure is 'pure' *and true* if and only if unmixed with pain. It would then be plausible to suppose that already in the *Republic* Plato considers a pleasure 'pure' if unmixed, and if pure true, so that unmixedness is a criterion of truth. This would, of course, have the uncomfortable consequence that he would have to say of some bodily pleasures that they *are* true, contrary to his aim and conclusion and/or supply us with two independent criteria of truth with no indication of priority.

6.5.5. The word translated 'pure', however has many nuances in Greek, such as those of clarity and freedom from pollution, connotations quite common in Platonic uses. To be sure of being taken in the *Philebus* way Plato would have to make it clear, as indeed he does in the *Philebus* by his comparison with pure white. There is notably no such elucidation in the *Republic*. On the other hand the *Republic* does in 583-4 supply an argument for opposing mixed pleasures to true, but it is not the simple fact of their being mixed. The point made is, rather, that the presence of pain makes people mistake a condition without pleasure or pain for one of pleasure. This characteristic of escapes from pain is a form of witchcraft and shows that these appearances are unsound so far as the truth of pleasure is concerned. Unmixed pleasures do not share this characteristic, but most pleasures, including those of anticipation, are like this, and those indulging them are like people thinking they are in the upper atmosphere, when in fact only moving to a mid-point: comparing pain and the absence of pain, they are deceived through their lack of experience of pleasure (585a). In none of this are we given an account of what constitutes a true pleasure so that we can see what the extent of their error is. It is simply agreed that there is a condition of absence of (pleasure and) pain which is not pleasure. But at 585a we are told that those who reach this mid-way stage are convinced that they have replenishment and pleasure (585a3) and this leads into the argument of 585b–e that a filling of what more is with what more is is a truer filling: the body *is* less than the soul and so are its fillings, so if pleasure is replenishment with what is naturally appropriate, the soul's replenishments will be truer pleasures than the body's. Only now do we get a ground for attributing truth, and so justify the claim of 585a3–5 that certain people are in error.

6.5.6. In short, the passage develops by taking some mixed pleasures, i.e. pleasures preceded by felt desire, which would be typical of a sybarite and which naturally suggest a replenishment model. These are argued to be deceitful on unsophisticated premises, but with examples suggesting sickness; the idea of replenishment is reinforced by the motion-language of the up-down-between analogy, so that the introduction of the replenishment analysis is very natural. But the only argument for lack of truth and purity has been one to the effect that antecedent desire leads to a clouded mind. That the mind *is* clouded could only finally be shown by showing that its judgment is false, and that would require an analysis of pleasure. So having at 585 characterized the mistake as supposing that one has pleasure and replenishment Plato goes on to show that the body never can be replenished truly. Consequently not only are the people in question wrong: anyone who thought they had achieved or could achieve genuine bodily replenishment would be wrong. But those experiencing unmixed bodily pleasures would at least have some approximation to replenishment without the added confusion of distorting anticipated absence of pain into pleasure. It is this last, not mixture itself, which is the ground for attributing lack of truth to mixed pleasures in the first part of the passage. Yet while this might be sufficient for attributing lack of truth, it does not follow that its absence is sufficient for attributing truth, though it will, of course, be necessary. It remains that lack of truth is argued for at this stage simply from the admission that there is a neutral state, without any analysis of the nature of pleasure.

6.5.7. In 585 we do get an argument, based on a replenishment view of pleasure, to show that bodily pleasures are less real than intellectual ones; and it is asserted in 586a–b that those who spend their lives in revelry will necessarily be involved in insatiable longings and mixed pleasures. These, presumably, are not the 'truest' possible for the relevant part of the soul mentioned at 586d–e.

6.5.8. The above account conceals a difficulty of interpretation, but what seems clear is that the main thrust of the passage is to argue that a class of pleasures (bodily ones) is to be downgraded on the grounds that they do not constitute genuine replenishments, and are thus bastard pleasures. Plato gives no sign of presenting a two stage proof, or rather of first providing a weaker and then a stronger thesis. The whole is presented as an argument that only philosophical pleasures i.e. pleasures of the intellect, are really true, and one would assume on a single criterion of truth. At the same time, however, it has to be acknowledged that Plato is primarily thinking of pleasures corresponding to various appetites. Thus the second proof refers back to the tripartite division of the soul and the desires corresponding to them, and the dispute is about the relative pleasantness of the pleasure of the *lovers* of wisdom, honour, money. Similarly the argument for the inferiority of bodily pleasure is conducted by reference to appetites such as hunger. Plato talks as though there are just three types of pleasure, those answering to the desires of the three parts of the soul (e.g. 587b14–c1), and as though only the intellectual ones were true, but it is not clear how the unmixed bodily pleasures such as those of smell, which are preceded by no felt lack, are supposed to fit into this analysis, or whether they are an unresolved anomaly. It is, of course, their presence in the text which makes people feel that there is an intended break in the argument. On the question of how, if at all, Plato felt that they fitted into his scheme, we find ourselves in unsettled, and, so far as we can see, unsettlable, disagreement.

6. The Problem of pure bodily pleasures

6.6.1. The problem can be highlighted by asking whether

the unmixed bodily pleasures mentioned at 584b are true or not. Two positions suggest themselves:

6.6.2. *Position (i)*. They are not (really) true. Plato must think of them, as of all pleasures, as fillings. They differ from other bodily pleasures in not being preceded by a felt lack. That there are such pleasures is a new point to Plato, and one on which he wants to insist in regard to the pleasures of learning (cf. 585b and the implications of 586b that mixture with pain is a mark of mere images of true pleasure). Nevertheless they will be fillings with what is naturally appropriate, and so will share with all bodily pleasures the defect of being less than genuine fillings. Since they do not, like those preceded by a felt lack, give rise to false judgement, they are less untrue than other bodily pleasures; still Plato cannot admit that they are simply true.

6.6.3. *Position (ii)*. They are true. When Plato introduces them he does so explicitly to convince us that not all pleasures are escapes from pain (584b). Now he has just been discussing people who erroneously consider that a state of quiescence which is neither pleasant nor painful is in fact pleasant. He seems to think that when we see this error we might erroneously suppose all 'pleasures' to be such states, but anyone supposing such a state to be pleasure is all astray as regards the truth of pleasure, so if these were all the pleasures there were, presumably no pleasures would be true, nor indeed, would there be any pleasures. So we get some examples of genuine ones and now (584c) we must not believe that escape from pain is pure pleasure. This seems to commit Plato to the reality of these pleasures, but it has to be admitted that they are left as something of an anomoly. For they receive no further discussion. They do not get placed in the image of the lower, middle, and upper spheres which seems only directed to pleasures from a condition of felt lack; nor are they fitted into the replenishment analysis. It seems, then, that Plato has noticed these examples, feels they are genuine, but has not integrated them into his general account. The suggestion of position (i) about Plato considering them as fillings is pure speculation.

6.6.4. It might seem that it should be easy to settle this question, and doubtless, if it were not for an obscurity in the crucial passage, it would be. If Plato clearly said that so-called escapes from pain were not pleasures at all, but states of quiescence, then it would be most plausible to maintain that he introduced pleasures of smell as examples of genuine pleasures. If, on the other hand, he clearly thought of the escapes as processes of fulfilment which are charged with lack of purity or truth in introducing a false opinion about the quiescent state, then the pleasures of smell will only be preferable for not introducing a false opinion. Since they involve no antecedent felt lack they presumably involve no opinion at all. This might make them less untrue, but would not involve Plato in thinking that they were true. Unfortunately the passage shows confusion on the crucial question of how he is thinking of escapes from pain.

6.6.5. At first (583c–e) we are introduced to people in a depleted state, looking forward to what is in fact a state of quiescence only, and *not* a pleasure, as pleasant. This is declared to be a false belief (583c4–5). The quiescent state is then said to appear, but not to be, pleasant, and these appearances are not healthy but witchcraft. We might want to say that the quiescent state is simply not a pleasure, and that falsity is an attribute of the belief. Plato's language declares that the state *appears* pleasant and that there is nothing healthy in these appearances. At 584b he seems to feel that what has been said might erroneously suggest that normally pleasure is cessation of pain. How could it? Only in that it has been suggested that what many dub pleasant is not pleasant at all but a state in which pleasure has ceased. In other words 'cessation' should refer to the state of having ceased. We then get the examples of smells and he concludes: 'Let us not then be persuaded that escape from pain is (a) pure pleasure'. It still ought to be that 'escape' refers to the condition of having escaped, but in his next paragraph Socrates says that pretty well the majority, and the greatest, of the so-called pleasures which get through the body to the soul are of this sort, escapes from pains. This remark suggests that he is taking 'escape' to refer to the process of escaping.

For, first of all, the most plausible candidates for bodily pleasures are eating, drinking, sexual pleasure; and secondly the language of getting through to the soul strongly suggests these processes rather than states of quiescence. The image of moving from a lower to a mid-way position reinforces this impression. At 584c9–11 we are told that the anticipations of these are in similar case. We are left in doubt, first, as to whether the anticipations are of the neutral state or the process, and secondly as to why they are in the same case. The most likely explanation is that these anticipations are pleasures in the *apparent* pleasantness of what is anticipated (584a7–10), and since they occur in a context in which escape is sought they are considered to come under the same account. The fact remains that we move, without any apparent awareness that it is a movement, from the point that those in depletion mistake a neutral state for a pleasant one, to the view that we should not therefore consider cessation of pain to be pleasure, to the view that escapings from pain are not pure pleasures, to the view that the antici-pations of such are for the same reasons not. This may be understandable (see 6.7.2), but it undoubtedly involves con-fusion. For present purposes the important point is the failure sharply to distinguish escape from pain as the condition of having escaped, from escape as the process of escaping. In so far as one attends to the first one is inclined to take it that escapes from pain are not pleasures at all: in so far as one considers the process of escaping, the moving upward of the analogy, one is inclined to think of them as attempted replenishings whose failure in truth, so far as the immediate context is concerned, comes not in failing to be pleasures altogether, but in being associated with false judgment. If the first is right, pleasures of smell look like being given as examples of genuine pleasure; if the second, they are only given as lacking the encouragement to false judgment inherent in the others. The truth, however, seems to be that Plato just does not make sharply the distinction that might make one interpretation more likely than the other. Consequently what he would have replied to the question: 'Are the pleasures of smell true?' must remain shrouded in mystery.

6.6.6. On either view, however, one anomaly remains: gradations of truth of pleasure are not determined solely by the criterion of relative reality. While the false judgements made by one in depletion looking forward to release are false because of error about replenishment, the falsity itself seems to add further to the lack of truth/reality of the pleasure, according to position (i). This need not be so on position (ii), but there we have some true pleasures which do not win their place in virtue of being real fulfilments.

7. Mixed pleasures and insatiability

6.7.1. Despite the anomalous results of the remarks on unmixed bodily pleasures, it is clear that Plato's main concern is with the pleasures pursued by the different classes of person, and that the burden of showing the relevant bodily pleasures to be inferior as a class rests on the argument that there are no genuine bodily replenishments. What is not so clear is just why Plato thought them not to be genuine. To judge from 586a–c, it seems that while it may be that Plato does not take the simple fact of mixture as showing lack of truth/ genuineness, he does think that mixed pleasures are intimately related to insatiable desire. This insatiability highlights the impossibility of proper replenishment and so the distant removal of these pleasures from true pleasure.

6.7.2. Yet no argument is supplied for supposing that replenishments of felt lacks are less stable, or real/true, by the replenishment criterion, than those of unfelt ones. This suggests that while Plato felt that there is a connection, he has not yet worked out what it is. This is reinforced when one reflects on the state of confusion in 583–4. Here, as we have seen (6.6.5), three points seem to be run together without their interrelationship being sorted out. It is remarked first that people in distress mistake the condition of release from distress for pleasure, secondly, that most bodily pleasures are escapes from pain (mixed) and, thirdly, that anticipatory pleasures are in the same case. The implication of the first point would seem to be that the sick, say, are liable to believe that health is a pleasure. Nothing follows from this about getting healthy being a pleasure, let alone a mixed one; nor about the patient's capacity to be pleased in advance at the prospect of his recovery. So nothing is shown about either mixtures or anticipatory pleasure. When most bodily pleasures are said to be escapes from pain, the point is presumably that of *Gor.* 494–7, that the pleasure of thirst-quenching requires the presence of the thirst that is being removed. Now of course the tendency of the quenching is towards a state where both pleasure and pain have ceased, but it seems false to suppose that those quenching their thirst necessarily misjudge the end state as a pleasure, and it certainly does not follow from the point about the end term of quenching. Similarly with anticipations. It is not clear that a thirsty person's pleasurable anticipation is even usually of the state of having quenched their thirst, so that these pleasures do not seem obviously in the same category as the first case; nor is the pleasurable anticipation of quenching one's thirst always a mixed pleasure. In the particular case of thirsty people, their anticipatory pleasure will no doubt be sharpened by their thirst. But people may anticipate with pleasure the prospect of downing a draught of cool beer later in the afternoon after a game of tennis. They are not presently in distress, nor anticipating with dread their future thirst. So these do not either seem obviously in the same category as the mixed pleasures. One can see how they·get conflated. One starts with people in a state of distress, say thirst, longing to be rid of it — a state that is not a pleasure. They take a drink, thus replenishing their lack. But what are they drinking for? Clearly to be rid of their thirst. If we concentrate on thirsty people it is easy to suppose (*a*) that they want to be rid of their thirst, (*b*) that their pleasurable drinking to which their want stimulates them terminates in the removal of thirst and (*c*) that before drinking, but still thirsty, they pleasantly anticipate the removal of their thirst. These can seem but three aspects of the same phenomenon. Concentrating on the thirsty person would be encouraged by the physiologically inspired model of pleasure. It seems to be a psychological fact that if one has a theory of, say, pleasure, it tends to determine one's choice and interpretation of examples. Some examples will doubtless have suggested the theory, and then the further examples that leap to mind tend in turn to be suggested by the theory, and so every example one can think of tends to confirm the theory. It is remarkably difficult, once one is attracted by a theory, to think up possible counter-examples or take them seriously. Plato seems to have been attracted by the physiologically inspired model, and this would tend to concentrate his attention on those examples that suited it. Although he is starting to consider pleasures of anticipation, the possibility that they require a different analysis is not explored. They are seen as occurring only in close association with the conditions of a standard example of pleasure, and assumed to come under the same analysis. Pleasurable anticipation is stimulated by present distress and aimed at its removal, as is the pleasure of replenishment.

6.7.3. This state of confusion would make it hard for him to be sure just what it was about mixed pleasures that made them especially hard to replenish. In the *Gorgias* the analysis was fairly close to its physiological origins. A depletion, which is an imbalance in the organism, is at once a form of distress and desire. The desire is the urge of the organism to right the imbalance which is/causes the distress. Pleasure is the righting of the imbalance or fulfilment of the desire. It is assumed that every imbalance is distressing and every such distress a desire. Clearly, the example of pleasures that are not escapes from distress, such as smells, will show (i) that a quite new analysis is needed, or (ii) that we must reject the view that all imbalances are distressing, or (iii) that we must reject the view that pleasure is the righting of an imbalance, or replenishment of a natural lack. Since the latter underlies Book IX of the *Republic* as an attempted single analysis, Plato should not want to accept (i) or (iii). Instead he should take the second line. There is, however, no resultant examination of the relation of desires to lacks. It is enough that we can have desires/lacks which are not distressing, and these the philosopher has.

6.7.4. The example of smells, then, should force us to free imbalance from distress, but Plato does not make that point. The importance to him seems to be that it draws attention to a set of non-necessary bodily pleasures which are truer than most and might feature in a philosophical life. The only ground we are given for supposing them truer by the replenishment criterion is a remark at 586 stating that mixed pleasures are especially insatiable. The trouble is that no argument is given for supposing this. After all, if pleasure is replenishment with what is naturally suitable, that entails no distinction between replenishments of felt or unfelt depletions. It might be suggested that Plato's point is that whereas it is possible that at some time our minds will need no further information, so long as our bodies live there will be no time when they need no further food — an interpretation strongly suggested by 585b–d. But while Plato doubtless believed this, it is no help with the present problem. For if smells just fill an unfelt lack, since the body is in constant change, there is no filling such lacks once and for all either. If, on the other hand, smells are not susceptible of the lack/replenishment analysis, we should need, as we have pointed out, a quite different criterion of truth for them, and it would be a moot point whether any sense could be made of comparing the degrees of truth of these pleasures with those of any others. So how can the presence or absence of distress be made important?

6.7.5. What one is tempted to say is that distress is important because it prevents, or hinders, one from calm consideration. If one is very hungry, it is hard to raise dispassionately the question of whether or not to eat. But while this may import some degree of anti-rationality, it entails nothing about unsatisfiability. For that we might do better to concentrate on certain desires which are distressing if unsatisfied, but which seem such that however much of X one gets one wants more. Thus, the Calliclean and Thrasymachean ideal men are characterized as always wanting more. However much money or power or pleasure they have, they never reach a condition where if they could have more they would not want it. Their desires are forever pushing them to further achievements, and while a situation might arise where they have all there is to get, that will not mean that their desires are such that what they have in this situation would in all circumstances satisfy them, but simply that they have everything available in this situation. Any awareness of more things to be gained sets up a distress only assuaged by gaining them. Certain ambitions, addictions, and states such as gluttony can plausibly be pictured as fitting this sort of pattern. Moreover, in these cases desire seems to grow with indulgence. As one ambition is satisfied, that just sets up a greater yearning for yet more power, and as that distress is soothed by success a yet greater one is aroused.

6.7.6. These examples might certainly encourage one to associate desire and distress, and so mixed pleasures, with insatiability, and indeed in a sense of 'insatiability' such that any lacks satisfied by smells would be satiable. For with smells the replenishment does not cause a greater sense of lack, whereas in these examples replenishment always creates a desire/lack and so on *ad infinitum*. This would justify the greedy, war-mongering picture of 586. What these examples also do, however, is put a strain on either the tie between desires and lacks, or between lacks and imbalances. For the original theory of pleasure stuck close to its physiological base. Here the general picture was of a complex organism with a liability to imbalance but a built-in tendency to self-rectification. In the physiological literature the imbalance might come from either deficiency or excess of some element or condition (e.g. condensation or relaxation). It was unfortunate, perhaps, that in the non-medical literature a general characterization of imbalance as deficiency became current. For desires can readily be construed as aimed at remedying deficiencies, not so readily as aimed at rectifying imbalances. Still, the physiological model will tend to concentrate attention on those desires ('natural' ones?) which manifest the organism's innate nisus to self-rectification. Thus it is plausible to think of thirst as the organism's reaction to fluid-depletion and its move towards replenishment. It is nowhere near so plausible to construe a glutton's obsession with food in this way. There is no natural imbalance to whose righting the glutton's desire tends. Rather his desires tend to the production of imbalance. On the other hand, a glutton aims at something he does not have, that he lacks. So if one saw the difference, one might either claim that all desires are associated with lacks, but not all lacks are signs of imbalance; or, that not all desires are related to real lacks, for real lacks are cases of imbalance and not all desires are directed to righting imbalances.

6.7.7. In the *Republic*, Plato does not explicitly dissociate either desire from lack or lack from imbalance. It looks, in fact, as though he is hoping to have a straightforward extension of the physiologically inspired account of desire and pleasure. At the same time he seems to feel that in some way mixed pleasures are the least real pleasures because their correlative desires are furthest from being replenishable. No argument for this is given, and the only examples of 'bodily' desires which could be claimed to give mixed pleasures and yet be said to be insatiable in a sense in which unmixed ones were not, or were less so, are ones which do not happily fit with the physiological model. Yet, interestingly, Plato not only fails to contrast these with 'physiological' desire, he actually does tend to assimilate these desires to desires like hunger and thirst. The 'desiring' part of the soul is precisely the one whose desires are indulged by the sybarite, whose pleasures are not real pleasures. The typical examples are hunger and thirst, and yet the tendency of this part is to aggrandisement without end (cf. 439d, 442a–b, 586a–b, 588–589b). It seems that gluttony is viewed as the result of uncurbed satisfaction of hunger, and similarly with the rest. In that case it would be easy to suppose that the mixed pleasures were always replenishments of something like hunger in either restrained or unrestrained form. As the natural tendency of the desire in question is for more and more, if not restrained, it is insatiable. By contrast, unmixed pleasures, including intellectual ones, do not answer to any distress-stimulated desire. This assimilation of gluttony to hunger ought to result in the abandonment of the original model, for now hunger is not a restorative but a destructive force. It would be possible for Plato to agree to this but point out that the philosopher restrains this force for the good of the whole, so that it is only satisfied as required by nature, but in those cases yields true pleasures (relatively) in accordance with 585d11 (and cf. 485d). But in that case a pleasure's being mixed would have no bearing on its truth. A philosopher may satisfy his hunger only when appropriate, but will be hungry nevertheless, and still enjoy the meal.

6.7.8. The situation, in fact, seems to be as follows: in the *Gorgias*, Plato came under the spell of the physiologically inspired account of pleasure and needed a general account. The natural move was to try to extend it. That analysis in its original application was subjected to counter-examples. The result was that on the one hand the extension suggested a possibility of grading pleasure in terms of satisfaction capacity. On the other hand, the typical indulgences of sybarites were brought under the original account as bloated versions of desires such as hunger and thirst. The implications of this were not fully appreciated, but some of the counter-examples led to a modification of the original view so as to allow for depletion without distress. In the bloated forms the distress seemed closely associated with insatiability, and this suggests a tie between lack of distress and relative satisfiability. Further all mixed cases were assimilated to cases of antici-pation, so encouraging a picture of eager pursuit. In short, so strong was the influence of the original account of pleasure drawn from the physiologists' picture of the organism as to make Plato interpret examples with a superficial similarity as of the same form. The general state of confusion would encourage the feeling that mixed pleasures were the least true, while hindering precise explication of why. This deter-mination to bring everything under the one account is shown in a further way. As already mentioned, anticipatory pleasures are noticed only to be assimilated to releases from distress. All this is no doubt natural, but the assimilations can hardly be sustained. Their existence, however, may help to explain some of the oddities and obscurities in the development of the passage. For if we grant them, then we can see how Plato may have felt that mixed pleasures should be judged less true than unmixed ones by the genuine-replenishment criterion. For mixed ones will have an insatiability (of one sort) not attaching to unmixed ones. At the same time no physical ones will be as true (satiable, in another way) as any philosophical ones. The uncertainties about the notion of insatiability are perhaps illustrated by the brusque treatment of honour-loving pleasure. We are just told that similar points hold. There is no analysis of mixedness; just a suggestion of unbridled ambition and rivalry.

6.7.9. In short, cracks are beginning to show in the original theory at the time when, in its extended form, it looked so promising for preserving as much as possible from the *Protagoras* while being faithful to the changes initiated with the *Gorgias*. To what extent these cracks were visible to Plato at the time is uncertain. It will be argued that the *Philebus* shows awareness of some of them. For the moment, it is time to see how the extension works even if we overlook the cracks in the foundations.

8. Meeting the demands of the *Phaedo* and the *Protagoras*: a fatal ambiguity

6.8.1. The original account of pleasure associates pleasure with the process of replenishing. The obvious way to extend the picture is to find non-bodily lacks which can be replenished. We can now see people who are pursuing different styles of life as trying to meet different lacks. As the *Symposium* has it (204a) no one desires what he does not think he lacks. Pleasure is the replenishment of desire and only that which truly replenishes a desire is truly pleasant. Now everything is set up for showing the philosopher's superiority, since the objects of his pursuit are the only ones to give genuine replenishment. Unfortunately, there is a fatal ambiguity in this notion of replenishment. Suppose we take it, as the original account requires, that the pleasure consists in the replenishing. Then it ceases when the replenishment is complete. In that case, if the philosopher's desires can be genuinely satisfied, that means that the so-called process of replenishing genuinely and once for all replenishes. But then as life goes on and a philosopher acquires full understanding he will be wise, and, as *Symp.* 204a declares, in that case he will no longer desire wisdom. Since these desires/lacks are now satisfied there is no further replenishing of them to occur. So the more successful a philosopher is, the sooner his life will cease to be pleasant. This considerably weakens the argument that his life will be pleasanter. Alternatively, one might take the pleasure/replenishment equation to mean that pleasure consists in being in possession of that whose absence would constitute a natural lack — in having what one wants. This would certainly secure the conclusion that the successful philosopher's life was pleasant, and even, by underlining 'being in possession', that it alone was truly pleasant. The cost, however, would be to cut off one's ties with the original account and leave one with the unsatisfactorily negative view that pleasure consisted in the absence of lacks, a view hardly consistent with the distinction made at 583c-584a. Furthermore, this second view is highly implausible when applied to the pleasure of quenching one's thirst, and the others with which the original account started.

6.8.2. In the *Republic* Plato shows no signs of seeing this ambiguity. He needs to combine two verbally similar but mutually incompatible theses: (*a*) that pleasure consists in the process of replenishing deficiencies, and (*b*) that pleasure consists in possessing what one's nature needs. The difference can be concealed by the wording: that pleasure consists in the replenishment of one's natural needs. He needs thesis (*b*) to supply any argument for the general greater pleasantness of the philosophic life, but it is thesis (*a*) that seems to be held of bodily pleasures when they are said to be flights from distress. The image of the vertical line associates pleasure with upward *movements*, which again suggests a process version of replenishment. The language of 585c is doubtless ambiguous, but if Plato wanted it and traded on it he was guilty of deliberate equivocation.

6.8.3. It might be felt that Plato must have seen this distinction on the grounds, first, that it lies behind the *Gorgias* argument that pleasure and pain cease together (496-7), secondly, that it is implicit in the *Republic* point about the sick mistaking the end term of the replenishment process for a pleasure and, thirdly, that this is surely the point made at *Symp.* 204a.

6.8.4. It is, of course, not true that a person who explicitly makes a distinction always bears it in mind or always sees that it applies where it does. Still less is it true that a person who produces an argument which points to a distinction always sees where it points. Now in the argument of *Gorg.* 496-7 Socrates argues that pleasure and distress, in the cases they have been considering, cease together. Thus, the hunger and the pleasure of eating and the desire to eat all exist together and cease together. And surely the reason for this, one might feel, is that the pain and desire come from the lack, the pleasure from the replenishing. But when the replenishing is finished not only is the lack removed but the replenishing also really is finished. So if pleasure consists in the replenishing, this must cease with the completion of the replenishment, for there is all the difference in the world between the process of replenishment and the state of repletion.

6.8.5. Yet while the replenishment thesis could no doubt have been developed to argue for the conclusion in this way, the interesting fact is that it is not. It is treated as a fact of observation that they cease together. Of course, the whole use of the physiological model seems to one with hindsight to cry out for this distinction between process and end. Once it is made the view of the organism's nature does not so obviously support the view that all pursue pleasure, but suggests that perhaps we pursue the pleasureless state. But that does seem to be hindsight, and the *Gorgias* develops no such position. Indeed, the contrast between the philosopher and the sybarite in the pitcher images at 493-4 also misses the opportunity. The contrast is not between the state of fullness and the process of filling, but between a situation where the process might succeed and one where it is doomed to failure. This might, indeed, suggest contrasting these *processes* as really and not really filling processes, but that move would just distract attention from the other contrast.

6.8.6. Similarly, with the *Republic* passage, one might hope to explain that recuperation aims at a state of repletion which is distinct from a process of replenishment, and therefore cannot be a pleasure. But we have already seen (cf. 6.6.4-5) that this passage itself exhibits the confusion between process of escape and condition of having escaped.

6.8.7. With the *Symposium* one could, of course, start arguing about relative dates, but it is not in fact necessary. For the point in the *Symposium* is that if A has X and knows he has X then he neither lacks X nor thinks he lacks X. But if A desires X he at least thinks he lacks X. So if A knows he has X he does not desire X. If we assume that a philosopher will know he has understanding if he has it, then a successful philosopher will no longer desire understanding. Since he no longer has the desire one is tempted to feel that he can no longer satisfy it and so no longer experience pleasure. But this further step is not taken, and requires the very sharpness of distinction between replenishment and repletion which cannot yet without argument be attributed to Plato. If he had had a sharp appreciation of it, he would have seen that his remarks in the *Symposium* entail that if pleasure consists in the process of replenishment, then neither the gods nor the wise take pleasure in wisdom. If he did not, then he could think of the wise as no longer wanting wisdom because that desire is fulfilled, and since they cannot lose their acquisition their pleasure is stable and complete.

6.8.8. There seems, then, no reason for supposing that at the time of writing the *Republic* Plato had become aware of the importance of the distinction between the process of replenishment and the end state of repletion. There is consequently no reason to doubt that he did conflate the two accounts of pleasure mentioned earlier, helped no doubt by the fact that the terminology of fulfilment contains the necessary ambiguity. As we shall see, the vital distinction was certainly noticed by him later and may well have been part cause of later developments.

6.8.9. It seems, then, that the *Republic* contains an ingenious attempt to salvage the table-turning elements in the *Protagoras* view while giving grounds for not giving value to 'lower' pleasures simply in virtue of their pleasantness. The method is to extend the lack/replenishment model to other than physiologically based examples and then argue that only the favoured cases deserve to be called replenishments. Since every pleasure is a replenishment, only 'real' replenishments are 'real' pleasures — and surely what is really pleasant is pleasanter than what is not? Quite apart from the initial plausibility, and the seductive ambiguity of 'replenishment', 'fulfilment', or 'satisfaction', the very neatness of the way in which the account yielded the results which Plato felt a correct account ought to yield must have made it not only attractive but convincing.

6.8.10. There are, however, signs of more than just an extension of an old view to meet a new problem. Examples are now on the table which do not appear in the *Gorgias*, those of pleasures unpreceded by distress and pleasures of anticipation, which are both thought of as ones the view should cater for in its unextended form. Their presence is an omen. They are unsatisfactorily dealt with, and it was not likely that Plato would rest satisfied. In addition there are unsatisfactory elements in the overall account that were not likely to escape attention for long. One interesting fact about the *Philebus* is the extent to which Plato takes up points on which the *Republic* is unstaisfactory, and develops a relatively rich array of examples which would break the chains of the physiologically inspired model. To see this it will help to have the unsatisfactory points listed.

9. Unsatisfactory points in the *Republic* account

6.9.1. *The original model.*
Even with those pleasures with which one would hope the original account would cope, problems are starting to arise because:

(i) While the sybarite clearly experiences pleasures of anticipation, these do not seem to fit the repletion account.

(ii) The admission of undistressing physical pleasures both raises the question of how extensive they are and also the question of how physical pleasure is related to insatiability and lack of tranquillity. If the blame is to be put on some distress element, this needs elaboration.

(iii) The existence of pleasures not arising from distressing antecedents can only be wedded to a view that pleasure is the replenishment of a lack or depletion, if we allow that not all lacks or depletions are distressing. This should lead in turn to a query about the equation of pleasures with replenishments.
(iv) This might well in turn raise the question of the relation of desires to lacks, and so of the equation of a view of pleasure as replenishing lacks and one of it as replenishing desires. It at least seems slightly strange to say of a person who suddenly is delighted by a beautiful scent that he had wanted to smell it; but not so strange to suggest that it pleased him because it answered some need in his nostrils.

6.9.2. *Extended Model*

(i) The treatment of the pleasures of an honour-lover is very unsatisfactory. The *Phaedo* position that lovers of honour are lovers of the body (68c) is not retained, but nor is much said of these pleasures.
(ii) The replenishing account only allows of intellectual pleasures of acquisition (e.g. learning) and this is related to
(iii) The lack of distinction between the process and the end term of replenishment.

6.9.3. *Repercussions.*
If he developed these difficulties then

(i) It would come to seem increasingly difficult to give an overall account of pleasure that would accommodate all pleasures, and
(ii) The abandonment of this particular one would mean abandoning the consequent version of how we assess relative pleasantness.

6.9.4. It will be argued in what follows that Plato did indeed respond to these problems, and that the grand design of the *Republic* position on hedonism is abandoned in favour of a position that is subtler though in many ways necessarily less satisfying, in the *Philebus*.

10. A note on 'truth'

6.10.1. In Book IX Plato aims to show that only a philosopher's pleasures are 'true' (*alēthes, panalēthes*). Clearly a part of what he means is that they are genuinely or really pleasures, and the terms get coupled with one for 'really' (*ontōs*), which in turn is related to the expression for what is, in contrast to what is in process. Since the truth, which is the object of intellectual desire, *is* as opposed to being in process, a certain amount of punning takes place in this passage. Leaving puns aside, the thought seems to be that a firm lasting container filled with firm lasting contents can truly be said to be filled, whereas when one has a non-stable container and volatile contents it is only in a dubious sense to be called a filling at all: can one fill a hair-sieve with liquid? So far it might seem that to talk of pleasures as true is to say that it is true of them without qualification that they are pleasures, though of course with the important addition that degrees of pleasure are a function of the capacity of filled and filler for genuine filling, and perhaps also of degrees of fulfilment in the relevant mode. Yet there is clearly more to it than this. For the argument in 583–4 is at least as concerned with the false judgment of the subject as with the failure of something to be a pleasure. One feels that Plato wants to suggest that untrue pleasures introduce an element of illusion and false judgement into life and that this is part of the allegation that they are untrue. In that case 'true'/'untrue' are implying more than just 'real'/'not real'. A full-bloodedly true pleasure will be not just really pleasant but a pleasure that is a proper part of a life dedicated to the truth, and a full-bloodedly false one a pleasure that is not just not really pleasant but bemuses the mind with false judgments as to what it is. In the *Philebus* Plato shows signs of distinguishing the sense of 'true' as applied to beliefs and judgments, from its sense as equivalent to 'genuine', but even there the extent of his success is uncertain (see Appendix A).

Chapter 7

Philebus

1. The period after the *Republic*

7.1.1. After the *Republic*, the three main discussions of pleasure occur in the *Timaeus*, *Philebus*, and *Laws*. In *Tim.* 64-6 there is a treatment of bodily pleasure where the simple equation of pleasure with replenishment is abandoned, and to which we shall have to return in discussing the nature of Plato's theories. There are also at 69 some rude remarks about pleasure, where the word is obviously used in its restricted sense. If we want to know how Plato stood on the problems left by the *Republic* we have to turn to the *Philebus* and *Laws*. It will be assumed that that is the order of composition of the *Philebus* and the relevant parts of the *Laws* and they will be discussed in that order.

7.1.2. In the dialogues before the *Philebus*, while it is obvious that hedonism has been exercising Plato a good deal, and that he has been influenced by outside views of philosophers and others, there is no sign from the dialogues of vigorous general philosophical activity on the subject. This is not to suggest that there was none. There is some evidence that some followers of Socrates took a hedonistic line and others a very austere one. Thus we have found (see 1.1.1 and 2.3) some reason for putting Aristippus in the first category and Antisthenes in the second. Evidence of these views is fragmentary, and it seems likely that in so far as these schools were active during Plato's lifetime there was no very vigorous argument for the positions, nor extensive analysis of pleasure. In that case it would not be surprising that up to the *Republic* there are no allusions to vigorous rival schools of thought. It must, however, be acknowledged that agnosticism is really the safest position on the question of vigour. What is clear is that Plato is not clearly reacting to them. He would not, indeed, react a great deal against Antisthenes, with whose

suspicion of bodily pleasure he had a good deal of sympathy.
As to Aristippus, if he held the view (cf. DL II.86) that
pleasure is a gentle motion, pain a rough one, then while
Plato might oppose his devotion to bodily pleasure as the
good (ibid. 85), he never criticizes the analysis of pleasure.
He does indeed (*Rep*. 583e9–10) speak of both pleasure and
pain as movements, but this view is accepted rather than
criticized, and is quite unrelated to Aristippus. The latter's
view is, as we have seen, quite different from the medically
inspired Platonic view, where violence of motion does not
cause pain, but all depends on the motion's direction.
Violence intensifies either pleasure or pain according to
whether the motion in question is towards or away from
natural balance. Of this 'motion' view of pleasure there is a
good deal in Plato, but of that attributed to Aristippus
nothing. There is, indeed, rejection of attachment to bodily
pleasure, but not in a form that allows us to consider
Aristippus as the specific target.

7.1.3. It is, indeed, worth wondering why one should
suppose that Plato must have been very familiar with
Aristippus' views, or thought them worth arguing against if
he was. The fact that two philosophers have been associates
of a third or that they have practised in the same town is no
guarantee that they either understand each other or appreciate
each other's importance. Bertrand Russell could apparently
read Wittgenstein's *Tractatus* and misunderstand it, and the
works of Russell and Wittgenstein are not filled with criticism
of each other's views. Yet we have no reason to suppose Plato
and Aristippus to have associated as closely as these two, nor
to suppose that the usual conditions of mutual interest and
understanding were suspended in their case because they
were ancient Greeks. So although we may suppose that there
were followers of Socrates who developed hedonistic views
and others who developed the more austere side of Socrates'
teachings, and although these trends clearly exerted influence
in ancient Greece, leading to the Cyrenaic and Cynic schools
respectively, there is no sign of any direct notice of them on
Plato's part at least before the *Philebus*.

7.1.4. It is said, however (cf. DL VIII. 87), that some time in the early 360s Eudoxus transferred his school to Athens, and he at some time propounded a form of hedonism and put forward arguments for it, a number of which are recorded by Aristotle. This probably either stimulated, or coincided with, the development of anti-sybaritic and more generally anti-hedonistic views, of which we get explicit mention in the *Philebus*. It looks as though pleasure became one of the fashionable philosophical topics in the 360s, and as the *Philebus* is written after the development of some of these views, and arguably in reaction to Eudoxus, consideration of Plato's views as expressed in it requires some consideration of these other positions.

2. The *Philebus*: general view

7.2.1. First, however, it will be helpful to get a general picture of the *Philebus*. We shall avoid entanglement in the intricate question of interpretation of the so-called meta-physical passages, for which see Gosling (5). The dialogue is concerned, to begin with, with the question whether the good life is a life of pleasure or intelligence. Protarchus takes over the thesis that pleasure is the good as can be seen from the fact that all animals pursue it. Socrates holds the intel-ligent life to be better. Socrates has a problem with Philebus' thesis, that while pleasure seems to be a single thing, 'it' is in fact many. He cannot be said to prove this position, but he is clearly portrayed as rejecting the view that pleasures resemble one another in virtue of being pleasures. Pages 11–15 are taken up with making this point, and in pages 15–20 Socrates purports to illustrate how any worthwhile discipline finds a unity in opposites, so that there is nothing to be surprised at in pleasure's situation. At this point the discussion changes tack. Socrates remembers hearing that neither pleasure nor intelligence is the good, and he and Protarchus agree that the good for man is a life that includes both. The dispute is now as to which is 'more responsible' for the good life. The next section, from 23–30, takes up this question and Socrates argues that the good states are produced, if at all, by intel-ligence, which works by imposing order in whatever area it is operating in. The ordered result is a good of some kind: a melody in music, health in medicine, and so on. Similarly, in human life, it will be intelligence that produces the right ordering that makes the life good. Pleasure has no such role. At this stage it is agreed that intelligence has the greater responsibility for the good life, and so, strictly the question set at 20-3 is settled.

7.2.2. Fairly clearly, however, the question that is in fact answered is one about their respective productive roles. Further, the question has been tackled at a very abstract level, with no consideration of specific pleasures or intellectual activities. It remains perfectly possible, first, that while intelligence is needed to bring about a good life, what gives it value is its pleasantness; and secondly that any pleasure is as good as any other for this purpose. In his discussion of the role of intelligence Socrates has, indeed, tried to make these positions unattractive. In 28-30 the activity of human intelligence is portrayed as allied to that of the divine intelligence, and we are doubtless meant to feel that that is what gives value to the intellect and that certainly there are many pleasures which would be below its dignity. This is at best done by suggestion, however. At 32c-d Socrates asks whether all pleasures are to be welcomed into the good life, or only some. The discussion from 30-66 is taken up with this question and also, towards the end, the question of what gives value to a life. The first is answered by a detailed analysis of various forms of pleasure. In 30-2 there is analysis of the pleasures of physical 'replenishment'; in 32-44 of the pleasures of anticipation which are spoken of as mental pleasure mixed with physical pain. From 44-7 there is a discussion of the views of some contemporary experts who consider pleasure always to be mixed with distress. This leads on to a discussion of pleasures mixed with pain that are experienced 'by the mind alone', such as malicious laughter, love, indignation, and so on. This discussion takes us from 47-50. There follows a brief treatment of unmixed pleasures in 51-3 which is followed in turn by a discussion of another contemporary view hostile to pleasure in 53-5.

7.2.3. At this point we get an analysis of various forms of

knowledge (55-9) leading to the decision (60-4) as to what forms of pleasure and knowledge are desirable. Pleasures which are necessary and ones unmixed with pains are the only pleasures allowed, while all forms of knowledge are admitted if underpinned by dialectic. At this point it is decided (64-6) that it is the order akin to intelligence that mainly gives a life value, with a minor contribution being made by a very select band of pleasures.

7.2.4. It is notable that in this whole section from 30-66 it is the sorts of pleasure that might characterize a vulgar hedonist that come in for the bulk of the criticism: physical pleasures resulting from righting some distressing condition; anticipatory pleasures which involve looking forward from a state of distress; pleasures of emotional excitement. The treatment of these is interspersed at 33, 43, and 55 with suggestions of the possibility of a preferable life free of such pleasures, and with two discussions of the views of contemporary experts, one of which is declared hostile to the pleasures of Philebus and his friends (i.e. physical ones), and the other of which declares pleasure in general not to be good. Desirable and permissible pleasures receive very short notice. The whole is not so much a discussion of various forms of pleasure as an argument that a certain collection of pleasures is undesirable. When these have been dismissed it is easier, with what is left, to get the view accepted that pleasure has only a small part to play in making a life desirable.

7.2.5. The dialogue, then, falls into two main sections: a shorter one from 11-30 where it is argued that while intelligence has the role of organizing the good life, pleasure is no more than something of which intelligence must ask what sorts and how much are to be included; and a longer one where it is argued that the sorts of pleasure Philebus would espouse are undesirable, and that the activity of intelligence not only brings about the good life, but because it is much the same thing as order in life, can be pretty well said to constitute the value of such a life.

3. The dissimilarity of pleasures

7.3.1. The above might suggest that in the first section Plato only distinguishes between the roles of intellect and pleasures in terms of producer and product. In fact there is another theme stressed in this section: the thesis that pleasures are unlike each other. From 12c to 14a Socrates tries to shake Protarchus from the position that pleasures resemble each other in virtue of being pleasures. He concedes that the single term suggests that pleasure constitutes a unit, but claims that pleasures differ as chalk from cheese. Protarchus objects that the differences are of source merely — for surely in so far as they are pleasures they must be alike. Socrates counters with the analogies of colours and figures: no one would say that white and black were alike as colours, nor a square and a circle as figures. One might feel (cf. Dybikowski (3), p. 447) that 'the "opposition" of pleasures does not logically exclude their resemblance or similarity *qua* pleasures' and that it is therefore preferable not to attribute to Plato the view that there is any further degree of dissimilarity than that later envisaged between true and false pleasures. Here it is important to distinguish between what Plato wanted to hold and his success in sustaining it. It is the first with which we are concerned; and here it is worth noting that Plato makes Protarchus in effect take Dybikowski's line. After Socrates has tried to get him to acknowledge dissimilarity from 12c-13b and allow in consequence that some pleasures are bad, Socrates says 'Yet you will admit that some are unlike each other at least, and that some are even opposites of others', to which Protarchus replies, in Dybikowski's words almost: 'Not at all, at least not *qua* pleasures.' It is just this stance that Socrates then stigmatizes as showing philosophical naivety. This is not the place to pursue the philosophical rights or wrongs of Socrates' rejection (for some analysis of its inadequacies see Gosling (5), pp. 73-80). The point at issue is whether Plato is prepared to allow that in virtue of being pleasures, pleasures resemble one another. On this it seems clear that Plato is not and that he considers it important to resist the move. Not only does he make Protarchus slow to accept the point that pleasure and forms of knowledge do not each form a single class in virtue of similarity (thus underlining the importance of it); but he offers in 16-18 illustrations from respectable disciplines of how you can justify putting dissimilars into a single class without (obtusely) claiming that they therefore resemble one another.

7.3.2. The importance of this is as follows: if we accept the models of music and grammar, then the problem for someone wishing to live a good life is not how to produce as much as possible of a single product, but rather how to select from and blend into a harmonious whole opposing and dissimilar elements among which are opposing and dissimilar pleasures. If we accept that different pleasures are as variously contrasted as vowels, labial, and guttural speech sounds, it becomes hard to see how we can simply refer to pleasure to see whether a successful life has been produced. It would be just like referring to sound as the criterion of successful speech. Just as there it is the principles of combination that are important, so in the moral life. This prepares the way for the later point that it is order and proportion that makes a good life good: pleasure cannot be the criterion of worth. Nor, indeed, can it be used as a criterion at all. There is no clear interpretation to be given to the notion of a life of pleasure other than that of a life densely packed with some pleasures or other — but there is an indefinite variety of such lives describable. So this first section purports to undermine the possibility of using pleasure as a criterion for deciding how to live; and by its insistence on the variety of pleasures opens the way to the question of which pleasures are to be selected. The variety and opposition of pleasure makes it hard to see what could be made of the hedonist's answer that those pleasures should be selected which lead to the pleasantest life; and it is interesting that the only interpretation given in the *Philebus* to 'pleasanter' is 'more purely pleasant' which means 'pleasant with less admixture of pain'. No interpretation is offered for a comparison of the pleasantness of two pleasures which have no admixture of pain.

7.3.3. In short, while the *Philebus* contains the familiar hostility to sybaritic pleasures, it also moves from the earlier

position that pleasure could be used as a criterion and if
properly used would yield the good life. This seems to stem
from the insistence on the variety of pleasures and the
rejection of the idea of similarity. This seems to be held in a
very strong form which would disallow even the kind of
common formula of the *Republic* account in terms of replenishment of natural needs. That the account indeed is no
longer acceptable seems fairly clear. While in the *Republic*
pleasures of anticipation are confusingly assimilated to ones
of replenishment, in the *Philebus* at 32c they are said to
constitute a distinct class, and no attempt is made to give
anything approaching a replenishment analysis of them. Even
standard replenishment examples no longer receive an unqualified replenishment analysis. At 43 it is argued that not
all replenishments are perceived; only the 'big' ones are
perceived and it is these which produce pleasures (cf. 43a–c
and 33d–34a). Similarly, no replenishment analysis seems
appropriate for malicious pleasure discussed in such detail
from 48–50, nor is any offered. It seems clear that in the
Philebus Plato has no general formula to encapsulate the
nature of pleasure; and that he does not use the *Republic* one
either in his account of any but pleasures of physical replenishment or in his account of comparisons of pleasure. It
seems probable that because of his views on the dissimilarity
of pleasures he actually thought that no such account was
available.

7.3.4. These changes partly resulted from problems in
supplying answers to the question 'What is X?' for certain
values of X. The later dialogues show an increasing interest
in these problems and in the analogies of the philosopher's
task with skills of combination. Partly, also, they must have
resulted from the closer attention to a richer range of
examples. There is a marked contrast between the cursory
confusing mention of anticipatory pleasures in the *Republic*
and the elaborate discussion of three distinct cases of falsity
in the *Philebus*; between the brusque assertion that pleasures
of the spirited element can be assimilated to the *Republic*
account (cf. *Rep*. 586c7–d2), and the detailed discussion of
malicious enjoyment which is to stand as typical of the

spirited element's pleasures and which does not, it may be noted, bear out the *Republic* claim.

7.3.5. Not only is a greater variety of examples discussed, but also the analysis is taken deeper. It was noted earlier that Plato fudged the distinctions between a lack and a pain and between a lack and a desire. In the *Philebus* both contrasts are made. At 43 the distinction is made between a state of physical depletion/replenishment and pleasure or distress. For the latter we need perception of the former. So we can no longer equate lack and distress, nor replenishment and pleasure. At 33c ff., leading up to his account of false pleasures, Socrates, as part of the contrast between physical and anticipatory pleasures, embarks on an analysis of physical desires. These are said not to be identical with a distress coming from perception of a lack, but to be movements towards replenishment stimulated by memory of how this lack was previously met. So it is no longer possible to equate either lack in general or felt lack with desire, since neither is sufficient for it.

4. Mixed pleasures and insatiability

7.4.1. It was noted, in discussing the *Republic*, that Plato seemed to think that pleasures unmixed with distress might not be insatiable, and that adulteration with distress was somehow connected with insistent and barely controllable pursuit. In the *Philebus* (44-7) we hear of some experts on pleasure whose position Socrates does not accept, but whom he considers allies. Their view on pleasure is confined to physical pleasures and they consider them all to be of their nature mixed (for a fuller discussion, see the next chapter). Presumably Socrates differs from them both in holding that there are pleasures of the soul alone and that there are unmixed pleasures. They will only be effective allies, however, if they are partially right — and it seems likely that Plato accepts that certain physical pleasures are mixed with distress, and that they tend to violent and irrational extremes of the sort described. In 46 we have an account of the way these pleasures tend to extremes which relies upon the compresence of pleasure and pain. This account might seem to explain how (some) 'impure' pleasures tend to give rise to insatiable desire: their satisfaction brings about an opposing depletion whose satisfaction in turn reinstates the original depletion and so reactivates the original desire. Thus the satisfaction of a desire in these circumstances contains the seeds of the desire's return. In short, the *Philebus* offers a reason for supposing, what the *Republic* took for granted, that mixed pleasures, in contrast to pure ones, have some inbuilt tendency to excess, while limiting the thesis to mixed physical pleasures. Doubtless, it is not fully successful. It is not clear, for instance, that thirst, though mixed, is insatiable in the required way. Still, the problem is faced and taken further; and at least unmixed pleasures will clearly not be prone to this sort of immoderate disturbance.

7.4.2. Again, with unmixed pleasures, we find more importance attached to this class (cf. 44d, 50e–51e), and pleasures of sight and hearing are added to those of smell. There is now clearly a grading of more and less 'divine' pure physical pleasures, and while those of smell would be susceptible of a replenishment analysis, the partially aesthetic pleasures of sight and hearing look far less likely candidates for such treatment.

5. More adequate analysis of examples

7.5.1. So far we have considered mainly the treatment of pleasures which in the *Republic* are lumped together as susceptible of similar treatment, and which might be thought obviously covered by the unextended medical model. In the *Philebus* a richer range of examples is examined in more detail in a way which strongly suggests that Plato actually became dissatisfied at points at which he ought to have become dissatisfied. In the *Republic* there was an attempt to extend this model to produce a theory for all kinds of pleasure. The list of examples supposedly covered by the typical case of malicious enjoyment (cf. 47e1, 50b–c), makes it clear that Plato now thinks he has an account of a wide range of pleasures, which would include those of the *Republic*'s spirited element. While he thinks he can show that they are mixed, there is no attempt to show that a replenishment model could be made to accommodate them, nor does the analysis make such a project look at all hopeful. Nor, again, does he try to show that these are connected with insatiable desire (cf. *Rep*. 586c–d).

7.5.2. If we turn to intellectual pleasures, we find similar signs of development. In the *Republic* only the pleasures of learning seemed to be envisaged, the pleasures, that is, of its acquisition, not of its exercise. These are still allowed in the *Philebus* (52), and secured from the see-saw disturbance of mixed physical pleasures in being declared to have no essential connection to a prior experienced thirst for knowledge. But there is also mention of the pure pleasures of virtue and knowledge. At 63e the forms of knowledge are being asked what pleasures they would like to live with. They let in the pure pleasures already mentioned, which include those of acquiring knowledge, and *in addition* those accompanying health, temperance, and every excellence – which must include wisdom. At 66c4–6 the pleasures following on the forms of knowledge are given value. So Plato is now re-cognizing intellectual pleasures apart from those of acquistion. Although he gives no account of their nature, it is hard to see how he could give a plausible replenishment account. On the other hand, once he has distinguished them from the others, he can allow the life of an accomplished philosopher to be pleasant (and even the pleasantest of going options (cf. *Laws* 734d)) and escape the embarrassment caused by the replenishment model in leaving such a life pleasureless just because replete.

6. Process and end

7.6.1. It looks, then, as though further consideration of examples which he might have hoped to cover by his extended model made that extension less attractive. That this was so seems even more likely when we consider the second set of contemporary experts whose views he considers. The details of this view will be considered in the next chapter. What is clear is that they relied upon making a very sharp distinc-tion between something aimed at, an end state, and the end state itself, and put pleasure into the first category. This distinction is precisely the one which, we claimed, Plato needed to blur if he was to pull off the trick of showing, in the *Republic*, that the philosophic life is pleasantest. In the *Philebus* he claims these thinkers as allies. Once again, this is presumably because he considers that they have a germ of truth in their theory. The most likely candidate here is the point that pleasures of replenishment, whether physical or otherwise, are well classified by this view. But if Plato has come to appreciate sharply the distinction between a process towards an end and an end, he must have appreciated the distinction between coming to acquire and being in possession. It is not likely that he would have seen and, in a limited area, welcomed the view of these thinkers without realizing that a successful philosopher could not be leading a life of acquiring knowledge — so that if his life was pleasant it must be a pleasure that was not a replenishing.

7.6.2. So it looks as though by the time of the *Philebus* not only has Plato done a good deal more thinking on the subject of pleasure, but also the more detailed analyses would make the *Republic* model quite unattractive. Further, the very variety disclosed might well make anyone doubt whether any general account, even of the schematic sort offered in the *Republic*, could ever be found. So the actual enquiries concerning pleasure would chime in with quite general misgivings about hunting for similarities in certain types of case, to make Plato sceptical of the possibility of finding an account. Certainly the *Philebus* contains none, and arguably by that time Plato thought it a sign of innocence to look for one. A musician studies sound; but he does not look for a general account of sound, but for ways of combining its opposed elements. Even if pleasure were what life's musician studied, he would not hunt for a general account of pleasure, but for ways of combining its opposed elements. Alternatively, doing that is all that giving an account of pleasure could be. Pleasure is something organized by an art, or of no value. Any art governing it thereby supplies an account of its 'nature'.

7. Degrees of pleasure

7.7.1. Going along with this general shift of aim is a loss

of an account of degrees of pleasure allied to an analysis of its nature. The account of relative degrees is now simply a matter of relative purity, and this makes it impossible any longer to dub intellectual pleasures as generally pleasanter than physical ones. On the *Republic* view, a life spent smelling roses would be a life of unmixed but bodily pleasure, and for this latter reason it would be less pleasant than a philosophic life. In *Philebus* terms it would be impossible to make a relative grading. We could, of course, ask whether in fact we can sustain a life of pure physical pleasure, and so we might rule out some describable options as not attainable; but we cannot grade the describable options as relatively pleasant if they both contain nothing but unmixed pleasures. Consequently, if we set ourselves the task of setting out the pleasantest describable life, we shall not any longer be sure, if we succeed, of coming up with the best. For there are many 'pleasantest describable lives'.

7.7.2. So Plato's approach to pleasure has developed. In some ways he has become more appreciative. There is a slightly greater tolerance of a slightly wider range of pleasures; the pure physical pleasures and pleasures accompanying health are upgraded, and those of virtue and the exercise of knowledge added. On the other hand, the hostility to the old enemy is as fierce as ever, and he has finally abandoned the table-turning position that if you do your research on pleasure adequately the resulting pleasantest life will be one of virtue. This is not to say that he no longer thought a virtuous philosophic life the pleasantest of the real-life choices, but simply that he had given up the view that one can use pleasure to guide one's calculations.

7.7.3. There is little doubt from a reading of the *Philebus* that it is written against a background of a good deal of philosophical activity on the topic of pleasure. In no earlier dialogue do we get an explicit allusion to other developed views on its nature and value. In the *Philebus* two such views are referred to, and indeed described, and we shall argue that probably Philebus' position on the value of pleasure is derived from the thesis of Eudoxus. This background we shall

examine in the next chapter. It might help to end this one by
laying out schematically the suggested weaknesses in the
Republic account alongside the *Philebus* contrasts.

Republic	*Philebus*
(1) *Original Model* has problems	(1)
(a) with anticipatory pleasure;	(a) gives a detailed analysis of anticipatory pleasures and distinguishes them sharply from those of physical replenishment;
(b) with the relation of physical pleasure to insatiability.	(b) offers an explanation of why *some* mixed pleasures lead to insatiability;
(c) with pure physical pleasures which suggest that not all lacks are distressing;	(c) contrasts lacks/replenishments, with pains/pleasures, which involve perception;
(d) with the relation of lacks and desires.	(d) explicitly distinguishes desire from the condition of depletion.
(2) *Extended Model* is inadequate because	(2)
(a) its treatment of honour-loving pleasures is too cursory;	(a) gives honour-loving pleasures a detailed analysis that does not support the *Republic* statement;
(b) it allows only intellectual pleasures which are acquisitive;	(b) allows of other intellectual pleasures;
(c) it fails to distinguish between the process of replenishment and its achievement.	(c) underlines the contrast between end-directed process and end.
(3) *Repercussions* are	(3)
(a) difficulty of giving overall account of pleasure;	(a) the difficulty is seen and embraced as a virtue;
(b) consequent adjustment of account of relative pleasure.	(b) a new account of how to judge relative pleasantness is given.

Chapter 8

Between *Republic* and *Philebus*

8.0.1. As we remarked in the last chapter, there seems to have been considerable philosophical activity on the subject of pleasure between the *Republic* (probably mid-360s) and the *Philebus* (probably some ten to twelve years later). The very richness of the *Philebus* suggests it, even if there were not the open reference to other theorists. Also, it seems likely that the dialogue as a whole is a response to the work of Eudoxus, who is said to have worked in Athens some time in the 360s.

8.0.2. It will be easiest to assess the case for Eudoxus' influence after considering the other two, explicitly mentioned, sets of theorists. The first of these are considered in 44-6, the second in 53-5. It has often been supposed (cf. Schofield, and references) that the view recounted in the first passage is that of Speusippus. We shall return to that question when we come to Aristotle (see Ch. 12). For the moment, the question is: precisely what is their position?

1. The naturists

8.1.1. They are sometimes referred to as physicists on the ground that they are said to be experts on nature at 44b9-10. This may, however, simply refer to the fact that they had a special view about how to determine what the nature of anything is (44d7-e4), and as this view is quite general, with no special tie to physics, they will here be referred to as the naturists, to leave the dispute open. The view in question, that if we wish to discern the nature of anything we must consider it in its most extreme form, could attract a physicist who believed in such elements as the hot and the cold, or equally a medical man who thought that the nature of black bile was best studied in its most extreme and violent operations, or, again, a moralist studying the nature of reason over against desire.

8.1.2. These theorists are somewhat puzzling, so we shall start with a rough sketch of the passage in order to isolate the problems for discussion. Just before they are mentioned, Socrates and Protarchus have agreed on the existence of an intermediate state when a person experiences neither physical pleasure nor pain (42d–44a), amending the earlier account of physical pleasure and pain in 31–2 so that instead of being considered as processes of restoration and disruption they are thought of as perceptions of these processes (for further discussion of this passage see Ch. 10). Since not all these processes are perceived we may allow the body to be in perpetual process while also allowing the person not always to be in a state of either pleasure or pain. At 44a12–b3 Socrates gives Protarchus an opportunity to go back on this amendment, and when Protarchus expresses puzzlement at the suggestion, Socrates says that Protarchus does not know who Philebus' real enemies are. These are people (44b9–c2) who say either

(i) there are no pleasures, and what Philebus calls pleasures are only flights from pain or

(ii) pleasures are not *real*, but what Philebus calls pleasures are only flights from pain, or

(iii) what Philebus calls pleasures are not pleasures but only flights from pain.

They then proceed to study the nature of pleasure by considering its most extreme and intense forms, concluding that these are all as much examples of distress as of pleasure and are in fact escapes from distress.

8.1.3. The problems to be considered are

(*a*) why does Socrates give Protarchus the opportunity to abandon the amendment of 42d–44a?

(*b*) what do the theorists think about pleasure? and connected with both

(*c*) just why are they Philebus' real enemies?

With regard to (*a*) it seems fairly clear that Protarchus is not being told that his thesis is safer if he sticks to the amendment, but is being given the option of abandoning it to save his thesis that pleasure is the predominant value. Quite apart from the way the conversation goes, the naturists are going to attack the pleasures of the body as witchcraft (44c-d), as characteristic of an overweening rather than temperate character (45d2-4), of a degenerate rather than excellent state of mind or body, (45e5-7), and as being always mixed with pain in intense form (46a8-c4). This attack could only carry conviction if it was possible to live some life that did not consist of these pleasures or pains. If the amendment of 42d ff. is abandoned, then we are left with the position that pleasure and pain are just the processes of restoration and disruption, and the possibility that the Heracleiteans are right in saying that everything is in a state of flux. In that case we should have to refute Heracleiteanism if we were to hold that any life was possible that did not simply consist in a succession of (mixed) pleasures and pains. The amendment, on the other hand, clearly allows for a life where few or no bodily pleasures or pains are experienced. Consequently without the need to challenge the flux theory at the physical level, the possibility is conceded of a life free of Phileban pleasures. Thus Philebus' real enemies are given a foothold.

8.1.4. We now have a partial answer to (c): these people are enemies of Philebus because they can put before us an alternative life. But they also attack the contents of the sybaritic life, and it is here important to see what they think about pleasure, and that means seeing whether they take any of the three options in 8.1.2. or some other. Here it is easiest to start with the second suggestion, that their view is that pleasures are not real, but that what Philebus calls pleasures are only flights from pain. This would suggest that these theorists are operating with a Platonic-style distinction between what is real and what is in process. In that case their objection is that pleasure occurs at the level of process, not at the level of reality, whereas what is worthwhile occurs in the stable, non-process operations of the mind free of the body's turbulence.

8.1.5. The objection to this view is that while these thinkers may have held this position there is no indication of it in the *Philebus*. The amendment of 42d ff. does indeed purport to dodge a difficulty in the view that everything is in process. But the amendment only secures the possibility of a life undisturbed by *bodily* processes. No argument is supplied for supposing that this life is one of utter stability where no process occurs, nor is this part of the attack made by the naturists. Their complaint is not that Philebus' pleasures are all processes, but that they are escapes from pain and always pleasure/pain mixtures — this is the main point — and also associated with degenerate states of mind and body and with a tendency towards uncontrolled madness. This has similarities with the stance in the *Phaedo*, but it lacks its use of the contrast of body/becoming with soul/being, as well as supplying arguments not found in the *Phaedo*. There is, in fact, no ground for importing any such Platonic-sounding point. No doubt what we know of them is consistent with such a point — except that the treatment of 'nature' fails to associate it with stable being — but many positions might agree in their fear of bodily pleasures and the characterization of their menace, while differing in the arguments for that characterization.

8.1.6. If their point is not that Phileban pleasure or pleasures in general fail to attain the unchanging stability of the real, it might be position (iii), that what Philebus calls pleasures are not really pleasures. Certainly this fits Socrates' opening remarks which could be translated (44b9–c2) 'Socrates: "People who are said to be great experts on nature, who deny they are pleasures at all." Protarchus: "How?" Socrates: "They say that all these which Philebus and his friends call pleasures are escapes from pain." ' The discussion then proceeds to an examination of Philebus' pleasures aimed at showing that they are not really pleasures, strictly speaking, but pleasure/pains. This becomes clear when we study their true nature in their extreme forms, for then the element of distress which we might overlook in milder forms stands out unmistakably. The discussion, of course, tends to use the word 'pleasure' in a restricted sense a good deal of the time. Thus when at 44e7–45a2 Socrates says that if we want to discover the nature of pleasure we must consider the most extreme forms and proceed to analyse them, 'pleasure' is being used to refer to those items sponsored by Philebus. The aim of the argument is going to be to justify the original claim of 44c1–2 that they are not really pleasures. The air of paradox, that pleasure is shown not to be pleasure, is superficial only and not, in the context, misleading.

8.1.7. This argument can only proceed if it is known what real pleasure is. So it is tempting to suggest (see Gosling (5), p. 231) that the naturists thought that there were real pleasures, but that Philebus' candidates were not among them (compare the *sophoi* of *Rep.* 583b). This would give them some resemblance to the Plato of *Rep.* IX. For since the only ground given for denying the title 'pleasure' to Philebus' indulgences is that they are mixed, the implication is that experiences that lacked all distress element and were pleasant would be genuine pleasures. They would presumably be trying to reject the *Republic* counter-example of smells as distress-free bodily pleasures through the thesis on nature: even these pleasures only show their true colours in intense form, and ecstatic pleasures of smell are ones that make one hardly able to contain oneself, and so introduce some element of distress. This would leave them holding that genuine pleasures can only be non-physical ones. But now the criterion of genuineness is not the *Republic* one of real filling of lacks, but the one that Plato will adopt in the *Philebus* of freedom from admixture with its opposite. They could, then, be holding that real pleasures occurred in the state where bodily turbulences did not get through to the soul, but were not to be found in sybaritic activities.

8.1.8. If this were so, then they would be in a strong position over against Philebus, in that not only could they claim that his sort of life does not really contain any pleasure, but also offer a life where pleasure really is to be found. Their hostility, in fact, is not to pleasure, but to the indulgences of a Life of Pleasure. If they could not offer this possibility, an opponent might naturally feel that a life where pleasure could only be got mixed up with pain was preferable to one where it is not found at all. While this line of opposition

is still perhaps open, it is not obvious that someone who
thinks pleasure is the good can without more ado make that
his ground for preferring a life with no real pleasure in to one
with.

8.1.9. Despite the attractions of this, there are considerations that tell in favour of position (i). The difference
between positions (i) and (iii) is this: that while position (iii)
allows for the existence of real pleasures, position (i), trading
on the same conception of real pleasure, argues that there are
none, and there are indications in the text that this is what
the naturists' position was. To begin with, while the sentence
at 44b9–10 can be translated as suggested at 8.1.6 in a way
that looks forward to the following sentence, it can also be
translated: 'Socrates: "People who are said to be great
experts on nature, who altogether deny that there are any
pleasures."' This would fit with 45c7–8 where the wording
suggests that the same point is referred to, and which reads:
'For we say we must consider what nature it [pleasure] has
and what those say it is who say that it is not at all.' There is
no natural way of supplying 'pleasure' after 'who say that it
is not . . .'. In that case it looks as though the naturists are
denying that there are any real pleasures and this seems to be
borne out by 51a, where Socrates says he disagrees with these
people who say that all pleasures are cessations of pain,
but makes use of them to make the point that many pleasures
are only *apparent*. This suggests that the naturists made the
mistake of reading 'all' for 'many'.

8.1.10. As we have seen, the translation of 44b9–10 is not
conclusive. The point at 51a is only conclusive if we have to
take 'pleasure' in an unrestricted sense. But we have already
seen that in the naturists' attack the word must commonly
be used in a restricted sense to refer to the sorts of pleasure
favoured by Philebus and his friends. There is no compulsion, therefore, to take 51a as attributing to the naturists a
general position about pleasure. It need only be a position
about bodily pleasures, or at least the pleasures that Philebus
likes. Presumably a sybarite would like sweet scents, and
Socrates is going to hold that these are genuine enough

pleasures. So it is perfectly possible that he is simply declaring his disagreement with the naturists about bodily pleasures, and it is all these merely that they are declaring to be releases from pain in accord with 44c1–2.

8.1.11. In fact, the issue hinges on 45c7–8. 'For we must consider what nature it [pleasure] has and what those say it is who say it is not at all.' Yet this sentence is peculiar on either view. The antecedent of 'it' in both 'what nature it has' and in 'it is not at all' must be 'pleasure'. At first one might be tempted to take 'pleasure' in its restricted sense. It is, after all, the nature of the Phileban pleasures that is under discussion. But then on neither view are the naturists denying that there *are* Phileban pleasures. What they are denying is that these are really pleasures. So one might try the suggestion that 'pleasure' be taken as referring to real pleasure. Then we are being told that we must consider the nature of real pleasure and what sort of thing those say it is who hold that there is none. Now on view (i) this would be a perfectly sensible point to consider. One would want to ask the naturists what their concept of pleasure was such that they denied there were any pleasures. But 'pleasure' as it occurs at 45c5 as the antecedent of 'it' seems to refer to Phileban pleasure, not the real variety, and perhaps more importantly, no consideration is in fact given to the naturists' views on the nature of real pleasure. All we get is consideration of the nature of Phileban pleasures which are, *ex hypothesi*, not real pleasures at all. To make this sentence clearly fit position (i) it would be easiest to amend '*tina*' to '*ti*' in 45c7, so as to read 'For we say we must consider what nature it has, and what those are saying who say it is not at all.' Then the point would be that an examination of the nature of pleasure as found in practice would bring out clearly just what the naturists' point is.

8.1.12. If we take position (iii) the sentence is awkward, because we have to supply a suppressed occurrence of 'pleasure' so as to be able to understand 'For we say we must consider what nature it [pleasure] has, and what those are saying who say it is not *pleasure* at all.' Once again, emendation would ease matters. If we could suppose '*HDONHN*' to have fallen out, and read '*MH HDONHN EINAI*' for '*MHDEINAI*' (writing *H* for ēta), this would make explicit what otherwise has to be understood, and the shift from a restricted to unrestricted use of 'pleasure' is no more difficult than in 44c5–d1.

8.1.13. Emendations are, of course, possible, but it is nice to be able to dispense with them. It seems fairly clear that the naturists use the fact that a set of occurrences are pleasure/pains to support their contention that 'there are no pleasures'. This certainly tempts one to suppose that their thesis is that pleasure/pains are not really pleasures. One difficulty encountered is that *either* the naturists by 'pleasure' mean 'bodily pleasure', in which case surely they are not denying that this exists; *or* by 'pleasure' they mean 'real pleasure' in which case it is odd that we do not get a consideration of the nature of 'real pleasure'. If, on the other hand, we try translating throughout as though their point was that bodily pleasures are not really pleasures, 51a is distinctly awkward. Suppose, however, we abandon the view that the naturists are using 'pleasure' either in a way that restricts it by sense to bodily pleasures, or in a way that commits them to the existence of real ones or using 'real pleasure' so that only some non-bodily experiences could be. Suppose that the only pleasures whose existence they recognize are bodily ones, or that what pleasure there is is to be found in bodily ones; but that at the same time they hold that for any *F*, if there are any *F*s there must be things that are *F* and not also the opposite of *F*. This is not a totally unattractive view. One may admit that some men are wise sometimes, but hold that there are no wise men on the ground that all men are sometimes foolish; or that there are no cures for social ills in that every cure of one ill produces another ill, so that there are no cures. Now this does not look too hopeful on pleasure, even if the only pleasures we recognize are bodily ones: for although many such pleasures come out as pleasure/pains, there are surely many examples where no distress is involved. It is here that the view on determining a thing's nature comes into its own. If one wishes to discover the nature of black bile, then one should observe its operation unhindered by the checks imposed by the other elements in the body. This is a matter of discovering its tendency, or perhaps extrapolating from a series of cases of increasing dominance of black bile. Similarly with bodily pleasures. One may get cases where no distress is observable, because of the checks imposed by other desires or whatever. But these examples do not reveal the nature of the pleasure in question. For that we have to see the results of an increase in power of that pleasure. The claim now is that all pleasures are such that in their true colours they are mixed up with distress. One may get particular examples of undiluted pleasure, but only because the pleasure is frustrated of its natural development. We need to look at *intense* pleasures of smell. Of its own nature the pleasure is not isolable from distress. So just as there are no genuine cures of social ills, there are no genuine pleasures. By contrast there are genuine pains: that is to say, there are pains which when left unchecked are unadulterated by pleasure. So while there are pains, there are no pleasures, but only pleasure/pains. The importance of this 'observation' will be that someone like Philebus who advocates indulgence in pleasures will turn out to be advocating the development in power of a class of tendencies not to pleasure but to pleasure/pain. It all sounds very nice until we recognize the true nature of pleasure. Once we do recognize it we see that the hedonist road is one to distress as much as pleasure and one to madness and degeneracy generally.

8.1.14. This interpretation yields a version of position (i) but seems to avoid the earlier difficulties. The naturists do not believe in the existence of some real, non-Phileban pleasures, nor do they have an account of the nature of pleasure according to which bodily pleasures could not count. They think that bodily pleasures are all the pleasures there are, and their view of the nature of pleasure is such that they think all pleasures are mixed in their true nature with pain. So we do get their view of the nature of pleasure. But on the assumption that if X is F and the opposite of F then it is not an F, the conclusion is that if we examine the nature of the only candidates for pleasurehood we find them not to be pleasures at all.

8.1.15. This view has obvious similarities to views expressed in the *Phaedo* and *Republic* on bodily pleasures, but differs in not recognizing any other pleasures, in making no use of any contrast of being and becoming, and in having a theory on discovering something's nature. Plato could hardly, in the *Philebus*, accept the naturists' general account of pleasure, nor even (cf. 51–2) accept their view as a correct account of bodily pleasures. But he probably did think that it was characteristic of sybaritic bodily pleasures to be associated with strong desires and to have the violent tendencies supposed by these thinkers; so that in their account of these pleasures they were substantially right and could be used as allies against Philebus.

2. The subtlers

8.2.1. The second view explicitly mentioned and attributed to others in the *Philebus* is that attributed in 53c–55a to certain subtle thinkers.

8.2.2. The passage develops as follows: Socrates mentions a supposedly familiar view that pleasure is a process of coming to be. This he expands by pointing out that there are two classes, one of things that are in themselves, the other of things aspiring to members of the first class. The first class deserves our respect, the second is deficient. In general terms, the first class consists of those things or states for the sake of which other things happen, the second of those processes that aim at members of the first class. The contrast is then expressed as one between being and coming to be/bringing into being, and illustrated by such examples as boat : boat-building, health : drug-taking. The first category is then identified with that of goods (goals), and the second is therefore not that of goods. Consequently, if pleasure is a process of coming-to-be, it will be for the sake of something else; it will therefore fall into the second category and cannot be a good. Anyone holding this view will ridicule those who hold that pleasure is the good, for they will be advocating a life full of hunger and thirst as proper subjects for the curative coming-to-be of pleasure. Indeed, since one can only come to be from a state of deprivation, such people will spend their lives pursuing deprivation/destruction as much as coming-to-be. They will, paradoxically, not want the good state at which the process of coming-to-be aims.

8.2.3. The view described relies upon a not very precisely characterized distinction between two categories. It is clear, however, that the contrast is not just between a process and its end term. Death is an end term of fatal disease; but dying is a process of ceasing, not coming, to be, and so death is not in the category of being, nor dying in that of becoming (cf. 55a, where destruction is opposed to coming-to-be). All the end states are good states. The word '*genesis*' (becoming) used here, then, is not a stand-in to refer to a condition of flux embracing both coming-to-be and passing away; nor is the contrast of *genesis* with *ousia* (being) a contrast between change and stability. Boats are not, by Platonic standards, permanent stable objects, but they are not either, in the terms of this theory, processes of producing or coming to be anything.

8.2.4. It may be, as Aristotle suggests (*EN* 1173b13–15), that this view developed from a consideration of pleasures of nourishment, but he implies that it was intended as a general view of the nature of pleasure, and this is the suggestion of the *Philebus*. Many candidates have been put forward as the holders of this view (see Bury's note to 55b13 for some) and some (e.g. Guthrie, V, p. 455) think that Plato himself espoused the view. The only ground for this last is that Plato treats them as allies and does not, as he does with the naturists (51a) explicitly dissociate himself from them. On the other hand, it is a view which has obvious affinities with a replenishment view — though the terminology is calculated to highlight an ambiguity which that of replenishment might conceal — and at 32c pleasures of replenishment are contrasted with pleasures of anticipation as a separate kind. No attempt is made to give any kind of replenishment analysis of these last, nor of the pure pleasures of virtue. Since earlier Plato had been inclined to use the replenishment analysis generally, the absence of it in these cases in the *Philebus* is almost certainly significant, in which case it is equally improbable that he thought that a *genesis* account could be generalized to all pleasures. Even with regard to bodily ones he would want to add in the condition about perception. On the other hand he probably did think that most bodily pleasures, especially those favoured by Philebus, did arise from processes of coming-to-be. Consequently something like the oddity that the subtlers see in making pleasure the good would attach to those who, like Philebus, make physical pleasures their goal.

8.2.5. As to other candidates, the evidence seems altogether too slight. The suggestion of Poste and others that Aristippus is meant does not sit happily with the tradition that Aristippus thought pleasure to be the good, (cf. DL II.85–7), especially as this amounts to saying of each pleasure that it is a good (*telos*, goal). Where there is less evidence, refutation is more difficult, but certainty also.

8.2.6. To see the form of this view more sharply it is help-ful to look at the differences between the subtlers and the naturists, a process which also protects one from the tempt-ation to identify them. The differences can be conveniently summed up under five headings.

(i) The aims of the two schools are different. The naturists aim to show that Philebus' pleasures are degenerate and not really pleasures, whereas the subtlers aim to show that no pleasure is good. For the first pleasure (physical) is bad, for the second just not a good (goal).

(ii) This leads to a consequentially different account of pleasure. For the subtlers pleasure cannot be a bad thing, since it is a process to a good state, from, presumably, one relatively deficient. The thesis is simply that it cannot in itself be a proper final object of pursuit. The naturists, on the other hand, see pleasure negatively as a flight from pain, but not towards a good condition. On the contrary, the flight characteristically brings further opposed disruption, setting up further desires. Pleasure is seen as a result of excessive physical disturbance, and so as a symptom of disorder.

(iii) The naturists argue of a set of pleasures that they are not pleasures at all, strictly speaking: but these would be paradigms of pleasure for the subtlers — in fact, if Aristotle is right, the ones most naturally cited as evidence for the view (and cf. *Phil.* 54e). The fact that they are flights from pain would for the subtlers have no bearing on the question of whether they were pleasures (what makes them pleasures is not what they are flights from, but what they are processes to), whereas for the naturists it is sufficient to show that they are not pleasures.

(iv) This last point also indicates a difference in their conceptions of the neutral state. The neutral state of the naturists is not at all what pleasure aims at, but what pleasure and pain equally disrupt; whereas for the subtlers the neutral state is one where the processes of pleasure are completed. For the naturists, the process of pleasure has no natural terminus, and the neutral state is one of anaesthesia in respect of physical alterations. It is this last that enables the naturists to duck the threat of Heracleiteans holding that the body is in constant flux. They can claim the existence of a neutral state while admitting flux. But the subtlers' neutral state is not so safe. An Heracleitean would presumably say that the processes of coming-to-be can only achieve some passing approximation to a state of completion: there is no achievable completion. It may be sensible to try so to approximate, but it is an illusion to think that there is a life, or even part of a life, where that completion is attained.

(v) There is not one single argument attributed to both sets of theorists.

8.2.7. In view of these points, together with the fact that Plato describes them differently and nowhere suggests that they are the same, we must conclude that they are different views. By Aristotle's time there is reason to suppose that some further view is developed taking points from each of these positions, but the naturists and subtlers are forerunners of that development. They do not already embody it.

8.2.8. We have already seen that the main thrust of the naturists' argument is anti-sybaritic, so putting them in the tradition of the *Gorgias*, the *Phaedo*, and Antisthenes. The subtlers' position is more radically anti-hedonistic as it makes every pleasure a sign of imperfection. This is achieved by grasping firmly a point about the physiologically-inspired account of pleasure that had hitherto been obscured. As remarked earlier (cf. 6.8) the use of the physiological model to argue that all organisms aim at pleasure has to conflate the process of correction of imbalance and the state of balance. It is the latter that is most plausibly presented as what the organism by nature aims at. If one makes the distinction, one has to choose between the two accounts of pleasure implicit in *Rep*. IX (cf. 6.8), and if one retains the equation of pleasure with the process of replenishment the conclusion follows that Plato's argument in the *Republic* for the (superior) pleasantness of the philosophical life must fail. So far from the pleasant life and the philosophically perfect life being identical, the philosophically perfect life as described in the *Republic* would be less pleasant than any other life because it would contain no pleasure at all. The life of greatest pleasure would be achieved by pursuing perfection constantly in the hope of never achieving it.

8.2.9. This position, then, not only contains arguments not found elsewhere in Plato, but shows a grasp of a distinction whose absence brings confusion to the *Republic*. It also bears an interesting relation to Eudoxus. The third argument attributed to Eudoxus by Aristotle (*EN* 1172b20–3) is that that is especially chooseable which we choose not because of something else (*di' heteron*) nor for the sake of something else (*heterou charin*); everyone agrees that pleasure is like this; for no one asks what is the point (*tinos heneka*) of enjoying oneself, as though pleasure is chooseable for its own sake. For what it is worth (not a great deal), two of the expressions for purpose (*charin*, *heneka*) appear in the subtlers' exposition. More important, their position is clearly dramatically opposed to Eudoxus'. Whatever may be true about what questions people ask, every pleasure is in fact for the sake of something else, and an organism only goes in for it as a means to achieving its end term, a condition when the point of the pleasure process is achieved and the pleasure is over. So whether or not it was specifically devised in opposition to Eudoxus, or resulted from ruminations about the

Republic or grew up independently of either, this position in fact underlines a distinction not made in the *Republic* and produces an account of pleasure which entails that Eudoxus' supposed observations must be wrong.

8.2.10. It might be objected to this last point that the subtlers only have a view about pleasure as tending to an end term, and nothing follows from this about the intentions or purposes of those who indulge in pleasure. Eudoxus, on the other hand, holds that pleasure is the goal of every living thing, so in fact the subtlers' view has no bearing on that of Eudoxus. Such an objection, however, supposes a degree of precision on the part of both the subtlers and Eudoxus for which there is no evidence. The exposition in the *Philebus* leaves it indeterminate whether being and good are end-terms which in some way make sense of certain processes, or whether they are what certain living things are out to pursue. Similarly with Eudoxus, it is left quite unclear in Aristotle's report what the observations were on which he based his view. It is plausible to suggest that commonly animals pursue what they have learned to be pleasant and avoid what they have learned to be painful. It is also not implausible to suggest that the general tendency of reactions such as jealousy, anger, devotion to young, and so forth is to secure a continuance of pleasant life. The undertaking of unpleasant and even dangerous activities can thus be brought under the pleasure-umbrella. But of course the thesis has changed from one about self-presented goals to one about the normal outcome of the pursuit of normal goals. Since the only 'general observation' which plausibly supports the Eudoxan thesis is one that makes this sort of conflation, it is quite probable that he was guilty of it, and that the subtlers' position would be thought to be in opposition to Eudoxus'.

3. Eudoxus

8.3.1. At the time of the *Philebus*, then, Plato is encountering two anti-hedonist positions, each backed by a theory of the nature of pleasure. But the opposition in the *Philebus* is a hedonistic thesis, and one which Plato thinks it worth while to attack with a wealth of argument not given to the subject in any previous dialogue. Some extra stimulus had been given to discussions of pleasure. This (cf. DL VIII.86–91; Proclus, *In Primum Euclidis Elementorum Librum Commentarii*, B.39) was probably given by Eudoxus of Cnidus (cf. 7.1.4). According to Aristotle (*EN* 1172b9 ff.), he argued that pleasure is the good on the grounds that

(i) all animals, including men, pursue it, and what all pursue is the good;
(ii) all animals and men avoid pain as evil, and the opposite of pain, pleasure, must therefore be good;
(iii) pleasure is never for the sake of something else: no one ever asks 'why enjoy yourself?';
(iv) if pleasure is added to anything it makes it better.

He is also said (*EN* 1101b27–31) to have argued that pleasure is prized, not praised, just as the good is. The point here is not altogether clear, and Aristotle interprets Eudoxus rather than cites him. It is plausible, however, to suggest that the point is that with other goods we praise them because of the benefits they yield, whereas with pleasure this is not the case. This suggests that this consideration might have supported argument (iii) above. For it seems to suppose that whereas people might cite pleasure as what justifies their praise of *X* and so gives point to pursuing *X*, no one praises pleasure because there is no further reason for pursuing pleasure. This might have been thought to imply, what Aristotle considers lacking in Eudoxus' position, that there is nothing that can be added to pleasure to make it (more) desirable.

8.3.2. At first sight this might seem to be a rehash of the hedonism of the *Protagoras*, but further consideration reveals important differences. To begin with, in the *Protagoras* Socrates is simply addressing himself to human beings, and his procedure is to challenge an honest man to acknowledge any other final end. Eudoxus, on the other hand, relies on the supposed observation that all animals, whether rational or not, pursue pleasure, and this is regarded as supporting the conclusion that pleasure is *the* good (compare *EN* 1172b9–15, 1172b35–1173a5). In other words pleasure is not shown just to be one goal among many, because the goal of one species, but to be the sole claimant to the title of goal with any goal-pursuing being. He also supports this with an argument from general pain-avoidance and the consideration that pain is opposed to pleasure. While arguments (iii) and (iv) doubt-less rely on facts about human beings' judgements they are not found at all in the *Protagoras*. Of course, in so far as 'pleasure' is taken in the *Protagoras* to mean 'maximization of pleasure' it will follow that no one will be able to supply a further end to give point to pursuing pleasure; but it is perfectly possible to ask of any individual pleasure what the good of pursuing it is. The point is not, however, made in Eudoxan terms, by appeal to the fact that no one asks a given question. Similarly it will follow from the *Protagoras* view that an addition of pleasure will make something better; but again, Socrates does not start with that as a premiss, but works to it as a conclusion.

8.3.3. Further, in the *Protagoras* the word 'pleasure' is used sometimes to refer to individual pleasures, but when pleasure is identified with the good the word is obviously equivalent to 'maximization of pleasure'. This is not only obvious to the intelligent reader, but Socrates seems clear that what he has shown to be the good is pleasure maxi-mization. By contrast, it is quite unclear from Aristotle's reports how Eudoxus' thesis is to be construed and con-sequently what his supposed observations were. A plausible observation-claim might be that for any animal on any occasion it is attracted to some object if and only if that object appears pleasant to it, and it is averse from it if and only if it appears painful to it. But this allows for simul-taneous rival attractions or aversions, and leaves any thesis about *the* good very weak indeed. It might, then, be strengthened into a thesis about the animal being most attracted to what appears most pleasant to it, thus importing some notion of comparative pleasantness. To get a reasonably strong thesis about the good, however, we need to move further. For so far we have it simply that the pleasantest-seeming of various rival prospects will attract most on each oc-casion. It may still be that as pleasures differ, animals have different objectives on different occasions. This might be met by requiring that on each occasion that most attracts which seems to be pleasure-maximizing. This secures some unity of objective, even if the cost is some loss of plausibility as an observation claim. Even so, it could still be that each species has its own pleasures, so that 'pleasure is the good' amounts only to 'for each species its good is the maximization of its specific pleasures'. For a stronger position we should require that there is something whose maximization all species pursue. Unfortunately, it is quite unclear how strong a thesis Eudoxus thought he was arguing for. On points on which it is clear where Socrates stands in the *Protagoras*, it is quite unclear where Eudoxus stands. Now this might be just because our information about Eudoxus is briefer, but it also appears that at least Plato and Aristotle found him unclear.

8.3.4. According to Aristotle, Eudoxus' views were very influential, not so much because of the arguments for them as because Eudoxus' own sobriety suggested that he put forward his views not as a pleasure-lover but because that was where the truth lay (*EN* 1172b15–18). This suggests that Eudoxus was not taken as arguing for some special refined notion of pleasure, or as advocating a life of temperance as really the pleasantest. His thesis was so expressed that it could be, and commonly was, taken as in favour of the pleasures from which a temperate person refrains, so that his temperance argued lack of temperamental bias in favour of pleasure. All this would make Eudoxus important in Plato's eyes, since his views were not simply of academic interest but were being used to support sybaritic hedonism. Further the *Philebus* shows signs of Eudoxan arguments. Thus Philebus' position relies on supposed facts about all animals (cf. e.g. 11b4–6, 60a7–11, 67b), which recalls argument (i) of Eudoxus. Then at 20–2 Plato argues that pleasure cannot be *the* good because if you add intelligence to a life of pleasure you improve it. Now Eudoxus argues that if the addition of *A* to *B* makes *B* better then (i) *B* cannot be *the* good and (ii) if this is true of everything to which *A* is added, then *A* *is* the good. Plato uses consideration (i) to show that since intelligence added to a life of pleasure makes it better, then a life of pleasure cannot be the good (and at least on Eudoxus' argument intelligence would be the good); and in arguing that the good has to be complete and adequate in itself in effect rejects consideration (ii), which is clearly invalid. So, first, this section constitutes a neat turning of Eudoxus' argument against his own position. But, secondly, Aristotle's report in *EN* 1172b28-32 suggests that Plato's argument was a riposte to Eudoxus, and made against him the correct point that the good must be complete — a point which is itself perhaps implicit in Eudoxus' own argument (cf. *EN* 1101b27 ff.) that only pleasure is prized. It cannot be said to be certain that Plato's point is in response to Eudoxus, but the report of it comes in Aristotle's account at the end of the description of Eudoxus' argument in a way which suggests that Aristotle viewed it as such. Thirdly, the argument of *Phil.* 20-2 as to what makes life more perfect is conducted in terms of what makes it a more acceptable object of choice. Once again, this is a pertinent consideration in relation to Eudoxus, since if the point is accepted that intelligence makes a life of pleasure better/more desirable, then it is conceded that humans, at least, do not make pleasure their prime good, and so Eudoxus' general observations about living things' attitude to pleasure must be wrong. It also follows, of course, that it is false that everything is referred to pleasure when it comes to praising: everything is referred to the good (mixed) life, which is prized, and pleasure will be up for praise.

8.3.5. When we come to the second argument, that pain is avoided as evil, and so pleasure as its opposite must be good, we get no direct consideration of it in the *Philebus*. We do, however, get some consideration of relations of pleasure and pain which suggests a stance. Thus the account of some physical pleasures and pains begun at 31 and modified at 43 and used in 44-7, sees them as inextricably related, but so related that while in a way they are opposites (i) characteristically pleasure A, which is opposed to pain A' gives rise to pain B' whose opposite pleasure B gives rise to A' and (ii) there is a condition of freedom from such pains and their opposites, which is preferable (cf. 33, 43). This treatment suggests that Plato would feel that if you come down from the generalities and consider kinds of pleasure, the argument:

A is bad, *B* is the opposite of *A*, therefore *B* is good, is a bad argument. The consideration of the subtlers (53 ff.) suggests something similar. If Plato accepts that many pleasures are (in part) processes of restoration, then again he can accept that pleasure is in a way opposed to pain, but that the good is the condition, not the process, of restoration and so pleasure is still not a good. In general, closer consideration of types of pleasure can be seen as an antidote to the attraction of Eudoxus' point. In particular, Plato seems keen to stress that there is a third possibility of neither pleasure nor pain (32e–33b), a midway life between (the opposites of) pleasures and pain (43e). Now if there were no possibilities except pain, pleasure or some mixture, Eudoxus' position would obviously be extremely strong. Within such confines pain is clearly undesirable and pleasure alone without qualification desirable. But if we can find a third possibility, we could allow pleasure to be opposed to pain without inferring that it is good. It seems clear from Aristotle (cf. *EN* 1153b1–7, 1173a5–13; for a discussion see Ch. 12) that this became a standard move against this Eudoxan-style argument. It is of interest that the seeds are in the *Philebus* and that once again it contains just the kind of response which Eudoxus' argument would require.

8.3.6. The position is similar on argument (iii). Plato never turns on Eudoxus with an example of asking why one should enjoy oneself. But then, Eudoxus' point is not pellucid. In order to support his conclusion it has at least to be the point that there is no room for a request to justify or give the point of pursuing pleasure. It is fairly clear that once it is conceded that the good life is mixed and that the soul in its capacity as intellect has pride of place in it, then it must be possible to ask of pleasures whether they are justifiable, and what the point of them is, as is recognized at 32d and done at 61–3.

8.3.7. Part of the problem in getting precise rebuttals of Eudoxus' arguments (ii) and (iii) is that Plato has a more fundamental problem with Eudoxus. For Eudoxus' thesis seems to be couched in utterly general terms, and to acquire much of its allure from that fact. In the *Philebus* Plato shows a new and conscious determination to get away from the generalities and come to grips with cases. He thinks it a mistake to conduct the discussion in terms of pleasure and vital to consider types of pleasure. The importance of this is not far to seek. If Eudoxus' position is to remain interesting and useful, he will have to give some account of what constitutes a life of pleasure — otherwise he is not offering any useable goal in life. In Plato's view the task cannot be done using pleasantness as the criterion, since pleasures differ as chalk from cheese, some being opposed to others. We need a skill to produce a proper combination of pleasures, but pleasure supplies no yardstick for such a skill. The thesis that pleasure is to be put with sound among those things that need proper combination goes hand in hand with the view that, like sounds, pleasures vary and are some of them in disharmony. But once that view is accepted a general thesis about pleasure and its relation to pain is likely to seem unappealing: similarly any general view on asking the point of indulging in pleasure(s). Thus different types of pleasure simply have a different relation to pain: some are flights from it, some are always mingled with it, some have only an accidental relation to any pain, and so on. Similarly, some pleasures are (or are experiences of) processes with a goal, some would only be good to pursue under special conditions, others are part of the good life and have to be there to make it acceptable to humans. So Plato would have no straightforward position of acceptance or rejection of Eudoxus' arguments (ii) and (iii). Rather he could be expected to feel that it depended what pleasures one had in mind. He will not accept a general thesis like that of Eudoxus, but it is plain that in particular cases he would think it must be rejected.

8.3.8. Thus the *Philebus* seems geared to the Eudoxan position (for further arguments see Gosling (5), pp. 139–42, 166–77, 226–8), and granted Eudoxus' association with the Academy and the influence of his views, it is probable that Plato would think it necessary to look to them. On the other hand, it is quite implausible to cast Philebus as Eudoxus. To begin with Eudoxus was a highly intelligent man, whereas

Philebus is portrayed as rather stupid (e.g. 18a1-2, 22c3-4, and esp. 27e). More importantly, Philebus is obviously sybaritic in character (cf. 12b, 27e-28a), so that his especial enemies (44 ff.) are those who are hostile to bodily pleasures. Eudoxus, on the other hand, was, according to Aristotle, well known for his sobriety. The probability is, therefore, that Philebus represents those who used Eudoxan arguments for sybaritic conclusions, and the *Philebus* is thus a reaction to Eudoxus at one remove.

8.3.9. This suggests that the *Philebus* was written in the wake of the disturbance caused by Eudoxus, and makes it likely, but not certain, that the other positions referred to in the *Philebus* were also developed in that context. Of these the naturists are primarily opposed to any sybaritic derivatives of Eudoxus, but would presumably be committed to rejecting any attempt on Eudoxus' part to claim the existence of any other sorts of pleasure. The subtlers could admit pleasures other than flights from pain, but claim that all pleasures suppose some good beyond pleasure, so that pleasure cannot be the good. Both, however, are committed to the rejection of Eudoxan views, and both base their rejection on what is absent from our account of Eudoxus' view: a theory of the nature of pleasure. This is of some interest because, of course, some such general theory would be an obvious basis for countering Eudoxus. If Plato still held the *Republic* theory, he could have come close to Eudoxus, while staving off the sybaritic consequences; or, if he had been able to agree with the naturists or the subtlers, he could have rejected Eudoxus outright in a straightforward way. In fact his position is more complex. He clearly thinks that a Eudoxan ought to give an account of pleasure; that he would need to give some single overall account if he was to supply a criterion for deciding how to live; but that any such project is doomed in a way which makes it clear that some other criterion than pleasure is needed. He seems to think that no theory of the nature of pleasure is available, and that, rather than any theory, forms the basis of his attack. The other theorists are useful in that what they say is true of some subset of pleasures, and so they supply sticks for beating Eudoxus or Philebus, but are not in general adequate.

4. A review of Plato's development

8.4.1. If we now look back on Plato's development, we can see that he starts with no theory of pleasure, but an enlightened hedonist view. Growing Pythagoreanism makes him uncomfortable with that view, though its polemical advantages would not be lightly jettisoned, and he comes to appreciate the need for an account of the nature of pleasure. In the *Republic* he provides a theory which allows him to preserve the polemical attractions of the *Protagoras* together with the *Phaedo*'s hostility to bodily pleasures; and by this time he has started to consider a wider range of examples than was evident in the *Gorgias*, although manhandling them to fit his theory. At some time near to that of the composition of the *Republic* Eudoxus propounded his hedonistic thesis, and very probably the combination of that and the *Republic* gave rise to renewed discussion on pleasure. At least two theories were evolved, one even more hostile to bodily pleasure than Plato in the *Republic*, the other underlining a contrast which would reveal cracks in the *Republic* theory. The first would seem unacceptable to Plato because it takes all pleasures as flights from pain and ignores intellectual pleasures. The second would make him realize that he needed a new account for the pleasures of the good life. Yet each seemed plausible for the pleasures on which it concentrated. In the *Philebus* we get a considerable change. Plato turns to examining all the pleasures he wants to consider and discovers no theory to cover them all. But now a virtue is made of this fact: the hunt for similarities is a mistake, and one should recognize that any given skill will supply criteria for putting sounds, pleasures, or whatever it may be, into a unified category, but the criteria will be other than similarity. This view on the development of skills and forms of knowledge leads him to the view that pleasure may be something harmonized into a good life, but cannot be the principle of harmony which makes the life good. This agrees with the *Republic*; that pleasure is not what makes the life good. But there pleasure was useable as a criterion, and the hunt for the pleasantest life would in fact yield the best. That was achieved, however, via a theory of pleasure. In the *Philebus* the only measure of pleasantness is relative lack of admixture of distress. One cannot use that criterion to distinguish the pleasantness of activities which are unadulteratedly pleasant, so there is no longer any hedonistic way of downgrading bodily pleasures *en bloc*. One could still go in for the empirical enquiry as to whether there was only one possible life which was more densely packed with pure pleasures than any other, but no enthusiasm is shown for it. The idea that a pleasure expert would find the best life to be the pleasantest seems to have been dropped.

5. The *Philebus* and Aristippus

8.5.1. In the main body of the chapter we have expounded the case for supposing Eudoxus to be the main target of the *Philebus*. Clearly the evidence is no more than circumstantial, though in our view it makes for a persuasive account both of some of the moves in the *Philebus* and of Aristotle's strategy in *EN* X. It is only fair to note that a case could also be made out for Aristippus being the target. First, the appeal to what animals value is common to the Cyrenaics as well as Eudoxus. Secondly, they are said explicitly to have denied that pleasures differ from each other, which makes Plato's insistence to the contrary apposite (for both points cf. DL II.86-7). Thirdly, Aristippus, as portrayed by Xenophon. was clearly a sybaritic hedonist, so that one could easily suppose that Philebus is a stand-in for Aristippus, or was just a typical Cyrenaic (which might give some point to the name 'Philebus' (Love-boy) if, as commonly supposed, it is an invented name). Fourthly, (cf. 2.3.3), Cyrenaic reasons for rejecting pleasures of memory and anticipation just might explain Plato's insistence that false pleasures are none the less genuine for being false (cf. *Phil.* 37).

8.5.2. The main difficulty is our lack of evidence for the Cyrenaics at this period (cf. 2.3.2). Also, as we have seen (cf. 7.1.2-3), there is no sign of Plato taking any Aristippan view seriously up to this date. Similarly, Aristotle shows no sign that Cyrenaics were making any impact, whereas he is quite clear that Eudoxus was. The *Philebus* would have to be the evidence for the importance of Aristippus, leaving us with the oddity of a large splash with no ripples. Eudoxus, on the other hand, is better evidenced, fits slightly better into the *Philebus* argument, and far better into the picture of Aristotle's development. On the point about false pleasures, of course, the Cyrenaic objection was based on the non-presence of past and future. Even if they inferred to the unreality of the resultant pleasure, it remains that they do not have a special doubt about false pleasures, but a general one about anticipatory ones. Finally, the argument of the *Philebus* is not against someone who holds that each individual pleasure is the goal, but against someone who holds that man's goal is a *life* of pleasure (cf. 11d, 20-3, 43). The Cyrenaics, on the other hand, are reported as holding that the individual pleasure is the goal, not the good life, even if it is conceived of as a collection of pleasures. This would fit their concentration on present pleasure and discounting of memory of past or anticipation of future ones (cf. DL II. 87-90). If these philosophers are his opponents, Plato shows no sign of appreciating the importance of what apparently was one of their main points.

Chapter 9

Laws

9.0.1. The *Laws* presents two problems for present purposes. First, it is open to dispute just what the temporal relations are between the composition of the *Philebus* (or various parts of it) and that of various parts of the *Laws*. Even the fact that Plato was polishing the *Laws* when he died is no guarantee that some of the sections on pleasure were not next in line for revision to make them consistent with the *Philebus*. Secondly, the *Laws* is a large-scale political, jurisprudential document, not given to the sort of detailed philosophical analysis found in the *Philebus*. It is therefore difficult to judge from remarks made there whether they should be taken as complete and precise statements, or as simply sufficient for the purposes in hand though doubtless requiring more careful statement under philosophical pressure. Consequently if one finds views in the *Laws* that do not seem straightforwardly in accord with those of the *Philebus*, they may represent Plato's final view, they may represent an earlier one due to be brought in line with the *Philebus*, or they may just be forgiveably imprecise statements.

9.0.2. The two main sections to be discussed are 653–70 and 732–4, and here we find the following apparent differences from the *Philebus*: first, (660–3), we seem to be told that the good life is pleasantest (and cf. 733–4), and (663c) that a good man is a better judge of pleasure than a bad one, but also (667) that it is not pleasure that makes pleasant things good; further (733b–d) we are said all to want pleasure and the pleasantest life, and any other view shows ignorance. Now all these points sound very like the *Republic*. So either Plato has gone back on the *Philebus* and thinks he can, after all, give criteria for maximum pleasure which show the identity of the pleasantest life with the good life, or we have a pre-*Philebus* section of the *Laws*, or these remarks can be interpreted to conform with the *Philebus*.

9.0.3. The last project is certainly not hopeless. After all, the *Philebus* claimed to show only that if you set out on the open sea of describable lives armed just with a criterion of pleasantness, you would only be able to exclude some; there would remain a large number of equi-pleasant options. But if we start with a pre-determined selection of describable lives it might be quite easy to decide that the good life was pleasanter than the rest, and so that the pleasantest of these lives and the good life were identical. Now a limitation to the practicalities does seem to be part of the *Laws* discussion (cf. 733d3–5), and the competition is not between all describable lives, but the small subset that constitute the actual options in which Plato considers that people are in fact interested. Further, the *Philebus* admits that we all want a pleasant life and this is interpreted (61) as committing one to saying only that we all want a truly pleasant life, i.e. one as pleasant as possible. All the *Philebus* does is claim that there are other features that make a life desirable to us, and this is not rejected in the *Laws*.

9.0.4. Even the use of the appeal to the good man as judge can be accommodated. At first it might seem to have no place in the *Philebus*. After all, we are all supposed to be able to follow the arguments there. They are not beyond the capacity of a Callicles or Thrasymachus. There is no need to be a good man or a philosopher to see that unmixed pleasures are less adulterated than mixed ones and so 'truer' and pleasanter. But of course what in the context of the *Philebus* might be doubted is whether the good man had any pleasures at all, and if so, whether his pleasures are unmixed. No appeal is now possible to a general theory of pleasure as what accords to natural needs. We have to rely on the good man. He is needed to judge not whether pure pleasures are pleasanter than mixed ones, but whether his life is one of pleasure at all, and if so, whether of pure ones. Also, he judges the correct mixture of pleasures in the good life.

9.0.5. There remains, however, a doubt that arises from the second difference from the *Philebus*. At 657c the Athenian Stranger gets agreement that we rejoice (and enjoy ourselves) when we think we are doing well, and when we rejoice (enjoy ourselves) we think we are doing well. In other words, the occasions when we enjoy ourselves are just and only the occasions when we think we are doing well. This remark is introduced to help us establish a criterion for distinguishing between correct and incorrect uses of music and entertainment. The criterion (658e ff.) is going to be the good man. The point is that various art forms delight us and we become assimilated to what delights us. It now emerges that coming to delight, say, in warfare is coming to think that when engaged in war we are doing well, and coming to think that is coming to delight in warfare. It follows that there will be good pleasures as well as bad, and that the good ones will simply be those of a good man. A good man will think he is doing well just and only when he is. All other men are, in their pleasures, involved in a greater or less degree of delusion. The coincidence of pleasure with thinking one is doing well is the crucial point in establishing that there is a rightness and wrongness of pleasures. Only those who are thinking that they are doing well when they are are commendable, and so the good man is the criterion.

9.0.6. This gives rise to a doubt on the point in 9.0.4 because the result is that while the good man is the criterion, the reason why he is, and the way in which he is, is not that suggested as fitting well with the *Philebus*. The *Philebus* does not, either, carry any suggestion that a person enjoying himself thinks he is doing well and conversely, though there is nothing, either, to entail rejection of this. Indeed, it would make good sense of the declaration (40c) that the wicked for the most part experience false pleasures. It would only be really awkward for the *Philebus* if it was proposed as an account of the nature of pleasure. If it were, then Plato would have, in the *Laws*, an analysis of pleasure which he lacked in the *Philebus*, one different from that of the *Republic*, enabling him to develop thoughts about the connection of pleasure with perception and with belief that are started in the *Philebus*. The trouble is that it is very difficult to assess the status of the remark in the *Laws*. It is not presented as an answer to the question 'What is pleasure?' but as a general

truth about people who enjoy themselves. Even if it reflects
new thoughts on Plato's part, we have no detailed elaboration
of them. At worst, then, we simply have an observation
unrelated to any view on the nature of pleasure, at best
evidence of a new view on the nature of pleasure but one that
was not, for anything we know, worked out in any detail.

9.0.7. Either way, however, the remarks in the *Laws*
might have played a suggestive role, and it is interesting to see
what sort of view of pleasure they might suggest. Clearly, any
account in these terms would be very different from those of
the *Gorgias* or *Republic*. An equation of pleasure with the
conviction of doing well at once introduces the possibility of
error with every type of pleasure. Granted that the aim is to
do well, it supplies a criterion for selecting among pleasures,
in that it seems natural to prefer correct beliefs about when
one is doing well. It does not, however, yield any way of
distinguishing between pleasures in terms of pleasantness.
Not even mixed pleasures can be downgraded in the straightforward way made possible by the *Philebus* view. A person
who enjoys relieving an itch just as much believes (rightly or
wrongly) that he is doing well as someone who enjoys
philosophizing. Pleasures can only be false in the way in
which the *Philebus* claims that anticipatory pleasures can be,
in virtue of falsity a judgement. Yet (663c–d) the good man
is supposed also to be a judge of the relative pleasantness of
the lives. With a suitable view of human nature and what constitutes doing well, it would be easy to develop a view to
explain how the life of the good man was more densely
packed with pleasure and less interrupted by distress. The
Philebus view on physical pleasures, that they are perceptions
of restorations, might be developed so that all pleasures were
perceptions or operations of one's nature, or rather, judgements on perceptions. Now some perceptions are mixed, and
the related judgements in conflict. A person relieving an itch
must be judging both that he is doing well, and that he is
doing badly. This might be explained by reference to the
condition of natural turmoil, where some things are going
wrong, others right. In a state where all is going well there is
no perception of things going ill to distract one's judgement

or to make the simple judgement that one is doing well inaccurate. But in the case where one judges one is doing well but is also in distress one may deludedly think one is doing as well as is possible even while admitting that in some respects one is doing badly. In that case one's life will always contain distress, whereas those in good condition will always be correctly judging that they are doing well, and so their lives will be pleasanter. In this way, just because a good life is one where one's nature operates perfectly, a good life will be fullest of pleasure.

9.0.8. The point is not that Plato has this all worked out, but simply that the remarks in the *Laws* would be the natural starting-point for such a way of thinking, and while it is not identical with that of *Nichomachean Ethics* X it is not too difficult to see how it might be refined and developed into that sort of view. So while one cannot use the *Laws* for attributing any precise form of development to Plato, the remarks on pleasure there suggest a possible starting-point for reflections of which one culmination could be Aristotle's view in Book X of the *Nichomachean Ethics.*

9.0.9. There is one final intriguing fact to be mentioned. The connection between pleasure and belief that one is doing well does not in fact originate with the *Laws*. An ancestor is found in Socrates' mouth in Xenophon's *Memorabilia* IV. viii. 6-8. Socrates there says that he thinks that those live best who best care to become as good as possible, and those live most pleasantly who perceive their improvement, while to be aware of worsening must make life less pleasant. Once again, this is not put forward as a theory of pleasure, but as a general truth. It is, however, an interesting view. The tradition on pain which seems most to have influenced Plato related it to something going wrong with the organism, and the related view of pleasure sees it as generally at least an improvement. The usual picture of replenishment is of a move towards a good condition. This could easily have developed into a view of pleasure as the perception of improvement or of doing well. Such a development would not have sat well, however, with Plato's suspicion of bodily pleasures, which goes more readily with a view which ties pleasure to desire. If pleasure is what answers to desire, bodily desires will direct one to bodily interests, and one can view that as no good thing. One would certainly not have to view pleasure as a *perception* of something going well. On the other hand Plato could have been happy with a view that pleasure was, or involved, a belief that things were going well. That leaves wide open the possibility of error, and with a slight modification of tense could accommodate the pleasures of recollection, day-dreaming, and anticipation allowed for in the *Philebus*. In fact, however, he seems to have been unsettled, in the central dialogues, between a view of pleasure as replenishing natural lacks — which suggest it is good — and as answering desires — which allows some to be bad. Nor does the idea of incorporating any notion of thought or perception come to the fore until after the *Republic*. While the context of the introduction of perception in the *Philebus* is the position of the naturists, who do not consider pleasure good, it is quite likely first that Plato did not accept their position as a general account even of bodily pleasure, and secondly that he would himself add the perception condition to the view about replenishments in 31-2. In that case one would expect him to hold that those pleasures are perceptions of something good so far as it goes. It is implausible, however, to take a perception account for all pleasures, and it is quite a step from perception to belief.

Chapter 10

The Nature of Pleasure

10.0.1. So far we have taken it that Plato tends, as it is sometimes put, to think of pleasures as activities indulged in,
rather than effects of activities, and it might be worth
spending a little time trying to clarify this. To begin with,
there is a question of preferred idiom. In a modern context it
is sometimes felt to be important whether a philosopher
tends to put his points in terms of a person's pleasures, or in
terms of the pleasure got. The point is that if we are asked to
list someone's pleasures we should naturally mention such
things as golf, listening to music, cooking, making people
unhappy — and these are all activities or experiences of the
subject. Someone who starts from this idiom will very likely
tend to think that what entitles all these activities to be
called pleasures is some fact about their place in the subject's
life, or the way in which they are approached. By contrast,
someone who uses idioms of pleasure being taken in, or
derived from or accompanying certain experiences will tend
to think of pleasure as an effect caused by various activities.
The contrast is not in fact, of course, a singular/plural one,
since a person of the second sort may well think that each
activity causes a specific sort of pleasure. The important
contrast is between thinking of pleasure as somehow identical
with the activity, or as being an effect caused by the activity.
The second most naturally suggests (to the modern ear) some
feeling accessible only to the subject, whereas the former
suggests (but no more) a way to construe pleasure as open to
public observation.

1. Plato's idioms

10.1.1. How a person thinks of pleasure may be influenced
or hinted at by the idioms they favour, but it is shown in
their theoretical comments and arguments; and here it will
make a difference whether their concern is with conceptual

analysis or with some other form of theory. We shall therefore first consider briefly Plato's linguistic habits and then at
greater length his theoretical statements. Greek contains, and
Plato uses, a variety of idioms describing pleasure as resulting
from the activity enjoyed, or from some source. Thus habits
are spoken of as 'having pleasures' (*Rep.* 538d); pleasures
'accompany' virtue or 'follow' vice (*Phil.* 63e), or 'come
from' sources (*Phil.* 12d; *Rep.* 581d) or 'come through'
media (the body: *Ph.* 65a); certain processes 'make' or 'give
rise to' pleasures (*Phil.* 43c). These idioms Plato uses freely.
Also on occasion 'pleasure' is used as though it were almost
a synonym of 'desire' (*Rep.* 431c-d, 558d, 574a). This is
doubtless helped by the tendency to use the word to refer to
prospective pleasures, or inducements, as in the passages cited
in 10.8.2. Then again, at *Gorg.* 499e we are told we must
perform good pleasures, and at 496e drinking is said to *be* a
replenishment of a need and (thereby) a pleasure (cf. *Rep.*
439d7-8, 585d11). 'The pleasant' (*to hēdu*) and 'pleasure'
(*hēdonē*) are often used interchangeably (cf. *Gorg.* 495a;
Hp.Ma. 299d1-5), suggesting a blurring of enjoyment and
what is enjoyed. In certain passages (*Phil.* 31d-e, and 32a-b,
the *Gorgias* and *Republic* passages cited above) some
'activity' is said baldly to be a pleasure. Finally, Plato uses
the verbs '*chairein*', and '*hēdesthai*' without objects to refer
to episodes of enjoyment (e.g. *Gorg.* 498a-b, 497c).

10.1.2. In short, Plato uses a wide range of idioms,
(though none of them equivalent to the English one of talking
of a person's pleasures). Sometimes the verbal form 'suggests'
that pleasure is distinct from what is enjoyed; sometimes an
identification is made; often, even when he speaks of *causing*
pleasure the form of words suggests neither identification nor
distinction clearly. Thus when in the *Protagoras* we are told
that health is good because it leads to pleasure (354b), it is
quite open whether these are enjoyed activities or the
pleasures to which such activities give rise. None of these
idioms seems to determine his way of thinking of pleasure.

2. Plato's theoretical comments: *Protagoras*

10.2.1. It is more to the point, then, to see what Plato's

theoretical remarks commit him to. In the *Protagoras*, as has been pointed out, we do not, surprisingly, get a theory of pleasure at all. It might, however, be felt, as suggested but not firmly adopted by Irwin (Irwin (1), p. 111) that the traditional empiricist view of pleasure as an introspectible feeling would be an obviously appropriate one to fit the ambition of measurement put forward in the *Protagoras*. Of course, Socrates might have been content to treat all pleasures as equally pleasant and restrict the measurement of relative pleasantness of lives to the measurement of periods during which pleasure occurred. But in fact (356b, 357a–b), the doubling of a word for greater size with one for greater number suggests that pleasures are to be compared not only for their fruitfulness in giving rise to other pleasures, but also for their intrinsic pleasantness. In that case Socrates will need to have a homogeneous view of pleasure, sufficiently so at least to make comparison possible. It might, then, be tempting to treat it as a sensation like warmth, but quite inappropriate to treat it as though it were like experience of colour.

10.2.2. It would be a mistake, however, to think that this was the only option. If one thought of pleasure in terms of filling natural lacks, then activities could be compared not only in respect of the degree to which they led to a life of natural fulfilment, but also in respect of the degree to which they succeeded in filling the lack they purported to fill. The truth, of course, is that we have no idea how Socrates proposed to do his measuring. It would, after all, seem obviously possible to compare the pleasantness of activities and courses of action, prior to having any theory of pleasure. It is nevertheless worth noting that other views of the nature of pleasure would seem to have just as much, if also, in the end, just as little, change of yielding a method of measurement as the familiar sensation model. As Plato never shows any inclination to the latter, but does show attraction to the fulfilment model, there can be no presumption that at the time of the *Protagoras* he would take pleasure to be a sensation.

3. Plato's theoretical comments: *Gorgias*

10.3.1. When we come to the *Gorgias*, there are the first

signs of a theory of pleasure. As we have already said, this is not an analysis of the concept of pleasure, but an attempt to give a quasi-physiological account of what constitutes pleasure. It is unclear whether this is intended as a general theory of pleasure or simply as an account of bodily ones. For present purposes it is unimportant. It seems that at least Plato is offering an account of pleasure that suffices for the cases that Callicles is interested in. In this context, arguing that pleasure and pain occur together, Socrates says (496e1-2) 'But drinking is a fulfilment and a pleasure.' The view sketched does not seem to take pleasure as something caused by fulfilment, but as consisting in fulfilment.

4. Plato's theoretical comments: *Republic*

10.4.1. In the *Republic*, as argued in Chapter 6, we have a generalized replenishment view of pleasure. The argument of 585a-e for the greater reality of intellectual pleasure depends directly on equating pleasure with fulfilment. If Plato were thinking of pleasure as caused by fulfilments nothing would follow as to the pleasures not being 'real' from the fact that the fulfilments were not; whereas if pleasures just are fulfilments, 'unreal' fulfilments are 'unreal' pleasures.

5. *Timaeus* and *Philebus*: pleasure and sensation

10.5.1. This same equation is made in the *Philebus* in the first account of physical pleasures in 31-2. There Socrates says (31e) 'Hunger, being a dissolution, is a pain? . . . while eating, being the return of fulfilment, is a pleasure?' – and the equations are repeated in the following paragraphs. This account of bodily pleasures as replenishments is modified in 43a-c. It is pointed out that living things do not perceive all processes, such as growth; most such things escape our notice. So we should not have said simply that the changes to and from produce pleasure, but only the large changes. Since the introduction of perception might suggest that Plato is moving to a sensation or feeling view of pleasure, it will be worth examining this passage in some detail.

10.5.2. The main point is fairly clear: if replenishment either constitutes or is a sufficient condition for pleasure, then we should enjoy all replenishments and, in the context, on the supposition of constant physical process, life would be a constant succession of pleasures and pains. In fact, however, many go unperceived. The clear implication is that in these cases there is no pleasure, so that perception is a necessary condition of pleasure. This leaves it still unclear whether Plato considers pleasure to be a form of perception or whether he thinks that pleasures are a subset of physical replenishments, those perceived by the subject, rather as taxis form a subset of motor-cars, those that carry passengers for a fare. In the latter case Plato would still be thinking of pleasures as the physical replenishments, but in the former he might be thinking of them as observed feelings aroused by the processes.

10.5.3. One certainly might expect Plato's point to be that pleasure is not a bodily change, but a function of the soul, but that might simply be twentieth-century prejudice. The *Phaedo* allots many pleasures to the body, but then the *Phaedo*'s body has many mental attributes such as desire and perception. The concept of body employed there is not one of matter in contrast with consciousness. In the *Republic* the *Phaedo*'s bodily desires form the lowest part of the soul, and often the word for pleasure is used pretty well as a synonym for 'desire' (cf. 10.1.1). Then in *Tht.* 156b pleasure comes in a list of perceptions. So while Plato may not previously have realized the importance of insisting that pleasures are *'psuchic'* rather than bodily affections, his language suggests that he took it for granted that they were (cf. also *Rep.* 462c10–d5, 583e9–10, 584c4–6).

10.5.4. If we return to the *Philebus* passage, we find certain verbal echoes with an earlier passage discussing perception. To translate so as to capture the echoes, 43b1–5 runs as follows:

Socrates: . . . but now you tell me whether a living thing which undergoes something always perceives everything it undergoes, and we are never oblivious of our growth or undergoing any of these things, or whether quite the contrary is the case.
Protarchus: Absolutely the contrary; we are oblivious of almost all such things.

Compare this with 33d:

> Soc.: Take the things the body undergoes on various occasions. Let's suppose that sometimes they are extinguished in the body before reaching the soul, so leaving it not undergoing anything, while sometimes they penetrate both and as it were set up a quake in each and both together.
> Prot.: I give you that assumption.
> Soc.: And we shall be right to say that the soul is oblivious of those that do not penetrate both, but not oblivious of those that do.

Socrates then explains that 'oblivious' must not be confused with 'forgetful', and suggests a change of terminology:

> Soc.: Instead of calling the soul oblivious when it undergoes nothing from the quakes of the body, I want you to substitute 'lack of perception' for 'oblivion'.
> Prot.: I see.
> Soc.: When soul and body, jointly undergoing one effect are jointly moved, it would surely be right to call this movement perception?

10.5.5. In both cases we have the situation envisaged of bodily processes of which the soul/subject is unaware, in contrast with others. In the earlier, more elaborate, passage, it is clear that the situation of joint arousal is perception: if sound waves penetrate to the soul so that soul and body are both moved, then we have a case of hearing. Presumably, if the body were unmoved we should have a delusion, if the soul, no experience at all. The second passage is far briefer, but seems to be deliberately recalling the earlier one first by noting the lack of perception of many processes, secondly by using the language of undergoing, and thirdly by using the language of oblivion. This, together with the general similarity of the situations, suggests that Plato is thinking of pleasure (bodily pleasure, that is) as a case of perception.

10.5.6. This is borne out by the treatment of bodily pleasure in the *Timaeus*, 64–5. Earlier, at 61c–d, Plato has made it clear that in discussing such things as heat one has to discuss both the soul and perceptive powers and the constitution of bodies, but that he is first going to concentrate on the physical aspects. At 64a, he says that the major part of the common undergoings relating to the whole body is the cause of pleasant and painful things 'and all those things which, having obtained perceptions through the bodily parts have pains and at the same time pleasures following in themselves. Let us consider the explanations of every perceptible or imperceptible undergoing as follows:' – we then get a general discussion of perceptions so far as physical causes are concerned, with the *Philebus* allowance that some of the processes will remain unperceived/imperceptible. (For the terminology of perceptible replenishment in the *Philebus* see 51b). As to pleasure (64c7), this is caused by mass return of bodily parts to their natural states. 'All those things which have acquired minor withdrawals and depletions, but massed and extensive replenishments, becoming imperceptive of the depletion but perceptive of the replenishment, provide no pains for the mortal part of the soul, but the greatest pleasures' (65a1–6).

10.5.7. It seems clear from this that Plato is here thinking of bodily pleasures experienced by the soul under certain physical conditions, and thinking of it as a form of perception. The whole reads so like an elaborate version, appropriate to the context of the *Timaeus*, of the account of perception in the *Philebus*, as to make it virtually certain that the positions in the two dialogues are the same.

10.5.8. This still leaves the question as to how like perception Plato thought pleasure was. It does need here to be emphasized that the *Timaeus* account is explicitly limited to bodily pleasures experienced by the mortal part of the soul. In the *Philebus* too, the amendment is made to an earlier account of the bodily pleasures which are at 32b–c clearly marked off from others (and cf. 47d). There is no warrant for taking such passages as support for the view that Plato thought pleasure in general to be a feeling which the feeler perceived. There is, however, a problem as to just what it is of which bodily pleasure is a perception. In so far as the *Philebus* points out that many changes are not perceived, presumably to suggest that only when they are perceived is there pleasure, it looks as though bodily pleasures are the perceptions of replenishments. This is suggested even more strongly by the *Timaeus* passage where it seems that it is in becoming perceptive of replenishment that one gives pleasure to the mortal part of the soul. But one needs to be wary of that 'of'. If one thinks of hearing being the perception of sound, the 'of' seems to introduce a conceptually necessary object; if the perception were not of some sound it could not count as hearing. Further, one would expect someone possessed of the vocabulary of hearing and sound to know that what they heard were sounds. One would hardly expect one possessed of the vocabulary of pleasure to know that what they perceived was replenishment. On the other hand, one might think that in fact every bodily pleasure was the product of some bodily replenishment, rather as hearing is the product of the impact of sound waves, and so be prepared to say that the pleasure is a perception of the replenishment. In Plato's day there had not been reams of discussion on formal and other objects of perception and their relation to causal conditions for perception. Plato's own language is ambivalent. He will talk of the physical motions getting through to the soul, but also (e.g. *Tim.* 64b5-6) of the effect being an announcement to the intellect of the power of the agent. He may have thought that the natural nisus to pleasure and aversion from pain signalized a dim apprehension of the worth of fulfilment and the harm of depletion, and that the message thus dimly understood was recognized in its full import by one with the correct account of these pleasures. The latter could correctly be said to perceive the replenishment.

10.5.9. It seems, then, that either Plato has not thought through the question of what bodily pleasure is a perception of, or he assumed that it is of replenishment. What there is no ground for is the view that what he considers the object of the perception to be is a feeling of pleasure. Rather each bodily pleasure is a perception of/caused by some replenishment, and is experienced by a part of the soul, although as with other such *psuchic* operations, there has to be a related account of the physical processes. It is, after all, the mortal part of the soul that is involved, the soul in so far as it is embroiled in bodily life.

10.5.10. Because of a problem that arises later in discussing Aristotle (cf. 12.5), it will be as well to modify some of the final remarks, in so far as they suggest that Plato clearly thought that the soul did the perceiving. It seems clear that if one asked Plato, 'Are you saying that the body perceives or enjoys?', the answer would be 'No'. Various physical changes may have a causal role, but the body is not the subject. On the other hand, it is not so clear that if one asked 'Are you saying that it is the soul that perceives or enjoys?', the answer would be 'Yes'. Earlier, at *Rep.* 583e he has declared pleasure and distress both to be forms of motion in the soul; but when in the *Philebus* he gives his account of perception it is the joint motions of soul and body which are said to be perception, and so with bodily pleasure one would expect a similar dual condition. He is, of course, here and in the *Timaeus* not concerned with the question of the subject, but rather with an account of the nature of perception. As we have pointed out, for bodily pleasures, as for perceptions, both physical and *psuchic* disturbances are necessary, though the causal language might suggest that Plato at least partially considers the bodily movements, in giving rise to the *psuchic*, to be therefore producing pleasure. The fact remains that an account of bodily pleasure requires reference to bodily movements and these pleasures are not purely '*psuchic*'. One's feeling that it is really the soul that is the subject of pleasure might be reinforced by *Tht.* 184c–e, where Socrates asks whether we perceive *with* or *through* our sense-organs, and declares that it would be odd if all the senses did not converge on one sort of thing, the *psuchē* or whatever one should call it, something with which we perceived things perceived by the senses using the sense-organs as tools. Here the perceiving seems clearly thought of as a function of the *psuchē*, even if it has to do it by means of particular bodily parts to count as perception. It remains a question whether one can transfer this to the *Philebus* and *Timaeus*, and also whether a Greek reader could be expected to.

6. Identification of pleasure and 'activity'

10.6.1. We should now be in a position to see in what sense, if any, Plato identifies pleasure and activity, and whether he has a natural interpretation for the causal sounding idioms of giving and deriving pleasure. But first we need to ask just what counts as identifying pleasure and activity. For there are at least two possibilities. First, a person may be impressed by the thesis that if I am said to enjoy a game of golf there are not two occurrences attributed, the game and the pleasure, but just one, the game. The relation of game to pleasure is not a cause-effect relation between two events. Rather 'enjoy' indicates the mental set of the subject towards the object, the manner of approach to the activity enjoyed. So there is nothing to the pleasure but the playing, though it will, of course, be particular features of *this* playing that makes this playing a pleasure. In general, the expression for the object of the verb 'to enjoy' will give what the pleasure is, though the mere fact that the object satisfies that description (e.g. 'golf') is not of itself enough to show that it is a pleasure.

10.6.2. Plato certainly holds nothing so linguistically based. He might admit, say, that if it is true that A is enjoying ϕ-ing, then A is ϕ-ing with attention and vigour, but still feel that he has not yet been told what pleasure is. He wants a general account of the conditions such that just and only when they obtain do people do the things they are doing with vigour. This last may be a correct account of what we are saying of A when we say A enjoys ϕ-ing, but it does not give an account of the nature of pleasure that will enable us to understand its role and importance in life. By contrast, 'pleasure is the replenishment of a natural lack' hardly tells us what a native English (or Greek) speaker purports to be saying of A in saying that A enjoys ϕ-ing. It would, however, amount to a claim that in fact any case of enjoyment is a case of filling a natural lack, as an examination of our nature and a review of the examples of enjoyment would reveal. It is this latter kind of thesis which Plato is putting forward in the *Gorgias* (possibly), *Republic* and, in a limited area, in the *Philebus*. It is also characteristic of the other theses of which we hear at the time such as the naturists' view that so-called pleasures are flights from pain, or the subtlers' that pleasure is a process of coming-to-be. What doubtless starts as a physiological account of the nature of pleasure gets generalized; but always we are given an account in terms of the subject's natural processes, not of those truth-conditions for a description which are used by a native speaker. Indeed, a similar point holds of requests for 'definition' in the early dialogues. Plato is not interested in what is meant by 'courage' or 'justice', but in the constitution of the soul in which it consists (cf. Irwin (1), Ch. III).

10.6.3. This being so, one would not expect Plato to identify the pleasure with the object of enjoyment, in any straightforward way. It is in fact noteworthy that although he does, e.g. in the *Gorgias* and *Philebus*, call eating and drinking a pleasure, it is always, as it should be, in a context where it is made clear that it is when they answer a lack that they are so. While there is no other activity apart from eating and drinking going on, that this is a case of eating is not enough to make it a pleasure. For that we need to be hungry. So if we are thinking of a pleasure as something taking place at some time, then it is one and the same occurrence as the eating or whatever; but more has to be true of it than simply that it is eating to constitute it as a pleasure.

10.6.4. It is because of this that Plato could quite naturally interpret the idioms of producing and giving pleasure. You do not produce pleasure just by giving someone food: if they are replete there is no lack to replenish. Pleasure (= (perception of) replenishment of lack) only comes from (is given by) eating if there is a lack so that the eating can bring about the replenishment of lack and, in the *Philebus*, if vigorous enough, perception of that replenishment (= pleasure). In this sense Plato might think of pleasure as an effect of activities enjoyed. However, first, it is a quite different picture from the traditional empiricist one, and secondly — a fact which illustrates this — he cannot, at the different periods, speak of replenishment of a lack or of perception of such replenishment, as causing or giving rise to pleasure. These *are* pleasures. So if we are thinking of 'replenishment of lack' (*Republic*) 'perception of replenishment of a lack', 'picturing a future pleasure' (*Philebus*) as typical descriptions of activities, then Plato will indeed identify these activities with pleasures, without demur.

7. Plato's interest in concepts

10.7.1. Yet while it is true that Plato is not overtly interested in analysing the concept of pleasure, there are arguments which look openly or implicitly to be about the meanings of ordinary expressions. Thus in the *Protagoras* (355b ff.) Socrates argues that showing that pleasure is the good is showing that 'pleasure' and 'good' are two names for the same thing. Consequently, in the exposition of the view that a person can do what he does not consider good because overcome by pleasure, either can be substituted for the other to produce absurdity. But saying they are two names for the same thing, it might be argued, is Socrates' way of declaring the terms synonymous. So it looks as though Plato is trying, however badly, to show something about the meanings of 'good' and 'pleasant'. This point seems to recur in the *Philebus*. At 60a–b Socrates describes the difference between himself and Philebus as that between holding that 'good' and 'pleasant' are two names for the same thing or nature, and holding that corresponding to the different names are two different things with different natures. This suggests that the argument at 55b is supposed to point up the absurdity of the suggested synonymy claim. For if 'pleasant' and 'good' mean the same, and pleasure is a psychological phenomenon (X is pleasant iff some being enjoys X), then it will follow that no state, say, of crops is good, but only the appreciation of that state, and that a brave man dying in agony is not good, and so on. These arguments suggest that Plato at least supposes that he and his opponents are in dispute about the meanings of terms. It may be that the arguments are shaky. The opposition is not allowed, for instance, to distinguish between 'good' as applied to ends and 'good' as applied to means and to equate 'pleasure' with the former only. The fact remains that it looks as though Plato is arguing that certain familiar expressions are or are not synonymous.

10.7.2. It is, however, rash to suppose that this is what Plato is doing, at least if this means attributing to him this view of what he is doing. After all, the *Protagoras* argument does not require the thesis that 'good' means 'pleasure maximizing'. It may be that 'good' should always be read as 'a good to X', and this be equivalent to 'an object of desire to X'. It is now a matter of discovery for each value of X what is an object of desire to it, and it may or may not turn out that pleasure is. The claim is that with humans we do on examination discover that pleasure is the only object of their desire. Anyone who realizes this will recognize the absurdity of saying of any humans that they did what they thought bad because they thought it would be pleasant. But the absurdity emerges not from realizing that 'good' means 'pleasant' but from recognizing that the only thing humans can take as a goal is pleasure. (Cf. Taylor (3), pp. 168–79 for a discussion.)

10.7.3. The same is true of the *Philebus* argument. If anyone says that pleasure is the only thing of value, then they must hold that crops, intelligence, and so on have no value in themselves, and that pain, even if experienced in the course of brave action, is always a *prima facie* sign of failure in life, just considered in itself. All this follows without benefit of a view that 'good' and 'pleasure' are synonymous, and while an opponent could account for calling these other things good the air of paradox remains in face of 'common sense', for it seems obvious that a crop's health (good condition) is not to be assessed by reference to human pleasure, that a good mind is assessed by non-pleasure criteria and that the nobility of courage is exhibited precisely in the bearing of pain. It may be, of course that Plato simply failed to distinguish between ' "A" and "B" are two names for the same thing' interpreted as meaning (i) 'A' and 'B' are synonyms and (ii) the extensions of 'A' (e.g. 'what an agent X thinks maximizes his pleasure') and of 'B' (e.g. 'what an agent X takes as his goal') coincide. But then if he does not make the distinction he cannot be portrayed as wanting to make precisely a point whose grasp requires a grasp of the distinction.

10.7.4. The arguments that look to be explicitly 'conceptual', then, seem at best to be not explicitly not. There are, however, other passages where one is tempted to say that what makes what Plato says seem true is a fact about language, although the point is not presented in those terms. This can be illustrated in a case from the *Republic*. In that work, as was noted in Chapter 6 (see 6.8.1–2), Plato tends to run together a view that pleasure comes in the process of replenishment and one that pleasure comes with the accomplishment of replenishment, i.e. when what one wanted is acquired. This latter version was needed to produce the conclusion that a successful philosopher's life is pleasant at all once he has acquired the truth. The conflation of the views is helped by the fact that both the process and the end term can be described as the replenishment of the desire or need. But this would not be so tempting if it did not seem obvious that those who have what they want must be pleased. Now in one sense it is truistic that if a person has what he wants that desire is replenished (or, in English, satisfied), for this need only mean that the objective that he set himself has been achieved. It does not follow, of course, that he must be pleased. But with regard to the last there is a common tendency to make pleasure on accomplishment a test of whether what is accomplished is what was really wanted. No doubt this move involves equivocation on 'wanting', but it remains that if, say, a person longs to be married and sees herself as the perfect embodiment of the role of wife and mother and then, when she experiences it, finds it constricting and a source of discontent, one common move is to say that it is not what she really wanted, after all. It may be held that she does not know what she wants, but a claim, say, that she really wants a more independent life frequently amounts just to the view that if she joined a women's group and took a job she would become pleased with life, and this latter would show that this different life is what she 'really wants'. The fact of a use of 'want' such that being pleased with what one has is a test of whether it is what one wanted (wants) makes it easy to think that a life where one has what one wants must be pleasant. It is very likely some such fact as this that makes it seem obvious to Plato that if he can show that a philosophic life is one where what the subject wants is achieved, then he will have shown that it is pleasant.

10.7.5. It is doubtless difficult to say whether one should consider the supposed fact a 'linguistic' fact, or a well-entrenched view about human beings that does not seem in need of evidence. If the latter, then the view tends to be so well entrenched that the required verbal manoeuvres have an air of obviousness that seems to make the points acceptable quite independently of consciously proposed theories, and the recurrence of familiar terminology serves to disguise the various shifts. In this way it seems likely that Plato's confidence in his position is reinforced by an implicit acceptance of the non-ambiguity of terms for 'want' and 'replenishment', and of the obviousness of a connection between meeting desires and pleasures that is so much a part of one way of thinking of what is wanted as to count almost as a fact of language.

8. 'Pleasure'-idioms and pleasure

10.8.1. If we grant that Plato's aim is to supply a general characterization of the natural conditions for the occurrence of pleasure, or to deny that such a characterization can be given, it becomes a good question what the correlate of these conditions is. So far this has been referred to as pleasure, and the assumption has been that we all know how to identify the members of the class of pleasures that have to be seen to conform to the conditions stated in the theory. Now, on the whole, where Plato is either telling us what pleasure is, or arguing that it takes different forms and so supplying objections to some accounts of what it is, no great problem arises. The pleasures in question are all examples of someone enjoying something. Thus there is enjoying quenching one's thirst, scratching one's itches, watching plays, looking at pictures, acquiring knowledge. Sometimes, however, this is not so obvious. If we take pleasures of anticipation (see Appendix A) it is not at all obvious that these are examples of enjoying something rather than just looking forward to enjoying something, though Plato (cf. *Phil.* 40a9–12) seems determined to construe them as enjoyments of picturing or pre-enjoyments.

10.8.2. This leads to two oddities. First of all, even if we confine ourselves to enjoyments, it is fairly obvious that the replenishment style of theory found in the *Gorgias* and the *Republic* has no chance, as it stands, of explaining the power of pleasure where this means its allure in advance. On this point we find Plato changing his stance. While in the *Republic* he boldly states that pleasures of anticipation are, like most bodily pleasures, escapes from pain, by the *Philebus* he has seen that replenishment alone will not explain the power of pleasure in anticipation. We need at least a supplementary account of memory of previous replenishments and belief in a future one. The second oddity is that Plato will not leave it there but seems to feel that since in some way pleasure is, in the anticipatory sense, now exercising its power, there must be some current enjoying which is the pleasure. Since the power of pleasure in education (cf. *Laws* 653a–b), or as the greatest incitement to evil (*Tim.* 69d) or, perhaps too, as what rivets the soul to the body (*Ph.* 83d) consists in its allure from the future, all such influence is to be explained in terms of some present enjoyment, a present gloating over the anticipated pleasure.

10.8.3. This might plausibly seem to rivet our attention and desire on the prospect, so that the attractive power of future pleasure is accommodated as the present power of an enjoyable anticipating. Yet while such episodes doubtless occur it is implausible to suppose that they exhaust the possibilities of anticipation. For one thing, a person may hope and work for certain pleasant experiences while jadedly unmoved at the time by pictures of the future. He may even be pleased to think that he is going to achieve his aim, and anticipate his holiday with pleasure, but this takes the form not of advance picturings but simply of a sense of relief that the daily round will not go on for ever and of a consequent greater cheerfulness. It looks as though Plato feels that if it is true of *A* that *A* is pleased, is getting pleasure, takes pleasure in something, then it must be true that there is something that *A* is enjoying doing or experiencing. This is not to suggest that he consciously tries to assimilate *prima facie* distinct expressions, but that he treats them all indiscriminately as examples of pleasure, and takes it that any pleasure is a case of enjoying something.

10.8.4. The same point emerges if we consider how it is

decided that spite or malice (*phthonos*) is both a form of distress and of pleasure, and similarly with love, anger, fear, and the rest. It is taken as just obvious that they are all forms of distress (*Phil.* 47e; see Xenophon *Mem.* III.ix.8 for the same assumption about *phthonos*), that a malicious person is pleased at the misfortunes of those around him (49–50), and that the person who laughs at his neighbour's misfortunes is clearly rejoicing at them. Consequently, it is clear that the malicious person is both pleased and distressed, and as this is the difficult case we can now take the same to be true of the angry or frightened person. What is of interest is to see just what might seem to make these points obvious. Certainly we are inclined to describe an angry or frightened person as distressed about something, and a person who rejoices or laughs at someone's misfortunes as pleased about them; also, on any given occasion a person who is angry or frightened may be feeling distressed and the malicious person enjoying hearing of or seeing someone else's calamities: but a person acting under the influence of malice is not thereby either feeling distressed or enjoying anything. They may, indeed, be pleased to think that they are causing someone else distress, say, by refusing them promotion, but nothing follows about enjoyment episodes. Plato's example obscures this because we are faced with a spectator chortling in a theatre. But someone who maliciously refused to recommend a subordinate for promotion would doubtless be described as taking pleasure in keeping him down, and being pleased to think that his opponent will never make any headway; consequently his malice will be 'a form of pleasure' — but he may be too eaten up with spite to enjoy anything any more. The considerations that lead one readily to classify this and other cases as both pleasure and distress are thus not just ones to do with enjoyment but with the possibility of using other pleasure expressions of them, which are not equivalent. Yet the applicability of these expressions is treated as sufficient to win membership of the class of pleasures.

10.8.5. In short, it seems that the phenomena which a theory of pleasure would, for Plato, have to explain, are all those phenomena which could correctly be described as examples of enjoyment, or being pleased, or taking pleasure, or . . . , the dots to be filled in with other appropriate pleasure expressions. There is no interest shown in whether or not these expressions are equivalent, or what the relationships between them are, though examples tend to get treated in a way that assimilates them all to cases of enjoyment.

10.8.6. The features discussed here were not peculiar to Plato. Part of the difficulty in interpreting Eudoxus is uncertainty about the range of 'pleasure', and neither side of the disputes about hedonism shows any interest in the possible ambiguities of the word, or the differences between expressions formed from it.

Chapter 11

Aristotle: The Contrast of Treatments

11.0.1. If we turn to the question of developments immediately after Plato, our main source is Aristotle, and if we are to use Aristotle as a source of information about the way discussion developed we have to reach some conclusions on the relationships between the treatments of pleasure in Books VII and X of the *Nicomachean Ethics*. What we shall be concerned with is what might be called their philosophical relationship.

11.0.2. Kenny's statistical researches (Kenny (4)) have, in our view, conclusively demonstrated that the so-called 'common books' (*EN* V–VII = *EE* IV–VI, termed by Kenny 'the Aristotelian Ethics') are stylistically much closer to the *Eudemian* than to the *Nicomachean Ethics*, and thereby established with considerable plausibility the hypothesis that those books, including the discussion of pleasure in *EN* VII, were originally composed as part of the *Eudemian Ethics*; nevertheless neither Kenny nor, to our knowledge, anyone else has suggested that stylometric study can contribute substantially to the question of the relative dating either of the ethical treatises as a whole or, more specifically, of the two treatments of pleasure. Given the absence from either discussion of any reference to the other, and the paucity of other indications of relative date (such as references to other Aristotelian works[1] or to datable historical events), one is left with arguments from likely philosophical development.

11.0.3. The principles here are hardly conclusive. A philosopher may grow worse with age, may become confused about points on which he earlier seemed clear, or mistakenly

---

[1] The reference to *Phys*. III.1–3 and V–VIII at 1174b2–3 shows merely that *EN* X is later than those portions of the *Physics*, which yields no conclusion as to the relative dating of the two treatments of pleasure.

think that he has seen a way round them, or simply fail to bear them in mind and apply them to the case in hand. So signs of greater sophistication in one work over another are not conclusive for the later date of the more sophisticated. Nor is the fact that more sophisticated opposition is dealt with in one work rather than another conclusive proof that one is later than the other. The opposition might have deteriorated rather than improved, or the philosopher might have come across the cruder views later but still think that they needed refuting. Still, there is a defeasible presumption that greater sophistication goes with a later date, and this will be assumed in what follows. As the main issues concern Books VII and X of the *Nicomachean Ethics* the main concentration will be on these. The *Magna Moralia* is considered in Appendix B. As a preliminary we give brief consideration to the evidence for Aristotle's early views on the topic.

1. The early Aristotle

11.1.1. With the exception of the *Rhetoric* (on which see below) no work other than the ethical treatises contains any but the most incidental reference to pleasure; yet the few brief allusions to it in the early works suggest at least an outline of the development of Aristotle's views. The nearest we come to any general account of the nature of pleasure is the statement in *Phy.* VII (generally agreed to be early) that pleasures and distresses are alterations in or of the faculty or organ of perception (*hai . . . hēdonai kai hai lupai alloiōseis tou aisthētikou*, 247a19). While the context indicates that this is intended as an account specifically of bodily pleasures (including, in a manner reminiscent rather of the *Republic* than the *Philebus*, pleasure in the anticipation and the recollection of such pleasures, a7–9), this statement is nonetheless interesting on two counts in particular. Firstly, in view of the prominence in *EN* X of arguments against any view of pleasure as a process of change (= *kinēsis*: for these arguments see 12.4–6, Ch. 16 *passim*) it is interesting that in what is perhaps his earliest account of pleasure Aristotle describes it as a certain kind of process of change, viz. alteration, i.e. change in quality. Secondly, the view of pleasure expressed in this passage is similar to, and presumably not independent of the account of certain bodily pleasures given in *Phil.* 42-3 and *Tim.* 64-5 (see 10.5), in which pleasure occurs when physiological processes (chiefly of restoration of bodily deficiences) give rise to *psuchic* 'motions', an account which is readily interpretable as the view that pleasure of that kind is the perception of those physiological processes. That such physiological processes played a similar role in Aristotle's early view is suggested, not merely by the antecedent probability that that view was derived from Platonic doctrine, but also by a reference to pleasure in another early work, *Posterior Analytics* 87b5 ff. Though the propositions about pleasure are cited there purely in the context of an example of a certain form of argument, Aristotle does say that they are true; hence we are justified in citing them as evidence of his own view. The propositions are 'The man who feels pleasure undergoes change' (or 'The man who is feeling pleasure is undergoing change') and 'Everyone who feels pleasure comes to be at rest' (or 'Everyone who is feeling pleasure is coming to be at rest'). It is natural (though plainly not necessary) to read these propositions as expressing the two main theses of the 'restoration' view of pleasure, viz. that pleasure arises from the process of restoring the disturbed balance of the organism, and that that process results in a state of equilibrium or rest.

11.1.2. It appears likely then, that at an early stage Aristotle accepted a view of pleasure as a perceived process of restoration of the natural state of the organism, and that that view derived from Platonic doctrine.[2] *Topics* 121a 27-39 (probably earlier than both *Posterior Analytics* and *Physics*) does indeed discuss an argument against that view, viz. that pleasure cannot be a process of change because it is not

---

[2] Though it is quite plausible that the *Philebus* and *Timaeus* are Aristotle's immediate source, we do not wish to exclude the possibility that the causal influence goes in the reverse direction. The emphasis in those dialogues of the necessity for the restorative process to be perceived represents a development from the view espoused in the *Gorgias* and *Republic*, and it is not out of the question that that development is itself a response to the early view of Aristotle. The plausibility of that hypothesis depends in part on one's view of the dating of the *Timaeus* relative to other Platonic works, on which scholarly opinion is still divided (see Guthrie, V, p. 243 n. 2).

(a form of) locomotion or qualitative change or any other kind of change, but without committing Aristotle himself one way or the other. His thesis is that someone who maintains that pleasure is a process of change must consider whether it is not locomotion etc., for it that were so, i.e. if pleasure isn't any *kind* of change, then it could not fall under the generic term 'change'. Plainly the passage carries no suggestion that he himself thought that pleasure was not a sort of change. Hence it does not require any modification to the picture of Aristotle's early view which we have derived from the passages in the *Physics* and the *Posterior Analytics*.

11.1.3. The 'Platonic' view is also adopted as a general definition of pleasure in *Rhet.* 1369b33–1370a1; 'let it be laid down that pleasure is a certain process of change in the soul, viz. a sudden and perceptible attainment of the natural state which belongs to it, and distress the opposite'. This formula contains clear verbal echoes of Platonic tests — the expression 'attainment of the natural state which belongs to it' (*katastasin . . . eis tēn huparchousan phusin*) recalls *Phil.* 42d 'when they (i.e. animate things) attain their own nature, we have accepted on the strength of our previous discussion (i.e. 31d–32b) that the attainment is pleasure', while the same section of the *Philebus* (43b–c) introduces the qualification that the process of 'attainment' must be perceived, a qualification which is maintained in Aristotle's description. The other condition specified, that the process should be 'sudden' (*athroan*) refers back to *Tim.* 64d 'the sudden return to the natural state is pleasant, whereas a gradual gentle return is imperceptible'. The force of the qualification lies in the contrast with 'gradual' (*kata smikron*, lit. 'in small stages'): in order to constitute a pleasure the process of restoration must be perceptible, and in order for that to be the case it must be concentrated within a short time in contrast with a process such as growth which is so gradual as to be imperceptible. In view of our other evidence of Aristotle's early adherence to the 'Platonic' view, this evidence of close Platonic influence would be quite unproblematic if it were clear that the *Rhetoric* was another early work. But in fact the situation is rather more complex, since

Rhet. II.23 contains reference to events which occurred in 338 and 336 BC, thus dating at least some portions of the work relatively late, while I.8 contains a reference (1366a23) to the *Politics*, which appears in the order of the Aristotelian corpus as the sequel to the *Nicomachean Ethics*. If Aristotle is taken as himself committed to the account of pleasure assumed in the *Rhetoric* the commentator has the choice of either attempting to justify an early dating for that work, or alternatively of formulating some hypothesis to explain Aristotle's readoption of the 'Platonic' view after his rejection of it in one or both versions of the *Ethics*. The former project is not hopeless. Düring has argued ((2), pp. 118-21) on independent grounds that the bulk of the *Rhetoric*, including the treatment of pleasure, dates from the period 367-347, when Aristotle was still a member of the Academy; his main grounds are the affinity of the work in thought, language, and content with the *Topics*, coupled with the frequent references to the *Topics* and *Prior Analytics*. Both references to events in the 330s come from II.23, which Düring argues on grounds of content to be a late addition. The postulation of a late revision can, of course, account for such other indications of later date as reference in II.8 to an event which took place in 341 BC and the reference to the *Politics* mentioned above, but it has the disadvantage of tending to make the hypothesis of early composition unfalsifiable. Further, it leaves unanswered the crucial question: why, if Aristotle was committed to the truth of his account of pleasure in the *Rhetoric*, did he not include a revision of that account in the light of the *Ethics* when he revised the *Rhetoric*?

11.1.4. The obvious answer is that his purpose in the *Rhetoric* did not commit him to the truth of his accounts of such concepts as pleasure, but in that case the question of the date of the work becomes irrelevant. In fact it is clear from the text that Aristotle regards the work as requiring only that degree of understanding of human motivation which is presupposed by its purpose, the provision of a systematic scheme of instruction on techniques of persuasion. Thus the orator who seeks to persuade the people to adopt some policy must have a grasp of generally accepted principles of evaluation, and hence of the concepts which compose them; for instance he must have an understanding of what constitutes *eudaimonia*, or what excellence of character is, sufficient to enable him to recommend courses of action by appeal to those acknowledged goals. But it is clear from the text that precise definitions of *eudaimonia* and of *aretē*, such as are attempted in the *Ethics*, are not required; neither concept is defined in the scientific manner by genus and differentia, but both in terms of a disjunction of popular views which are accepted without discussion. (For *eudaimonia* see 1360b14–18, for *aretē* see 1366a36–8. The latter definition, '*Aretē* is, according to the usual view, a faculty of providing and preserving good things, or a faculty of conferring many great benefits and benefits of all kinds on all occasions', is an elaboration of the traditional account proposed by Meno in Plato's dialogue of that name, 77b. It is hard to believe that Aristotle could ever have believed that to be a theoretically adequate account of human excellence, as distinct from an account adequate for persuasive purposes.) It is clear that the account of pleasure is to be taken in the same way, as a commonly accepted view sufficiently close to the truth to meet the orator's needs. It is significant that it is introduced by the caveat 'Our various definitions may be regarded as adequate, even if they are not exact, provided they are clear' (1369b31–2).[3]

11.1.5. We conclude, then, that while Düring's hypothesis has a considerable degree of independent plausibility, it is unnecessary for our enquiry to take up any position on the relative dating of the *Rhetoric* and the two *Ethics*, since the account of pleasure accepted in the former represents, not Aristotle's own view, but a current view accepted as adequate for the particular purpose of that work. While it is in fact quite likely that Aristotle accepted it at the time of writing the *Rhetoric*, the aim of the work did not require his acceptance, and consequently a change in his view of pleasure did

---

[3] For a fuller discussion of the treatment of pleasure in the *Rhetoric* see Lieberg, pp. 23–42.

not have to be incorporated in any revision of the work. Aristotle's mature view, which we now proceed to examine, can thus be seen against the background of early adherence to the 'Platonic' view, without the complication of a reversion to the latter at a stage subsequent to the composition of one or both *Ethics*.[4]

2. Books VII and X: general comparison

11.2.1. That there are differences between Books VII and X in their treatments of pleasure emerges clearly from an inspection of the following outlines.

Book VII. 1152b1-1154b34 (6½ pages of Oxford Classical Text).

1152b1-7   (1) *Introduction*
The philosopher must discuss pleasure, because he constructs the end. Also moral virtue is concerned with pleasure and distress, and most people attach pleasure to the good life.

b8-12   (2) *Various positions*
(i) No pleasure is good, in itself or incidentally.
(ii) Some pleasures are good, but most are bad.
(iii) Even if all pleasures are good, the good cannot be (a) pleasure.

---

[4] Evidence of what is presumably a transitional stage in the development of Aristotle's thought about pleasure is provided by a passage from the *Protrepticus* (fr. 14; Ross, pp. 50-1) which dates from the late 350s (Düring (1), pp. 284-6). In this passage Aristotle both argues for the supreme pleasantness of the theoretical life on the ground that 'actuality (*energeia*) which is complete and unhindered has enjoyment in itself, so that intellectual actuality is the pleasantest of all' and describes that actuality as 'filled with what is most real and always permanently containing its allotted completeness'. The first quotation recalls *EN* 1153a12-15, b7-17, the second is a clear echo of *Rep.* 585d11-586b4. This suggests that while Aristotle had already come to his view of pleasure as unimpeded actualization he had not yet clearly distinguished it from the Platonic view of pleasure as the making good of natural deficiences, or at least that he regarded the distinction of the two, which was to be a central theme in the *Ethics*, irrelevant to a popular work such as the *Protrepticus*.

b12–24	(3) *Arguments for those positions*
b12–15	(i) (*a*) Pleasure is a perceived *genesis*, and no *genesis* is an end (good).
b15	(*b*) The temperate flee pleasure.
b15–16	(*c*) The wise pursue absence of pain, not pleasure.
b16–18	(*d*) Pleasure hinders thought.
b18–19	(*e*) There is no skill of pleasure; but every good is the product of a skill.
b19–20	(*f*) Children and animals pursue pleasure.
b20–2	(ii) Some pleasures are base, harmful, diseased.
b22–4	(iii) Pleasure is a *genesis*, not an end.
b25– 1153a35	(4) *Aristotle's counter-arguments.*
b25–1153a7	Against (i) and possibly (ii). Many pleasures, bad on the whole, are good on occasion. Other 'bad' pleasures are not pleasures at all.
a7–17	Against (i) (*a*) and (iii). Not all pleasures are associated with *genesis*, some are actualizations and complete/perfect. In fact, pleasure is un-impeded actualization.
a17–20	Against (ii)
a20–3	Against (i) (*d*)
a23–7	(i) (*e*)
a27–35	(i) (*b–c*), (*f*).
b1– 1154a7	(5) *Positive view*
	Pleasure is the opposite of pain (evil) and so good. Speusippus' argument about opposites does not work. So the good might be (a) pleasure — and indeed must be since the good is unimpeded actualization (= pleasure). That all beings pursue it is evidence.
	People are misled because 'pleasure' has become attached to bodily pleasures.
a8–b34	(6) *The goodness of bodily pleasures*
	Why some mistakenly think that no bodily

pleasures are good. The explanation makes it clear why no one experiences pleasure without interruption.

Book X. 1172a16–1176a29 (11 pages of Oxford Classical Text).

1172a16–27	(1) *Introduction* Pleasure is important because of its role in education. Also, moral virtue consists in loving and hating what we should. Pleasure has a lifelong influence through its attraction. Also, there is much dispute on it.
a28–b8	(2) *Various positions* (i) Pleasure is the good. (ii) Pleasure is base.
b9–25	(3) *Arguments for* (i) The position of Eudoxus.
b26–1174a12	(4) *Arguments against* (i)
b26–35	(*a*) Intelligence added to pleasure makes it better (Plato).
b35–1173a5	(*b*) It is false that what all desire is the good.
a5–13	(*c*) Pain has two opposites, pleasure and the good.
a13–15	(*d*) Pleasure is not a quality.
a15–28	(*e*) Pleasure is indeterminate, the good determinate (Plato).
a29–b20	(*f*) Pleasure is a movement/*genesis*.
b20–31	(*g*) Some pleasures are shameful.
b31–1174a12	(*h*) Friends differ from flatterers in aiming at good, not pleasure; and some things we should want even without pleasure.
a13– 1175a3	(5) *Positive view* Pleasure is like perception: complete at any time. It is perfection added to actualization.

a3-

11.2.2. The difference in the introductions does not seem
significant for our purposes. The two differences which strike
one immediately are first, that the problems are set up differently (compare VII (2) and X (2) above), and secondly
that the accounts of pleasure are different (compare VII (4)
and (5) with X (5)) (the references here are to our outlines
of the books). In Book VII the question is whether any
pleasure is the good. In Book X whether pleasure is the good.
In Book VII pleasure is said to be unimpeded actualization,
in X perfection added to actualization.

11.2.3. The first difference might suggest a difference of
context, and this impression is reinforced when one considers
further differences. Of the anti-hedonist arguments considered
in Book VII that at (3) (ii) is answered in Book X along with
(i) (*a*). For the rest (i) (*b*), (*c*), (*e*), and (*f*), have no counterpart in Book X. (Strictly, nor does (i) (*d*), though it is in effect
met in Book X, cf. X (6), (iv) and (v).) Of arguments in Book
X, the consideration of Eudoxus has no counterpart in Book
VII, and of the arguments against holding that pleasure is the
good, X (4) (*a*), (*b*), (*d*), (*e*), and (*h*) have no counterpart in
Book VII. To this point we shall return. The apparent over-
laps are as follows:

1.   Both books have arguments against the view that pleasure is a *genesis*.
2.   Both consider the argument that pain may have two opposites.
3.   Both consider an objection from shameful pleasures.
4.   Both consider why humans cannot experience pleasure without interruption.
5.   Both hold that pleasure improves performance of what it is pleasure in.

Points 3 and 4 are not central in either book, but it is interesting that they produce different reactions in each. Point 1 is important in both books, and it has often been pointed out that whereas Book VII has a brief dismissal, Book X contains an additional battery of arguments peculiar to itself.

11.2.4. Then each book has a tail of its own. In Book VII there is (for Book VII) a long discussion of why people think that bodily pleasure is bad; in Book X there is a long discussion of how pleasures differ in kind in that, (*a*) pleasures of different actualizations differ and, (*b*) the pleasures of different kinds of animal differ. The first uses, the second leads up to, each book's different way of discriminating against some pleasures: Book VII does it mainly (but not entirely) by the contrast between what is pleasant by nature and what incidentally, Book X in terms of what is pleasant to so-and-so, and what is pleasant.

11.2.5. Finally, the discussion of pleasure in Book X is almost twice as long as that in Book VII, and the arguments on shared concerns are correspondingly longer.

11.2.6. It has commonly been felt that Book X is later than Book VII, partly because it is a more detailed treatment, partly because it contains interesting arguments that are not found in Book VII, and partly because it is thought that the analysis of pleasure given in Book X is a philosophical advance on that in Book VII. Of course, this set of considerations only supports a later date on the assumption that Aristotle was the author of both books. Those who sympathize with Spengel's arguments that Book VII was not written by Aristotle but by some follower can accommodate these views to a position that nevertheless dates Book VII later. First, however, one has to see what the differences amount to, and the procedure will be to consider first arguments for the greater sophistication of Book X, starting with those presenting the most dramatic contrast.

3. Books VII and X: the contrast: Owen's view

11.3.1. Most commentators who consider that there is a change take it to be a refinement rather than a radical shift (e.g. Ackrill (2), p. 33; Festugière; Gauthier and Jolif). Recently, however, Owen has argued for a far more exciting contrast marking an important difference of philosophical approach and so, on the assumption of identical authorship, signalling a significant change in philosophical direction. Briefly (for a longer criticism see Gosling (4)) the thesis is that in Book VII Aristotle is pursuing the hopeless quest of finding some feature which all members of the class of pleasures have in common, whereas in Book X he is asking the modern question 'What is it to say of someone that he is enjoying something?' Thus in Book VII we are told that pleasures are unimpeded 'activities' (*energeiai*) in accordance with natural capacities or dispositions. This looks like an attempt to characterize those performances that we enjoy and identify each pleasure with some performance that satisfies the conditions of being unimpeded and natural. By contrast, in Book X Aristotle rejects this identification (1175b30–5) as absurd, and his view that pleasure perfects 'activities' reflects this rejection. To say of a subject that he enjoys ϕ-ing is to attribute to him perfection in ϕ-ing, and the view on the nature of pleasure is not one about what the activities enjoyed have in common, but one about what it is to enjoy, viz. to perform completely, with full attention and vigour.

11.3.2. This would not, of course, emerge simply from the passages cited. Two further facts are significant about Book X. First, Aristotle shows an interest in arguments about how the verb 'enjoy' works which is quite absent from Book VII. Thus at 1173a15–23, in considering a Platonist argument that pleasure is indeterminate, he remarks that it is important to know whether they base their argument on premises about enjoying or ones about kinds of pleasure — which suggests that he is aware that some arguments, while apparently about phenomena, are better construed as about the concepts used to interpret the phenomena. This impression is strengthened in the passage that follows (1173a29–b20). Here we get the argument that while one can come to enjoy something quickly or slowly, one cannot enjoy it quickly or slowly, which is obviously a point about what it is or is not absurd to say. This is followed by the point that the proper subject of 'enjoy' is a person, not his body, (1173b7–13), whereas if pleasure was a replenishment of a bodily lack, since it is the body that is replenished it should be the body that does the enjoying. Again, the arguments in 1174a13–b14 seem to be trying to point out that ways of speaking that are appropriate to various forms of motion are quite inappropriate when applied to enjoying. All this indicates a new awareness on Aristotle's part that arguments on the nature of pleasure are commonly at least in part covert analyses of the concept of pleasure and so can and should be met by making the correct conceptual points.

11.3.3. All this new interest in the verb (and even occurrences of the noun can often be seen to be uses referring not to the class of things enjoyed but to what it is to enjoy them) is further indicated by the increased frequency of occurrence of the verb relative to the noun. Thus in Book VII the proportion of occurrences of the verb to those of the noun is 17:100, whereas in Book X it is 27:100, an increase of some fifty-eight per cent. Also the number of different verbs in Book X is far greater.

11.3.4. This version of the contrast between the two books leads, as one might expect, to a quite different view from the usual on the significance of the change in critical arguments. These are not now seen as new weapons for the old battles, but as new weapons for new battles. The old arguments are simply inappropriate for the new conceptual interests. We do not, in Book X, get a refinement on the answer to Book VII's question. We get a new question with its own answer. So the opposition is interpreted as answering the new question; and it is hardly surprising that the arguments, whether critical or constructive, that are needed for the new enterprise, are different from those that seemed appropriate to the old.

11.3.5. This position seems to be based on the following assumptions:

(i) that in 1175b30-5 Aristotle is rejecting the Book VII identification of pleasure and 'activity', specifically denying that to enjoy ϕ-ing is to ϕ under certain conditions;
(ii) that in 1174b14-1175a3 this refusal to identify has been made good, and that Aristotle is there claiming that no amount of information about the conditions of an 'activity' or its perfection as an 'activity' entails or is entailed by facts about the subject's enjoyment. Aristotle declares pleasure to be an added perfection, and this is his way of saying that to say that A enjoys ϕ-ing is not to say that A ϕs perfectly but to say something else about his ϕ-ing, to attribute to him a complete or perfect *doing* of it on top of standardly perfect performance;
(iii) that certain arguments show the appropriate interest in how the verb works;
(iv) that the statistics about verbs are significant;
(v) that the (main) opposition in the two books is the same, so that there is some puzzle about the replay of treatment unless we suppose that Aristotle is treating them in quite different guises.

Clearly points (i)-(iii) bear the main burden here, with (iv) and (v) playing a supporting role. As consideration of (iv) and (v) brings up some interesting points they will be taken up in due course (see 11.3.34-8, 12.) First, however, (i), (ii), and (iii) must be examined.

11.3.6. *(i) 1175b30-5: is Aristotle rejecting the Book VII identification of pleasure and 'activity'?* To take (i) first, the remark at 1175b30-5 runs as follows: 'the pleasures in them are more closely related to the "activities" than are the desires; for these latter are distinct both temporally and in respect of their nature, whereas pleasures are closely bound up with their "activities" and so inseparable that there is dispute as to whether (the) "activity" is identical with (the) pleasure. Yet (the) pleasure does not seem to be thought, nor perception (that would be absurd), but because they are not separated some people think they are identical'. The question is: what exactly is being rejected? Owen seems to want to say that the position of Book VII is rejected, and that this rejection marks the change of course in Book X. According to Owen Book VII uses the word '*hēdonē*' as equivalent to 'pleasure' in 'golf is one of his pleasures'. It says that golf is an 'activity' performed without impediment in accordance with a natural disposition. But Book X, according to Owen, uses 'pleasure' as equivalent to 'enjoyment', and while golf might *be* one of Jones' pleasures it is only one of the *things* he enjoys. His enjoyment is what he gets from or takes in golf. But in that case, in the Book VII use, it is not a mistake to 'identify pleasure and "activity" ' in the sense of saying that every pleasure is some 'activity' satisfying certain conditions. Nor can the Book X remark constitute a rejection of that position if '*hēdonē*' is used in different sense in Book X. Book VII will be saying that a man's pleasures are those 'activities' that he manifests without impediment in accord with a natural capacity, while Book X will be saying that a man's enjoyment is not an activity he enjoys. These are quite compatible positions, and the most that could be said of Book X would be that it is using '*hēdonē*' in a different way, and this remark is underlining the fact that when one uses it this way one cannot identify *hēdonē* with an activity under whatever conditions it is performed.

11.3.7. It should be noted, however, that the Book X remark might simply be saying that it is absurd to say that a pleasure simply is an 'activity' just because the two seem inseparable. For this would imply that any thinking or perceiving is a pleasure, which is absurd. But this would not be a rejection of Book VII either, for Book VII does not say that a pleasure simply is an 'activity', but that it is one that is in accordance with one's nature and is unimpeded. So on the

Book VII account the absurd consequence would not follow. It might be objected to this that no one, surely, would be tempted to identify pleasure and activity in this sense, so that it cannot be such a position that Aristotle is rejecting. To this it has to be pointed out that we only have to suppose that Aristotle took some people as disputing the question because it was apparently impossible to separate pleasure and activity. In other words, some philosophers found it difficult to isolate anything as constituting the pleasure apart from the fact that the subject is exercising a faculty. Now we do not have to suppose that they did more than raise the problem, and that Aristotle is simply pointing to the absurdity of one choice. But even if we suppose them in fact to have taken that option it has to be recognized that in the face of problems philosophers are all too capable of saying things which strike both other philosophers and non-philosophers as patently absurd. Certainly Aristotle is envisaging a view which strikes him as simply absurd.

11.3.8. Now the remark might, of course, be intended as a rejection of Book VII. Aristotle might, in other words, think of himself as using '*hēdonē*' in the same way and be declaring that it is a mistake to suppose that a pleasure is an 'activity' satisfying certain conditions. The trouble is that the remark which is supposed to show this mistake to be absurd signally fails since it omits all mention of the conditions which on the face of it save the position from absurdity.

11.3.9. It seems, then, that 1175b30–5, might signal a change in the use of '*hēdonē*', but might equally be just the rejection of an absurd view. In neither case would it be strictly a rejection of the position of Book VII, though on the first interpretation it might be a sign of a different enterprise from that undertaken in Book VII. So everything is going to hang on points (ii) and (iii). If it is clear from elsewhere that Aristotle is wanting to contrast questions about the activity enjoyed with questions about what it is to enjoy, then it will be tempting to take 1175b30–5 in Owen's way. Otherwise it will be at least indeterminate.

11.3.10. *(ii) 1174b14–1175a3: Aristotle's account of pleasure*. In this passage Aristotle spells out his account of pleasure. For Owen's view he has to be construed as saying that while if an 'activity' is perfectly performed it is (at least normally) enjoyed (and conversely), still, to perform perfectly and to enjoy are not the same. Enjoyment is an added perfection which always accompanies perfect performance, but is theoretically distinct. Thus, typically, when we say that some soprano sang perfectly, that she enjoyed singing is not among the criteria used; nor, if one says she enjoyed singing, is the fact that she sang perfectly one of the criteria used to establish that. It is a matter of (dubious) observation that enjoyment and perfection of 'activity' by the normal criteria go hand in hand, but in theory they could fall apart. Yet enjoyment is a sort of perfection for to enjoy ϕ-ing is to ϕ to the full so far as one can, with one's mind on it and heart in it. So if our soprano is enjoying her fine singing, not only is the singing fine, but, so to speak, her agency is at its peak; she is fully immersed in her doing. And so enjoyment is an added perfection. But to say that she sings perfectly is not to say or say what entails that she enjoys it, and to say that she enjoys it is not to say or say what entails that she sings perfectly. In short, Aristotle is introducing a notion of 'doing', such that to enjoy is to do things to the full (bring a *telos* to the doing), but not, in the ordinary sense, to do them perfectly.

11.3.11. The position relies heavily, as do many interpretations of this passage, on supposing that Aristotle treats the perfection of 'activity' as only a condition for pleasure, to which pleasure comes as a further, added, perfection of some sort. Yet it is impossible to find any such point in the passage. As it is important to see this, it will be worth going through 1174b14–1175a3 in some detail.

11.3.12. At the start, in a cumbersome sentence, Aristotle says: 'With every *aisthēsis* actualized in relation to a perceptible [*aisthēton*] and perfectly actualized when it [the *aisthēsis*] is in good condition and related to the finest of the objects that fall under the *aisthēsis* (for this especially is what the perfect actualization seems to be; it does not matter whether one says that it [the *aisthēsis*] is actualized, or the subject to which it belongs) then with respect to each [*aisthēsis*] the best actualization is that of the best conditioned subject in relation to the best of the objects that fall under it [the *aisthēsis*].' The word left untranslated, '*aisthēsis*', can be used to refer either to perceiving or to a faculty of perception. Clearly in this passage it is not used in the first way, for any perceiving is an actualization (*energeia*, 'activity') whereas here *aisthēsis* is spoken of as something of which there can be an actualization. Since it is conceived of as belonging to a subject it is also a particular sense faculty, not a type. We are next told that there is a pleasure corresponding to each sense faculty, the pleasantest being the most perfect, and the most perfect being that of a subject in good condition in relation to the best sense-object; and pleasure makes the actualization perfect. There is, however, a contrast between the way in which the pleasure makes the actualization perfect, and the way in which the sense-object and sense-faculty do so. These latter do so as efficient causes, and whenever percept and perceiver are in perfect condition pleasure will always occur. The former perfects in the way in which health does.

11.3.13. The important point for present purposes is that, throughout, *aisthēsis* is spoken of as something capable of actualization (cf. 1174b14, 17, 18), and it is said not to matter whether we say that the actualization is of the *aisthēsis* or the perceiver (1174b17-18, and cf. 29-30). Nowhere is the word used to refer to the actualization, perceiving. So when Aristotle says that a good condition of *aisthēsis* and sense object is either (1174b23-6) what makes the actualization perfect or (1174b30-1, 33-1175a3) what will always result in pleasure, he is not making perfect actualization itself a condition. This would be absurd in the first case, but it is also false in the second. In fact, perfect condition of faculty and object is said to be the efficient cause indifferently of perfect actualization or pleasure, but there is no stated contrast between perfect actualization and pleasure. The only place there is any hope of introducing any such contrast is in 1174b31-3, to which we must now turn.

11.3.14. This sentence has been the main source of trouble, and probably the points made in the last two paragraphs have been passed over because of what seemed the obvious point of this sentence which runs: 'But pleasure perfects actualization not in the way of a pre-existent condition, but as some added perfection, as the *hōra* to those in their prime.' Even here, however, it should be noted that what is contrasted with pleasure in the way it makes an actualization perfect is not the perfect actualization, nor indeed actualization at all, but the existing condition of the subject, and perhaps the object as well. In spite of this, commentators seem to have felt that Aristotle goes on to say that pleasure is an added, or supervenient perfection, and that this can only mean a further perfection added to the perfection of actualization. This feeling is reinforced by Aristotle's comparison with the bloom (*hōra*) of those in their prime. It is attractive to suppose that his point must be that those in their prime are thereby at their best, but then there is also a flush of full health which while not one of the conditions of good health, does tend to descend on those in their prime as an added glory, making the perfect even more perfect.

11.3.15. Now the word often translated 'supervenient' (*epigignomenon*) simply means 'being added'. In view of what has been said about the lead up to this sentence, it would be a very abrupt change on Aristotle's part suddenly to talk of adding perfection to perfect actualization. The sentence starts with 'Pleasure makes the actualization perfect', repeating the phrase of 1174b23, where it is straightforward making of actualizations perfect that seems to be in mind. One would expect the present sentence simply to mean that 'Pleasure makes the actualization perfect not in the way the existent condition does, but as some perfection does when added.' This would identify pleasure with what constitutes the perfection of the actualization, and would be in line with the earlier way of speaking of the existing conditions indifferently as causes of perfect actualization or of pleasure. The source of the trouble must, therefore, be 'the bloom of youth'.

11.3.16. The trouble at this point is at least partly one of translation. The word translated 'bloom of youth (*hōra*) comes from the word for a season. It comes to be used to refer to the right season or suitable time, and then for the spring-time of life, the healthy season, as it were, of humanity. There is no doubt that it also came to be used to refer to the beauty of those in the spring-time of life, but this usage had no predominance. Those in *hōra* were just those in the prime of youth, and only the context can make it clear whether '*hōra*' means the bloom on the cheek of youth or the spring-time of youth. Yet this makes all the difference in the present case. If it means the bloom, then Aristotle is, with what can only be unforgiveable suddenness, introducing the idea of some further perfection — the bloom — added to perfection — the prime of life. If, on the other hand, it means the spring-time of youth, then Aristotle is saying that pleasure makes an actualization perfect in the way that the spring-time of youth makes those in the prime of youth perfect. Some people pass from winter to autumn. To go through spring is to go through a season of perfection. So the spring-time of youth perfects those in their prime as a perfection perfects when added to that of which it is the perfection. In this case, there is no need for extra perfection piled onto perfect actualization. One per actualization is enough.

11.3.17. The above assumes that what perfection is added *to* is the actualization, and that Aristotle's point is that of course actualization is not a sufficient condition for pleasure — it has to be perfect actualization. It could, alternatively, be that pleasure produces perfect actualization by actualizing the perfect organ/object. These latter bring about perfect actualization as efficient causes, whereas the form (= actualization) added to the faculty-cum-object produces the perfection of actualization formally. In that case Aristotle will be thinking of health being the cause of being healthy when added to the body in good condition as its actualization. In the sentence concerning *hōra* Aristotle would be thinking of the prime of life as a condition whose actualization the *hōra* is. It is difficult to be sure in which of these ways Aristotle is thinking, nor does a decision make any substantial difference to the interpretation. On either view pleasure will emerge as simply perfect actualization (for further discussion see Ch. 13).

11.3.18. The question as to whether pleasure should be seen as the formal or final cause of perfect actualization will be discussed later (see Ch. 13). For the present it is worth noting that this equation of pleasure with the perfection of an actualization makes it crystal clear why (1175a21 ff.) pleasures differ in kind. Since actualizations differ in kind, what constitutes the excellence of two different actualizations must of course be different. If we take pleasure to be added to perfection in the way suggested earlier in terms of fuller agency (see 11.3.10) then of course what constitutes throwing oneself wholeheartedly into a novel will differ from what constitutes throwing oneself wholeheartedly into a bath. The main complaint here would be that this is sheer speculation as to how we are to interpret 'added perfection' and Aristotle does nothing to bring out how the conclusion follows. If, on the other hand, we take the 'bloom' metaphor seriously, and suppose Aristotle to be thinking that pleasure is an added indefinable glow attaching to perfect actualizations, it is far from obvious that glows of different actualizations must differ in kind — certainly not obvious enough to justify Aristotle's breezy remarks at 1175a21 ff.

11.3.19. It remains true, no doubt, that if it were clear from all the rest of the book that Aristotle is primarily interested in what it is to enjoy, where this means what is being said of A when it is said that A enjoys something, then one might have grounds for supposing that 'bloom' should be taken the other way, and that Aristotle overlooked the awkwardness of the shift because of his obsession with enjoyment. This brings us to point (iii), that a number of Aristotle's arguments show a novel interest in how the verb works, and that his use of the noun '$h\bar{e}don\bar{e}$' calls for the translation 'enjoyment' rather than 'pleasure'. With regard to interest in how the verb works there seem to be four relevant passages: (a) 1173a15–27, (b) 1173a29–b4, (c) 1173b5–12, (d) 1174a 13–b14. These will be taken in turn.

11.3.20. *(iii) Aristotle and the verb for 'enjoy'.* Before these passages are considered, there is a prior problem to be discussed. It is not clear what is needed to show the required interest in the verb. It is quite possible for philosophers to produce statements which are plausible in virtue either of certain facts about the common words used or about the way in which technical ones are being defined, although the statements are made in a form that might lull one into thinking that they expressed the result of observation. Thus 'human beings are unable to see sounds' seems a very plausible proposition. If it occurs as a list of human incapacities along with 'human beings are unable to fly, digest raw grass, lift ton weights' one might get the impression that the grounds for supposing it true are similarly observational. Suppose we agree, however, that it is true because no perception of sounds is going to count as seeing. Then we might claim either that the statement is misleading, because it is put in the material mode, whereas the truth contained in it would be more clearly expressed in the formal mode: 'No perceiving of sounds can count as seeing, whether by humans or anything else' (or perhaps better: 'No perception verb taking "sounds" or an equivalent as an object can be equivalent to "see", whether humans or others are the subject'); or that statements about ability and inability are subject to a wide range of styles of justification, and it is important to distinguish between cases where the justification is by appeal to the relations between the concepts used and those where it is not. For present purposes it does not matter which alternative we take. The point is that it is easy to produce a statement which is true in virtue of the terms used as though it was just a very obvious fact of observation. Someone who says 'We can no more paint an object red and green all over than we can see sounds' is not thereby showing an interest in verbs, nor an awareness of some distinction between empirically and linguistically based truths. He may simply be failing to make any distinction. He may indeed be producing points whose truth others think does derive from linguistic facts, but that is another matter. A sharp awareness of the possibility of producing linguistically based truths as though they were observationally based, and of the importance of not doing so, came late into the history of philosophy. Prior to that, it is rash to say of a philosopher who produces points whose plausibility derives, say, from facts about a certain verb, that he is interested in how the verb works, if this is meant to imply, as one would expect, that that describes how the philosopher views what he is doing. To justify this intentional ascription we should need some express comment on his part that this is a fact about verbs and not just of common observation about the phenomena the verbs are used to describe. Consequently, with Aristotle we shall want to know first whether the arguments and statements in question are acceptable only or partly in virtue of facts about the way the verb for enjoying works, and secondly whether Aristotle shows any awareness of this fact.

11.3.21. (a) *1173a15–27*. Here Aristotle is considering a Platonist argument to the effect that pleasure cannot be the good, because pleasure is in the indeterminate category, whereas the good is determinate. Pleasure is indeterminate because it admits of more and less. Aristotle remarks that if the Platonists judge this to be true from the enjoying, then no contrast with excellence is produced, since they clearly say people are more and less excellent; whereas if they are judging from the pleasures, they have their explanation wrong, since this only refers to the mixed nature of pleasures and not all pleasures are mixed. He goes on to suggest that pleasure is like health: it is a proper proportion to which individuals may approximate.

11.3.22. Now it would be possible to take Aristotle as saying that if the Platonists are basing their argument on the verb 'enjoy' they cannot get the required contrast, whereas if they are relying on an analysis of the nature of pleasure they can only make out their case for a selection of pleasures, since not all are mixed. But equally, Aristotle may be complaining that if the Platonists are relying on our capacity to enjoy in varying degrees, then their argument is weak because they themselves say we can be excellent in varying degrees, and then as above for the second point. The whole passage is fairly clearly geared to the *Philebus* or people who have accepted the *Philebus* position. For precisely this problem arises there. Plato first characterizes the indeterminate category (24-5) by its capacity to admit of degrees, but later (52c-d) distinguishes between measured pleasures and indeterminate ones, the latter being so because they are mixed with distress. One's impression at first is that it is the possibility of enjoying things in varying degrees that is the important fact, until 52c-d puts one off balance. The question now arises: is the truth that it is possible to enjoy things more and less a linguistically or observationally based truth? Now obviously it must make sense to speak of degrees of pleasure, but is that clearly sufficient? The answer is: not clearly. Plato may be thinking that with some things we cannot enjoy them more or less; that the pure pleasures are unvarying in their degree of enjoyability, and that if God enjoys himself he is not able to enjoy himself more and less, despite the fact that the verb allows of comparative modification. So the important point for getting pleasure into the indeterminate category might be that human beings are capable of varying degrees of enjoyment, and this is not a fact about the verb, but an important fact about humans, because it means that with them the question of the right degree arises. It is unfortunate that in the *Philebus* the admission that pleasure belongs to the indefinite category (27e) is not based on any premises or examples about pleasure. Rather Philebus is suddenly brought back into the conversation and asked whether pleasure and pain have a limit or are among the things which admit of more or less. He replies that they are among the latter since pleasure would not be completely good if it were not unlimited in number and degree. To begin with, this answer does not seem addressed to a question on the nature of pleasure. The point seems to be that only pleasure of an unlimited amount would be the complete good. Philebus is thinking of his ideal life rather than the more theoretical question. Secondly, he probably had sybaritic pleasures in mind. So we are not given as the ground for admission the fact that any pleasure admits of degrees, and it may be a deliberate cheat: Plato's use of Philebus may have been to hint that certain pleasures, the unmeasured ones of 52c–d, are what belong to the indeterminate; or he may have been confused.

11.3.23. If Aristotle is reacting to this position there is no reason to require that he is interested in facts about the verb rather than just facts about our capacity to enjoy in varying degrees. He goes on to suggest that as health is determinate, though it admits of degrees, so might pleasure be. 'The same proportion does not obtain in everything, nor even is there always a single one in the same thing, but it may be relaxed, yet continue to a certain extent and vary in degree. Something like this might be the case with pleasure' (1173a25–8). This does not sound like someone interested in the verb, but reads like an anticipation of an analogy with health in Aristotle's own account (1174b23–6). It seems, therefore, that this passage does not require us even to suppose that Aristotle's points rely on facts about the verb, let alone that that is how he saw them.

11.3.24. (b) *1173a29–b4*. Here Aristotle is arguing against those who say that pleasure is a movement. The objection is that speed and slowness are proper to every movement, whereas neither is to pleasure. It is possible quickly to come to enjoy something, but not to enjoy it quickly or slowly. It certainly looks here as though what makes all this plausible is apparent facts about what can sensibly be said. There is simply a problem about interpreting such statements as 'I enjoyed Beethoven's Fifth Symphony slightly faster this time than last, and am aiming to break the world record before long.' It can, of course, be taken as a hope to get through the Fifth Symphony very quickly while still enjoying it, but this is just making 'fast' or 'quickly' modify something other than the verb 'enjoy' and this seems necessary to make sense of the statement. (For further discussion see Ch. 16.)

11.3.25. So this argument does seem to hold simply in virtue of apparent facts about what it makes sense to say, or how the verb works. What is not clear is that that is how Aristotle sees it. He uses no expressions which make it clear that he considers himself as making remarks about how the verb works. For all we can tell it may have struck him as a very obvious fact about enjoying that one cannot, however hard one tries, either speed it up or slow it down. So while this passage takes us a step further than the previous one in the desired direction, it does not take us the final step required.

11.3.26. (c) *1173b6–12*. Here Aristotle objects to those who say that pleasure is a process of coming-to-be something. The complaint is that the analysis equates pain with lack of something integral to one's nature and pleasure with replenishment of the lack. But these are things that happen to the body, and since it is the body that is replenished, if replenishment is pleasure it should be the body that does the enjoying, whereas it seems rather that a person would enjoy something when replenishment came about. How might this seem to betray an interest in the verb? Well, it might be felt that what Aristotle says is true in virtue of the fact that 'body' is not a possible subject of the verb 'enjoy'. It makes no more sense to say 'This body is enjoying a meal' than to say 'The square root of two enjoys Bach'. The range of proper subjects of 'enjoy' is the set of sentient beings. It is this sort of consideration that makes it clear that it is the person, not the body, that enjoys things.

11.3.27. Yet we are not told why Aristotle thinks it is not the body that does the enjoying. He might have been reading *Phil.* 43a–b where Plato argues that pleasure cannot be equated with replenishment, but at best with perception of replenishment, and have inferred that as perception is not a bodily function it cannot be the body that enjoys. Or he might have been reading *Phil.* 34d–35e where Plato argues that it cannot be the body that desires. Of course Aristotle would not want to reproduce these passages exactly. In particular he preferred to speak of persons rather than souls doing things. The point is that this sort of background suggests arguments for supposing that the body does not do the enjoying, so that if a view entails that it is the body that enjoys, that view must be wrong. These arguments would not be relying upon linguistic facts about 'enjoy', (Plato asks us

to recognize the fact that not all replenishments are noticed),
but they are just as likely to be the basis of Aristotle's dismissal as any reliance on these supposed facts. That the *Philebus*
is in the background is perhaps suggested by the fact that
Aristotle goes on to say that the view he is opposing starts
from a consideration of pleasures of nourishment, which seem
to fit the proposed pattern, but not all pleasures are like this.
He proceeds to cite pleasures of learning, sensible pleasures of
smell and hearing and vision, memories and hopes. All these
are found in the *Philebus* and are, it has been suggested
(Ch. 7), just the examples which drove Plato from the
replenishment model.

11.3.28. (*d*) *1174a13–b14*. This is an obscure discussion
where Aristotle proposes to embark on his account of the
nature of pleasure. He starts by declaring pleasure to be
complete for any given time, like sight, and in contrast to
movements or processes of coming-to-be something. This
relies on a contrast that Aristotle makes in various places
between *kinēsis* (movement) and *energeia* (actualization),
(for a discussion see Ch. 16), and this in turn might seem to
be based on a distinction between different kinds of verb.
Aristotle thinks that a verb such as 'see' contrasts with one
like 'build' in a variety of significant ways. For instance, '*A*
sees *X*' entails '*A* has seen *X*' whereas '*A* builds *X*' does not
entail '*A* has built *X*'. As Ackrill brings out (Ackrill (1)), the
linguistic criteria do not seem altogether happy in that 'walks'
differs unfortunately from 'builds'. Also, it should be that 'enjoys' operates like 'sees', but if the present tense is the occur-
rent rather than the habitual one, it does not seem that '*A* is
enjoying *Mansfield Park*' entails '*A* has enjoyed *Mansfield
Park*': and if one modifies and says that '*A* is enjoying
Mansfield Park' entails '*A* has enjoyed some part of *Mansfield
Park*', the contrast with walking breaks down. For while 'I
am walking to London' does not entail 'I have walked to
London' it does entail 'I have walked some part of the way to
London'.

11.3.29. Now this may show only that Aristotle is
not very good at this game, but it does suggest another

possibility: that this is not the game that Aristotle is trying to play. He may be starting with a notion of *energeia* in contrast with *dunamis*. The latter, potentiality, is a crucial conception in talking of change. Every change is the actualization of some potentiality. That is only the case with changing, and therefore, complex entities (cf. *Met*. Λ 2, 6–7). God, by contrast, has no aspect of his nature which is at any time only in potency. He is, in fact, the perfect example of actualization, and reflection on his case makes it clear that with pure actualization there is no reason why it should not go on forever (cf. *Met*. Λ 6–7 and *EN* 1154b20 ff., 1175a3–10), it is completely what it is at any time (cf. *EN* 1174a14–15), it lacks nothing that might later perfect it (cf. *EN* 1174a15–19), if *X* is actualized, *X* has been actualized and so on (cf. *Met*. Θ 6). The various characterizations of *energeia* supposedly emerge as obviously attaching to it when one reflects on what a pure case of it would be. If one then reflects on the actualizations of the potentialities of complex natures, one notes that while thinking, say, is an actualization such that there is no reason why, because it is the actualization it is, it should come to an end, still with a particular complex nature there may be other potentialities which demand actualization and which will bring it to an end. On the other hand, some of the potentialities of changing things will be potentialities to effect changes, and the actualizations of these will be such that the more perfect they are the more certain they are to come to an end, and so they are of their nature imperfect actualizations. They are not merely actualizations of imperfectly actualized natures, but imperfect examples of actualizations.

11.3.30. If Aristotle is starting from this sort of conception of *energeia*, then while certain verbs will be handier than others for making the sort of point he wishes to make about *energeia*, the point he is wishing to make is not one about the behaviour of verbs. The fact that the verb 'enjoy' does not lend itself to such illustration (and Aristotle does not pretend that it does) would therefore not disturb him. It might still be that pleasure either is, or is related to *energeia*. In fact, of course, Aristotle's view of pleasure is one that is very unlikely to rely upon facts about how 'enjoy' works. For he is prepared

to confine the title 'pleasure' ('enjoyment') to a select set
of cases where subjects enjoy something, to those, in fact,
which a member of the species in good condition would
enjoy. All other cases are not really pleasures (*EN* 1176a10–
19). This is simply filling out the doctrine of 1174b14–
1175a3 where pleasure is tied to the operation of a subject in
perfect condition in relation to a perfect object. Whatever
else this doctrine may be, it is not one about the verb 'enjoy'.

11.3.31. What one gets, in fact, from 1174a13 onwards,
where Aristotle purports to be giving his own answer on the
nature of pleasure, is not an argument so much as an exposition. First, pleasure is declared to be like sight, and this
turns out not to be just an analogy and certainly not an
analogy between verbs. For sight is one form of perception
and it emerges that perfect perception (perfect eye contemplating perfect object of sight) is a pleasure, (or produces
pleasure, but see 11.3.10–17). Pleasure, in fact, is tied to
things like sight, thought, or 'contemplation' in that it
perfects these, and since these are not 'movements' or
changes nor will it be. This tying of pleasure to perfection is
used at the end of the passage to indicate how many enjoyments can be dismissed as not really pleasures, and the basis
of this is not that the verb 'enjoy' operates in a noticeably
different way in these cases, but that they are not perfect
actualizations of the sort of being in question.

11.3.32. The outcome of all this is that, of the passages
cited, only one seems clearly to rely upon linguistic facts
about 'enjoy', and even here it does not seem that there is
any reason to suppose that that is the way Aristotle saw
things. With other passages, there is either no reason to
suppose that the arguments rely upon linguistic considerations,
or reasons to suppose that they do not.

11.3.33. For completeness it is perhaps worth making a
few remarks on the claim that in Book X the noun '*hēdonē*'
is (predominantly) used to mean 'enjoyment' rather than
'pleasure' (cf. 11.3.6). For it is worth asking what would
show this. Certainly in Book VII (e.g. 1153b9–12) we seem

to be told that the unimpeded actualization of a capacity is a pleasure, whereas in Book X 'pleasure' is not used to refer to the actualization that satisfied certain conditions but to what perfects the actualization. Further, if the thesis that in Book X we have an interest in what it is to enjoy were established, then we should doubtless feel justified in taking '*hēdonē*' to refer to the enjoying of the actualization rather than to the actualization enjoyed. But suppose we take Book X differently. Suppose the contrast between Books VII and X is that the former asks whether any pleasure is a/the good, while the latter is asking whether what makes a life pleasant is what makes it good. If the answer to the question 'What makes life pleasant?' is: 'Its being a life of perfect actualization of the being in question', then the answer to the Book X enquiry is 'Yes'. The interest in Book X will not be (primarily) in pleasures, but in what makes a life or an actualization a pleasure and that might cause a shift in the reference of *hēdonē*, but not one that requires the translation of 'enjoyment' in Owen's sense. In fact, the nature of the shift depends entirely on the general interpretation of the book and is not independent evidence for the detail of interpretation.

11.3.34. (*iv*) *The relative frequency of verb to noun.* Despite all this, it remains that Owen's statistics about the relative frequency of verb and noun in the two books are correct. Although in face of the above one may not want to make this the basis of a thesis as radical as Owen's, it is at the very least an interesting oddity, and it is worth considering what significance it might have. Before this can be done perhaps it will help to have the facts. In Book VII the proportion of the occurrence of verb to noun is 17:100, of occurrences of verb to number of lines 1:20. In Book X it depends on what one allows as relevant verbs. Owen's figures include '*agapān*', a word meaning 'love' or 'desire', and '*terpein*', an active verb for 'delight', as in 'the view delighted her'. If we include these the respective figures for Book X are 27:100 and 1:12; if we exclude them they are 23:100 and 1:14; either way, this looks at least an interesting difference. In what follows the higher figure for the verb will be used.

11.3.35. One might, of course, produce general considerations that might explain the difference, but it is more interesting to consider the way in which the figures vary for a breakdown of Book X. For the frequency of the verb is most noticeable in certain passages. Thus in 1173a29–b20, where Aristotle is first criticizing the views that pleasure is a movement or coming-to-be, the relation of verb to noun is 66:100, and the verb occurs at a rate of once every four lines (1:4). Again, in 1175a21–b24, where Aristotle is arguing that pleasures differ in kind, the rates are 41:100 and 1:8, respectively. By contrast, in the rest of the book the figures are 17:100 and 1:20. In the two rogue passages together, the figures are 52:100 and 1:6. The figures for Book VII are 17:100 and 1:20, that is those for Book X without the two passages that show exceptional numbers for the verb.

11.3.36. The first of the exceptional passages is one where, as we have seen, Aristotle is relying on linguistic facts about the verb. In the second passage it is suggestive simply to try writing the examples adduced and points made while using only the noun. The resulting cumbersomeness suggests that the reasons for the verb are as likely to be stylistic as philosophical. This is a point which receives no elaboration in Book VII (1153a20–3 as against 1175a29–b16 in Book X, to take a strict view), and consequently there is no opportunity for generating occurences of verbs there. If, however, we compare the section where Aristotle elaborates his view in Book X, (1174a13–1175a3) with that where he gives his in Book VII (1152b25–1153a17), the figures are startlingly the other way. In Book VII they are 33:100 and 1:14, whereas in Book X they are 8:100 and 1:60.

11.3.37. Of course, by themselves these statistics would not prove very much anyway, and Owen only uses them as corroboration. The breakdown, however, suggests that they are very dubious corroboration. Nor is the variety of verbs used in Book X either significant or particularly surprizing. Book X is reacting to disputes concerning Eudoxus. The *Philebus* (11b4–5, 19c6–8) suggests that it was part of the case to equate a fair variety of nouns and verbs as equivalent for the purpose in hand, and very probably they were all used. It would not be surprising if Aristotle reflected facts about the literature. As we shall see, Book VII does not have the same background.

11.3.38. None of this, of course, explains the final fact relied on by Owen (point (v)), that Book X reacts to the view that pleasure is a form of coming-to-be in a way quite different from Book VII, and employs a battery of arguments of which there is no trace in the earlier book and which show a new degree of sophistication. This feeling that at least a great part of the opposition is common to both books, so that one can compare their reactions to the same views, is shared by a great many commentators. As the treatment of it will bear not only on Owen but on others as well, who often have a *mild* view of the contrast between the books, it will appropriately start a new chapter, and a passage to milder forms of the contrast.

Chapter 12

Speusippus

12.0.1. Professor Owen himself seems clearly to suppose only that the positions on pleasure as a process of coming-to-be criticized in the two books are identical. Others suppose in addition that Aristotle's main opponents are the same in both books. Obviously this is important for the question of developments after Plato as well as for that of the relationship between the two books. In what follows the case will be considered for supposing that in both books Aristotle's main opponent is Speusippus, Plato's successor as head of the Academy. This will require comparing the two books in some detail, including the views on pleasure as a process of coming-to-be. A clear view of Aristotle's opponents should help one to see the nature of his own stances in opposition to them. So the discussion should help fill in the post-Platonic picture and lead in to a discussion of Aristotle.

12.0.2. The argument for identical opponents in both books will be developed in its most extreme form. Different commentators (e.g. Festugière, Gauthier and Jolif, Joachim, Ross) differ in the extent to which they approximate to this extreme, but as the discussion will tackle the extent to which one can approximate this does not matter for present purposes.

1. The argument for Speusippus

12.1.1. The argument might be presented as follows: the *Philebus* is clearly a reaction to the impact of Eudoxus. On the other hand it paints a picture of sharp opposition to Eudoxus. It is likely that this reflects a situation in Plato's immediate environment, and that he is as it were adjudicating in the rather heated dispute in the Academy. We know from Diogenes Laertius (DL IV.4) that Plato's successor, Speusippus, wrote a book on pleasure. So it is likely that he, as a foremost member of the Academy, is represented in the *Philebus* dispute. Further, we can glean a little about the likely contents of that book from testimony about his views. Thus Clement of Alexandria (*Stromateis* II.22.133 = fr. 57 Lang) says that Speusippus thought the good to be a state of *aochlēsia*, lack of disturbance, tranquillity (and cf. *EN* 1104b 24ff. for a possible reference). This fits the position of Philebus' special enemies, the naturists (see Ch. 8) who clearly advocate a life free from the turbulence of bodily pain and pleasure. Further, Aulus Gellius (*Noctes Atticae* IX. v.4 = fr. 60i Lang) says that Speusippus held that both pleasure and pain are opposed to the good as evils. This position is recorded in *EN* X (1173a5–13), and the view there that pleasure and pain may be opposites and pain evil, without it following that pleasure is (a) good, is explicitly attributed to Speusippus in Book VII (1153b4–6). This again fits the naturists of the *Philebus*, for pleasure and pain are equally opposed to tranquillity, even though opposed to each other, and are equally deplorable. All this suggests that Speusippus held a position opposed to Eudoxus which is portrayed in the *Philebus*. The position there clearly thinks of pleasures as processes of physical restoration, and so processes of coming-to-be. The probability therefore is that those who think that pleasure and pain are opposed as evils and both opposed to the good, and those who think that pleasure is a process of coming-to-be, are one and the same — Aristotle's main philosophical rival, Speusippus. In both Book VII and Book X Aristotle is trying to defend a Eudoxan position against Eudoxus' main antagonist. The position is more carefully modified in Book X, but the main Eudoxan spirit preserved.

12.1.2. All this is, no doubt, circumstantial argument, but it builds up a plausible picture which avoids an unnecessary proliferation of opponents. Of course, not all the arguments mentioned by Aristotle are Speusippus', still less are all the opposing positions mentioned held by him. Thus Book VII (1152b1–24) mentions a variety of opposing positions, but the one considered most important is the one that can be attributed to Speusippus. Again, Book X actually mentions

Plato (1172b28), but it is the view that pleasure is a motion or process of coming-to-be that receives the most prolonged critical attention, so it seems clear that Speusippus dominates the discussions. The crucial link between Speusippus and the naturists of the *Philebus* can also be argued on largely independent grounds (cf. Schofield). For they are constantly referred to as difficult people The word used ('*duschereis*') is pointedly repeated in the discussion of them in a way that suggests deliberate allusion, and Aristotle has a tendency to use the noun '*duschereia*' for 'objection' or 'difficulty' more frequently when discussing Speusippus, which suggests that it was perhaps a favourite word of his. If so, this could explain its emphasis in the *Philebus*. This last argument, however, is at best corroborative.

12.1.3. Since in both books a Eudoxan style of position is defended, and both are fighting off the views of Speusippus as the main threat, it is obviously appropriate to compare the two books for success in meeting that threat. What strikes one is the greater detail of Book X, as though points felt at the time of Book VII were now mastered; the production of arguments in Book X that are not even hinted at in Book VII; and the attempt of Book X to say what pleasure is, not what a pleasure is, an attempt which shows a more refined and sophisticated approach.

2. A skirmishing point

12.2.1. To start with a mild skirmishing point: there is no presumption in favour of supposing that when a philosopher is considering arguments for a conclusion he has even primarily a particular fellow philosopher in view. He may have, of course, and he may even set up his problems by specific reference to some author. But suppose we imagine someone discussing views on physical objects. He might divide possible views by saying that some philosophers hold that objects are collections of actual or possible sense-data, others that they are the unperceived causes of sense-data, others that they are not sense-data but the direct objects of (most) perception that exist independently of perceivers. He might now list arguments in favour of the first type of position and mention, say, arguments from the occurrence of hallucinations, arguments from dream-experiences, arguments from changing perspective, arguments from what can be certainly known. It would be rash to infer that he had some particular philosopher in mind, or that he thought that any one philosopher relied upon all these arguments — Berkeley, Russell, Price, Ayer? They are all arguments for the type of conclusion being considered, but that is all. It is antecedently just as probable that Aristotle is considering a rag-bag of arguments for the view that no pleasure is a good, put forward by a variety of philosophers, as it is that he has a particular opponent primarily in mind.

12.2.2. It is more important, however, to ask how strong the evidence for Speusippus is. This seems to rely upon three points.

(i) The argument about opposites at Book X 1173a5 ff. is that attributed to Speusippus in Book VII 1153b4-6. This serves to get Speusippus into Book X.
(ii) The naturists in the *Philebus* can be identified with Speusippus and his friends.
(iii) The positions on pleasure as a process of coming-to-be that are criticized in Book VII and Book X are identical.

12.2.3. These are not independent points. The first, for instance, is partly supported by the evidence of Aulus Gellius in connection with the identification of Speusippus with the naturists, which in turn supports and is supported by point (iii). Still, there are considerations peculiar to each point and it is of interest to see how strong each is individually and to what extent they can give mutual support.

3. The argument from opposites

12.3.1. In Book X (1173a5-13) Aristotle considers some theorists who object to the argument that since pain is an evil, and pleasure is the opposite of pain, therefore pleasure is a good. The objection clearly takes the form of saying that A may have two opposites, B and C, and that these may be opposed not only to A, but to each other. This certainly sounds like the way out attributed to Speusippus in Book VII. He, too, claims that an evil may have more than one opposite. But there the similarity stops. According to Book X, the opposition argue: it does not follow that if pain is (an) evil, pleasure is (a) good; for evil can be opposed to evil and both to that which is neither. Aristotle agrees with the general point, but argues that it fails for the case in hand; because if pleasure and pain both belonged to the class of evils they would both be objectionable, or if they belonged to the class of that which is neither, neither would be objectionable, or both equally; but in fact the objectors clearly object to the one (pain) as evil and choose the other (pleasure) as good; and that is the form of the opposition of pleasure and pain.

12.3.2. There are problems about this passage. In particular it is not clear what is referred to by 'that which is neither'. The immediate context suggests that which is neither evil; the slightly wider context makes it possible that it is that which is neither good nor bad. Michael of Ephesus, in his commentary, (fr. 60g Lang) takes it the first way, holds the position to be that of Speusippus and declares that he uses the expression to refer to the good. But in that case, as Stewart in effect points out, we have a problem with the following sentence, where Aristotle says that if both pleasure and pain belong to the 'neither' category, then neither should be avoided, or both equally. For if 'that which is neither' refers to the good one would, first, not expect Aristotle to consider the possibility that both pleasure and pain were good and, secondly, not expect him to suggest that if they both were good they were either merely not to be avoided or were to be avoided equally! These remarks really only fit an interpretation of 'that which is neither' as referring to something which is not only neither evil, but not good either — 'neutral' as Ross translates it.

12.3.3. The majority of commentators take it that this passage refers to Speusippus, and that he thought pleasure and pain both to be evils. This gives rise to a great urge for emendation both here and in Book VII. It might be preferable, however, not to beg those questions. As it stands, the passage seems to envisage philosophers who are mainly concerned to say that pleasure and pain might both be in the same category, so far as goodness is concerned. If pain is evil, then pleasure might be evil too; if pain is neutral, so might pleasure be. Against Eudoxus the first way of putting the matter would be appropriate; but Aristotle's covering of the second suggests that the main thrust of the argument is that the fact that pleasure is opposed to pain does not justify one putting pleasure in a different value-category: they might both be evil or both neutral. All that does not seem to be envisaged is that they might both be good.

12.3.4. If we leave the passage unemended, then Aristotle is responding to philosophers who hold that pain and pleasure may be opposites, yet be in the same value-category. If we excise the remark about both belonging to the category of that which is neither, we have philosophers who hold that pain and pleasure are opposed as evil to evil. In either case they differ from Speusippus as mentioned in the unemended text of Book VII (1153b1-7). To begin with, Speusippus is cited not directly as saying that pleasure and pain are opposed as evils, but as using an analogy with 'larger', 'smaller', 'equal' to make the general point. It is true that the scholiast elaborates this with the claim that Speusippus thought pleasure and pain to be opposed as evils, and argued that with the virtues, the virtue was a mean with two opposing evils, and similarly pleasure and pain were opposed to the good state of painlessness. This is, however, in direct opposition to the text of Book VII as it stands. For Aristotle goes on to say that Speusippus would deny that pleasure is of itself an evil. Aristotle's point seems to be that if one accepted Speusippus' escape route one could avoid saying pleasure is a good, but only at the cost of calling it an evil; a consequence Speusippus would wish to reject. In other words, we have an *ad hominem* argument against Speusippus.

12.3.5. The interesting point here is, that whichever way we interpret Book X the position is different from that attributed to Speusippus in Book VII. With Book X unemended the opposition is not committed to thinking pain an evil;

whereas in Book VII Aristotle thinks that Speusippus' way out commits him to thinking pleasure an evil, and that can only be because he is confident that Speusippus thinks pain to be one too. With Book X emended the opposition hold that pleasure and pain are both evil, and so are different from Speusippus as described in Book VII unemended. The desire to have everyone agree has therefore led some (e.g. Grant) to insert 'one' (*tis*) in the Book VII passage, so as to read 'one would not call pleasure of itself an evil'. This would remove the denial from Speusippus, and so make it possible that he did think pleasure an evil. The cost is to attribute extraordinary obtuseness to Aristotle. In face of someone who, according to this view, does, vigorously, hold that pleasure is an evil, it is very lame to reply that one wouldn't say it was.

12.3.6. From the text as it stands, then, one would suppose that Aristotle is considering different positions in Books VII and X. In view of the general uncertainty, in the absence of quotation, of when later commentators are citing with the text before them, when giving way to the temptation to assimilate different philosophers for a neat historical outcome, it is probably best to suppose that Aristotle is considering different opposed views in the two books. Of course, since Speusippus, like any other philosopher, might have changed his position, it could be the same philosopher in each case. But the important question is whether the same position is opposed.

4. Speusippus and the *Philebus*

12.4.1. Let us suppose, however, that we do emend both books so as to bring them clearly into line with later reports of Speusippus. Can we find this Speusippus in the *Philebus*? The only possibilities are the naturists or the subtlers, since Plato himself is too tolerant to pleasure by far. But there is no reason to suppose that the subtlers (cf. 8.2) consider pleasure as an evil. It is not a good (goal), but it is a movement towards one, and so hardly a bad thing. The most likely candidates are the naturists. Their examination of the true nature of pleasure certainly brings it out as bad. Further,

both pleasure and pain are disturbing elements opposed to
the neutral state where neither is experienced, which might
be the painless state commonly said to have been identified
with the good by Speusippus. So if Speusippus held that the
good was a neutral painless (and pleasureless) condition, and
that both pain and pleasure were evils, it is possible that he
and his associates are the naturists of the *Philebus*.

12.4.2. If we make this assumption, however, it is difficult
at the same time to suppose that he held the view that
pleasure is a form of coming-to-be. We have already seen
(cf. 8.2.6-7) that the subtlers' view is not the same as the
naturists'. It is integral to the former view to see *genesis* as a
process towards a good in contrast to *phthora*, a process
away from the good. The process towards a good is then
sharply distinguished from the good towards which it is a
process. This is clearly still the point in the views cited in
Books VII and X. In Book VII (1152b13-15, 22-3, 1153a7-9)
the thinkers mentioned contrast the process to the end with
the end perfection (*telos*); and Aristotle's explanation of the
adoption of the term '*genesis*' is that pleasure was thought to
be a good thing (1153a15-16). In Book X the *genesis* theorists
consider the good perfect (*teleion*), pleasure, as a process,
incomplete or imperfect (*ateles*) (1173a29-31); and *genesis*
is contrasted with *phthora* (1173b6-7). Now clearly, anyone
making the contrast in this way will not think that pleasure is
a good (= goal), but also would hardly consider it evil. It is,
after all, a move to the good, and always better than the
starting condition. Nor is it likely that these thinkers considered pleasure and pain to be both neutral. In fact they are
unlikely to be the same as those mentioned in Book X who
refuse to accept the argument from opposites, whether we
emend the text or not, for they would hardly put pleasure
and pain in the same value category.

12.4.3. On the other hand, if we retain the text of Book
VII and suppose Speusippus was not prepared to call pleasure
an evil, then it would be consistent for *him* to hold a *genesis*
view. For, of course, a *genesis* theorist would hold that
pain is evil, the end state the good, and the *genesis*-process

neither an evil nor a good (goal). But that would break the identity between Speusippus and those who reject the argument from opposites in Book X. It would also break the identification of Speusippus with the naturists of the *Philebus* and ally him instead with the subtlers.

12.4.4. To sum up so far: the options are as follows:

(i) Speusippus and those opposing the argument from opposites in Book X are holding the same position; in which case neither is holding the view that pleasure is a *genesis* but both *might* be holding the position of the naturists of the *Philebus*.

(ii) Speusippus holds a *genesis* view, and does not hold the same position *vis-à-vis* the argument from opposites as those mentioned in Book X, and is to be found among the subtlers rather than the naturists of the *Philebus*.

(iii) (ii) except that Speusippus does not hold a *genesis* view, and so is not among the subtlers.

12.4.5. If (ii) is right, then it is of some interest to see how a holder of the *genesis* view might react to the argument from opposites. There are, clearly, at least two possible counters to the argument (cf. Gauthier and Jolif II (2), p. 823). First, as suggested by the Scholiast, one has a model like Aristotle's doctrine of the mean: the good is in the middle and the two extremes on either side are bad. Alternatively, the good is at one end, pain/evil at the other, and the *genesis* of pleasure in between. Either model justifies speaking of two opposites neither of which is (the) good, but both of which are opposite to it. Only the first suggests that both the other opposites are evil. If Speusippus adopted the second it would be possible for him to reject the argument from opposites while refusing to call pleasure either a good or an evil. In that case it becomes a good question why Aristotle thinks that his escape route would commit him to calling pleasure evil. In relation to this it has to be remembered that in Book VII Aristotle is operating (cf. 1152b26–31) with a distinction between things good without qualification and things good to so-and-so, on occasion, and so on. This would make him want to reject the *genesis* theorists' view that 'good' should be confined to things good as ends. If he was confident that he could do that, then he would be able to argue that any *genesis* on Speusippus' view while not a good without qualification, is always a good to the subject of it. Consequently, the only way to avoid the argument from opposites would be to adopt the other model. But that would involve saying that pleasure is an evil; a consequence which Speusippus would not want.

12.4.6. The result of this is, that if the rejectors of the argument from opposites in both books are the same, Speusippus does not loom large among the opponents in either book. But if they are not the same, it may still be that he is important if he holds that pleasure is a *genesis*, since that sort of view is considered important in both books. It remains, therefore, to see whether the positions mentioned are identical.

5. Pleasure as a *genesis*

12.5.1. As has already been mentioned, it is clear that Aristotle's responses are different, in that most of the arguments against the *genesis* theory in Book X are not in Book VII. It is also interesting to note that the descriptions of the views are not identical. In Book VII at the first mention of a *genesis* view (1152b12–15) and again in the rejection of such views (1153a13), the position is said to be that pleasure is a perceived *genesis*. The qualifying adjective does not appear in Book X. Nor, of course, does it appear in the exposition of the subtlers in the *Philebus*, the earliest exposition of such a view that we have. It is worth asking what the significance might be.

12.5.2. It will be remembered that in the *Philebus* (and *Timaeus*) Plato became dissatisfied with the straightforward identification of bodily pleasure with the physical process of restoration to a natural condition (*Phil.* 43, *Tim.* 64a–65b). For we should have to suppose that we had many pleasures of which we were unaware or underwent fewer replenishments than theory and observation would suggest. He says, therefore, that it is the big changes which produce pleasures or pains. Now a change is big just and only if it gets through to the soul; and the earlier account of perception makes it clear that with some physical motions they set up a concomitant *psuchic* motion, and the combination is a perception (*Phil.* 33d–34a). So the replenishments that are big produce pleasure, i.e. perceptions. (For a fuller discussion see Ch. 10.5.) Now this modification is applied to a replenishment, not a *genesis* view. It looks, then, as though by the time Book VII was written some theorist has taken the *Philebus* point, but preserved the *genesis* terminology because that underlines, as that of replenishment does not, the contrast with goal-goods. As we have seen, the terminology of replenishment contains ambiguity on the very point which the *genesis* terminology underlines (cf. 8.2.9).

12.5.3. It might seem that this is building a lot into Book VII, but it has to be recognized, first, that the word for 'perceived' is there, and secondly that at 1153a15 Aristotle tries to account for its presence. He does so by suggesting that '*genesis*' seems plausible because pleasure is felt to be a good thing (a significant remark if Speusippus is supposed to have thought it evil and also to have held the *genesis* view) and that 'perceived' should be changed to 'unimpeded'. Aristotle seems to be trying to correct a view which has some glimpse of the truth. If we remember the *Philebus* and *Timaeus* it is possible to see how he might have thought that 'perceived' played a role analogous to 'unimpeded' in his own theory. Someone holding an unmodified replenishment or *genesis* view faces the problem that not all *geneseis* are enjoyed. Aristotle holding that pleasures are actualizations of capacities faces a similar problem. 'Actualization' catches, correctly, the feeling, inadequately met by '*genesis*', that pleasure is good. 'Unimpeded' gives the condition which makes an actualization a pleasure — which is the role to be played in the new *genesis* theory by 'perceived' — it is being perceived that makes replenishments pleasures, as the *Philebus* argues. The proposed genealogy back to the *Philebus* therefore helps explain not only the occurrence of the word 'perceived', but Aristotle's view that 'perceived' should be changed to 'unimpeded'.

12.5.4. Is there, then, any significance in the fact that in Book X the word for 'perceived' does not occur? We certainly know that there were *genesis* views (e.g. the subtlers') which did not contain the modification. Yet it could be that the omission from Book X is not significant, that Aristotle could safely leave it out because his readers would be familiar enough with current views. There may, however, be more to it than that. For if the above account of the view opposed in Book VII is right, it is arguable that some of Aristotle's criticisms in Book X would be irrelevant to it, though relevant to an unmodified version like the subtlers'. The arguments consist of one against pleasure being any kind of motion (change), (1173a31-b4), including *genesis*, and one against the view that pleasure is a *genesis* or a replenishment (1173b4-13), with an explanation of how that view arose which contains a further objection (1173b13-20).

12.5.5. The first argument is that changes can be fast or slow, whereas pleasure cannot. Clearly if anyone simply identifies pleasure with some change, whether process of coming-to-be, or replenishment, then since these must be capable of occurring at different speeds, so must pleasure. So if pleasure cannot, it cannot be identified with any such change. It is not clear, however, precisely what kind of view is Aristotle's target here. There seem to be two possibilities. First, he might be making a general criticism of those who put pleasure into the category of *kinēsis* or change. In that case his objection would tell against Plato's view in the *Republic* (583e9-10) that pleasure is a movement in the soul, or in the *Philebus*, if he is there assimilating bodily pleasures to perception, since he holds perception to be joint *kinēsis* of body and soul. It would also tell against his own early views (cf. 11.1). There are two difficulties with this:

(i) It is fairly obvious, as Aristotle must have known, that the function of the expression '*kinēsis*' in these views was to assimilate pleasure to perception and assert that it is something going on in the soul. The obvious riposte to Aristotle's objection would be to say that these movements cannot be quick or slow; and to that Aristotle can only say that in that case 'movement' is the wrong word. That would not be an objection which bore on the substance of that theory.

(ii)   The theorists envisaged in Book X clearly do not use '*kinēsis*' in the innocuous sense of Plato and the early Aristotle, but in a way which contrasts a movement with the goal to which the movement tends. Movements so conceived must be capable of being quicker and slower, and so the objection would not be merely terminological; but nor would it be an objection to the position of Plato and the early Aristotle. This leads to the second interpretation of Aristotle's opponents, that they are precisely people who construed all pleasure as a process to an end term, and identified the pleasure with the movement. In that case it is far from clear that the objection can be transferred to people who hold that pleasure is a *perceived genesis*. Even if they retain the Platonic view of perception as a *kinēsis* in the soul they would not, as we have seen, have to consider the objection very seriously. If they did not retain that view of perception, they could hardly consider it an objection at all, but a straight *ignoratio elenchi*.

12.5.6. A similar ambivalence obscures the section (1174a13–b10) at the opening of Aristotle's own account where he insists that pleasure is not a motion/change and takes it that this shows the error of those who hold it to be a motion or a *genesis* (1174b9–10). As in the earlier passage (cf. 1173a31 and 1173b5) Aristotle takes it that if pleasure is not a motion/change *a fortiori* it is not a *genesis*. Once again, if the *genesis* theorists are identifying (bodily) pleasure with bodily replenishment it is probably views that pleasure consists in some physical motion/change that Aristotle has in mind or at least that it is a movement to an end term. Certainly his examples are all of this sort. If he had been objecting to philosophers who held that pleasure is like sight and perception generally and is something that goes on in the soul, it would not be obviously appropriate to argue that pleasure is like sight, complete, and distinct from a motion/change, without first arguing that sight is not a motion.

12.5.7. So there is some uncertainty as to Aristotle's target in his arguments about motion/change. The same is not true when at 1173b4 he turns to the view that pleasure is a *genesis*. Here the argument is to the effect that anything that comes to be, comes to be from some particular state, and it is into this state that it dissolves; so of that of which the coming-to-be is a pleasure the dissolution is a distress. But the replenishments and depletions in question are of the body, so it should be this that enjoys. In fact, however, the replenishment is not the pleasure — rather, when the replenishment occurs someone experiences pleasure.

12.5.8. Clearly this argument is a *reductio* aimed at people who consider that pleasure consists in certain bodily changes and purports to show that pleasure is not any bodily change, but at best the latter are an occasion for pleasure. Someone who, like Plato in the *Republic* (583e9-10), thinks that pleasure is a motion in the soul, or as in the *Philebus* or *Timaeus* assimilates it to perception for which the bodily occurrences are the occasion or cause (see Ch. 10), will simply concur with Aristotle's point. They, too, have seen that one cannot identify pleasure with the bodily replenishment. So if the point of adding the adjective 'perceived' was, as it had been suggested, to take on board the *Philebus*/*Timaeus* point, then the *genesis* theorists of Book VII would agree with Aristotle of Book X and, rightly, not consider their own views endangered.

12.5.9. Aristotle then (1173b13-20) offers an explanation of the growth of this theory. While in the *Philebus* the exposition of the subtlers' views contains no mention of replenishment (which appears only in 31-2), the mention of the pleasures which would lead them to ridicule the advocacy of a life of pleasure (54d-55a) suggests that perhaps they took bodily pleasures of replenishment as their model. Aristotle, anyway, considers that that is where the theory started and so he speaks indifferently of replenishment or *genesis*. He then remarks that this is plausible only of a subset of pleasures, and quite ignores the scholarly pleasures, pure pleasures of smell, hearing, and sight, of memory and hope. These, of course, are examples of pleasures which are not processes of coming-to-be. Equally they are examples of pleasures which are not perceptions of or caused by any processes of coming-to-be. So this consideration would tell equally against the theorists of Book VII. It is the only argument common to the two books.

12.5.10. In short: Book VII suggests a modification to the *genesis* view adding in the notion of perception; Aristotle is sufficiently aware of it to try to explain it; the likely ancestry is the Platonic addition of perception to replenishment for an account of bodily pleasures in the *Philebus* (and cf. *Tim*. 64a–65b); Book X gives no indication of any such modification; the anti-*genesis* argument peculiar to Book X would be irrelevant to the opposition in Book VII, and its presence in Book X could well be explained not by the relative sophistication of Aristotle but by the relative naïvety of his opponents; the only argument common to the two books is the only one clearly relevant to both *genesis* theories. In fact, the easiest explanation of all the differences is that the views opposed were different.

12.5.11. If we return to the question of Speusippus, it could be of course that he is the main opponent in each book, but only if he had changed his position. The fact should be faced, however, that we have altogether too little firm evidence about Speusippus to associate him with either position. The Speusippus of the commentators is like an inflatable ball, ready to accommodate any amount of hot air that any given scholar has at hand. When one reads Festugière after looking at the available evidence one feels that his deep intimacy with Speusippus must come from access to sources now lost to scholarship.

6. The differences between Books VII and X

12.6.1. If we look back to Chapter 11 the differences between the two books look even greater. The two main points of overlap now look like not being points of overlap at all. The arguments from opposites seem different, and so do the *genesis* views of pleasure. There remain as significant points of overlap

(i) the objection from the existence of shameful pleasures,
(ii) the puzzle as to why humans cannot experience pleasure without interruption, and
(iii) the point that pleasure improves performance of what it is pleasure in.

This degree of difference, however, creates an interesting problem. If the main opposition faced in the two books is the same, then the books can be compared for their success in dealing with it and the relative sophistication of the equipment used. But if we are right about the differences between the books, then they reflect a changing philosophical scene as much as development on the part of one author.

Chapter 13

Pleasure: Formal or Final Cause?

13.0.1 It might help at this point to review the state of the argument. In Chapter 11 we gave a sketch of the two passages on pleasure which suggested various points of divergence, while leaving some points of overlap. One attractive view is to hold that the points of overlap indicate the presence of a persistent opposition, and this enables us to explain at least some of the more interesting divergences in terms of developments in Aristotle's position. In the last two chapters we have been arguing that the divergences between the two books are greater than such a view would suggest. In so doing we hope to have done two things: first to have removed or at the very least weakened some of the grounds for supposing a change of view on the nature of pleasure, and in particular a growth in sophistication between Books VII and X; and secondly (cf. Ch. 11, especially 11.3.12–19), to have shown to be baseless what might be called the after-glow theory, the view that Aristotle in Book X thought of pleasure as a supervenient *je-ne-sais-quoi* rounding off perfect actualization. It remains to ask whether the books differ at all with respect to the view of pleasure presented. We shall proceed in two stages. First we shall consider the view that in Book X Aristotle considers pleasure to be the final cause of actualization, and shall argue for the more traditional view that he considers it the formal cause. We shall then be in a better position to ask what the difference amounts to. Our second stage will consist in arguing that the differences of terminology do not indicate a difference of view.

13.0.2. We have already argued that Owen's interpretation of Book X is unacceptable (cf. Ch. 11–12). Traditionally the difference has been seen as finer. In Book VII Aristotle sees pleasure just as unimpeded actualization, in Book X as something extra. Here there have been three styles of view. First, that of the majority of commentators (for references see

Gauthier and Jolif II (2), p. 839) holds that pleasure is the
formal cause of actualization; secondly, not always distinguished from this or the following has been the view (cf.
Gauthier and Jolif II (2), p 841) that pleasure is some subtle
extra perfection added to the perfection of actualization; and
thirdly, there is the view adopted by Gauthier and Jolif themselves, that pleasure is the final cause of (perfect) actualization.
We have already argued against the second view in Chapter 11
where we wrote as if pleasure was a formal cause. It remains,
therefore, to see whether Aristotle is treating pleasure as a
formal or final cause.

1. The four causes

13.1.1. In order to get the nature of this dispute clear it
will be necessary first to make a few remarks on the different
kinds of cause and then see what would be needed to settle
the issue. This is no place for a full discussion of Aristotle's
doctrine of cause. Briefly and dogmatically the essential
features are as follows. Aristotle held that if you ask the
question 'Why is X F?' there are four families of answers
available. Thus, suppose we are faced with a tall tree and ask
'Why is this tree growing so tall?' We might be told

(i)   it is made of such and such tissue (material cause),
(ii) it is a poplar (formal cause),
(iii) the gardener has been feeding and watering it (efficient
cause), or
(iv) to reach the light and encourage root growth (the final
cause).

The first of these appeals to the material of which the tree is
constructed and gives the material cause of growth, the
second to the form of object and gives the formal cause, the
third to the agency effecting the change and gives the efficient
cause, the fourth to the purpose or function of such growth
and gives the final cause. These are families of answer in the
sense that not every explanation has to take one or other of
these forms, but it does have to belong to a group structured
round one or other of these forms. Thus we might explain a
murderer's killing a certain man by saying that he mistook
him for the Prime Minister. This is not an explanation of any

of the above forms, but is grouped under (iv) because it is a failure of purpose. The act in question had a point, though the point does not successfully explain what happened. The explanation given is explaining what went wrong with the pursuit of the given goal. Similarly a person may walk as he does because he is blind. This does not give the formal cause, because blindness is a deformity; but the explanation depends upon the formal type of explanation in that it explains by reference to that as a standard.

13.1.2. Aristotle often makes remarks suggesting that in some sense causes of types (ii)-(iv) can be identified (cf. *Phys.* 198a24-6) and at other times that (ii) and (iv) can (cf. *Met.* H 1044a35-b1). For the present it is only important to see the plausibility of identifying (ii) and (iv) since this threatens to annul the present dispute. Suppose, then, we return to the example of the poplar. It seems plausible to suggest that if one had a full understanding of the nature of a poplar one would grasp its peculiar mode of growth and propagation with all its attendant needs. It would become clear what was good for a poplar, why it needed to grow high, and so on. In other words, one would have the final cause of the growth. Similarly, to know the final cause (cf. *GA* 731b23; *Phys.* 195a23-6) is to know why such growth is a good thing, and this involves knowing the nature of that for which it is good. In the case of a formal cause, the form of a poplar is what makes a perfect poplar. A form never explains bad functioning, but only good functioning. So if we can give a formal cause of the poplar's growing tall this will be because the poplar is in good condition, manifesting the poplar form by this growth, i.e. it will be a good thing for a poplar to grow so tall. Similarly, a final cause always gives a good state towards which the object is tending. All things are tending towards death, but this is not their final cause (cf. 8.2.3). This is given only when we have the good state of that thing, towards which it is its nature to tend.

13.1.3. In this way formal and final causes, at least with living things, look like being much the same. Yet if there is to be a dispute about Aristotle's view on pleasure they must be distinguishable, and the options exclusive. In other words, Aristotle's remarks that they are identical must be interpreted in a way that allows them to be different. How this might be will emerge more clearly if we consider the arguments for saying that pleasure is a final cause.

2. Pleasure as final cause: arguments and objections

13.2.1. There seem to be two (cf. Gauthier and Jolif, II (2), p. 839). First it is claimed that although the example of 'health' that is used by Aristotle as an analogue of pleasure could be an example of a formal cause, it is more likely to be an example of a final cause. Aristotle, does indeed, on occasion, use the way in which health makes something healthy to illustrate what he means by a formal cause (e.g. *EN* 1144a3–5; *Met.* Λ 1070a21–6, b28). Far more commonly, however, health is used as an example of a final cause (e.g. *EN* 1094a8, 1145a7–9; *EE* 1218b2–3, 18–22, 1249b11–13). Thus health explains the body's recuperative activities as their goal, the perfection towards which they are aiming, and it is in this sort of context that Aristotle most commonly cites it. It is more probable therefore that pleasure is being looked upon as that towards which the organism tends as a goal. Just as health, as a goal, causes the perfection of the body, so pleasure perfects actualizations as the goal at which a sentient nature aims.

13.2.2. Secondly, this is reinforced by the fact that Aristotle actually calls pleasure a goal. He uses the word '*telos*', one of his words for referring to the final cause, to refer to pleasure when at 1174b33 he describes it as supervenient perfection (*telos*). He would be guilty of gross incompetence if his example of health were of a formal cause. For he has set out to explain how pleasure perfects the actualization. The claim would be that he reminds us how health perfects the body as formal cause and then declares pleasure to be a final cause. In other words his illustration signally fails to be an illustration of the relevant manner of perfecting. All is well, however, when we realize that the illustration is in fact intended to be of health as a final cause. Then the whole passage is consistent.

13.2.3. The first argument is not, of course, one that could bear the whole weight of the thesis by itself. Indeed this is putting matters too mildly. This argument cannot really bear any weight at all. It must be among the most futile arguments to be found in the literature on the subject. For of course health might figure equally well as either formal or final cause. If we have two people, one of whom, A, is constipated, the other, B, is without digestive troubles, and ask 'Why is A having such trouble while B has none?' the answer may be not that B is being helped along by a mixture of medicaments, but that B is healthy. Here B's health is the formal cause of his digestive peace. Now A may well go to a doctor and the doctor advise him, and A's digestive organs undergo a reactive change as a result of treatment. All these occurrences may be geared to A's health, so that A's health may be cited to explain them all. But now it is being cited as final cause, as that to which they are all aiming. It is quite futile to ask 'But which is health really? Is it a formal or final cause?' For it is not in itself *really* either, though it may well be either. In other words, A's health may be a formal cause or a final cause, but it does not follow that these styles of explanation are identical. For saying on any given occasion that it is a formal cause is saying that health (in possession) is the form that in this case explains, while saying it is the final cause is saying that it is the goal towards which . . . . This does not entail that an explanation by reference to a form possessed is the same as one by reference to a goal. Typically they will differ. Thus typically a formal explanation explains why A is F by reference to the possession by A of the requisite form. But a final explanation typically supposes present lack of full possession. But of course, A's health, which is the final cause of his own activities and his body's reactions, will, once achieved, be the formal cause of a quiet life. Indeed, with living things the form is the formal cause of much activity just because it is what makes something act perfectly and its good state is what each thing aims at, and so the form is the final cause too of much activity.

13.2.4. Everything hangs, then, on the statement that pleasure is a *telos*, at least so far as evidence internal to

Book X is concerned. Yet as it stands this looks very weak. To begin with, the word '*telos*' is not a decisively purpose word like the English 'goal'. It means, equally, completion or perfection, and Aristotle commonly talks of the actualization of natural potentiality as *telos* (for examples of this use, e.g. *GA* 725b8, 736b4, 742b1; *de An.* 416b23; *Met.* Λ 1021b25). A being is incomplete in so far as it is in potency, is perfect in so far as it actualizes its nature, and so its actualization is its perfection (*telos*). So the use of the word is not decisive. Aristotle could be thinking that pleasure is the perfection of an actualization or condition rather than its goal.

13.2.5. Three further points about the Book X passage might make one hesitate about the final cause thesis. First the section where pleasure is called a *telos* is the end of a passage where Aristotle has been arguing that it is not a movement because, like sight, it is something perfect (*teleion*) and does not, like movements, aim at a *telos* and so become perfect only in achieving it. The use of '*telos*', '*teleion*' of sight in this passage is very much that of 'perfection', 'perfect' ('complete') rather than 'goal'. Secondly, the question that we are asking is not one of the form: 'For what does *X* φ?' The question is: 'What sort of thing is pleasure?' That it should be a form seems quite intelligible. That it should be the nature of something to be a goal is hard to make much of. So, indeed, is the idea that it should be the goal of an actualization (though see Ch. 16). Actualizations are perfections at which potentialities may, at a stretch, be said to be aimed and at which beings of course may aim. They are themselves, however, complete. The only apparent exceptions are imperfect actualizations, mentioned at *Phys.* 201b27 ff., but in the Book X terminology these would presumably count as movements. In general, then, only an imperfect actualization can be said to have a goal. There will, however, be that which makes an actualization perfect by way of form. Vision, for instance, may be perfect because of the relevant form, this being, of course, the form of animal whose vision is in question, which is what makes this sort of vision good vision for this animal. So the form that makes a given sort of life a good canine life is that whose presence is the actualization of the canine potentialities, including canine vision. Thus actualizations are made perfect by forms, but do not have goals. So the form may feature in formal explanations of them, but not in final ones. They may, however, be the final causes of activities aimed at perfecting actualizations, but that is a different matter. Thirdly, in the health illustration, health is the cause of *being healthy*, and this must surely be a formal explanation (*aitia esti tou hugiainein*: 1174b26).

13.2.6. The situation so far, then, is as follows: with living things one and the same thing is both the formal and the final explanation of behaviour, viz. the relevant form; but this is not to say that formal and final explanations are explanations of the same sort. So Aristotle's remarks identifying formal and final causes do not mean there is no dispute about pleasure. When it comes to the text of Book X one cannot argue from the frequency of Aristotle's use of health as an example of formal or final cause, since it must be capable of being either, according to context, nor does the use of the word '*telos*' tell us anything, since that indifferently means 'perfection' or 'goal' and, once again, a thing's '*telos*' may explain formally or finally according to context. Finally, health, in the illustration, explains being healthy, which is not an explanation by reference to purpose, but is a formal explanation.

3. God's pleasure a formal cause

13.3.1. It is important to realize that in his treatment of causes Aristotle is not simply concerned to analyse and categorize familiar ways of answering the question 'Why is X F?' Doubtless reflection on standard ways of explaining influenced his account, but he also has a view, partly inherited from Plato, as to the form an adequate explanation should take. This in turn is bound up with his overall view of the universe. The distinction of form and matter which underlies that between material and formal cause, is part of Aristotle's general account of change. Any change is coming-to-be something, and that implies that what changes is now potentially, but not yet actually, what it becomes (cf. e.g. *GC* 317b17 ff.). In general, only what is composed of matter and form can change; for matter is the potentiality for some other characteristic, and without that change is impossible. So changeable things are always composite (cf. e.g. *Met.* Θ 1050b15 ff., Λ 1069b15 ff.; *Phys.* 190b10–11). The heavenly bodies, which move eternally, have matter with regard to place (i.e. they are potentially at P_1 or P_2), but they are not, like normal natural objects, potentially in motion or at rest (*Met.* Θ 1050b15 ff.). An ordinary material object has the capacity to receive opposed characteristics and so to become or cease to be something; indeed its material constitution consists in not just a capacity but a tendency to change (*GC* I.3), while the form that constitutes its nature ensures a constant tendency towards the development in actuality of that form (*Phys.* II. 8). The unmoved mover is the perfection of being, that is he contains no potentiality to be anything else, but is the pure actualization of his nature (cf. *Met.* Λ 1072b), with no possibility of change. The rest of nature aspires after this perfection, but cannot attain it. Some things are in constant motion, and the process of coming-to-be goes on forever. The whole structure is one of imitation of the unchanging pure actualization of the divine (cf. *GC* 336b25 ff; *Met.* Λ 7.) Perishable beings cannot achieve true being, but the drive of their nature is to some approximation to it. In animate beings this is shown by the urge to procreation, achieving in the species a quasi-eternity unachievable by the individual (*de An.* II. 4).

13.3.2. The consequence is that final explanations are of two sorts. Any poplar will be geared to the manifestation of poplarhood, and its operations explained in that way; but poplarhood itself is a good in being some approximation to the perfect actualization of God, who is in this way the final cause of everything. So each kind of composite being aims at its own good, and has a good condition to which it can (intermittently) attain or between aspects of which it will change (cf. *EN* 1154b20–30); and there is one good, God, which all beings aim at; not that he can be attained, but he can be imitated, or be the point of their struggles.

13.3.3. Fairly clearly we have here an elaborate world view. God is at the peak, the perfection of actualization. The activity of the universe is motivated by love of him, and he is the basic final cause. Now plainly, if we are thinking of a final cause as explaining any change or motion, no final cause can apply to God. The description of him as pure actualization entails that he has no potentiality for change, and so there will be no change or motion to be explained. Yet God is stated by Aristotle to experience the highest pleasure in virtue of being the perfection of actualization (*Met.* Λ 1072b 13-30, and cf. *EN* 1154b24-8, 1178b7-28). It follows that in his case pleasure cannot be a final cause if a final cause is one that explains some change or movement. Yet any other version of a final cause makes it difficult to distinguish from a formal one. In short, it seems clear that God enjoys himself because pleasure is perfect actualization and God is the most perfect actualization. Since there is no sign of a different account of pleasure for God and humans it seems that Aristotle's view of pleasure, in Book X at least, is that it is perfect actualization. It follows, of course, that with humans it will commonly be the final cause of action. But it is the final cause because it is the form.

13.3.4. If the above is correct, then Aristotle believes that the 'real' pleasure of a thing of a given species consists in the perfection of actualization of the nature of the species, and that this in turn can be seen to be aspiring after that perfection of actualization which is the life of God. It is implicit in this that although, in a sense, every species has its own specific pleasures which it pursues, there is also a sense in which all species aspire after one and the same pleasure, in that they strive to approximate to the divine life. This is precisely what is suggested at *EN* 1153b25-32, where it is said that perhaps all living things pursue not the pleasure they think nor the one they would say they were pursuing, but the same one; for they all by nature have something divine in them.

13.3.5. When one says that pleasure is the formal cause of perfect actualization the question arises how one is thinking of forms. Is it the form of seeing that is the pleasure of

seeing? After all, it is a form that is a formal cause, and it
sounds a little odd either to call pleasure a form, or seeing.
The earlier exposition of formal causes was in terms of
'species'-forms. It would, of course be possible to opt for
agnosticism, but there seems no obvious reason why Aristotle
should not have thought of the 'species'-form as the form in
question. In God's case, it is the divine (perfect) life that is
the pleasure, and the form is not something added to life, but
its perfect actualization. With a being like man there will be
no episode of complete actualization. Only over a life could a
man manifest human nature; at any given time he will only
actualize aspects of it. So the form of man is only partially
manifested in particular actualizations. Still, in so far as these
are actualizations of human nature they are manifestations
of the form of man and it is their form that makes them
perfect actualizations of human nature. So with human
beings, the form in question that perfects 'activities' is the
form of man; and to talk of human pleasure and the form of
man (i.e. form of human life) is to talk of one and the same
thing. An account of the form of man is an account of the
good life for man which is an account of the pleasant life for
man.

4. The nature of pleasure in Books VII and X

13.4.1. We conclude, therefore, that in *Nicomachean
Ethics* X Aristotle is considering pleasure as the form of the
being in question, that is as the actualization of its nature. It
is now time to ask whether there is any significant difference
between Books VII and X in their views of pleasure. It has
been acknowledged that, as Owen points out, there is a
tendency in Book VII to talk of pleasure as what perfects
activities and so makes them pleasant. The question then is,
what sort of difference does this signify? This is of interest
at least in part because it has been commonly thought that
the Book X statement is slightly subtler, and so should be
taken as a later refinement (cf. 13.0.2). It has also sometimes
been thought that the opposite is true (cf. e.g. Webb).

13.4.2. Suppose we admit there is a terminological difference, and that whereas in Book X the interest is in what

makes actualizations pleasant in Book VII it is in the pleasant actualizations. One obvious reason for this could be the current state of disputes. At the time of writing of Book X Eudoxus and Plato dominate the discussion, and that dispute was over what makes the good life good. Eudoxus was for saying that it was its pleasantness, Plato for claiming (*a*) that some pleasures are bad, (*b*) that there are activities that are good not because they are pleasant, and (*c*) that what makes a life good is not its pleasantness but its order. To turn the tables on this critique it will be necessary to portray pleasure as what makes Plato's further activities good, as filling the role of order with respect to a life, and then to dismiss the bad pleasures. This will account for the criterion of reality for pleasures of Book X and also the interest in seeing them as what makes actualizations good. In Book VII the issues seem different. The point about different kinds of pleasure seems accepted on all sides. Consequently the issue is not whether pleasure is or is not the good but whether any pleasure is (the) good. The opposition may have a small selection of pleasures which it treats as the totality, but it is in no doubt about their plurality. The issue then is what should be allowed into the set of pleasures and whether any could be good.

13.4.3. Granting all this it is hard to see an incompatibility of substantial position between the two books. This can be seen by posing to each the other's question and seeing whether they would have to supply different answers. Suppose then that the Aristotle of Book X is asked: is any pleasant actualization a or the good? Clearly on the Book X view those actualizations will be pleasant which pleasure perfects or which are perfect. So the first question is: will the criteria for identifying pleasant actualizations differ from those of Book VII? We have already seen (cf. 11.3.12–16) that perfect actualization involves perfection of faculty and perfection of object. The first requires that the subject be in good condition for its kind, or in other words that it show a developed nature. This corresponds to the Book VII point that a pleasure is an actualization of a natural disposition, which is contrasted with something defective (cf. 1153a1,

1154b15–20). When it comes to perfection of object, this clearly entails a requirement for external goods. As has been pointed out perfect manifestation of perfect faculty is not sufficient for perfect actualization, and so a fine eye gazing at an ugly building is not a perfect actualzation of vision. Pleasure requires the provision of an appropriate environment. Now this is precisely what Book VII's lack of impediment requires (cf. 1153b16–19). Lack of impediment is required for perfect actualization which constitutes *eudaimonia* and external goods are required for lack of impediment. But lack of impediment entails pleasure, and so pleasure is required for *eudaimonia*. It also emerges from this passage that lack of impediment is needed for perfection of actualization, the other requirements being that one have a non-defective nature actualized. It seems, then, that the conditions that Book X would require for a perfect actualization are identical with those of Book VII, and if Aristotle had been asked whether any pleasant actualization was the good he would have had to say 'yes' (cf. 1177a22–7, b19–21), and for precisely the same reasons.

13.4.4. Suppose we reverse the procedure and ask the author of Book VII what makes an actualization into a pleasure in the formal way? Clearly he thinks the efficient cause of a pleasant actualization is perfection of natural disposition and perfection of object. But those do not simply produce an actualization. They produce a perfect actualization, and what is needed to make an actualization a pleasant one is, of course, that it be perfect, the actualization of a good nature without impediment, i.e. on a perfect object. Consequently, even allowing for the terminological difference it seems that each book would be committed to giving to the other's question an equivalent answer, and there seems no cause to suppose greater sophistication of position in the one than in the other.

5. The terminological differences

13.5.1. It should be noted, however, that the above suggests that the terminological difference implies a greater difference than in fact it does. The air of contrast comes from

speaking of forms as what, when added to actualizations
(or faculties and objects), perfect them. This suggests that a
form is not an actualization but can be added to one to
round it off and perfect it, like some tune-up additive to
one's motor oil. But this is a quite un-Aristotelian way of
thinking of forms. It is part of his reaction against the
Platonic way of talking to reject this implication and insist
that a form is an actualization (cf. *Met.* Θ 1050a4–b3, esp.
a15–16, b2–3). The form of dog is not added to something to
actualize it; rather a dog is considered with respect to its
form when its actualization is considered. But just as actualization is prior to potentiality, so perfection of actualization
is prior to partial actualization. The operations of imperfect
natures are only to be called actualizations by benefit of
some relation to perfect actualizations. A mediocre dog is
imperfect in form, but a perfect dog is in perfect form simply
in virtue of actualizing perfectly. This means that speaking of
actualization may not be enough for speaking of form, for we
should add the qualification 'perfect'. But this is an addition
in definition. There is not an added, formal, element in
reality that is stuck onto the actualization. The form is the
perfect actualization. Consequently, when Book X speaks of
pleasure as perfection added to actualization this does not
imply that it is something other than an actualization, but
that it is not just an actualization but a perfect one. Consequently the contrast with Book VII evaporates.

6. The difference in context

13.6.1. It seems, then, that Book VII shows no contrast
with the position of Book X. The changes are not in the
position but in the opposition, and therefore in the way the
issues are set up.

13.6.2. On any hypothesis about the relative dates for
Books VII and X it would seem that there is a difference of
atmosphere in their respective philosophical contexts. There
are indeed in Book VII those who think some pleasures very
desirable but not bodily ones or those with regard to which
the intemperate man is intemperate (1154a8–21). (If these
people objected to all bodily pleasures, as the discussion

suggests, they cannot include Plato (cf. *Phil.* 51).) Predominantly, however, the arguments considered are to the effect
that no pleasure is good — six arguments are cited as against
two for the view that not all pleasures are good and one for
the view that pleasure is not the good. The arguments that no
pleasure is good mostly seem to rely on taking 'pleasure'
to refer to bodily pleasures. The view that pleasure is a
perceptible *genesis* does not have to be confined to bodily
pleasures, but the *Timaeus* and *Philebus* suggest that that is
where it got its origin. The argument that a temperate man
avoids pleasure has any force only if 'pleasure' is confined
to the pleasures with which temperance is concerned. The
position that the wise man pursues a painless life, not a
pleasant one, is backed up by the point that pleasure disturbs
thought, and cites the effects of love-making (cf. *Phil.* 65e–
66a). The objection that children and animals pursue pleasure
again seems to have bodily pleasures in mind. Consequently
the point has to be made that these objections cover bodily
pleasures only (1153a29–35), and the question is raised, that
does not occur, naturally, in Book X, as to why bodily
pleasures have so monopolized the name (1153b33–1154a1).
Even those who think that some pleasures are very desirable
are portrayed as very hostile to bodily pleasures, and seem to
suppose that most people will think bodily pleasures more
desirable, so that they need to be attacked. This is why,
presumably, it is thought important (1154a22 ff.) to explain
just why bodily pleasures are thought to be so much more
desirable. Of this, again, there is no sign in Book X, but the
context of Book VII is one where bodily pleasures have
assumed considerable importance so that philosophers are
either talking as though they were all the pleasures there are,
or at least as though it has to be insisted that there are others
and that though bodily ones form the majority, they are
none of them desirable. The significance of these differences
we shall discuss later.

Chapter 14

Aristotle and Eudoxus

14.0.1. If we are right so far, Books VII and X of the *Nicomachean Ethics* show no disagreement on the nature of pleasure, but considerable difference of context. In this chapter we propose to concentrate on Book X. First, armed with the interpretation we have offered of the account of pleasure contained in it we shall examine Aristotle's position in relation to Eudoxus and Plato, and secondly we shall consider the place of this view in the *Nicomachean Ethics* as a whole. The first discussion will clear the ground for the discussion in Chapter 15 of the different contexts of the two treatments of pleasure. So far as the second is concerned, since the views on pleasure in the two books are identical, and since the *Eudemian Ethics* is in essential agreement with the *Nicomachean* in its other remarks on the importance of pleasure, we trust that what we have to say about Book X can be transferred to Book VII and accommodated to whatever view one has about the relation of either treatment to either *Ethics*.

14.0.2. It is sometimes thought (e.g. Festugière, pp. XVI-XVIII) that Aristotle rejects the Eudoxan position. For at 1174a8-10 he seems to acknowledge that pleasure is not the good, and on the grounds, presumably, given in the previous sentences, that we should not choose to live a life of childish pleasures even if it were free of distress, and that there are things such as knowledge, memory and excellence that we should choose even if no pleasure accrued. He clearly thinks it is difficult to get free of Eudoxus, as he in effect states at 1175a10-21, where he says that it is hard to decide whether we choose life for the sake of pleasure or vice versa. It remains that he rejects the equation of pleasure and the good, although he agrees that the pleasantest life and the good life are identical.

1. Did Aristotle reject Eudoxus?

14.1.1. Yet matters are not so clear as this. If Book IX 1170a13–b8 is to be taken in conjuction with Book X, it looks as though the remarks on the difficulty of saying whether we want life because of pleasure or pleasure because of life are intended seriously. That is to say, it looks as though Aristotle may have thought that correctly interpreted there was no assigning of priority to one over the other. For 'life' has to be taken as referring to the kind of life in question. With humans this means perceiving and thinking, not just staying alive. So the question becomes: do we want to live a life of thought and perception because it is pleasant or want pleasure because it is or leads to thought and perception? But life so conceived is something good and pleasant in itself, as also appears from the fact that everyone pursues it; and is to be chosen, especially by the good, because it is good and pleasant to them. The whole passage takes it that if we are considering what is pleasant in itself and what life for a given species consists in, then wanting life (i.e. the actualization of the species' nature) and wanting pleasure (i.e. what is in itself pleasant to that species) amount to the same thing, and there would be the same air of redundancy whether one said that one wants a full life because it is in itself pleasant or that one wanted what is in itself pleasant because that is a full life.

14.1.2. It looks then as though in Book IX Aristotle really does not think the issue settleable, because he does not think there is really an issue. This might incline one to take the remarks of Book X as seriously meant, if it were not for the apparent rejection of Eudoxus, but on this it is important to note that it falls short of outright rejection. We are still at this point with the rehearsal of opinions about pleasure, which is only declared over in the following sentence (1174a 11–12); and Aristotle only says that it *seems* clear that pleasure is nót the good, nor is every pleasure choiceworthy, but that some, varying in kinds or sources, are chooseable in themselves. Now the 'seems' could, of course, give Aristotle's judgement, but the immediate reminder that this concludes what is *said* about pleasure and distress makes it unlikely. Further, while he does later endorse the view that pleasures

differ in kind, (cf. 1175a21–1176a29) there is no taking up
of the view on sources (1173b25–8, 1174a10–11); and the
view that not every pleasure is choiceworthy (1175a9)
is only accepted in a qualified form, in that un-choiceworthy
ones turn out not really to be pleasures, because not pleasant
to the good man (1176a3–29). Not everything, then, governed
by, 'it seems clear . . . ' is endorsed by Aristotle, and so one
cannot assume that one element is intended to be endorsed.
In fact, at the end of this listing of views some have been
rejected in the course of exposition, while others are left in
unresolved opposition. Thus Eudoxus' claims (a) that everything pursues pleasure and so it is the good, (b) that everything avoids distress as evil, and so pleasure as the opposite of
distress must be good, and (c) that that is especially choiceworthy which is not chosen for the sake of something else,
are all left unchallenged. Similarly, Plato's counter-argument
that a pleasant life with intelligence is preferable to one
without is left unrefuted. Then we get a series of rejected
objections until we come to those who complain that some
pleasures are shameful (1173b20). Here various possibilities
are sketched without any being selected. Similarly the final
considerations about children and about knowledge are left
unargued, and that brings to an end the positions hostile to
the view that pleasure is the good. One is left, at this point,
in some disarray. There is no counter-argument to the
position that all pursue pleasure, but there is a rejection of
the position that what all pursue may not be the good
(1172b35 ff.). So that leaves a Eudoxan argument holding
the field. But Plato's counter-argument is also in the field.
Nowhere later is an explicit mention made of this conflict,
and what might have been an opportunity is missed
when at 1175a18–19 Aristotle sets aside the question of
whether we want life for pleasure or the other way round.
The suggestions that shameful pleasures are not really
pleasant and that pleasures differ in kind are both taken up,
but not the view that pleasures are choiceworthy in themselves but not from those sources, which, indeed, seems
inconsistent with Aristotle's final position. It seems, then,
that failing an unambiguous endorsement within the passage
we can infer nothing, but have to wait to see what Aristotle's
final position can do with these points.

2. Kinds of pleasure in defence of Eudoxus

14.2.1. Now as remarked earlier (cf. 8.3.7), it seems that Eudoxus put forward his views in a way that seemed to suppose that pleasures did not differ in kind, and that Plato thought that their mutual difference, not to say opposition, was something that was important to insist upon against Eudoxus. But Plato only makes this point with respect to different pleasures of different activities. Aristotle also takes up this point at length, but he adds the point (1176a5 ff.) that pleasures differ by species. Not only is the pleasure of debauchery distinct ·from the pleasure of intellectual discovery, but the pleasures of pigs differ from the pleasures of horses or humans. Clearly he has taken Plato's point and developed it. He also takes from Plato a verbal manoeuvre, that of distinguishing between real pleasures and others and equating relative reality of pleasure with relative pleasantness (cf. 1176a15-19, 1174b14-23). But all this Platonic influence is used to produce a Eudoxan-sounding conclusion. For it emerges that the important way for pleasures to differ in kind is by species. Different human pleasures do differ in kind, but so do human pleasures from porcine ones, and human pleasures are those specific to the human race. For judging these we do not, of course, rely on what degenerate members of the species enjoy (1176a15-16). What pleases someone in an advanced state of yellow fever does not figure among the pleasures specific to man, but what pleases the well-developed human (cf. 1170a13 ff., esp. 19-25). It is these things that are really pleasant, and so pleasantest. (This last is inferrable from the statement in 1174b19-23 that the most perfect actualizations are pleasantest). So Aristotle has devised a way of talking of real pleasures and relative pleasantness which enables him to hold the following points: each living thing by nature aspires to its good state, that is to the perfect actualization of its potentialities; but this means that it desires a certain kind of life; this life is one that contains the real pleasures of that species, and so is the pleasantest life attainable by that species; so each living thing wants/pursues the pleasantest life possible to it, and each particular desire, being aimed at the actualization of some potentiality, is directed at some pleasure. Plato's point about kinds of pleasure is thus accommodated, but instead of leading to an abandonment of Eudoxus is used to produce an adaptation of that position which is clearer and stronger. Aristotle's view on the nature of living things together with his extra point about the ways pleasures differ in kind combine to protect Eudoxus against Plato.

3. Aristotle and the *Philebus*

14.3.1. It is also interesting to note the antithesis between Aristotle and the *Philebus* on pleasure. In the *Philebus* pleasure is said to be indeterminate, something that needs· ordering. This view can seem plausible for two reasons: first, the simple fact that a life contains pleasures seems insufficient for showing it to be good; it is the selection and ordering of pleasures that is important; this order, which determines the arrangement, is what makes the life good. Secondly, some pleasures seem of their nature liable to get out of hand and to need the imposition of control if they are not simply to disrupt the good life. On the first, Aristotle can say that this seems so only if we fail to recognize the criterion of reality for pleasures. Once we recognize this it becomes clear that pleasure is what perfects an actualization, and, in relation to a life, what perfects the actualization of the nature in question. It is, in fact, on the determinant side of the determinant/indeterminate distinction, bringing determinateness to life by making it the perfect one of the relevant species. It thereby ensures a determinate form of actualization of each potentiality. This is implicit in the 'perfection' account of pleasure, is suggested in the consideration of the *Philebus* indeterminacy point (cf. esp. 1173a23-8), and is explicit in Book IX (cf. esp. 1170a19-25). As to the second point, the criterion of reality can be used again, in that the sorts of pleasure envisaged (e.g. at *Phil.* 52c) can be dismissed as not really pleasant. So pleasure is able in Aristotle to play a role analogous to that of the determinant in the *Philebus*. The point that if indeterminate it would not be the good seems to be taken, and so an analysis is devised which enables it to cross the boundary. Hence at 1173a23-8 he holds that Plato's arguments would not stop one assimilating pleasure to health, which he proceeds to do at 1174b25.

4. Resolution of difficulties

14.4.1. In all this, Book X seems carefully worked out to save Eudoxus from his critics, foremost among whom are Plato and the subtlers of the *Philebus*, with, of course, some later developments as well. If one looks at other hostile points left unresolved in the opening consideration of views, it again emerges that Aristotle's final view has an answer to them. Thus Plato's point, that a life of pleasure is made more desirable if intelligence is added, relies upon supposing that a human being living an unintelligent life could nevertheless be living a life of pleasure. But this ignores the point about pleasures of species. For such a human would not be living a life of human pleasures and so not a life really pleasant for humans; and since life for humans means a life of perception and thought it would not be living a pleasant life. Once this point is taken it becomes clear that at *Phil.* 20-2 we are given a false choice. The same goes for the point at 1174a 1-4, that no one would choose a life of childish pleasures or shameful pleasures. Since these would not be pleasant to him, it would therefore not be really pleasant and a person desiring such a life cannot strictly be said to be desiring pleasure or a pleasant life (cf. *EN* 1176b18-30; *EE* 1235b30-1236a6). Consequently this objection will not trouble Eudoxus as revamped by Aristotle. Again, the point that we should desire vision, memory, knowledge, and the excellences (1174a4-8) even if no pleasure followed begins to look strange. For, of course, we should desire good vision and memory, and the exercise of these on appropriate objects. But now it sounds strange to suggest that we should want these even if no pleasure accrued when it emerges that the perfections of these actualizations just are (human) pleasures. It consequently becomes obscure just what is being suggested by the counter-factual condition. This also shows that Socrates has no alternative when he opposes a life of intellectual exercise to one of pleasure; for proper intellectual exercise is a pleasure for any being capable of it.

14.4.2. It seems, then, that in Book X Aristotle is primarily concerned to defend a Eudoxan position against its critics, and that while the state of play is not exactly as it was left by the *Philebus*, the dispute as discernable there is clearly still exerting a considerable influence. It is also noticeable that Aristotle does think he can answer the question 'what is pleasure?' in a way of which Plato seemed to have despaired in the *Philebus*; and it is this that enables him, like Plato in the *Republic*, to tie his criterion of reality of pleasure to his analysis of the nature of pleasure.

5. The account of pleasure and the defence of Eudoxus

14.5.1. The analysis that Aristotle offers is quite unlike anything in Plato up to the *Philebus*. Of course, there would be suggestive elements. The view of nature that Aristotle has is in line with a common Greek tradition embracing most pre-Socratics as well as Plato. What is novel is the equation of pleasure with perfect actualization of potentialities. This serves to make pleasure an object of desire, (since all desire their good), while at the same time allowing that they may occur undesired — that is, without having been specifically desired prior to their occurrence. This move to assimilating pleasure to good operation may have been partly suggested by Plato's remark in the *Laws* (cf. 9.0.5) that a person enjoys himself if and only if he thinks he is doing well. As it stands, this clearly allows for people really to enjoy themselves even if they are doing very badly. While one could criticize such people as living in a fool's paradise, their folly would consist in thinking that they were doing well, not in thinking that they were enjoying themselves. Anyone who wished to hold a closer tie between pleasure and actually doing well might suggest that pleasure simply consisted in doing well. But this would be open to two objections; first, it seems peculiar to suggest of someone who thought he was doing very badly that he could be anything but displeased, and perhaps peculiar to suggest that he might normally still enjoy himself, (being pleased and enjoying do not get distinguished by Plato or Aristotle); secondly, this seems to allow for a person enjoying himself without realizing it — since one can do well without realizing it — and this has commonly been thought impossible.

14.5.2. Now Aristotle is talking of living things, and primarily humans, in the *Nicomachean Ethics*. The actualizations he speaks of are potentialities specific to the beings in question. Any human who is thin is potentially fat, who is standing is potentially falling. But these potentialities are common to non-sentient beings, and the perfect actualizations of these are not pleasures. It is the actualizations of perceptive and thought potentialities that are pleasures. One might think that these could be actualized without one's realizing. If a person absorbed in conversation neatly side-steps a puddle without realizing it, then surely their visual capacity was actualized although *ex hypothesi* they did not realize it. Whatever the truth may be here, in Book IX Aristotle seems clearly to hold that with humans at least if perception or thought is actualized the subject realizes that it is actualized (1170a29–b1 and cf. *de An*. III. 2). Now it does not follow, of course, that if A is actualizing a given potentiality perfectly A realizes that it is perfect, or even thinks that it is good. But Aristotle does seem to think (1176a9–12, 1099a7–11) that to enjoy X is to love X or to be fond of X, and this seems to involve taking it as an object of desire, or a good. Consequently one would expect him to hold that if A enjoys X, A is fond of X and so thinks having X a good thing. In other words, one would expect him to hold that if A enjoys X, i.e. is actualizing well in respect of X, then A will think his actualizing in respect of X to be a good thing, that is a good actualization. Aristotle's position, however, still allows for error about enjoyment. For all that follows is that if A is (really) enjoying X, then A's actualization approximates in some degree to perfect actualization. It does not follow that there is some degree to which it both does approximate and A believes it to approximate. So a person enjoying something will be actualizing a potentiality with some approximation to perfection, but he may well believe that it is perfection itself, or he may (although it is less clear that Aristotle could accept this) be actualizing perfectly while considering his actualization only moderately good. The outcome is that Aristotle can take Plato's hint on the connection of pleasure with belief in well-doing and get all the advantages of tying pleasure to perfection of actualization while preserving the plausible view about belief.

14.5.3. Plato is not the only philosopher against whom Eudoxus needs to be defended. As has been remarked, the subtlers of the *Philebus* would be diametrically opposed to Eudoxus. Not only is their thesis that no pleasure can be a good the clear contrary of Eudoxus', but it involves outright rejection of his third argument, that pleasure cannot be for the sake of anything else. Aristotle goes to considerable trouble to refute them first in the passage explicitly given to their rejection and then when he begins to expound his own view (cf. 12.5).

14.5.4. If we consider Eudoxus' four arguments, we get the following situation:

(i) The principle that what all pursue is good is accepted in the initial consideration of views (1172b35–1173a5). Whether all pursue pleasure is there left in abeyance.

(ii) The argument that pain is evil and avoided and so its opposite must be good is upheld (1173a5–13).

(iii) One major set of objections to the point that pleasure is never for the sake of anything else is met when the subtlers are refuted.

(iv) Plato is acknowledged to be right in his objection that the good must be perfect, i.e. such that nothing, if added to it will improve it. Eudoxus' principle that X is the good if its addition improves anything is rejected.

14.5.5. Since, in pursuing its own good any living thing is pursuing a good life, that is a life of perfect actualization of its specific capacities, the account of pleasure as perfection of actualization ensures that all beings do pursue pleasure. Since no one pursues the good for the sake of anything else, since it is all that could be desired, Eudoxus' third point is made good. Plato's point that pleasures differ in kind is accepted, but is turned from an objection into a defence, since it emerges that all pursue pleasure in the sense that the members of any species pursue the pleasures of that species, that is, aim for the best life of that species. As has been pointed out (cf. 14.4), Aristotle can now reject the dual suggestion of the *Philebus* that (*a*) there might be a human life of intelligent activity without pleasure or (*b*) that there might be a life of (human) pleasure without intellectual activity.

14.5.6. When one reflects on the way in which Eudoxus' thesis is saved, while many of the essentials of Plato are preserved, one can only admire the subtlety and ingenuity of the Book X treatment. It is a classical example of Aristotle 'preserving the truth' in his predecessors.

6. The role of pleasure in the *Nicomachean Ethics*: explaining the facts

14.6.1. It should now be possible to see the connection between the official account and remarks on the importance of pleasure found in the other books. It is tempting when thinking of Aristotle on pleasure to take the two treatments in Book VII and Book X in isolation. If one does this it is easy to ignore the introductory remarks to each discussion and take the passages as primarily concerned to give an account of the nature of pleasure. This has become a stronger temptation recently among English-speaking philosophers since the subject of pleasure has intrigued many as giving rise to interesting problems in the philosophy of mind. Further, Aristotle's treatments have been influential in these discussions. Yet this leads to a risk of distorting Aristotle. For one point that has emerged is that Aristotle is not primarily concerned with the question 'What is said of *A* when it is said of him that he enjoys some *X*?' nor even with the question 'What has to be true of *A* if in the vulgar use of the words it is going to be true that he enjoys something?' His prime interest is ethical, and his purpose to show that in some sense pleasure is the good. This leads him to select certain pleasures and reject others as not really pleasures although undoubtedly it would be true to say of the subjects in the usual use of the Greek word for 'enjoy' that they were enjoying something. Shameful pleasures of masochists or sadists are enjoyed although according to Aristotle they are not real pleasures.

14.6.2. Of course Aristotle's theory does imply a partial theory about the conditions under which enjoyment occurs, but he is not interested in it so much for its power to do that as for its power to yield the result that pleasure is the good, and to explain the importance of the topic of pleasure for the moralist and political theorist. It is true, however, that Aristotle thinks that there are certain facts about pleasure which any theory ought to be able to explain, and some of the facts at least would be of just as much interest to a philosopher of mind as to a moralist. Thus he thinks that in fact the pleasure of ϕ-ing improves one's ϕ-ing and it is only other pleasures that would prove a distraction. He also thinks that in some sense pleasure is an object of desire pursued for its own sake. Other facts are more directly ethical. Thus it seems obvious (1099a17 ff.) that a good man must take pleasure in acting well, and that the good life must at least be to some extent pleasant. The theory has to explain all these facts, and it also has to justify certain positions, such as that virtue is concerned with pleasure and pain, and explain what is true in the various views on pleasure that various thinkers have put forward.

14.6.3. We shall consider later (cf. 14.9) whether the supposed facts are facts. For the moment it will suffice to see how the theory would explain them, and what light it throws on Aristotle's view on the importance of pleasure. To begin with, however, it may help to explain the qualification 'partial' at the beginning of the previous paragraph. Remarks in 1174b14 ff. about relative degrees of pleasure might suggest the following picture: when a perfect faculty is operating on a perfect object, there is the highest pleasure. Pleasure can occur, of course, in less perfect conditions, but the degree of enjoyment is a function of the degree of excellence of actualization, which is in turn a function of the degrees of excellence of faculty and object. If neither of the latter has any excellence then there is no pleasure. Now we might hope that this would also cover 'unreal' pleasures. After all, if someone is sick and enjoys something that would revolt them if well, it remains that some part of the constitution is in good order and the object enjoyed might be held to be a not wholly inappropriate object for that element in the constitution. So while a person in good condition would not enjoy it, there is some approximation to good condition, and it is this that explains such enjoyment as occurs.

14.6.4. This, however, sits ill with some of Aristotle's remarks. To begin with, he seems in 1176a8–29 to want to say that shameful pleasures should not be called pleasures. At the same time (1175b24–9) he seems prepared to allow that there are bad actualizations, with bad pleasures. This might seem to suggest that his view of pleasure as a perfect actualization resulting from a combination of good faculty and good object is only intended to apply to the pleasures of the species, the real pleasures. In so far as there is a general theory of pleasure, a pleasure is a (full?) actualization of potentiality. If it is a deplorable actualization of a deplorable potentiality (e.g. sadism) then it is a deplorable pleasure. If excellent, then excellent and a real pleasure. There is no call to think of sadistic pleasures as approximations, however faint, to perfection.

14.6.5. A possible compromise solution goes as follows: Aristotle does not have to hold that all pleasure is an approximation to perfect actualization, but on the other hand he does not have to think that bad actualizations can be detached entirely from man's nature, so that while there are real pleasures which are actualizations of human nature there are bad ones that are not. He could hold that the man in good condition is central for understanding pleasure, but that non-standard cases are non-standard in different ways. A sick man may be seen in terms of some good part of his nature struggling towards proper actualization. A sadist, on the other hand, may be seen as actualizing a corruption of something good, as perhaps suggested, but no more, by the language of 1176a20–2: 'It is not surprising if what he finds offensive is pleasant to someone: for there are many ways in which men are corrupted and damaged.' In that case we should have to say that wherever pleasure occurs either some natural potentiality is perfectly actualized, or is achieved as well as possible under imperfect conditions, or is corrupted and is actualized as well as possible in corrupt form. No doubt there are lurking dangers of trivialization here but it could be kept interesting so long as allowance was made for the theoretical possibility of showing an actualization to be bad but not a distortion of something good. Then the explanation of sadism might be that it is a feature of a fully developed man to enjoy the exercise of proper power and authority. It is the tendency to this that a sadist displays, but he has a wrong conception of the admirable exercise of power. We can see how it is related to the good man's, and his practices are doubtless pleasant because they conform to this incorrect conception, whereas they would revolt him if he had a proper conception. His condition has some relation to perfect actualization and perfect object, and if that relation did not hold there would be no pleasure.

14.6.6. Even so, Aristotle would seem only to have a theory covering enjoyments of people whose enjoyment has to be explained by reference to some failure to be normal. There are, however, on the face of it things which people enjoy which they do not enjoy just because of some deformity, nor is it obvious that failure to enjoy them would show some failure to reach a standard of full development. Thus some people enjoy collecting things, while others have no interest in acquiring collections of anything. Some people enjoy teasing puzzles, others are quite indifferent to them. It seems hard either to require of a good man that he enjoy collecting either stamps or farthings or old books or . . . , or to hold that anyone who does enjoy such things is in some way defective, so that these things are not really pleasant but only pleasant to someone in this unfortunate condition.

7. The ethical function of the theory

14.7.1. The fact is that Aristotle is not really setting himself to work out the conditions under which A will enjoy X, for any A and X. His prime interest is in whether pleasure is the good, and if his theory allows him to deal with objections to that he is happy enough. But the obvious objections there come from pleasures of sick people or bad people and so the important thing is to be able to cover these cases. So far as idiosyncratic pleasures go they may be manifestations of some general faculty and under that heading count as species-determining activities.

14.7.2. *Pleasure and distraction*. Granted this limitation, he will be able to explain the fact about distraction. For if pleasure is (somehow related to) perfect actualization, then of course the more a person enjoys playing the flute or solving a problem, the more perfect the actualization, whereas if a person is distracted they will do these things worse. But other pleasures will distract, for another pleasure is always a relatively perfect actualization of another potentiality, and with beings limited as regards the number of potentialities that are co-actualizable these will fight for domination. So if Aristotle is enjoying solving a problem and overhears Plato playing the flute, his listening to the flute will become relatively perfected, which will, of course, compete with the perfection of his problem solving. This is going to be an important point for Aristotle, for it means that the right pleasures (the real ones) so far from being avoided must be cultivated, since they will improve the actualization of good potentialities, and this affects his educational programme.

14.7.3. '*A enjoys what A is fond of*'. Then it seems to him in some way obvious (cf. *EN* 1099a7–14; *EE* 1235b19–1236a16) that that is pleasant to *A* of which *A* is fond, and that somehow Eudoxus is right that every living thing pursues pleasure. The first will make it obvious that a good life must be pleasant to a lover of virtue, if achieved. The account of pleasure makes it clear how this, of course, must be so. For what the lover of virtue (excellence) achieves is a life of perfect actualization, viz. pleasure. Also the theory explains how Eudoxus is right. For since every living thing by nature aims at the best life possible for it, and that is precisely the really pleasant life for it, each living thing by nature aims at what is really pleasant for it. On the other hand there are various sorts of natural deformation which either make something unusual good for the subject in its special circumstances, or make the subject mistake its good and pursue some degenerate end. In these circumstances, something other than what is really pleasant is enjoyed, but still what the subject is fond of is pleasant to *it*. It does not follow that it is really pleasant, but this simply means that corresponding to the distinction between real and apparent good must be one between real and apparent pleasure. It remains that what *A* is fond of is pleasant to *A* and that if *A* is in good condition what he is fond of is the same as what is really pleasant; and that all living things pursue pleasure in that (*a*) they all pursue what is pleasant to them and (*b*) the 'true' object of their pursuit is what is truly pleasant, i.e. the perfect actualization of their natures.

14.7.4. *Pleasure in virtuous action.* In the light of this it becomes clear that a good man must take pleasure in his good actions (cf. *EN* 1099a7–20; *EE* 1249a18–21). For if his actions are good then they are done in the right circumstances, for the right reason, from the right disposition, to the right extent, and so on. In other words, they are actualizations of a well-developed nature in relation to the proper objects. But in that case the actualizations are perfect, and so pleasant. It might be complained that surely a really virtuous person would, for instance, stand by a friend who had been publicly disgraced even at the cost of himself suffering obloquy and shame. Yet he would hardly enjoy it, and there would surely be something almost masochistic about doing so. The point will be taken up in the next chapter. For the moment it is enough to note that it is a very un-Aristotelian conception of excellence. It is no part of the picture of an ideal man to supply him with disreputable friends, nor are they proper objects of an affectionate nature. That is to say, it is not by reference to such persons that one understands the function of affectionate tendencies. They are to be understood in the context of the bond between good men. Of course, a person whose nature is well-developed may be fond of someone who falls on bad times. For instance, his friend might have been disgraced through an unjust accusation. In that case because of his good condition he will suffer more than most. Similarly, the function of the intellect is to be understood in relation to universal truths and valid arguments. A good mind may be brought into contact with falsehood and invalidity, and will suffer from the contact more than others. Yet while such suffering may be a measure of the excellence, intellectual or moral, of the subject, it is not in such circumstances that human excellence is seen to flourish, nor why it is excellent understood. For this, one needs to see human nature developed in its proper environment. There one sees that nature in relation to its proper objects, and its value shows clearly. This is why the actualization of man's nature (*eudaimonia*) requires external goods (*EN* 1099a31-3), that is proper conditions apart from its own condition of character. In the examples above it is the failure of these conditions to obtain that makes the actualization not one that will enter as a paradigm in a description of *eudaimonia*, just because it does not display human nature in ideal operation but only struggling with un-ideal circumstances. But the same failure would lead one to expect it was not a pleasure. Aristotle would think that choosing such examples as ones that especially show excellence was like demonstrating the merits of a mowing machine by trying it out on brushwood: it may be that only a very good mowing machine would break down so quickly, but it is a bizarre illustration of its excellence, and that means its operation in proper conditions. Everyone expects the best life to be pleasant, and Aristotle's theory explains how indeed it must be, for the good man will obviously enjoy his virtuous acts.

14.7.5. *Ethics concerned with pleasure and pain.* Finally it becomes clear how everyone's suspicions and Aristotle's declarations that ethics is concerned with pleasure and pain are right. Some of the truth in these views is unexciting. Thus (*EN* 1104b16-18; *EE* 1220a35-8) the use of punishment illustrates the point. For punishment is a form of cure; and all cures work through opposites; but punishment cures by means of distress, and so must be counteracting the (vicious) pleasure. But also Plato (cf. *Laws* 643c-d) declared pleasure and distress to be basic educational material. An educationalist should enable children to enjoy and disenjoy in a way that will lead to their loving what is good and hating what is bad. As put here it is quite possible that Plato is simply thinking that one should, say, make mathematics fun for children, so that they like doing it until such time as they come to see its value and do it for its own sake and not just because they enjoy it. The initial pleasure might consist in various games associated with numbers, and not be precisely enjoyment of mathematics. The important point is that with the young all pills should be sugared. Within Aristotle's theory, however, getting people to enjoy the right things (*EN* 1104b11–13, cf. *EE* 1227a39–b12) will simply be training them to develop their faculties and exercise them on appropriate objects, which is directly educating them to excellence. Pleasure is thus not just a tool. If you succeed in getting people to enjoy the right things, then just because you have got them to actualize perfectly you have got them to perform in accordance with excellence and so have brought them to the good life. Real enjoyment is the whole aim of education.

14.7.6. Then ethics is concerned with the regulation of actions and passions. So far as actions are concerned it is its function to work out what the good actions are. But these are the actions of a good man. They are also more. Munificence for instance, is a virtue, but clearly can only be exercised in certain sorts of social context where there are exceptional wealth and deserving objects of munificence. The virtues require external goods for their manifestation, and so we come back to the point that concern about right acts turns out to be concern for actualizations of perfect dispositions on perfect objects, i.e. pleasures. When we turn to passions, Aristotle seems to think that every passion has correlative pleasure and pain (*EN* 1104b13–16, cf. *EE* 1220b11–15) or that they are all ways of being pleased or distressed (*EN* 1106b16–21). He might be thinking one of two things. First, the point might be that obviously to feel grateful is to be pleased about something, to be angry or afraid to be distressed about something. So every passion is either a way of being pleased or a way of being distressed. But also they involve judgments on what it is good to receive, or should be resented or avoided. Clearly it will be an educator's job to inculcate the right views on these matters and so, quite generally, get people to be pleased and distressed by the right things. Alternatively, he might think of each passion as, according to circumstance, a form of pleasure or distress. Thus it is the very same passion that makes one pleased at the sight of justice, distressed at the sight of injustice, pleased at the recognition of security, distressed at the recognition of danger. Once again, the same educational significance would attach to getting the passions rightly directed.

8. The accommodation of obvious facts and current views

14.8.1. In short, the view of pleasure enables Aristotle to account for what he considers to be obvious facts and to accommodate views on the value of pleasure both as a goal and in education that were common in his day. In the latter respect, of course, his view does not show all his predecessors to have been right, only to have been some way along the right road. His own position is a subtle and thorough-going vindication of the insights of Eudoxus, though with a view of the nature of pleasure which should secure him against the unworthy suspicions of pleasure-loving from which Eudoxus' views seem to have suffered. For it is one of the noticeable facts about Aristotle's defence of Eudoxus that he preserves large amounts of Plato too. He can preserve, of course, Plato's hostility to sybaritism, but also Plato's preference for tranquil pleasures and his association of the good life with the divine life. For on Aristotle's view pleasure goes with perfection of actualization, whereas change and becoming are contrasted with perfect actualization. So the highest pleasures attach to the most perfectly actualizable, that which is by nature least liable to change, *theōria*. The remark of Book VII, that pleasure is to be found in tranquillity rather than motion is fully consonant with the position of Book X. Further, *theōria*, which is the highest pleasure, is also the actualization of what is most divine in us. Of course in Aristotle's view God is not so active as in Plato's, but it remains true that the highest form of human life is that which approximates to the divine life — but that is one and the same thing as approximating to the pleasantest life.

14.8.2. In all this no question has been raised as to the status of the supposed facts that Aristotle purports to explain. Yet just as Plato (cf. 6.7.2) showed signs of being ruled by theory in his selection of facts, so Aristotle's view of the facts seems to be heavily influenced by his theory. We conclude this chapter with an assessment of the success of his theory in accounting for the facts.

9. Aristotle's facts

14.9.1. The type of criticism that can be levelled at Aristotle can be illustrated by considering three examples: first, his view that pleasures do not hinder 'activity', secondly, the position that the good man takes pleasures in his virtuous acts, and thirdly, that A is fond of just and only what is pleasant to him. In each case it looks as though Aristotle takes something as obvious which his theory brings out as true, and whose truth it perhaps even explains. Yet in such cases it becomes difficult to determine to what extent the truth seemed obvious and so presented a requirement on the theory and to what extent the theory, seeming increasingly acceptable, made it seem obvious that these were the facts. In Aristotle's case his theory must have seemed so neatly to meet so many *desiderata* as to set up a bandwagon effect.

14.9.2. *Pleasure and distraction.* To begin with Aristotle's position looks like a general truth of observation. Of course, in a sense, pleasures are a distraction, and so if, say, one is thinking particularly of those that make up a life of pleasure, it is natural to think of them as distracting one from the good life and so hindering the actualization of one's nature. On the other hand a little reflection suggests that even if we concentrate on these pleasures they serve as hindrances only to other activities. The pleasure of serious music may hinder one's enjoyment of an ice-cream or vice versa, but surely the pleasure of listening to serious music confirms rather than hinders one's listening. If, with Plato and Aristotle, we allow for a wider range of pleasures, this point still holds. The more a person is enjoying a book the more concentrated his reading is likely to be. It is the intrusion of other pleasures that is likely to distract or prove a hindrance. Consequently one would expect that if a good man enjoys his good acts, the greater his pleasure the better, for so far from hindering his performance it will promote it.

14.9.3. The more one considers such examples the more convincing it can seem. And yet, as Urmson points out, someone engaged in research may become so excited as barely to be able to continue. The pleasure of discovery may be so great as to send him to his pipe and result in feverish pacing to and fro in order to calm him for further progress. So the (or at least a) pleasure in discovery may after all hinder one's intellectual actualization.

14.9.4. It might be complained that we need to distinguish between enjoyment of intellectual discovery and pleasure at the realization or illusion that one is succeeding at it or engaged in it. It is only the first that Aristotle has to hold prospers the activity. The second is not an *oikeia* pleasure, one peculiar to the activity. Yet if he took this line Aristotle would be faced with a choice: (*a*) he could allow there to be pleasures associated with an actualization, and in some sense pleasures *of* that actualization, which were not themselves enjoyments of that actualization and which did not fit his analysis, or (*b*) he could show how Urmson's example is an enjoyment which does fit his analysis. The first should obviously seem objectionable, so how might he fare on the second? The examples cited to make the facts seem acceptable in advance of theory certainly do best if described in English in terms of enjoyment, and one might expect that when described in Greek they would be interpreted in ways appropriate to the English notion of enjoyment. Is it plausible to describe Urmson's restless excitement as enjoyment? What, for instance, is he enjoying? Well, one might suggest, thinking to himself what a clever fellow he is, how marvellously everything is starting to fit into place, and so on. Certainly a person could be distracted from his speculations by the enjoyment of such thoughts, but there do seem to be different possibilities here. After all, the person distracted by such thoughts does characteristically want both to day-dream and get on with his work. He is pulled in two directions. But Urmson seems to be describing someone in a different state, someone who is not wanting to think how clever he is and so on, but who is so excited/pleased with his progress that he both wants to get on but is taken all of a dither and cannot. His frustration is not from being pulled in two directions, but from being disabled by his pleasure from going in the one direction he wants to go. If we think of someone's pleasure in making progress with some delicate physical operation, as in surgery or in a balancing act, the point becomes more obvious.

14.9.5. Even if we stay with examples of enjoyment Aristotle's point is open to question. Suppose Jane is attending a review. If she enjoys it she will presumably enjoy the jokes. If she is a giggly type her enjoyment of the jokes will take the form of laughing. If she laughs a lot that will impede her listening to the jokes. So what happens if she is helpless with laughter? Has she stopped enjoying the show? It sounds unlikely. Does she not enjoy the joke she is laughing at? But it is because she enjoys it that she laughs. Yet surely she cannot be said to be *enjoying* the joke? Certainly there is some oddity about this continuous present to cover her laughter once the joke is finished. Even if we bring in memory, she may have forgotten what the joke is. Then what is she enjoying? Perhaps she is enjoying laughing. Yet that seems an odd statement, for it suggests that laughing is sufficient for the enjoyment, and there seems no reason to suppose that Jane is an easily pleased person who simply has to laugh to enjoy herself. Her laughter is the form her enjoyment of the joke takes. Yet this is just the trouble, for she is helpless with laughter and in that state very likely has trouble remembering precisely what the joke is. In short, it is difficult to find an actualization such that this enjoyment furthers it and is in some way the enjoyment of it. Listening and laughing seem the two best candidates and both are objectionable.

14.9.6. Now the point is that these examples make Aristotle's 'facts' seem less obvious. Of course, Aristotle might now refer to his theory and claim that he can in these cases isolate perfect actualizations that these pleasures are and which they further, but then these cannot be the actualizations with which we should intuitively associate the pleasures. Thus it may be that laughing is the actualization of Jane's nature that is perfected. But this will mean that the theory will have to separate the laughing from the enjoyment of the joke, and so bring out that contrary to our expectation there are two pleasures here. In that case the theory is requiring a re-description of the facts in order to stop them being recalcitrant. That is another way of saying that it is not initially obvious that the facts are as Aristotle claims so that it is in favour of his theory that it would require them to be like that.

14.9.7. In addition, it has to be remembered that the above contains only speculation as to what Aristotle might say in face of these examples. In fact, of course, he does not consider them. This suggests that possibly the theory made it easier for him to think of examples that confirmed it and so was governing his selection of examples. One small point also suggests that in this area it influenced his view of the facts. For he cites in his favour the point that at a play those who are fond of sweets eat sweets more when the play is poor, less when it is good (*EN* 1175b10–13). The point is that as one's play appreciation is actualized one's sweet activity diminishes, as one's sweet activity increases one's play appreciation diminishes. Yet this suggests a selective view of the sweet-eating evidence. Children, for instance, will indeed eat sweets when bored; but often sweet-eating also increases with growth of excited involvement, so that in times of tension a bag may be demolished almost without the child's realizing it. Nor could Aristotle object that then the child did not enjoy the sweets, whereas he is talking of pleasures. For he is only talking of pleasures in respect of their correlation with augmented or diminished performance of activities described without reference to pleasure. The counter-example simply shows that a heightening of one activity may diminish the pleasure of another even if it does not diminish the activity.

14.9.8. In short, Aristotle's facts are not obviously facts. There are examples of pleasures which are not obvious cases of enjoyment that fail to fit his view; and there are enjoyments which fail. This suggests that, without noticing, Aristotle is ignoring examples not conforming to the enjoyment model, and within the latter ignoring those which do not fit the theory, as well as misconceiving some of the facts he cites in his favour. On the first, a closer attention to differences of expressions might have helped, but for the rest it is a wider range of examples that is needed.

14.9.9. *Enjoying virtue*. That a good man should take pleasure in his virtuous acts might have seemed acceptable to Aristotle independently of theory for two different sorts of reason. First, the common opinions suggest it. Thus many people think pleasure is the good, and although they equate this with taking some pleasures only, and some of them dubious pleasures at that, as the good, still their taking that as the description of their good cannot go for nothing. Then others at least admit that the good life must be pleasant, and others again assert that pleasure is the good in some more refined sense than the vulgar opinion. It is thus a widespread human opinion that the good life is a pleasant life. But in judging the good life for any species of animal we have to discern what is generally pursued and work out the norm on that basis. With humans what they say they are after, especially on reflection, must also be held to carry weight. They are not likely all to be wrong about what they aspire after, or in their conception of the good for man. So the presumption is that the good life is at least pleasant, and so that the good man will enjoy his life, and so (many of) the activities of his life.

14.9.10. Secondly, common criteria for virtue suggest it. The first consideration is just the fairly weak one that the good life must be pleasant. But at *EN* 1099a17–20 Aristotle says that no one would call a man just or liberal who did not take pleasure in just or liberal acts. In other words, he thinks that there is an obvious and well-accepted criterion for virtue which ensures that a man will only be allowed as virtuous if he takes pleasure in the acts of virtue. It is interesting to ask what such an obvious criterion might be. The English 'take pleasure in . . . ' has been used because like the Greek verbs it is ambiguous. Thus one might so use the expression that '*A* takes pleasure in ϕ-ing' is true if and only if '*A* enjoys ϕ-ing' is true. Yet this would yield a highly implausible doctrine of virtue. As we shall see in a moment, in Aristotle's view courage is shown primarily in face of death in battle, but it is not very plausible to suppose that a really brave man will revel in dying in battle, the more so the slower, more agonizing, and more noble his death. It does, however, seem plausible to suppose that a brave man should not grudge risking his life in a noble cause, nor drag his feet resentfully towards death, making a fuss about it (*lupoumenos*) at every step. He should go gladly to his death, and even, at a slight stretch, take pleasure in such noble deeds. This last will more easily fit the Greek words than it will the expression 'take pleasure in . . . ', but the latter might stretch to equivalence with 'do gladly . . . ' and so approach 'do willingly'. Of course, such a criterion will seem more obviously acceptable if one thinks of virtue as shown not in the struggle for mastery but in the condition of having achieved it, but that is precisely what is characteristic of Greek conceptions of *aretē*.

14.9.11. If Aristotle saw it this way, then he should realize that showing that a good man will gladly do his virtuous acts is not equivalent to showing that he will enjoy any of his acts let alone his virtuous ones. Consequently, while in some sense pleasure may characterize the good man's actions, it is not in the sense of enjoyment, although this would be what the first set of common opinions mentioned would suggest. This raises the possibility that Aristotle is ignoring the difference between '*A* ϕs with pleasure' and '*A* enjoys ϕ-ing'. The question is, which wins?

14.9.12. If one turns to Aristotle's treatment of courage, it looks as though he is interpreting 'the good man takes pleasure in good acts' as 'the good man enjoys doing good acts'. Otherwise it is difficult to understand the problem he gets into at *EN* 1117a29 ff. On the other hand courage is an obvious difficulty for anyone who holds that a good man enjoys his virtuous acts, especially if he holds an Aristotelian view of the good man. As Aristotle points out in the passage cited (and cf. *EN* 1115a25-35), courage is displayed at its height in undergoing death in war for a noble cause. But a good man, being rational, will reasonably be very distressed at the prospect of death, since death is the loss of life and *ex hypothesi* he has a better life to lose than others. So far we might infer that either a brave man will not willingly sacrifice his life, or that the experience will be distressing rather than enjoyed. It is his solution that suggests that he is thinking in the latter way.

14.9.13. What Aristotle does, is to draw an analogy with wrestlers or boxers. He suggests that the *telos* (goal, completion) of courageous action is pleasant, but the surrounding circumstances distressing. Similarly, to a boxer the goal, the crown and so on, is pleasant although the blows are painful. Since, he says, the goal is small (*sic*), it seems to have no pleasure. If this sort of thing holds with courage one could hold that the *telos* is pleasant but is diminished by the distressing circumstances, and so pleasant actualization is not found in all the virtues except in so far as the *telos* is achieved (1117b15–16).

14.9.14. It is not clear at first sight what is going on here, but the boxing analogy does not look very appropriate if there is a problem about doing things gladly, at least not as developed by Aristotle. Of course, reference to a crown of victory might explain very well why a boxer was pleased to box, and why he gladly continued to the very end. There might be a problem as to how anyone could be pleased to embark on a wholly unpleasant enterprise; but once we realize the pleasure in prospect there is no great problem. Aristotle, however, puts the difficulty strangely. He says that the goal is diminished or small (*mikron on to hou heneka*) and so seems not to be pleasant. This suggests that his problem is about the boxer enjoying the bout. The bout has a point which is pleasant, but the pleasure it supplies in the course of the bout is very little. No doubt. Indeed one may suspect that a boxer might not have it in mind at all in the course of the bout and get no pleasure. It looks as though Aristotle is thinking that he must get a *little*, but that the pleasure really comes with the accomplishment of the goal. But, of course, it is not his fighting gladly that comes with the accomplishment of his goal. Rather that is when he will really start enjoying himself. This has some plausibility applied to boxing, and we have the official doctrine that pleasure comes in the completion of the activity. The application to courage, however, is problematic. Aristotle hopes to have shown that with some *aretai* pleasant actualization does not arise, except in so far as the *telos* is achieved.

Presumably courage is accommodated because we can see that the brave man is like the pugilist; he is so beset with distress, that the *telos* is diminished, and pleasure has to await its achievement. Unfortunately the analogy is weak at the crucial point. The plausibility of the pugilist example lies in the fact that receiving the crown happens when the distress is all over, and so it is natural to think that the pleasure comes then, and that by then the pain must be over. But for the brave man the *telos* is *to kalon* — the noble. It is not some crown in some future life, after the suffering is over. On the contrary, nobility is achieved precisely in facing death, and nothing seems either good or bad to a dead man (*EN* 1115a26-7). It is precisely this prospect of an end to life and so to his good that makes the prospect of death so distressing for a good man (1117b9-13), but it is just here that his courage shows in choosing the noble in preference to these goods. What makes the death noble is presumably that it is undergone in battle for a noble cause. But granted those conditions, the acts of risking and undergoing death surely already achieve nobility. There seems to be a stark choice; either the *kalon* is not integral to the act but only achieved as a later crown after death, or it is integral to the act and is achieved precisely by it. If the first, then in many cases of real courage only a fool (and therefore never a good man) could suppose the noble to be or to be going to be pleasant, since *ex hypothesi* nothing is pleasant to a dead man and the noble is only achieved with death. If the second, then since pleasure is present in proportion to achievement of the end, the brave man must reach his peak of enjoyment on the point of death. (This is, indeed, the implausible thesis propounded in Book IX (1169a18-26).) For while he will have been achieving nobility perhaps for some little time prior to that, the height of nobility, and so the *telos* of his act, is achieved at this final moment of glory. Consequently courage cannot be one of the *aretai* where pleasure does not characteristically occur.

14.9.15. It looks, then, as though Aristotle is interpreting the view that a good man must take pleasure in his good acts as meaning that he would enjoy them. This is indeed what one would expect him to think that his theory shows, and it is also what seems needed to explain the way in which he sets up and tries to solve the problem about the brave man facing death. So we have an agreed 'fact' that the good man takes pleasure in his good acts, which looks as though it should be taken as the fact that a good man is expected willingly to do good acts; it gets taken by Aristotle as the supposed fact that a good man in some way enjoys his good acts, and then has to be shown to be true in the obvious difficult cases. Here again, then, Aristotle is not showing any great concern for nuances of idiom, or varieties of expression, and very likely it is his overall theory that makes him interpret the expressions in a way that makes them say something that his theory would lead him to expect to be true.

14.9.16. *Fondness and Pleasure*. As already noted, Aristotle seems to think that it is obvious that what a person is fond of is pleasant to him, and conversely. This is explicitly said the one way round at *EN* 1099a7 ff. There Aristotle says that what each person is fond of is pleasant to him; so horses are pleasant to a horse-lover, sights to lovers of sights, justice to lovers of justice. At *EN* 1176a10–12 he says that the same things delight some and distress others, and are distressing and hateful to the latter, pleasant to and beloved of the former. This equation of things pleasant to one with things of which one is fond can seem so obvious as not to bear questioning, and it looks as though this obviousness strengthened Aristotle's convictions. Afer all, to say that a child is fond of toffees and that it enjoys toffees seem to be two ways of saying the same thing; that a man is fond of a given woman's company and that he enjoys it seem similarly equivalent and so it goes on. The Greek prefix *philo-* seems in part to mean 'fond of . . . ' and so encourages a like assumption of equivalence. It also conveys the sense of 'lover of . . . '. Here again, if a child loves toffees it seems clear that it enjoys them, and one's only doubt about the converse comes from 'love' being rather stronger than '*philo-*' so that not all enjoyment may deserve so strong a characterization. But the love element introduces a suggestion of pursuit, so that a person who sets his heart on something is a lover of it. Consequently the truism that what A is fond of is pleasant to him seems to support, or show to be obvious, the view that what a person sets his heart on is pleasant to him. Now this is ambiguous as between (a) what A sets his heart on is attractive to A, and (b) what A sets his heart on he enjoys on achievement. The first is more plausible than the second, though the second is what Aristotle's theory purports to show. The outcome of this is that there is some difficulty here in determining what the supposed fact is. 'What A is fond of is pleasant to A' seems capable of at least the following interpretations:

(i) A enjoys the things A finds enjoyable.
(ii) A enjoys those things on which A sets his heart.
(iii) A is pleasurably attracted to those things on which A sets his heart.

Now (i) seems safe enough, but not in need of any theory to explain it; (ii) seems often to have been assumed, but seems highly dubious. Its plausibility seems to come from the feeling that A should be pleased at achieving the things on which he sets his heart. But this is not the same as attributing enjoyment and is in itself, though plausible, dubious. It only looks like being obvious if one emasculates the notion of being pleased so that pleasure is entailed by accomplishment of (approved) objectives, or strengthens the notion of setting one's heart on so that lack of pleasure is taken to show that one's heart was not set on it after all. Otherwise it seems possible for someone as a matter of grim duty to set his heart on keeping to a hunger strike to the end, and not be pleased when he finally succeeds, but dead. The strengthening of 'set one's heart on it' suggests (iii). This has now to be acknowledged as only one way of setting one's heart on something. Even so, a successfully enthusiastic hunger-striker would still seem to show it not to be a general truth.

14.9.17. So only (i) seems to give a fact, whereas it is at least (iii) and probably (ii) that Aristotle's theory 'explains'. The failure to note the ambiguities of the original statement would help confirm his belief in the theory. For the theory does seem to explain how what a being is basically aiming at is what is (really) pleasant to it, and, as we have seen, can accommodate some misconceived objectives. Further the obviousness of the supposed fact might have helped Aristotle in believing that the good activities are really pleasant. For it is of the nature of every member of a species to tend to the good operations of that species, and so, as that is what each member really wants, the achievement of it must be what is really pleasant to it. What it thinks it wants will merely seem pleasant to it. Yet if normal criteria for pleasure are being observed, reflection might have made this dubious. A good wolf will teach its young to hunt with great persistence and devotion, but apart from a prior theory there seems no ground for attributing to it enjoyment of the exercise. It will naturally tend to this behaviour as good species behaviour, but there is nothing to bear out the correlation of this with pleasure.

14.9.18. There are doubtless many other examples that could be selected where Aristotle's theory seems either to have influenced his selection of examples or his interpretation of supposedly obvious truths, or to have blinded him to some ambiguity in the proposed obvious statements. These however should be enough to show that Aristotle was not very much taken up with analysing the senses of expressions. What primarily confirmed him in his view on pleasure was the way it fitted into his overall view of nature, the way in which, true to his methodological principles, it enabled him to exhibit the truth in his predecessors, and perhaps especially the way in which it enabled him to preserve the basic tenets of Eudoxus while adapting them to Plato's criticisms and allying them with some major Platonic views.

Chapter 15

The Contents of Books VII and X
of the *Nicomachean Ethics*

15.0.1. In the last two chapters we have been arguing that there is no reason to suppose any change of view on Aristotle's part as to the nature of pleasure or its relation to the good for man. While the *Eudemian Ethics* does differ in nuance from the *Nicomachean*, in that, for instance, there is in the former work no such clear statement that what X is fond of is pleasant to X as that in *EN* 1099a, still such positions seem to be implicit, and if we suppose either treatment of pleasure to be inserted into the *Eudemian Ethics* this view would be reinforced. Consequently we can see no reason to suppose a change between the two ethical works. On the other hand a considerable part of our argument has been to the effect that the two treatments of pleasure suppose more difference of context than has commonly been believed. This suggests the intriguing question: what, if anything, does this show about the order in which the two treatments were composed? We are unable to find any decisive arguments from a comparison of the books. The whole question is, of course, part of the wider problem of the contents of and relationship between the *Eudemian Ethics* and the *Nicomachean Ethics*. So prevalent, however, is the assumption that the treatment of pleasure in Book X is the later, more refined treatment, that we shall in this chapter argue for the view, which we consider at least as plausible, that Book VII is responding to a later philosophical context than Book X.

1. The *genesis* theorists

15.1.1. We shall start with a puzzle raised by the differences between the views on pleasure as a *genesis*, and their relationship to the *Philebus*. The view rejected in Book X could well be that of the subtlers of the *Philebus*; for the latter seem simply to equate pleasure with the process of coming-to-be, which in the case of bodily pleasures would be a bodily process and so the argument of Book X would tell against them. The theorists of Book VII, on the other hand, find no direct reflection in the *Philebus*.

15.1.2. As we have seen (cf. 11.1.1–15), there is evidence that Aristotle himself might well have been of this number, in that at least he seems to have been attracted to the view that pleasure is a perceptible change, even if he does not adopt the terminology of *genesis*. In that case he must have appreciated that the introduction of the term 'perceived' was part of a rejection of the identification of pleasure with the physical process of restoration, and so have realized that the first argument specific to *genesis* in Book X missed the mark. As we have pointed out (cf. 12.5.4–6) it is not quite clear what sort of view is being attacked by the Book X critique of pleasure as a *kinēsis*. If the views identify pleasure with some physical *kinēsis*, then the same problem holds. If they are just views which consider pleasure to be processes to some end, whether physical or not, the position is less clear. What does seem clear however, is that if they consider pleasure to be a *perceived* process, and perception to be a *kinēsis* then the objection is not likely to frighten the opposition.

15.1.3. Whatever the truth about the *kinēsis* theorists the puzzle remains. In Book VII (where, incidentally, there is no mention of *kinēsis*) a view is criticized which introduces the term 'perceived' in addition to *genesis*; in Book X no such addition is there; Aristotle must, from early on, have understood the significance of the addition; his specific argument against *genesis* theorists in Book X is only relevant against a view which lacks the addition; Book VII, which has the addition, lacks the irrelevant argument. Aristotle himself, in his early days, held that pleasure is a perceived process, though not using the language of *genesis*.

15.1.4. One possibility is that in Book VII Aristotle was criticizing theorists to whose views his own had recently been very close. The argument he adduces will in fact be sufficient against any *genesis* theorists. By Book X he had thought of an argument that would also demolish the subtlers of the *Philebus*, and by then this view was becoming prominent. Alternatively, he had this new argument, and the old one, that many pleasures are not associated with process anyway, is seen as looking after *all genesis* views, whether 'perceived' is added or not.

15.1.5. There are at least two oddities about this. First, the Book X objection is so close to the reason for introducing the term for 'perceived' in the first instance that it is unlikely that Aristotle thought of the argument only later. Secondly, while not impossible it is surely improbable that a *genesis* view lacking the modification 'perceived' came into prominence when one containing the modification was available. A more likely history is that the subtlers' view remained prominent until people had assimilated criticisms derived from Plato's *Philebus* and *Nicomachean Ethics* X, then they realized that by availing themselves of the *Philebus/Timaeus* addition of '*perceived*' while retaining the general category of '*genesis*', they could retain the polemical advantages of their analysis, while avoiding the Platonic/Aristotelian objections to identifying the pleasures with the processes that give rise to them. In that case the likely story is that Book X is reacting to the earlier situation, Book VII to the later.

15.1.6. Yet this has its problems, too. Since Aristotle himself seems to have held a perceived-process view in his early days, surely he must have realized when he wrote Book X that there was a more powerful view available than the one he refutes, that is, the one he recently held? Granted that his own view was not stated in terms of *genesis*, his account of the *genesis* theory uses the terminology of restoration characteristic of his own earlier view, and it would not require much imagination to see that a perceived *genesis* view could easily be generated and less readily rejected. So why rest content with refuting an inferior opponent? One possibility is that Aristotle is primarily concerned with refuting known views outside his school and not with refuting his own previous errors. So perhaps there was, at the time of Book X, no known school of other thinkers outside his school putting forward a perceived-process view. Plato, after all, proposed such a view as an account of physical restorative pleasures only. So it may be that up to that time Aristotle was alone in trying to generalize it. Only later did others marry the perception conditions to a specifically *genesis* view.

15.1.7. Granted the early history of Aristotle's views, together with the likely import of the term 'perceived', there remains a puzzle about why he produced the arguments he did against the positions he did in Books VII and X, in whichever order he wrote them. For present purposes it is enough to note that the treatment of _genesis_ theories does not demand one ordering rather than the other.

2. Eudoxus and Plato

15.2.1. None of this is more than suggestive, but it does encourage one to wonder more generally about the philosophical contexts of the two books. Once one does this, one contrast strikes the eye: the apparently different relationships to Eudoxus and Plato. In Book X the opposed views are that pleasure is the good and that it is base (*EN* 1172a27–31); but it is the positive thesis and its denial which receive most attention. The setting of the dispute recalls the setting in the *Philebus* and other Platonic writings, and the main proponent of the positive thesis is Eudoxus, of whose main arguments we are given a résumé. Plato is mentioned by name for an argument against Eudoxus (1172b28), and one of the main theses of the *Philebus*, on the indeterminacy of pleasure, is rejected at 1173a15–27. As we have seen (cf. 8.3.7, and for further discussion 14.5), Plato had considered it important, probably against Eudoxus, to insist that pleasures differ in kind. In Book X this point is elaborated (1175a21 ff.) to underline the positive value of pleasure in the activity enjoyed and to bring in the point that some apparent pleasures are not really such. As has been argued (cf. 14.5) this enables Aristotle to accept Plato's point while using it to defend a Eudoxan-sounding position, and indeed Book X can be seen as developing a view subtly adapted .to reconciling these great predecessors. In short, while there are other philosophical positions, some mentioned in the *Philebus*, others not, which are influential at the time of Book X, the Eudoxus-Plato dispute is a live and influential one and Book X is clearly Aristotle's working out of his position on it. By contrast, neither philosopher gets mentioned in Book VII. At 1153b 25–32 one main Eudoxan argument is mentioned, but it is simply adopted, not put forward as part of a position in question. Similarly, it is simply taken for granted that pleasures differ in kind: the view does not have to be argued nor seem to have any air of excitement. Eudoxus has been absorbed.

15.2.2. When we turn to consider Plato we find that he too has receded into the shadows. If we look at the list of arguments supporting the view that pleasure is, quite generally, not good, we find nothing that requires that Aristotle has Plato in mind. The reference to house and housebuilding in the allusion to the *genesis* view recalls the *Philebus* mention of ships and shipbuilding — but then the *Philebus* is there recounting someone else's view, so this does not show that Aristotle had Plato in mind. Then the objections that the *sōphrōn* flees pleasures and that pleasures impede thought might be held to recall the first the *Phaedo*, the second, more precisely, *Philebus* 63c–d, where the forms of knowledge reject many pleasures on this ground (and cf. 65c for pleasures of love-making). But Aristotle is citing these as arguments supporting the view that pleasure is just in general bad. The argument from the *sōphrōn's* behaviour must be that the *sōphrōn* would not flee from anything good, but he does flee pleasure. For the conclusion to follow it must be held that he flees all pleasures. But not even in the *Phaedo* does he do this, for he indulges in pleasures of the intellect, and in the *Philebus* this is more obvious still. So Aristotle could hardly have Plato in mind unless he had misunderstood his works. A similar point holds with regard to hindrance to thought. One could well suppose that the naturists of the *Philebus* hold such a position, but Plato is quite clear that only *some* pleasures should be rejected on this ground while others are admitted as part of the good life.

15.2.3. The only apparent pointers to Plato specifically are, first, the second class of opponents who hold that while some pleasures are good, most are bad, which recalls Socrates' remark to that effect (*Phil*. 13b1-2), and secondly, the objection that there is no skill (*technē*) of pleasure. As to the first, it is not a very exciting position to hold and was probably quite common. Even if Aristotle has Plato in particular in mind it is noteworthy that this does not constitute the main opposition in Aristotle's eyes, and that no uniquely Platonic argument for supposing that most pleasures are bad or that no pleasure is *the* good is considered.

15.2.4. As to the objection that there is no *technē* of pleasure, this might at first hearing seem to recall the *Gorgias* (463d ff., 501 ff.) where those engaged in *empeiriai* are said to be concerned with pleasure and have no *technē*, which is concerned with good. But it is not stated there that there *is* no *technē* of pleasure. The most that can be inferred is that a *technē* concerning pleasure would say not which pleasures were pleasantest, but which were best. In this sense there is no *technē* of anything but goodness. Again, in the *Philebus* (23-30), the intellect, with its knowledge and skills, is in some sense concerned with order, whereas pleasure is something on which order has to be imposed. By reflection one could extract a view that music is a skill concerning melody, not sound, of which there is no skill; and since pleasure is analogous to sound there will be no skill of that either. On the other hand, one could also infer that music and grammar (*Phil*. 16-18) are both skills concerning sound — in which case there may be a skill of pleasure, for all we know. One can see how either could be developed from the *Philebus*, but neither way of speaking seems expressly sanctioned by that dialogue. It may well be that members of the Academy developed the *Philebus* in this direction, but it can hardly be traced in any clear form to Plato.

15.2.5. So Platonic views do not seem to figure as important protagonists in the context of Book VII. The only other likely reference to Plato is at 1154b26-8, where it is said that pleasure occurs not only with motion but with tranquillity, indeed in the latter rather than the former. This could be a reference to *Rep*. 583e9-10, where it is said that pleasure and pain are both movements in the soul, or, more probably, to *Laws* 657c8–9, where it is said that we cannot be in tranquillity when enjoying ourselves. There is, however, too little made of the point for us to be able to say with any confidence at whom, if anyone in particular, it is directed. It anyway hardly constitutes one of the main fighting points of the book.

15.2.6. In short, while in Book X Eudoxus and Plato are clearly important parts of the philosophical context with which Aristotle is trying to come to terms, in Book VII he seems to have absorbed his lessons from these, and other figures on the philosophical scene are absorbing his attention. So arguably while at the time of Book X the disputes evidenced by the *Philebus* are still fresh, by Book VII the forms of opposition have developed and other positions predominate.

3. If Book VII is earlier

15.3.1. If we take the Book VII treatment as earlier, we have to suppose some combination of the following: when writing Book VII Aristotle was unaware of the positions treated in Book X, or he thought their proponents unimportant; there was a range of views not influential at the time of the *Philebus* which he considered important when writing VII but decided to ignore in writing X; the more sophisticated version of the *genesis* view, opposed in Book VII, was not thought worth refuting by the time of writing Book X, or had been abandoned by its proponents in favour of the more naïve and vulnerable version refuted in Book X. Now it is almost incredible that Aristotle should either have been unaware of the disputes between Eudoxus, Plato, and others, or have thought them unimportant. Book VII would therefore have to date from very early in Aristotle's career, before the Eudoxus/Plato disputes erupted; it would then constitute a confidently non-Platonic view at a period when other evidence suggests he had not yet worked it out (cf. 11.1). Nor is it likely that once perception had been incorporated into a *genesis* view of pleasure it should be dropped in favour of the bald, subtlers' version. A more probable, though far from certain, account would place Book X in the aftermath of the Eudoxus/Plato disputes, with Aristotle trying to preserve the truth in both positions. By the time Book VII was written Aristotle felt those earlier issues had been settled. The *Philebus* point about kinds of pleasure had been accommodated to the view that the good life was the life of (real) pleasure. A modified form of Eudoxus' principle that since all pursue pleasure it is (the) good can be accepted. Now other philosophers dominate the scene, who are inclined either to think of pleasure in terms of bodily pleasure, or to think that bodily pleasure is bad. While we do not consider these arguments conclusive, we do consider that this view gives at least as plausible an account as the currently favoured ordering.

4. If Book X is earlier

15.4.1. Suppose, then, we take it that the Book X treatment of pleasure is closest in time as well as relevance to Plato, what picture do we get of the intervening period, or at least of the state of play at that period? To begin with, of course, both Eudoxus and Plato are still live influences. On the other hand, there are other influences. Someone has suggested that what everyone wants is not the good. In the *Philebus* the testimony of animals is rejected in favour of that of the wise (67b), but then at 20–2 Socrates has extracted the admission that intelligent beings want more than just pleasure. Aristotle is considering people who do not make this point (1173a2–3). Then there are those who argue that pleasure and pain are opposed as evils. In the *Philebus*, both the naturists and the subtlers have the materials for such a view. The naturists consider pleasure and pain as opposing movements both hostile to the good; the subtlers have pleasure as a process between evil and good. But while the seeds are there, there is no clear statement of the principle, nor awareness shown of the kind of position mentioned in Book X. Probably this development came in the interval. Then there is the objection that pleasure is not a quality. This has no obvious ancestry in Plato. But the view that 'pleasure' does not specify a way in which pleasures resemble one another, together with the contrast of determinant/indeterminate, might well have been developed in this direction. The notion of quality developed by Aristotle gets its sense by reference to answers to the question: 'What is it like?' Anyone accepting the *Philebus* point would probably feel that '*X* is pleasant' or '*X* is a pleasure' do not tell us what *X* is like. On the other hand, since 'healthy' stands for a determinate form of physical organization, '*X* is healthy' will tell us what *X* is like. In general, terms for good states will indicate what something is like, while terms for indeterminates will not. This is, however, at least a development. Then there is the argument from shameful pleasures (1173b20 ff.). There is perhaps a hint of this latter at *Phil.* 65c-66a, where pleasure is dubbed a liar, shameful, and so on, but there is no suggestion there of any developed position, certainly not to the effect that no pleasure is (a) good.

15.4.2. Again, the remarks of *Phil.* 63d-e on the distracting, disruptive power of many pleasures could easily lead someone who concentrated on bodily pleasure to develop the view that pleasure was a distraction and hindrance, and the elaborate argument that pleasures help their own actualizations might be a reaction to that. The *Philebus*, however, does not contain that general objection to pleasure, and the presumption is that it emerged later. Indeed in the *Philebus* itself (63e) it is acknowledged that the pure pleasures, which include some bodily ones, are congenial to the intellect.

15.4.3. Finally, Book X criticizes, along with the view that pleasure is a *genesis*, the view that it is a movement. This *could* be a reference to *Republic* IX, or it could be that Aristippus is in view. The arguments, on one interpretation, operate equally against any view which equates pleasure with some form of movement or change, whether in virtue of its direction or its force. Aristotle does not write as though he took 'movement' as another term for '*genesis*', (although *genesis* is a form of movement) and one must allow that he might have had other views in mind. Since, however, the theorists in question use the notion of movement to refute the view that pleasure is a good, the presumption is that they were relatives of the *genesis* theorists.

15.4.4. In short, while many of the issues alive at the time of the writing of the *Philebus* are still influential there are new developments, and some of the old positions no longer predominate. In particular the naturists get no mention, although if they were still a significant force one might have expected that view on how to discover the nature of something to have received some criticism. In contrast to Book VII it is still the dispute over Eudoxus that dominates the question of pleasure.

5. An objection

15.5.1. An obvious objection to the suggested ordering would go as follows: if Book VII is later than Book X we have to suppose a context of greater philosophical crudity at the later date. For although on the one point of considering pleasure as a *genesis* there might have been some refinement, the general picture is one of deterioriation. In the period of Book X Aristotle is not much engaged with people who think that there are only bodily pleasures or that all bodily pleasures are bad, and the influence of Plato's work would make that intelligible. We are now asked to believe that at a later period many of those considered worth refuting have regressed from the lessons of Plato and are ignoring the distinctions he had so painstakingly established. This would go against our earlier presumption that a later date will go with increased sophistication. That presumption is, however, defeasible, and in the present case there is some historical evidence that things had developed in that direction by the late- and post-Aristotelian period. Further it is possible to explain why this should have been.

15.5.2. Already in the *Philebus* there is evidence of philosophers in contact with Plato who were hostile to bodily pleasures *en bloc*, and of others who were simply opposed to pleasure at least to the extent of denying that it is a goal. The Cynic philosophers Antisthenes, Diogenes and Crates also held an austere view of pleasure and reputedly were known to the Academy (cf. Diogenes Laertius' lives of these). The fact remains that Plato himself is only hostile to certain bodily pleasures and is insistent on there being a large number of non-bodily 'pure' ones. So Plato and Eudoxus between them ensured a fair enthusiasm for pleasure in Academic circles and some enthusiasm for some bodily ones, with no inclination to equate pleasure with bodily pleasures generally.

15.5.3. Plato's successors in the Academy, on the other hand, seem to have become a little more severe. We have seen (cf. Ch. 12) that it is difficult to be precise about the details of Speusippus, but Clement of Alexandria's description of him as holding that the good for man is a state of tranquillity (*aochlēsia*), suggests an ideal of freedom from the disturbances of bodily pleasures and distress. The implication of the reference in *Nicomachean Ethics* VII is that he refused to say pleasure was a good, even though unwilling to declare it an evil. It is at least plausible to suggest that he was inclined either commonly to use 'pleasure' with its restricted, bodily reference, or deliberately to confine the title to those indulgences. This suggests a more severe view than that in Plato's *Philebus* or *Laws*.

15.5.4. In Academic circles, then, there seems to have been a veering to a more severe view of the good, so that it is quite likely that members of the Academy are among those referred to in *EN* 1104b24–5, as defining the virtues as *apatheiai* (states of being unaffected). Between Plato's death in 347 and Aristotle's in 322, Eudoxus' advocacy of pleasure had passed to the Lyceum and the rival Academy had failed to keep Plato's balance and had reacted towards greater austerity. It seems to have been the influence of Crates the Cynic and then of Polemo at the Academy under which Zeno came when he transferred from Cyprus to Athens in 312/11 (cf. DL VII.1). These and the many Socratic books that his father is reported to have brought home from Athens probably explain the equation of virtue with knowledge, the tendency to use '*hēdonē*' for an irrational disturbance that should be suppressed, and to equate '*chara*' (= joy) with a stable state in accordance with nature (DL VII.110 ff.). Zeno's stoicism develops various non-Aristotelian schools of thought on the value of pleasure, all more pessimistic than Plato.

15.5.5. Another sign of changing times is Epicurus who set up a school in Mytilene in about 311 and transferred to Athens about 307. Here there are Democritean as well as Academic influences but once again there is a view of many bodily pleasures as disturbances to be avoided, and an apparent tendency to equate pleasure with the absence of pain. The views of Zeno and Epicurus show some relation to those mentioned in *Nicomachean Ethics* VII which put forward the *alupos* (painless) life as ideal and contrast pleasure with what either the wise or temperate man can pursue. Such views hardly sprang from nowhere and were doubtless encouraged by developments in the immediately preceding period, say 330–310. This is the sort of development which Book VII of the *Nicomachean Ethics* seems to reflect, but which is not nearly so pronounced in Book X.

15.5.6. It still remains an odd development. Surely, one might think, anyone who had read Plato, let alone Aristotle, must have taken the point that there are other than bodily pleasures; that among bodily pleasures many are neither disturbing nor such as to arouse disturbing desires; and that the pleasures of someone in a good state are as delightful as any and not uncommon. Finally, Plato's polemics against those who confused absence of distress with pleasure should have warned people off the assimilation. For although his strictures are not aimed at those who make the conflation part of a theory, but only at the common habit of people in a distressed state, the point was that these people made a mistake about the nature of pleasure.

15.5.7. Various considerations may have conspired to help the change. To begin with, one of the attractions of Plato's and even more of Aristotle's position is that it not only allows for pleasures of intellect and virtue, but enables one to argue to their greater pleasantness. As *tours de force* they are breathtaking, but would be liable to lose conviction on reflection. For the result is produced in each case by means of a highly artificial criterion for degrees of pleasantness which seems to have little to do with even a wise man's reports of enjoyability (for further discussion cf. Ch. 17). It may be that Aristotle's lyricism on the exquisiteness of the pleasures of philosophizing came from his own experience and convinced him that God's life must be even more enjoyable. It is not likely to have been the experience of many. Consequently one would be left with at least three obvious possibilities. First one might recognize that contemplation was not notable for enjoyment but was obviously superior to other activities, and infer that pleasure was not a part of the best activities. This might encourage one to think of pleasure as something really alien to the highest life and only manifested in lower activities. Secondly, one might hold that whatever held with contemplation was so different from what obtained with profligate pleasures as to deserve a different name. Contemplation brings joy, say, rather than pleasure. It is not pleasanter than dissipation, because not pleasant. Pleasure is an irrational reaction and should be deplored. Thirdly, one might recognize the lack of excitement in contemplation and think that good but consider only the familiar more vulgar pleasures as pleasures; thinking the good to be pleasure would be taking it to be a life of such pleasures unadulterated by turmoil or distress. The life of an excellent man is free of distress; the life of a profligate is one of turbulent pleasures which are partly distressing and also are fertile of further distresses. So the good life is pleasantest. The first of these ways is the sort of direction taken by those who thought virtues forms of *apatheia*, the second the sort taken by Stoics, the third by Epicurus. All have it in common that the greater pleasantness of individual activities is no longer asserted. The hedonistic position relies solely on a comparison of lives, and uses as its criterion of relative pleasantness relative lack of distress. All these moves would reflect a determination to stand by a preference for virtue and wisdom. The attempt to use hedonistic premises to defend the excellent life has been abandoned except in the Epicurean case, where it is achieved by a new view on what the greatest pleasure is.

15.5.8. So one suggested reason for the change is the sheer implausibility of the earlier views on degrees of pleasure. A second might come from a consideration of the nature of bodily pleasure. As Urmson points out, Aristotle's treatment of bodily pleasures in Book X takes pleasures of perception as paradigms, and it is not easy to see how those of replenishment are to be treated. In Book VII it looks as though the view is that in, say, pleasures of recuperation, what is important is not replenishment but the operation of some healthy natural element (cf. *EN* 1152b33–1153a2) — thus keeping the notion of actualization. But this does not give a very clear thesis, for there may be many actualizations of healthy parts (a good deal of digestion for instance) which go unnoticed and so are not pleasant. If actualization is here, as with perception, to entail perception of actualization (cf. *EN* 1170a25–b7), Aristotle will be committed to a quasi-perceptual account of restorative functions, and it is not clear how it is going to be made plausible. Restorative functions do not seem, either, to be defining elements of the life in question (cf. *EN* 1170a16–21), whose actualization is (real) pleasure. In fact a philosopher might well feel that a host of pleasures, especially bodily ones, are better described in terms of perception of changes in the organism. But then it seems that they are quite different in nature from whatever it is that the philosopher experiences — especially if Aristotle is right to associate this with lack of change. So surely it ought to be given a different name, even if we are inclined to talk of pleasure in both cases.

15.5.9. The first consideration, then, was that it did not seem plausible to describe many (or any) of the best activities as pleasurable, so that a different name should be devised. This would be based upon experience of the activities in question. The second consideration is that examination of the nature of the activities shows them to be so different that it would be patently misleading to preserve the same name for both. Once again, one might simply infer that pleasure is to be rejected, or that a different name from the 'pleasure' family should be reserved for the stable, reputable activities, or assimilate 'pleasure' to 'painlessness', with a revised view of the pleasant life.

15.5.10. These considerations both come from dissatisfaction with earlier attempts to show that hedonistic
premises lead to a preference for excellence. A part of that
argument was some form of the thesis that the good person is
the standard or judge of real pleasure. The difficulties of such
a thesis will be discussed in Chapter 17. Suffice it to say that
it is not likely to have been a thesis with a wide appeal.

15.5.11. Apart from the philosophical dissatisfaction
there were probably politico-social reasons for the change. In
Plato's day there was still a tradition of the political usefulness
of academic men. It was not uncommon for *sophoi* (wise
men) to be called in to advise on the political organization of
a city and Plato himself was much engaged with the affairs of
Syracuse. This interest in political organization was conceived
of as part and parcel of being a philosopher, and so when in
the *Politicus* (Statesman) he distinguishes between 'practical'
and *'gnōstic'* knowledge, this is not a contrast between
practice and theory, but between forms of knowledge where
the knowledge resided in the production of things and the
techniques of production, and ones which are concerned with
direction and oversight and involve general considerations of
how things should be (cf. *Pol.* 258c–259d). The higher form
of knowledge is still very practical and Plato generally
assumes that a philosopher will be engaged politically.

15.5.12. This was not *simply* a matter of an odd educational tradition. In a small city state with a roughly
democratic constitution an individual could exert some
political influence and his power to argue would be important.
Educators would be looked upon as supplying the latter, and
their views on the nature and function of the state and the
good for man would have an influence on those they taught.
An individual teacher might reasonably expect to have more
far-reaching practical influence than his present day counterpart, unless the latter starts some fashionable movement. But
even a person devoted to ideals of rigour and intellectual
honesty might have felt that there was some scope in ancient
Greece.

15.5.13. With the rise of Macedon matters changed. Important decisions affecting people's lives were taken at a less local level. By the time Alexander had conquered an empire the political situation had changed radically. Although the empire broke up after his death it was divided only into four. The old city-states did not regain their importance. Aristotle could still write the *Nicomachean Ethics* and the *Politics* with the city-state as man's ideal environment, but the next generation was unlikely to have a similar view. An increasing sense of political impotence was fertile ground for views encouraging withdrawal from political engagement and resignation at one's inability to produce great changes. Stoicism and Epicureanism were doubtless partly the effect of this change, and both, with their views of the wise man as self-sufficient and relatively immune to the world's changes, fitted a growing mood of the period. Of course ideals of self-sufficiency were already there in Plato's generation, and in Aristotle's, but both Plato and Aristotle saw the ideal in a political context. The post-Aristotelian generation emphasized the untrustworthiness of the lower passions and of ambition, and the ideal tended, especially with Epicurus, to involve withdrawal from these in favour of an individual calm and self-sufficiency. This would make it natural to be suspicious of many bodily pleasures and to prefer some ideal of freedom from distress and disturbance.

15.5.14. In short, there are plausible philosophical and socio-political explanations for the changing attitudes to pleasure which seem to have taken place, and it is easy to see Book VII of the *Nicomachean Ethics* in the context of a later stage of development of this change.

Chapter 16

Kinēsis and *Energeia*

16.0.1. In the exposition so far it has been taken as relatively unproblematic what Aristotle means in calling pleasure an *energeia*, and why he is so confident that it is one. In particular we have offered no discussion of what ought to be an illuminating passage in *EN* X in which he distinguishes *energeia* from *kinēsis*. In the present chapter, therefore, we shall consider what light if any can be got from this and other passages elsewhere in Aristotle's works where this contrast is made.

16.0.2. In two passages in *EN* X Aristotle argues that pleasure is not a process of change (*kinēsis*) on the grounds that pleasure either lacks some features which necessarily characterize all such processes, or possesses some feature which cannot characterize any such process. In the first passage (1173a31–b4) he argues that it cannot be a process of change, because any such process may appropriately be described as fast or slow, but pleasure cannot be so described. In the second (1174a14–b14) he argues as follows:

(i) Pleasure, like seeing, is complete in every moment at which it occurs, whereas every process of change proceeds in distinct stages, and is hence complete only when all stages have been gone through. But when all stages of the process have been gone through, the process itself is over; hence at any time at which the process is still going on, it is incomplete.

(ii) It is not possible for anything to undergo change otherwise than for some stretch of time, but it is possible to have pleasure (*hēdesthai*) under that condition, for something which occurs at a moment (*en tōi nun*, lit 'in the now') is a complete whole.

(iii) There is no process which is the coming into being of any whole, e.g. a unit; therefore there is no process which is the coming into being of pleasure.

16.0.3. These passages, together with passages in the *Physics*, *Metaphysics*, and elsewhere which relate to them, have generated some critical discussion and provided a starting-point for some modern theory of the classification of verbs.[1] Much of that discussion, while of considerable interest in its own right, is remote from our main concern. In this chapter we shall confine ourselves as far as possible to exegesis and criticism of Aristotle's views as expressed in these passages, examining wider aspects of the distinctions drawn therein only in so far as they aid our understanding of the contribution of these passages to his treatment of pleasure.

1. The *kinēsis-energeia* distinction(s)

16.1.1. Fundamental to the distinction he is making is his distinction between actuality (*energeia* or *entelecheia*) and potentiality (*dunamis*). An acorn is not actually an oak, but has the potentiality to be an oak; a lump of ice is not actually liquid, but has the potentiality to be liquid. For any predicate *F* which does not signify a process of change[2] anything which is not actually *F* but is potentially *F* realizes that potentiality only by undergoing a process of becoming *F*, i.e. of changing from not being *F* to being *F*. Aristotle's general term for that process of change is *metabolē*, of which the principal kinds are coming-to-be and ceasing-to-be (substantial change), growth and diminution (quantitative change), alteration (qualitative change) and locomotion (change of place). He sometimes uses the term *kinēsis* as interchangeable with *metabolē* (e.g. *Phys*. 261a27–36), but more frequently uses it as a generic term for the three main kinds of non-substantial change (e.g. *Phys*. 192b13–15). *Kinēsis* is then the process by which certain kinds of potentiality (especially the potentialities to have a certain quality, to be of a certain size and to be in a certain place) are converted into actuality. Aristotle's main motivation in his discussion in the *Nicomachean Ethics* is opposition to any view which sees pleasure as consisting essentially in the subject's undergoing

---

[1] See Kenny (2), Ch. 8; Potts and Taylor; Ackrill (1); Penner (2); Pickering; Graham.

[2] This qualification is necessary to avoid an infinite regress of processes: cf. *Phys*. 225b33–226a6.

any process of change, e.g. the making good of any bodily or *psuchic* deficiency. Rather, as we have seen, he takes pleasure to consist in a certain kind of actualization (in the sense of being actual). The kind of actualization in question is actualization in perfect conditions; thus enjoying thinking is actually thinking when one's mental faculties are operating in top gear and the object of one's thought is something appropriately elevated. And since the state of actually being F is always to be distinguished, not only from the state of potentially being F, but also from the process of becoming F, any account of pleasure which gives the essence of pleasure as some process of becoming must be rejected.

16.1.2. The criteria which Aristotle uses in the passages cited to distinguish pleasure from any process of change are well suited to this basic distinction. Every process of change, being a progression from an initial state in which the subject possesses a certain characteristic only potentially to a terminal state in which the subject possesses that characteristic actually, takes some time, however short, to be completed, and proceeds via a series of distinct intermediate stages. Since any such process takes time, it must always be possible in theory to measure the amount of change relative to the time taken to complete the change, i.e. to characterize the change as fast or slow. (We pass over complications arising from the relative nature of the predicates 'fast' and 'slow'.) When, on the other hand, a subject actualizes some potentiality, i.e. for some F actually is F, the description of it as actually F describes it not as proceeding to any terminal point, but as being at the terminal point of the process of actualization.[3] And the predicates 'fast' and 'slow', which qualify processes from one state to another, lack application to the static concept of being at the end-point of such a process. The main argument of *EN* X relies on the contrast between the serial character of processes and the non-serial character of states in which processes terminate. At any moment at which the process is under way, some stage or stages are yet to be completed; hence any stage which has been completed

---

[3] This point is subject to the restriction on the range of replacements for 'F' made in 16.1.1.

(e.g. laying the foundations of a house) is different both from any stage yet to be completed (e.g. fixing the roof-timbers in position) and from the complete process (i.e. building the house). By contrast, at least some states which realize potentialities are non-progressive. Aristotle's example is that of seeing: when someone sees something his capacity to see that thing is fully realized at every moment at which he sees it; his seeing it never has to wait for the completion of some further stage of itself to make it a complete bit of seeing, in contrast with a bit of housebuilding. There, as long as the builder is engaged on it there is some building left to do; hence the building (i.e. the process) is never complete until it is finished, whereas the seeing is complete at any moment at which it is true that the subject sees whatever it is. Aristotle asserts that pleasure shares this non-progressive character with seeing. It is as yet unclear whether he thinks that that is so because both seeing and pleasure are actualizations, and all actualizations are non-progressive, or because seeing and pleasure belong to a special kind of actualization one of whose characteristics is that they are non-progressive. In either event, pleasure will not be a process of change, because, it is assumed, all such processes are progressive.

16.1.3. In elucidating the main argument of *EN* X.4 we have virtually found ourselves making use of the grammatical criterion which Aristotle uses to distinguish *kinēsis* from *energeia* in *Met.* Θ 6. The general topic of that book is actuality and potentiality: after discussing potentiality in Chapters 1–5 he begins the discussion of actuality in Chapter 6. He does not offer any general definition, but illustrates the concept by instances: the builder who is actually engaged in building (by contrast with the builder not so engaged), a waking man (by contrast with a sleeper), a finished artefact (by contrast with the unformed material) are all instances of actuality in contrast with potentiality. At 1048b6–9 he makes the revealing comment that not all cases of actuality are alike; some are cases of change (*kinēsis*) by contrast with the potentiality for such change, others are substances by contrast with the matter of which they are composed. The foregoing examples provide cases of each kind: actual building is a change (Aristotle uses the term *oikodomēsis* to refer indifferently to the change which the materials undergo, i.e. being combined in certain ways, that is to say being built, and the activity of the builder in bringing about that change (*Phys.* 201a16–18)) as opposed to the potentiality for that change which characterizes the unorganized materials; a house is an actual substance as opposed to the bricks etc., which are *that* substance only potentially. Particularly noteworthy is the statement that some instances of actuality are instances of processes of change. Of course that is exactly what we should expect; how else could the capacity of e.g. a plant to grow be actualized otherwise than in the actual process of growth? Yet in what appears to be an appendix to the chapter Aristotle distinguishes *kinēseis* from *energeiai*[4] in a way which suggests that the kinds are exclusive. *Kinēseis* and *energeiai* are distinguished as kinds of *praxeis* (normally translated 'actions', but better rendered as 'things which subjects do', since e.g. seeing and becoming healthy are not on an ordinary view actions); the former are described as actions which have a limit (*peras*), as not strictly *praxeis* or at least as incomplete *praxeis*, and as *kinēseis* on the ground that every *kinēsis* is incomplete. The latter are described as having their end or completion (*telos*) in themselves and as being strictly speaking *praxeis*. Aristotle gives what is in effect a single grammatical test to distinguish the two kinds, viz. that if a verb which characterizes a subject is such that the present and perfect tenses are true of the subject simultaneously, then the verb signifies an *energeia*, and if that is not so, the verb signifies a *kinēsis*. Thus seeing and thinking are *energeiai*, because as soon as '*A* sees *Y*' is true '*A* has seen *Y*' is also true, as soon as '*A* is thinking of *Y*' is true '*A* has thought of *Y*' is also true. Building on the other hand, is a *kinēsis*, because it is not the case that '*A* has built a house' is true as soon as '*A* is building a house' is true. There has been some disagreement among commentators on whether Aristotle's point is that for *energeiai* the present tense entails the perfect, but does not do so for *kinēseis*, or rather that for *energeiai* present and

[4] These are the plurals of *kinēsis* and *energeia* respectively.

perfect are compatible, whereas they are incompatible for *kinēseis*. Aristotle's insistence, both here and in *EN* X.4., on the completeness of *energeiai* as opposed to the in-completeness of *kinēseis* should be sufficient to settle the question. In both passages the central point is that no process of change is complete while it is occurring, but achieves its completion only when the end-state towards which the process is directed is reached, i.e. when the process itself is over. By contrast, in the cases of *praxeis* such as seeing 'the completion is contained in them' (*Met.* 1048b22);[5] 'they do not lack anything which, by occurring later, will complete their nature' (*EN* 1174a15–16). Given that the function of the perfect tense is to express the thought that the state or action which it introduces is complete, it follows that Aristotle's thought must be that for *kinēseis* the present tense excludes the perfect, wheras for *energeiai* it entails it. The classes of *kinēseis* and *energeiai* seem therefore to be exclusive, though not exhaustive.

16.1.4. This immediately presents a difficulty, for we have seen that Aristotle counts at least some *kinēseis* as themselves *energeiai*. But in fact the difficulty is worse than our discussion has so far indicated, since in the case not just of some processes of change, but of every such process, the actual process is the actualization of potentiality to undergo that change. Indeed Aristotle's definition of *kinēsis* is that it is the actuality (*entelecheia*) of that which is something potentially, as such, i.e. the actuality, *as potentially F*, of what is potentially *F* (*Phys.* 201a10–11). The sense of this obscure formula is given by Aristotle's examples: the bricks and mortar piled on the building site are not actually a house, nor are they actually being made into a house, but they are capable of being (*a*) a house and (*b*) made into a house. The completed house is the actuality of potentiality (*a*), the process of being built is the actuality of potentiality (*b*). In that process the materials actualize fully their character of being capable of being built; hence it is as capable of being

---

[5] In Aristotle's technical terminology *energeia* (lit. 'in-act-ness') is inter-changeable with *entelecheia* (lit. 'having completion in').

built (*hēi oikodomēta*) that they may be said to be actualized
in the process of being built. But that process, as we have
seen, is always incomplete as long as it is being undertaken;
hence change can be said to be incomplete actuality (*Phys.*
201b31–2, 257b8; *Met.* 1066a20–2). In contrast, the actuality
which consists in the completion of a process is actuality
properly so called (*De An.* 431a6–7).

16.1.5. Every process of change is, then, an actualization
(i.e. a being actual) of a certain kind, i.e the actuality of the
potentiality which a subject has for undergoing that kind of
change.[6] That kind of actualization Aristotle calls incomplete
actualization. At the same time every process of change is a
process towards a state of complete actualization, and is
distinct from that state. This dual aspect of every *kinēsis*
accounts for the apparent inconsistency in Aristotle's application of his grammatical test to the verb 'change' (*kineis-
thai*). At *Met.* Θ 6 he lists that verb among others which
satisfy his criterion for signifying processes of change: 'these
(i.e. slimming, learning, walking, and building) are *kinēseis*
and incomplete; for one does not at the same time walk and
have walked, nor build and have built, nor become and have
become, nor change and have changed' (1048b30–3). The
point here is that something which is undergoing a change has
not completed *that* change (see above, 16.1.3). But Aristotle
believes that there is no first moment of change; hence anything which is changing at any time must already have been
changing for some time (however short) previous to the time
at which it is changing (*Phys.* 236b32–4). But that is to say
that change satisfies the criterion for *energeiai*, viz. that when
the present tense of the verb 'is undergoing some change' is
true the perfect tense 'has undergone some change' is true.

---

[6] It is also, of course, an actualization (in the sense of becoming actual) of
another potentiality in the subject, e.g. getting hot is the becoming actual of a
thing's potentiality to *be* hot. But when Aristotle describes *kinēsis* as incomplete
energeia he should not be understood as describing change as the incomplete
process of a potentiality's becoming actual. For his account of *kinēsis* is not that
it consists in anything's *becoming* actual, but in the potential's *being* actual:
' . . . when the buildable, in so far as we describe it as such, is in actuality, it is
built, and this is building; and similarly with learning, healing, etc.' (*Phys.* 201a
16–18).

There is no inconsistency between this passage and *Met.* Θ 6. There the point is that any process is incomplete while it is in progress; in the *Physics* passage the point is that anything which is actually changing has already actualized some change. What looks like the same point can be made in English by exploiting the difference between the perfect and past continuous tenses: someone who is painting the ceiling has not yet painted it, but must have been painting it for some time. Yet that can hardly be exactly Aristotle's point, not merely because Greek has no continuous tenses, but more significantly because that account loses the distinction, central to Aristotle's thought, between the process described as a process from not-*F* to *F* and the same process described as the actualization of the potentiality for a certain sort of change. In our example the process is described in either case as painting the ceiling (thereby specifying its terminal points), and the difference is that whereas it is false that the painter has painted it, it is true that he has been painting it. But that distinction is unavailable to Aristotle, lacking continuous tenses. His point is that whereas the man who is painting the ceiling has not painted it, in so far as he is painting it (and thereby actualizing his capacity to paint) he has painted (has done some painting). The point holds generally for *kinēseis*: a man running from Athens to Sparta has not done that run, but has done some running, an actual slimmer (i.e. one engaged in slimming) has not yet reached his target weight, but has slimmed, and so on.

16.1.6. There is, then, no inconsistency in Aristotle's treatment of *energeia* and *kinēsis*. Nor is there any reason to suppose that either term is ambiguous. When *energeia* contrasts with *dunamis* (= potentiality) it means 'actuality' and Aristotle correctly counts every actual process of change as an instance of the actuality of some potentiality. And when Aristotle distinguishes *energeiai* from *kinēseis* as distinct sorts of *praxeis*, the sense of *energeia* is precisely the same. The point he is making is that among things which subjects do we can distinguish the undergoing of change from the realization of potentiality. Every instance of the former is an instance of the latter, though not *vice versa*: John's seeing the Parthenon and Mary's thinking of Pythagoras' Theorem are not instances of change. There is thus a distinction between two kinds of actuality, actuality properly so called (*energeia haplōs*) whose instances are not also instances of processes of change, and incomplete actuality, whose instances are instances of processes of change. But that distinction does not require a distinction of different senses of the word *energeia*. Indeed, Aristotle's exposition appears to exclude that suggestion, firstly because he introduces the term in contrast with *dunamis* via examples of both kinds of actuality (*Met.* Θ 6 1048a35–b9), and secondly because, as we have seen, his single grammatical test for *energeiai* fits verbs picking out either kind of actuality.

16.1.7. There is thus not a single contrast between *kinēsis* and *energeia* but two. Firstly there is the contrast between change and actuality as such, between the process by which a potentiality comes to be realized and the state of its being realized. While no event is an instance both of potentiality *P*'s *coming to be* realized and of potentiality *P*'s *being* realized every event which is an instance of *P*'s coming to be realized is an instance of the being realized of a different potentiality *Q*, viz. the potentiality to come to be in the state which is the realization of *P*. Secondly, there is the contrast between processes of change and complete actualizations, i.e. states or events which are (*a*) realizations of potentialities and (*b*) not themselves (under any description) processes of change. It must be acknowledged that the existence of these two contrasts, rather than of a single contrast, does not emerge with complete clarity from Aristotle's exposition.

2. The application of the distinction(s) to pleasure

16.2.1. This puts us at last in a position to consider the relevance of the *kinēsis-energeia* distinctions to the treatment of pleasure. When Aristotle argues that pleasure is not a process of change by in effect showing that it is a kind of actualization, which of the two contrasts just distinguished is he trying to make? If it is the contrast between change and actualization as such (sometimes referred to subsequently as 'the weaker contrast') then his point must be that what constitutes enjoying something is not undergoing some change, but realizing some potentiality. It would not, of course, follow that the event described was not also an instance of a process of change. Thus John's walking to the pub and John's enjoying walking to the pub need not be different events, but might, on some occasions, be the same event described differently, in the first case as an instance of change (viz. locomotion), and in the second case as an instance of a certain sort of realization (viz. realization in perfect circumstances) of the capacity to walk. If, on the other hand, the contrast is that between change and complete actualization, then Aristotle appears to be committed to the view that John's walking to the pub and his enjoying walking to the pub are distinct events, the former an instance of change (and hence not an instance of complete actualization), the latter an instance of complete actualization (and hence not an instance of change).

16.2.2. It is hardly to be expected that Aristotle's text will provide an explicit answer to this question. Firstly, we have seen that Aristotle himself does not clearly distinguish the two contrasts. Secondly, he lacks the concept of an event such that he could ask the question 'Is John's walking to the pub the same event as John's enjoying walking to the pub, or a different event?'. We must therefore look for an answer firstly to the arguments which he uses and secondly to the wider context of his theory of pleasure. His first argument, viz, that pleasure cannot be a *kinēsis* because one cannot have pleasure quickly or slowly, whereas all *kinēseis* may be described as fast or slow, does not differentiate between the two contrasts, since the premises of the argument viz, that the adverbs 'quickly' and 'slowly' modify verbs which pick out processes but not the verb 'enjoy' are compatible with its being the case that the same event is describable both as a process and as an instance of enjoyment. But that is not to say that Aristotle may not have intended that argument to support the stronger point that 'enjoy' picks out a kind of complete actualization. His second main argument, viz. that pleasure, like seeing, is complete at any time it is instantiated, whereas any process is incomplete as long as it is occurring, might be thought to tell in favour of the stronger contrast. For if the pleasure has already occurred while the walk is still going on, then the pleasure and the walk occupy different stretches of time, and must therefore be different events. But that argument depends on ignoring the temporal specifications which apply alike to the walk and to the enjoyment. Pleasure is complete at any time in just the sense in which walking is complete at any time, viz. that as soon as 'he is enjoying himself' is true 'he has enjoyed himself' is true (just as 'he has done some walking' is true as soon as 'he is walking' is true). Hence if this argument showed that John's walking to the pub and John's enjoying walking were distinct events, when the walking that he enjoyed was a walk to the pub, it would equally show that John's walking to the pub was a distinct event from his walking, when the walking that he did was a walk to the pub. Since that is absurd, we must allow that this argument too is compatible with its being the case that some enjoyments are the same events as *kinēseis*. But once again that does not exclude the possibility that Aristotle's intention may have been to show that 'enjoy' like 'see' picks out a kind of complete actualization.

16.2.3.   Aristotle's third argument (1174b7–9) is similarly indeterminate between the two contrasts. This argument is: no *kinēsis* can occur at a moment (for every process requires a stretch of time for its completion), but pleasure can occur at a moment. Therefore, pleasure is not a *kinēsis*. This argument may be taken in either of two ways depending on how the minor premiss is understood. (*a*) That premiss states that some instances of pleasure are instantaneous events (being pleased to learn something might be a plausible example). In that case those instances would be instances of complete actualization, but the general point about pleasure would have to be that pleasure is not as such a process of change, i.e. the weaker contrast. (*b*) That premiss states that, if someone enjoys himself for a time he enjoys himself at every moment during that time (by contrast with processes of change where, in Aristotle's view, a subject undergoing such a process for a period cannot be said to undergo it at any moment during that period, but merely for sub-periods within

that period (*Phys.* 234a24-31)). As with the argument
dealing with 'quickly' and 'slowly', this argument, were it
sound, could show only that the description of an event as a
process of change has different implications from the description of an event as an instance of pleasure, from which it
does not follow that the event which is the process of change
is not the same event as the event which is the instance of
pleasure.

16.2.4. A similar indeterminacy characterizes the fourth
argument (1174b9-14). Commentators disagree on whether
the conclusion of this argument is that pleasure is not a
process of coming-to-be (*genesis*, see above 16.1.1), or that
there is no process of coming-to-be *of* pleasure, and consequently dispute over the correct reading of the text at various
points (for details see Gauthier and Jolif II (2), pp. 836-8).
On either interpretation Aristotle is again insisting, as in the
second argument, that pleasure is complete at every moment,
and again illustrating his point with the example of seeing, a
complete actualization. Consequently the conclusion of our
examination of the second argument applies to this argument
also.

16.2.5. The upshot is that none of Aristotle's arguments
has to be interpreted as directed towards the stronger conclusion that no instance of pleasure is an instance of a process
of change. On the other hand, only one subsidiary argument,
the third, appears clearly directed to the weaker conclusion,
and that interpretation requires one reading of a premiss
whose sense is disputed, while the alternative reading gives an
interpretation closer to that of the second main argument,
which, together with the first and fourth, is indeterminate
between the two contrasts. Our overall choice of interpretation must, therefore, be made, if at all, on the basis of more
general considerations of Aristotle's theory.

16.2.6. These considerations appear to tell in favour of
the weaker interpretation. We have seen that in both Book
VII and Book X Aristotle's conception of pleasure is that it is
a kind of perfection, viz. the actualization under perfect

conditions of the capacities proper to each nature. Mary's enjoying playing the Moonlight Sonata is not an extra event supervening on her playing it under ideal conditions, but is playing it under those conditions. But playing the Moonlight Sonata is a *kinēsis* by all Aristotle's criteria: it consists of a sequence of distinct stages, is complete only when it is over and can be done quickly or slowly.[7] Hence, if he is to count her enjoying playing the sonata as a case of pleasure, he cannot maintain that the event which is her enjoying playing it is not an instance of incomplete actualization. Rather the point is that in describing her as enjoying playing the sonata one is viewing the event which is both playing (*kinēsis*) and a realization of the capacity to play (*energeia*) under the latter aspect, by specifying the circumstances in which that capacity was realized. Aristotle's thought may perhaps be that when someone enjoys e.g. playing a piece of music, what he really enjoys is exercising his musical capacity, the playing of the particular piece being merely incidental to the enjoyment; hence what he enjoys will be complete even if he has to break off before he finishes the piece, and so for all apparent cases of the enjoyment of *kinēseis*. That view, if indeed it is Aristotle's, is pretty plainly wrong, since it is essential to many kinds of enjoyment that they are enjoyments of activities which proceed by stages from a beginning to an end. Thus while one may indeed enjoy every move in a chess game, it is likely to be essential to one's enjoyment that one sees each move as contributing to the development of the game from start to finish, and if the game is left unfinished one's enjoyment is no less curtailed than the game itself. If that is Aristotle's view then the contrast he is arguing for could perhaps after all be that between *kinēsis* and complete actualization, since, he might argue, enjoyment will consist in the perfect exercise of e.g. chess-playing capacity, which is realized non-serially, and is therefore complete actualization. But one could defend that position only at the cost of

---

[7] It is nonetheless obscure what kind of *kinēsis* it is, since it does not fit happily into any of the kinds which Aristotle distinguishes. It is not a case of *genesis*, since it has no end-product, nor is it a case of locomotion, qualitative change, or quantitative change. But if Aristotle were to deny that it is an instance of any kind of change, despite satisfying his criteria, the *kinēsis-energeia* distinction would collapse.

insisting on the distinction between on the one hand enjoying exercising the capacity to be playing a game of chess and on the other enjoying exercising chess-playing capacity. The former realization is by Aristotle's criteria an incomplete actualization, like the realization of the capacity to be engaged in building a house, since it is the process of playing a game of chess (building a house). The latter realization is complete, since it is the activity of being a chess-player or, (equivalently) of making chess moves. Yet the distinction has now been brought close to vanishing-point, since a chess-player is essentially one who engages in the process of playing games of chess, as a musician is one who engages in the process of playing pieces of music and a housebuilder one who engages in the process of building houses. Hence it would surely have to be admitted that the standard exercise of musical capacity is the playing of a piece, and of chess-playing capacity the playing of a game. But those activities are *kinēseis*; hence in saying that those pleasures are not *kinēseis* Aristotle must be contrasting the aspect under which they are enjoyed (i.e. incomplete actualizations) with their character as *kinēseis*. It appears, therefore, that Aristotle can both recognize such serial activities as music as pleasures (*EN* 1175b3–6) and insist that the enjoyments of those activities are not *kinēseis* only if he is upholding the weaker of the two contrasts which we have distinguished.

3. Evaluation of Aristotle's arguments

16.3.1. Let us take it, then, that the conclusion which Aristotle might hope to establish by these arguments is that what constitutes enjoying oneself is the actualizing of some potentiality (whether in a complete or an incomplete actualization) in ideal circumstances, not the undergoing of any process of change. How strong are the arguments themselves? The question is not whether the conclusion is true, but whether the arguments support it. We shall consider only the first two arguments, for the third and fourth are manifestly defective, the third because it depends on the false premiss that a subject cannot be said to be changing at any moment within the period over which it is changing, the fourth because it contains (whether as premiss or conclusion is irrelevant to our enquiry) the proposition that there is no coming-to-be of pleasure, which is both false and inconsistent with Aristotle's statement at 1173a34–b1, that whereas one cannot enjoy oneself quickly, one can come to enjoy oneself quickly, just as one can become angry quickly. What, then, is the force of the non-applicability to pleasure of the qualifications 'quick' and 'slow'? One difficulty affecting this argument is that it is not clear that the premiss is true. Various sentences look as if they contain the predication of 'quick', 'slow', and similar terms of enjoyment, e.g. 'He slowly savoured his drink', 'I don't like to hurry my pleasures'. It may be suggested that in these cases 'fast' and 'slow' qualify the activity which is enjoyed, not the enjoyment of it. Thus slowly savouring one's drink is drinking slowly and enjoying drinking, or perhaps enjoying drinking slowly; the pleasures which are hurried are the things enjoyed, not the enjoyment of them. But it is not obvious that in the first case what is slow has to be the drinking; might not one drink at normal speed, while dwelling lingeringly on the delights of the drink? Here the adverb seems to be qualifying not the drinking, but the drinker's reaction to or assessment of his drinking, i.e. his enjoyment of his drinking. To take another case, suppose that a woman has a regular pattern of sexual enjoyment, with three regularly-spaced orgasms, but that the time taken to achieve this pattern varies; why should she not be described as enjoying sex more quickly on some occasions than on others? A difficulty here is that, taken literally, that description requires that she have the same amount of enjoyment each time, and there are well-known difficulties in quantifying enjoyment. But those difficulties are not insuperable, at least for a single individual; thus our Kinsey-type subject might report that she enjoyed each occasion of sexual activity equally, irrespective of its duration, and that report might be taken as establishing that she experienced the same amount of enjoyment on each occasion. In that case there does not seem to be any objection in principle to the view that a given amount of enjoyment may be achieved in more or less time, i.e. relatively slowly or quickly.

16.3.2. The second main argument (1174a14–b7), from the premiss that pleasure is complete at every moment at which it occurs, is even weaker. We have already seen that in the case of a progressive activity such as playing the Moonlight Sonata or reading *Mansfield Park* we have just as much reason for counting the enjoyment as progressive as for counting the activity as such. The enjoyment of playing the first movement is distinct both from the enjoyment of playing the second and from the enjoyment of playing the whole piece, and the last-mentioned enjoyment can be had only by playing the whole piece (cf. 1174a19–b5 on temple-building and walking). The only test of those suggested by Aristotle which tends to separate such activities from the enjoyment is the speed test; i.e the second argument has no independent force.

16.3.3. The distinction between *kinēsis* and *energeia* thus contributes little to Aristotle's attack on process theories of pleasure. Of the four arguments which rely on it, three depend on false premisses, and the fourth on a premiss that is at least dubious. There is, moreover, a deeper flaw in the whole project. Our analysis of Aristotle's concept of *energeia* has shown that the most that he could hope to show is that what constitutes enjoying oneself is not undergoing some change, but realizing some potentiality. Since the test for the distinction is in effect a grammatical one, that is ultimately a thesis about the meaning of *hēdesthai* etc.[8] But process theories of pleasure such as that of the *Republic* or the subtlers in the *Philebus* are not theories about the meanings of the words for pleasure, but theories of the real nature of the phenomena which we pick out by those words. Such theories cannot be refuted by any demonstration that they fail to capture the sense of the ordinary words, but only by a demonstration that the conditions which they specify fail to be satisifed in some clear instance of the phenomena which they purport to explain. We have already come across counter-examples to process

[8] This is not, of course, to say that Aristotle regarded the thesis as one about the meaning of pleasure-words, rather than about the nature of pleasure. See above 11.3.19–32.

theories of pleasure in such cases as pleasures of memory, of anticipation and of the possession of e.g. knowledge. The nearest Aristotle's arguments come to refuting process theories is by suggesting further counter-examples; thus the pleasure of seeing the Himalayas for the first time cannot plausibly be accounted for as an instance of any physiological or psychological process. But the arguments themselves provide no refutation of the theories against which they are directed. They thus constitute an interesting example of the limitations of arguments from ordinary language as applied to theories in the philosophy of mind.

Chapter 17

The Criterion of Real Pleasures

17.0.1. As has been repeatedly observed in this study, both Plato and Aristotle emphasize the diversity of pleasures. Animals of different species, and men of different temperament, upbringing, physiological condition, etc., find pleasure in radically different types of object and activity, and, in the latter case, are likely to express conflicting judgments on the pleasantness or unpleasantness of any particular kind of object or activity. One possible response to this situation is to espouse a form of relativism concerning pleasures: every case of pleasure is a case of something's being pleasant to someone or something, and questions such as 'Is mathematics really pleasanter than ludo?' or 'Which is the pleasantest sort of life?' are dismissed as improper. Unless one is also prepared to espouse a corresponding form of relativism concerning goodness, the adoption of such a position must involve the abandonment of any connection between pleasure and goodness. Since both Plato and Aristotle maintain some connection between the two, both have an interest in discriminating between pleasures, e.g. in showing that some pleasures really are pleasures, whereas other purported pleasures are not pleasures at all, or are so only to a limited extent, or with some qualifications. An important part of Plato's treatment of this topic is his discussion of false pleasures (see Appendix A). While that discussion is intended to exclude many kinds of putative pleasures from the good life on the ground that they are unreal or false, it does not appeal to the judgment of any particular sort of person as decisive in discriminating real/true from unreal/false pleasures. In *Rep.* IX, however, (580d–583a) Plato makes such an appeal to establish that the philosophic life is pleasanter than the life of ambition and the life of bodily appetite, while Aristotle makes fairly frequent use of a similar criterion, especially in the *Nicomachean Ethics*. In this chapter we shall examine the use of this pattern of argument by Plato and Aristotle, considering, among other things, whose judgment is appealed to, what the judgment is supposed to establish, and whether either Plato or Aristotle is successful in his use of this pattern of argument.

1. The criterion in *Republic* IX

17.1.1. At 580c9 Plato concludes his first argument in support of the thesis proposed for examination at 544a5-8, viz. that of the types of men whose characters correspond to the various types of political organization, the best man has the most completely satisfactory life and the worst the most completely unsatisfactory (*ho aristos eudaimonestatos kai ho kakistos athliōtatos*). This first argument (576b11-580c9) consists of the presentation of the contrasting pictures of the best and worst types of men, the former the 'Platonically just' man who enjoys total psychic harmony in that all his lower impulses are harmonized under the direction of the intellect informed by knowledge of the Good, the latter the 'tyrannical' man (i.e. the man who is totally enslaved to the satisfaction of one of his lower appetites) who actually rules as a tyrant. Both aspects contribute to the total misery of the latter's life. In so far as he is enslaved to appetite, he will be constantly at war with himself, since the better parts of his nature will resent the domination of the worst, and his life will be a chaos of uncoordinated, insatiable desires (cf. discussion of *Gorgias* above, Ch. 4). In so far as he is an actual tyrant, he will be friendless and in constant fear. The conclusion that his life is the most unsatisfactory or unfortunate of all follows from the fact that such a life does not satisfy the agent's desires at all; he is 'of all men the most needy and poor in reality . . . burdened with fear throughout his life, full of convulsions and pains' (579e1-5). The emphasis here is on the unsatisfactoriness of his life to the agent; it doesn't in fact give him what he wants, viz. the satisfaction of his bodily appetites, and it does produce in him states which he is assumed, like everyone else, to wish not to experience, especially distress and fear. Plato's picture does indeed suggest a man too far gone in slavery to the passion of the moment to form any reflective judgment at all, but in so far as the rational element is still active in him he resents his domination by his lowest impulses and is full of shame (577d–e). So the tyrannical man has a life that is *athlios* (wretched) — his life is not at all as he wants it to be, in contrast with the philosophic man whose reason is satisfied, and who therefore (441e ff.) sees to the proper operation of all parts of the personality. The latter, being temperate, is one in whom the desires and wisdom of the nobler part of the soul rule (431c–d). Since to each 'part' there is a desire (580d7–8) and reason sees that each 'part' is properly developed, the philosopher's life will be satisfactory in the sense that all his desires (i.e. each kind) will be catered for.

17.1.2. As was pointed out in 6.3.2, this argument for the superior *eudaimonia* of the philosophic life cannot be considered by Plato to be a proper proof, since it lacks the required reference to the form of the good. In fact the 'proof' concluded at Book IX.580c is the continuation of the argument of Book VII which is itself picking up the question of Book IV.445 as to whether it pays to be just. Now Book IV.445 is in turn recalling us to the challenge of Glaucon and Adeimantus in Book II, and reminding us that the account of the formation of the city, and the analysis of the parts of the soul with its description of justice, is supposed to be telling us what it is that justice itself does to the soul to make it worth choosing (358b). Glaucon and Adeimantus, in asking Socrates to show that the just man is more *eudaimōn*, or that justice is good, are wanting to be shown that it is something that we would, if we understood its nature, pursue and want for its own sake (357). So Glaucon portrays justice as a second best (358e–359b) — no one is willingly just (360c5–8) — and suggests that a thought experiment will reveal that if one were in a position to do as one wished one's desire would lead one to injustice (359c). The tripartite division of the soul, being at least a distinction of desires, indicates that what we want is a more complex matter than this picture suggests. Plato can consequently suggest that only a properly organized life can meet all our desires, and, through his view of the imperialistic tendencies of bodily desires, that complete indiscipline will lead to a person's least of all doing what he wants (compare 359c with 577d, 579e). In short, by Book IX

Plato hopes to show that the just/philosophic life is good in itself, *eudaimōn*, in the terms set by Glaucon and Adeimantus, and that involves showing it to answer to our desires better than the unjust life.

17.1.3. The first argument might claim to show the superiority of the just/philosophic life over the unjust, but it shows the superiority of the just life only in the weak sense that in that life all natural desires are satisfied. Perhaps the fully unjust life has been shown to be totally unsatisfying, but it remains possible that it is more satisfying to curb intellectual desires in pursuit of ambition than to pursue the dull harmony of philosophy. The second and third arguments are to prove the just life's outright superiority.

17.1.4. At first sight it might seem odd for Plato to use arguments for the greater pleasantness of the philosophic life to prove its greater *eudaimonia*. But this oddity evaporates when we remember that he is proving this latter on Glaucon's terms, and that pleasure is thought of as replenishment of (natural) desire or need. This last becomes clear later, in the third proof (cf. 585d11), but Plato has already coupled pleasure and replenishment (e.g. 439d8, 442a6-8, 485d) and the introduction of the second proof (the first in terms of pleasure) at 580d-581 clearly envisages the pleasures of the different parts as coming with the replenishment of their desires. A proof that a life is pleasanter, therefore, is a proof that it is more desire-filling and so something more desirable ($\neq$ ought to be desired). It thereby becomes a proof that the life is more *eudaimōn* as that thesis is understood by Glaucon and Adeimantus. This does, however, highlight a peculiarity of Plato's view of pleasure: the pleasantness of a life, as the notion is used in Plato's second and third arguments in the comparison of lives, is not determined purely by the attitude of the agent to the activities which make up his life or to his life as a whole. Herein lies the crucial difference between Plato's conception of a really pleasant life and the ordinary conception of happiness. In setting up the second argument Socrates is careful to acknowledge that each of the three types of man will insist that his own life is the pleasantest of all (581c7–10). The argument does not proceed by way of showing that the Platonically just man's life is pleasanter *to him* than the life of the ambitious or the appetitive man is *to him*. Rather, accepting that each man's life is fully pleasant *to him* it tries to show that the just man's life is pleasanter *tout court* than the others. The argument thus requires a standard of pleasantness *tout court* by reference to which the inferior man's judgement that his life is completely pleasant to him is shown to be, not indeed false, but irrelevant to the question of which life is the most worthwhile. Socrates claims that the judgement of the just man as to which life is pleasantest provides that standard; we have now to consider his grounds for that claim.

17.1.5. It is worth observing that the parties to the dispute as to whose life is the pleasantest are not the five 'political' types, the comparison of which extended into the first argument, but three types classified by reference to the tripartite division of the soul, viz., the intellectual, ambitious, and bodily-appetitive types. This should cause no difficulty. The basic question (see above, 6.4.1–3) is which kind of life most truly satisfies the agent's desires. In order to answer that question we must classify the principal kinds of desires, a classification which is provided by the tripartite analysis of the soul, which is at least in part a distinction of fundamental types of motivation. The 'political' typology is merely an elaboration of this more fundamental scheme of motivational analysis, e.g. the 'oligarchic' man is described as one whose primary aim is money-making, which is treated as a function of the appetitive element, but who restricts himself to the satisfaction of necessary bodily appetites (553a–554a). Hence in asking which of the three basic types of man has the pleasantest life Plato is not losing sight of his original question, viz. which of the five political types has the most worthwhile life. Since only the 'aristocratic' man is intellectual, and the other four inferior types are merely more specific kinds of ambitious and appetitive men, the answer which is to emerge from the second and third arguments, viz. that the intellectual man has the pleasantest life, implies the answer to the original question, viz. that the aristocratic man has the most worthwhile life.

17.1.6. The argument itself is extremely simple. On any disputed matter the best judge is the man who excels in experience (sc. of the matter in hand), intelligence (*phronēsis*) and reason (*logos*) (582a4-6). But the intellectual excels the two other types in all three respects. First, with respect to experience, he has experience of the two other kinds of pleasure, whereas the ambitious and appetitive men are without experience of his pleasures. He has experienced appetitive pleasures from his childhood onwards, and he has experienced ambitious pleasures in his enjoyment of the praise of his fellow intellectuals for his intellectual successes. On the other hand 'it is impossible for anyone but the philosopher to have tasted how much pleasure there is in the contemplation of reality' (582c7-9). Then, since intelligence and reason are the attributes which distinguish the philosopher from the other types of man, he naturally excels with respect to those also. Hence he is the best judge of pleasures, and consequently his judgement that his own life is the pleasantest is to be accepted as establishing that it is pleasantest *tout court*. Similarly, his judgment is decisive in awarding second prize in the contest of pleasantness to the life of ambition, since it is more like his own life than is the appetitive life, and consequently in relegating the latter to third place (583a6-11).

17.1.7. Our first question, viz. what it is that the philosopher's judgment establishes to be the case, appears to admit of a straightforward answer. It establishes that his life is the pleasantest of all lives, that is to say, the pleasantest absolutely, not just the pleasantest for him. But while that is stated perfectly plainly in the text at 583a1-3, there is a certain problem as to what status the philosopher's judgement assigns to the inferior pleasures. Are they simply not as pleasant as his, or are they rather not really pleasant at all? Consequently, is the philosophic life simply the pleasantest of three pleasant lives, or is it the pleasantest life of the three in so far as it alone contains real pleasures, or perhaps in so far as it contains the highest proportion of real pleasures? The question is raised, of course, by the fact that the third argument attempts to establish that only the philosopher's pleasures are really pleasures (for details see above Ch. 6). Now we should not automatically read that view of inferior pleasures back into the second argument; Plato might be proceeding cumulatively, arguing firstly that the worst man is the unhappiest of all, secondly that the best man has the pleasantest life of all (even allowing that other kinds of life really are pleasant), and thirdly that in fact only the best man has any real pleasures. There is, however, some textual evidence to suggest that the latter thesis may itself be part of the conclusion of the second argument also. Firstly, at 581d10–e4 the philosopher is said to consider inferior pleasures, in comparison with the pleasures of philosophy as 'very far from pleasure'. Secondly, at 582e8–9 Glaucon asserts that necessarily *ha ho philosophos . . . epainei alēthestata einai*, which may be rendered either as 'the things that the philosopher praises are the most real' or as 'what the philosopher says in praise (sc. of what he praises) is the truest'. Given the former rendering it is immediately implied that the inferior pleasures are less real pleasures than those of the philosopher. That implication is not contained in the latter rendering, but when we recall that part of the philosopher's praise of his own pleasures consists in describing their rivals as 'far from pleasure' it follows that on either rendering the philosopher counts the inferior pleasures as less than fully real. It appears then, that while the principal conclusion to be established by appeal to the philosopher's judgement is that his is the pleasantest life of all, it is also implied that no other life is really pleasant. For, asked whether the appetitive and ambitious lives are pleasant, the philosopher must say 'No', since those lives would not be pleasant to him; hence by the principle that the philosopher's judgement decides what is the case absolutely, those lives are (absolutely) not pleasant. Some inferior pleasures may perhaps be, or approximate to, real pleasures; we may recall the statement that in the case of the philosopher each part of his soul enjoys the best and most real pleasures of which it is capable (586e4–587a1). But a life given over to inferior pleasures is not a real instance of a pleasant life. Since the judgement of the philosopher is set up as a standard for the comparison of *lives*, it does not, therefore, determine which of a number of really pleasant things is pleasantest; rather, it determines which of a number of putatively pleasant things (i.e. lives) is really pleasant. To that extent it is correctly described as a criterion of real pleasure.

17.1.8. We must now consider the soundness of the argument. Given the truth of the premisses that the best judge of any disputed matter is the man who excels in experience, intelligence, and reason and that the philosopher excels all other men in experience of pleasures, intelligence and reason it plainly follows that the philosopher is the best judge of any dispute about pleasures. It might be objected that from that intermediate conclusion it does not follow, as Plato's argument requires, that whatever judgement of relative pleasantness the philosopher makes must be true; the best judge need not be infallible. But the force of this objection disappears when we recall that 'the philosopher' designates a type of person, not an individual; cf. 'in disputes about which is the best vintage, the expert wine-taster is the best judge'. While no individual expert is infallible, in any sphere where expert judgement is the criterion of correctness, the agreed judgement of acknowledged experts must be taken as authoritative. Any criticism of the argument must, therefore, be directed at the truth of the premisses. With regard to the first premiss, while it is true that, other things being equal, A is a better judge of any disputed question than B if A is more experienced, more intelligent, and more rational than B, there are certain areas of dispute, notably those of connoisseurship, where intelligence and rationality are much less relevant than highly developed discriminatory capacities. This point is of some significance, in that it might be claimed with some plausibility that disputes about the relative pleasantness of different ways of life are much more matters of taste than of rational judgement; hence if they are to be settled by appeal to the judgement of experts, the expert in question should be someone more like a wine-taster than a philosopher. The first premiss, then, may be criticized on the ground that, while purporting to state sufficient conditions for superior expertise in any area, it ignores conditions necessary for expertise in some areas where the philosopher's particular merits are irrelevant. Hence the claims of the philosopher are unduly favoured from the outset.

17.1.9. Further difficulties arise about the second premiss, that the philosopher excels the other types of men in experience, intelligence, and reason. Plato offers no arguments for the superiority of the philosopher in intelligence and reason, but takes it for granted. Argument is, however, required, for Plato nowhere explains why someone of the highest intelligence might not prefer to pursue the goals of ambition or appetite. He was, it is clear, convinced that anyone who had attained the degree of insight into the nature of things which accompanies the full development of intelligence and reason must see that the goals of appetite and ambition are worthless compared to those of the intellect. But this very argument is presented as part of the proof of that crucial proposition: the only plausible ground on which the goals of ambition and appetite might be thought to be superior to those of intellect is pleasantness, but by this and the subsequent argument they are denied even that superiority. Plato is, then, faced with a dilemma: either he gives an independent proof of the comparative worthlessness of the goals of the ambitious and appetitive lives, in which case the appeal to the philosopher's judgement is otiose, or he fails to do so, in which case the appeal itself fails, since one of its premisses is insufficiently supported.

17.1.10. Nonetheless, the appeal to the philosopher's judgement must stand or fall with the claim that he excels the other types of men in experience of pleasures. For the objection of the previous paragraph could show no more than that men of the other types might be as intelligent and as rational as philosophers. If Plato can show that, typically, the philosopher has more experience of pleasures than the others, then, failing some further argument to show that the other types of men are typically more intelligent and rational than philosophers, he will have made out a strong case in favour of his reliance on his appeal to the philosopher's judgement. This might even go some way towards meeting the objection which we brought against the first premiss, since the notion of experience might perhaps be extended to include discriminatory capacity; it must at least be conceded that the latter is likely to improve as the former is widened. The claim to superiority in experience is therefore crucial.

17.1.11. But the claim cannot be sustained. For Plato has to show that the philosopher has *sufficient* experience of the pleasures of the other types of life to count as rejecting them on the basis of experience, whereas the other types of men lack sufficient experience of his pleasures to reject them on the basis of experience. But all that he urges is that the philosopher must have had *some* appetitive pleasures and some ambitious ones; as regards his negative thesis he says that the money-loving (i.e. appetitive) man *need* not have had any philosophical pleasures and that it would be difficult for him to do so even if he wanted to, but in contrasting the philosopher with the ambitious man he says that no one but the philosopher *can* have the pleasure of contemplating reality. It is obviously open to the partisan of appetite or ambition to reply that, in order to have experience of a type of pleasure sufficient for the purposes of this argument, it is necessary to experience those pleasures in their most developed form, and to pursue them with the degree of enthusiasm that the devotee gives them. Hence you can't claim to know what the pleasures of appetite are really like if all you know is how much you enjoyed afternoon tea in the nursery, or how much you like your refreshing glass of milk after a strenuous bout of dialectic; only the man who can really appreciate a debauch or an orgy knows what *the pleasures* of appetite are like. A similar point can be made of ambition. Plato then faces a dilemma: either really experiencing the pleasures of a given way of life itself requires that one prefer those pleasures to any other throughout one's life, or some less stringent condition is adopted. In the former case it is a necessary truth that no one has experience of the pleasures of any way of life other than his own, since anyone who abandons one way of life for another thereby shows that he did not really appreciate it. This position is of course destructive of the claim of the philosopher, or of anyone else, to have experience of the pleasures of more than one way of life; no such criterion is available. If, on the other hand, some less stringent condition is adopted, it will be impossible to establish other than empirically the asymmetry between the experience of the philosopher and that of his rivals which the argument requires. Suppose, for instance, that the following condition were accepted as necessary and sufficient; someone has experience of the pleasures of a given way of life if and only if for some part of his adult life he has made those pleasures his predominant pursuit. It cannot now be claimed *a priori* that the philosopher and he alone has the necessary experience, thus defined, while as an empirical claim it lacks any plausibility whatever. The same result holds if the condition is weakened still further, e.g. if it is sufficient that one should occasionally have experienced full-blown examples of the pleasures of each way of life. It might perhaps be claimed in favour of the asymmetry that, while it is contingently possible to experience occasional full-blown appetitive and ambitious pleasures without living the corresponding way of life, it is necessarily impossible to experience full-blown philosophical pleasures without being a philosopher, since an essential element in such pleasure is one's synoptic understanding of reality. But (*a*) there seems to be a similar conceptual impossibility in isolating full-blown pleasures of ambition from an ambitious way of life, (*b*) it has still not been shown that someone who had achieved such a synoptic view might not thereafter abandon the philosophic life for one of its competitors. If that possibility is excluded by stipulation, then we are back in the first situation, in which there can, by definition, be no experience of more than one way of life.

17.1.12. The claim that the philosopher excels the other types of men in his experience of pleasures must therefore be rejected, and with it the claim that the philosopher's judgement provides the criterion of what is a really pleasant life. The claim to superior experience cannot be maintained as an *a priori* truth, while as an empirical claim it has neither adequate support in Plato's text nor any inherent plausibility. On reflection this result ought not to be unwelcome to Plato, since the claim that the philosopher judges by experience what is a really pleasant life and what is not has highly embarrassing consequences. Does the philosopher really pronounce his life more pleasant than a life of perverted or sadistic pleasures from experience of both kinds of pleasures? As a good man, the philosopher must surely be without experience of those activities at all, not to speak of experience of *the pleasures* of those activities. It is a natural response to such examples to maintain that one does not need experience to disqualify such ways of life from counting as really pleasant. They are not really pleasant in themselves, one is inclined to say, but are pleasant only to someone in a corrupted or diseased state, rather as honey may taste bitter when one is sick. Here the implied criterion of what is really pleasant is not the judgement of the man of experience, but the judgement of the man in a state of physical or psychic health, i.e. the man whose physical and/or psychological components are organized and functioning in the way they ought. In view of the fact that we were led to postulate an appeal to such a criterion by consideration of difficulties which Plato's criterion was unable to cope with, it is all the more interesting that this, rather than experience, is the criterion which Aristotle regularly relies on in discriminating pleasures. We must now consider his use of it, with a view to deciding whether it is ultimately more successful than Plato's appeal to experience.

2. Aristotle's use of the criterion

17.2.1. As a preliminary, it is worth noting one passage (the only one, to our knowledge) where Aristotle alludes to something like the Platonic criterion. This is *EE* 1235b31 ff., where Aristotle, as a prelude to his discussion of problems concerning friendship, makes his standard distinction between on the one hand what is good or what is pleasant without qualification, and on the other what is good or pleasant only in a qualified way, e.g. good for an invalid, pleasant to someone of perverted tastes. We call good for the body without qualification what is good for the healthy body; amputation may be good for a diseased body, but the question 'Is amputation good for the body?' is properly answered 'Not good for the body as such, good only if the body happens to have a diseased part which must be removed'. The same distinction is made for 'pleasant', first of all for physical pleasures (e.g. the pleasanter wine is the one which is pleasanter to the man whose palate is in good order, not to the man who has ruined his by boozing, as evidenced by the

fact that boozers sometimes add vinegar to their wine to pep
it up) and then for pleasures 'in the soul', i.e. presumably
pleasures of games, conversation, the arts, etc. Aristotle then
adds, with reference to both kinds of pleasure, that what is
without qualification pleasant is what is pleasant to normal
adults (lit. 'to those who are in an established state') not to
animals or children, adding the comment 'at least while we
remember both (sc. sorts of pleasures, i.e. those of childhood
and adult pleasures) we prefer the latter'. He concludes by
stating that as an animal or child stands to a normal adult, so
the bad and stupid man stands to the good and wise (*phronimos*) — the latter finds pleasant what is in harmony with his
dispositions, and those things are good and fine.

17.2.2. Of the many questions raised by this interesting
passage, the most immediately relevant concerns the force of
the comment quoted above. Is Aristotle here suggesting that
what is without qualification pleasant is determined by the
judgement of the normal adult rather than that of the child
because the adult has experienced both kinds of pleasures
and prefers his own? I.e. is he here relying on the Platonic
criterion of experience to discriminate between pleasures?
That suggestion is open to the objection that the criterion of
experience applies only to the contrast between adult and
child, not, obviously, to that between adult and animal, nor
to that between good man and bad. Yet the adult is explicitly
contrasted with the child *and* the animal, and that contrast
(presented as one rather than two) is said to be analogous to
that between the good and the bad man. In view of this (and
of the fact that the comment is connected to the statement
of the criterion not by 'for' or 'because' (*gar*) but by 'at least'
or 'at any rate' (*goun*)), it seems best to take Aristotle's
remark not as an explanation or justification of our taking
the adult's judgement as deciding what counts as without
qualification pleasant, but as an incidental comment; since
(Aristotle assumes) we value what is unqualifiedly pleasant or
good above what is so only with some qualification, we find
that our ordinary evaluations confirm the identification of
the criterion of unqualified pleasantness, in that we value
adult pleasures above those of childhood. Aristotle is not,

then, asserting or implying that certain pleasures count as un-
unqualified pleasures in virtue of the fact that they are
preferred by the man with the greatest experience of
pleasures. Here, as in the *Nicomachean Ethics*, he maintains
that unqualified pleasures are determined as such by the
preference of the man in sound condition of body and soul.
The fact that experience confirms his judgement serves
simply to confirm that the criterion is the correct one for the
discrimination and evaluation of pleasures.

17.2.3. Turning now to Aristotle's use of that criterion,
we should first ask why it is important for him to distinguish
between qualified and unqualified pleasures. Firstly we must
take account of his doctrine of meaning. Impressed by the
relativity of predicates such as 'good' and 'pleasant', Aristotle
recognizes that the questions 'Is X good?' and 'Is X pleasant?'
are as they stand ambiguous, requiring to be disambiguated
by unpacking the predicates into 'F absolutely' and 'F with
such and such qualification' (to this person, in these circumstances, etc.). This process of disambiguation requires
(reasonably) clear criteria for the application of the specific
predicates. Further, in the case of any predicate which is
applied both with and without qualifications, the unqualified
use is primary, e.g. understanding what it is for something to
be good for a sickly body presupposes the understanding of
what it is for something to be good for the body *simpliciter*, i.e. for the healthy body, since things are good for the
sickly body in so far as they cause it to approximate to the
state of the healthy body. That understanding requires a
grasp of the conditions necessary and sufficient for the
primary application of the predicate. So the complexity of
the concept requires that the investigation of pleasure
proceed via the distinction of qualified from unqualified
pleasure. The investigation of pleasure is, of course, essential
to the main purpose of Aristotle's ethical enquiry, the
identification of the good for man and the conditions under
which it can be attained. As we have seen, he inherits from
Plato and Eudoxus a debate on the relation of pleasure to the
good for man; according to one extreme position it simply is
the good, according to another it is not merely not *the* good,

but not good in any respect. The distinction between qualified and unqualified pleasures affords an elegant resolution. Some at least of the anti-hedonist arguments are effective only against qualified pleasures, such as those of the sick or the wicked, while unqualified pleasure has at least a strong claim to be identified with the good for man. Again, Aristotle consistently acknowledges an obligation to preserve as much as possible of ordinary beliefs; one such belief which his theory must show to be true is the belief that the life of *eudaimonia* is a pleasant one (*EN* 1099a7; cf. 1152b4–8). Given the identification of the life of *eudaimonia* as the life of excellent activity, the acceptance of the judgement of the physically and psychologically sound man as the criterion of unqualified pleasure and the requirement that one is not a good man unless one enjoys acting well (1099a17–20), it necessarily follows that the life of *eudaimonia* is not merely pleasant, but unqualifiedly pleasant. (On the question of whether this result is achieved at too high a price see below, 17.2.7.) Since unqualified pleasure is the highest grade of pleasure, the life of *eudaimonia* wins top marks in respect of pleasure as in other respects. The fact that a depraved man finds depraved activities pleasant is no objection, for their being pleasant *to him* does not count against their being unpleasant *simpliciter*, since they are unpleasant to the good man (1173b20–5, 1176a19–24). The results which Aristotle reaches by the use of his criterion are, then, of the highest importance for his whole project; but is the criterion itself sound?

17.2.4. If the criterion is to work, two conditions must be satisfied. Firstly it must be possible to identify the physically and psychologically sound man independently of the fact that he takes pleasure in those things of whose pleasantness his judgement provides the criterion, and secondly persons thus identified should agree, broadly, in their judgement of what is pleasant and unpleasant. The necessity of those conditions becomes apparent when we consider the perceptual analogies on which Aristotle regularly relies in proposing the judgement of the good man as his criterion of pleasures. Thus if we stipulate that to be sweet just is to taste sweet to the healthy man, we must be able to identify the healthy man other than as the man to whom things which are sweet taste sweet. For if we have no other way of identifying him, our proposed criterion gives the result that to be sweet is to taste sweet to the man to whom those things taste sweet which are such that they taste sweet to the man to whom ... ; that is to say, the criterion cannot even be stated. It might be suggested that we might identify the healthy man by indirect ostension, as the man to whom some previously identified kind of thing, e.g. sugar, tastes sweet. But that implies that we already know that sugar is sweet, and that we use that knowledge to test the correctness of each man's perceptions. But if we know, prior to identifying the healthy man, that some kind of thing is sweet, we do not need to appeal to the judgement of the healthy man as a test of whether things are sweet. Plainly, we identify the healthy man via our general theory of health and human functioning; the healthy man is he whose organs are functioning as they should do and whose general condition is up to standard, and that is something which can be more or less objectively established, independently of the functioning of the particular sense for whose object the healthy man's perception provides the criterion.

17.2.5. But surely a man might be otherwise perfectly healthy, yet suffer from a malfunctioning of the sense of taste to such an extent that such things as sugar and honey tasted bitter to him? Here we have to ask why we are entitled to talk of malfunction. That description is justified in cases where a sense or an organ functions less *well* than it should, or than it standardly does. A sense malfunctions when its possessor is unable, by the use of that sense, to make discriminations which other users of that sense standardly make; hence we count e.g. colour blindness a malfunction of vision. So if our hypothetical man was unable to discriminate honey and sugar from e.g. aloes, we should be justified in describing him as suffering from a malfunction of his sense of taste. But if he was just as good as normal people at discriminating sugar from other things, while describing it as tasting much more like aloes than ripe strawberries, he would not be correctly described as suffering from a sensory defect; still less if he could discriminate fine nuances (of bitterness, naturally) in the taste qualities of sugar all of which tasted indistinguishable to normal people. Such a man, though not indeed defective, would be atypical, and we might amend our proposed criterion of sweetness by counting as sweet those things which taste sweet to the typically healthy man. Here we see the importance of the second condition, that there should be broad agreement between our 'standard observers'; in this instance their qualification to be standard observers is purely statistical, viz. that they constitute a substantial majority among healthy tasters. The less substantial the majority is supposed to be, the less compelling is the claim that the judgement of the majority is the criterion of what is really the case. Thus if, say, one otherwise normal person in four reports that sugar tastes bitter to him, there is little substance in the claim that it really is sweet (cf. Bennett's phenol-thio-urea example). In any case this modification of Aristotle's criterion is inapplicable to the case of pleasure, since he would be unwilling to admit that there might be atypical good men who just happened to enjoy depraved or brutish pleasures.

17.2.6. The refusal to admit this possibility is no mere squeamishness on Aristotle's part; rather it is central to his theory of human virtue. For virtues and vices are states of character, and the best indication of states of character is the pleasure we take in some things, the unpleasantness we find in others; so the man who abstains from bodily pleasures gladly (*chairōn*) is temperate, but the man who does so reluctantly is licentious, the man who faces dangers gladly or at least not unwillingly (*mē lupoumenos*) is courageous, the man who does so unwillingly is a coward (1104b3–8). States of character involve both actions and affective states (*pathē*), and hence perfect character requires that the two be harmonized under the direction of the intellect to the pursuit of the good. There could not, therefore, be an 'atypical good man' who just happened to like depraved pleasures; for such a man's desires and consequent pleasures and pains would be out of phase with his judgement of what was best, irrespective of whether he actually indulged his 'atypical' tastes. If he did indulge them he would be enjoying bad actions, while if he abstained from indulging them he would be doing good actions (i.e. abstaining from bad pleasures) contrary to his inclinations; in neither event could he be a good man. Aristotle states this emphatically at 1099a17-20; 'someone who does not enjoy (or 'rejoice in' (*chairōn*)) fine actions is not a good man; for no one would call just the man who does not enjoy acting justly, or generous the man who does not enjoy generous actions, and similarly in other cases.'

17.2.7. Aristotle's criterion thus fails to satisfy the first of our two conditions (17.2.4), since it proves impossible to identify the physically and psychologically sound man independently of the fact that he enjoys those very pleasures of whose reality his enjoyment is the criterion. (Since the satisfaction of the second presupposes the satisfaction of the first, Aristotle's criterion in fact satisfies neither condition.) It might seem that Aristotle could overcome this difficulty fairly easily, in that he could provide an independent identification of the sound man without dislocation of his system. Why not, for instance, identify the sound man as the man who does good actions, and then identify as real pleasures the things that he enjoys? But, as we have just seen, that would distort Aristotle's thought by locating goodness of character wholly in the sphere of action, in contrast to Aristotle's own conception of goodness as consisting in the harmonious integration of intellect, action, and affective states. Further, even if that point were set aside, it does not seem that good actions can themselves be identified independently of the identification of the good man. For, as is well known, good actions are those which manifest a state of character which is 'in a mean', e.g. self-controlled actions manifest a state of character which is neither too given to indulgence in bodily pleasures nor insufficiently appreciative of them. But what counts as being too given to pleasures, or insufficiently appreciative of them, is said to be determined by the judgement of the man of practical wisdom (*phronimos*; *EN* 1106b 36-1107a2). Hence the identification of good actions presupposes the prior identification of the *phronimos*, from which it follows that our proposed modification is impossible within the Aristotelian system. It is worth adding that, at least in the *Nicomachean Ethics*, Aristotle does not attempt the independent identification of the *phronimos* which his system requires.

17.2.8. The same problem recurs in Aristotle's use of the contrast between things which are pleasant by nature (*phusei hēdea*) and things which are only incidentally pleasant (*kata sumbebēkos hēdea*), e.g. things which are pleasant to someone who happens to be in a certain abnormal condition. Aristotle uses this contrast at *EN* 1099a7 ff. as part of his argument for the conclusion that the virtuous life is in itself pleasant (see 17.2.3). Most people's pleasures, he says (a11–15), conflict because they are not of that sort (i.e. pleasant) by nature, but the lover of noble things finds pleasant things which are pleasant by nature; and virtuous actions are of that kind (i.e. pleasant by nature), so that they are both pleasant to those people and pleasant in themselves. It is not altogether clear what is meant by the statement that most people's pleasures conflict, since the verb (*machetai*, lit. 'fight') is used here without a complement, requiring the reader to supply from the context the specification of what it is that most people's pleasures conflict *with*. The point may perhaps be that they conflict with one another, in that they arise from a disturbance of the proper, balanced state of human nature; in that event Aristotle is making the additional assumption that disturbance of the proper state produces a condition in which conflicting impulses compete with one another for satisfaction, rather than one in which the agent's motivation leads him in a uniform, but wrong direction. An alternative view, which perhaps fits better with the actual context, is that most people's pleasures are said to be in conflict with what is naturally pleasant. But whichever interpretation is adopted, the chief interest of this passage for our enquiry lies in the fact that this argument fairly clearly presupposes that what is pleasant by nature is an objective matter, and in particular that it is independent of the judgement or preference of the lover of noble things. It is hard to read this argument otherwise than as recommending the pleasures of the noble life on the ground that the noble man's preference reflects what is really preferable; it is noteworthy that a13 reads 'the things which are pleasant by nature (subject) are pleasant to the lover of noble things (predicate)' and not 'the things which are pleasant to the lover of noble things (subject) are pleasant by nature (predicate)'.[1] Yet it is the latter reading which would be required if Aristotle were here making the point that things pleasant by nature are *constituted* as such by the preference of the noble man.

17.2.9. The argument of this passage, then, requires that there be a criterion of what is pleasant by nature independent of the preference of those who actually enjoy such things. That immediately threatens the status of the judgement of the good or sound man as a criterion of what is really pleasant. To refer back once again to our perceptual analogy, if sugar is sweet by nature, independently of how it tastes to anyone, then it needs to be explained just how the perception of the normal taster can be relevant to determining whether it really is sweet. Perhaps we might suggest that, while there is some objective fact of the matter in virtue of which sugar actually *is* sweet by nature, the only way we have of *telling* that it is is that it tastes sweet to the normal observer. Realism about tastes (and, by analogy, about pleasures) might then be claimed to be a position similar to realism about, say, the past; the realist claims that certain events actually happened, but the only way we have of telling that they happened is by consulting our memories and other indirect records. Just as the experience of remembering and of looking up records is held by the realist to give us access to the objective past, so the experience of the man in sound condition give us access to the realms of objective tastes and pleasures. A position of this kind is attractive in so far as we can actually give content to the notion of the alleged objective fact to which we have only indirect access. We can certainly do this in the case of the past, as we see from e.g. the fact that we *understand* the hypothesis that our memories and records might be systematically erroneous. But it is doubtful whether any meaning attaches to the hypothesis that salt may as a matter of fact be sweet. Aristotle would, then, be

---

[1] Cf. 1170a14–16. 'It has been said of the good by nature that it is good to the good man (*tōi spoudaiōi agathon*) and pleasant in itself.'

on shaky ground if he attempted to defend his position on pleasure by the adoption of a 'realist' strategy of this kind.

17.2.10. Does Aristotle in fact even attempt to specify what makes certain things pleasant by nature, independently of their being enjoyed by the man who is in sound condition? The concluding paragraphs of the discussion of pleasures in *EN* VII (1154b9 ff.) might perhaps be interpreted in this sense. Here he is discussing the question why bodily pleasures are commonly held to be the most desirable form of pleasure, and in the course of his discussion draws the familiar distinction between on the one hand pleasures which are experienced when one gets rid of a painful state of bodily deprivation, and on the other pleasures which involve no distress. The latter, he says, belong to the class of things pleasant by nature and not incidentally. Restorative pleasures such as those of convalescence are pleasant incidentally, in that what is strictly speaking enjoyed is the activity of some part of the organism which remains in a healthy condition, and which happens to lead to restoration of the proper state and hence health. The pleasure of satisfying one's thirst is, then, strictly speaking, pleasure in the exercise of the capacity of assimilation of liquid (or perhaps pleasure in the perception of the exercise of that capacity). The fact that the act of assimilation restores the proper balance of bodily elements and so eliminates the distress of thirst is an incidental feature of the situation, just as the fact that a statue is made by a man with knowledge of music is an incidental feature of the situation which is properly to be described as the making of a statue by a sculptor (who is, incidentally, a musician). By contrast (b20) 'things pleasant by nature are those which bring about the activity of such and such a nature'. Thus the eating of grass in good condition brings about the activites, such as cud-chewing and digestion, proper to the nature of the cow, and is therefore by nature pleasant to the cow. Here it might seem, we have a preference-free test for things which are by nature pleasant to man; if we find things which bring about the activities proper to human nature, then we shall have found the things pleasant by nature to man. But the search for things which bring about the activities proper to human nature takes us back again to the preference of the *phronimos*; for the activities proper to human nature are those which constitute the *ergon*, the function or characteristic activity, of man, i.e. in the first place the intellectual excellences and in the second place the excellences of character such as courage and temperance. Now we have already seen first that in the *Nicomachean Ethics* Aristotle defines excellence of character in terms of dispositions of the *phronimos*, and secondly that excellence consists not merely in doing what the *phronimos* approves but in doing it in the right spirit, i.e. gladly or with enjoyment. Hence in the practical sphere the description 'things which bring about the activities proper to human nature' is co-extensive with 'things which bring about activities which the *phronimos* enjoys'. It is clear that we have no way of telling which things are by nature enjoyable other than by observing what the *phronimos* enjoys; what is less clear is whether, as we have suggested, Aristotle may have thought that the enjoyments of the *phronimos*, rather than constituting certain activities as pleasant by nature, give us access to the objective truth that those activities *are* pleasant by nature.

17.2.11. In this connection a crucial, though ultimately indecisive text is *EN* 1113a25 ff. where Aristotle is discussing the question whether the object of wish is what is in fact good, or what each person considers good. His answer is that in the unqualified sense wish is for the good, but in the case of each person his wish is for what he takes to be good. He continues 'In the case of the good man the true good is wished for, but in the bad man's case anything at all, just as things that are really healthy (subject) are healthy (predicate) to bodies in good condition, but different things (sc. are healthy) to sick bodies, and similarly with bitter and sweet and hot and heavy things etc., for the good man judges each sort of things aright, and in each sort of things the truth seems (sc. so) to him. For each disposition has its own fine and pleasant things appropriate to it, and the good man perhaps differs most in that he sees the truth in each kind of things, being as it were the standard and measure of them.' In this passage we find expressions suggestive of the view that the good man's judgement reflects an independent reality, side by side with others which suggest that it constitutes that reality. In favour of the former we have the statements that the good man sees the truth in each sort of things, and that things that are really healthy are healthy to the body in good condition (cf. 1099a13, and above 17.2.8, and contrast *EE* 1235b33–5 (17.2.1) which reads 'we say that the things which are good for the healthy body are good for the body without qualification, but not things good for the sick body, e.g. drugs and amputations'). In favour of the latter we have the fact that Aristotle illustrates his thesis by examples of sensible properties at least some of which (viz. bitter, sweet, and hot) fit the latter interpretation more naturally, and, above all, the description of the good man as the 'standard and measure' of how things are. (The use of the word 'measure' (*metron*) in this context (repeated at 1176a17–19) could hardly fail to recall the famous dictum of Protagoras 'Man is the measure of all things' the point of which was precisely to deny the existence of any reality independent of how things appear to the individual. Aristotle might then be thought to be proposing the revised formula 'The good man is the measure of some things'.) The mingling of these contrary indications in the course of a few lines would most reasonably be taken to suggest that Aristotle had not formulated the question with which we have just been struggling, viz. 'Is there an objective fact that certain things are pleasant (sweet etc) by nature, which is revealed by the judgement of the good man, or is it rather the case that those things are pleasant because the good man judges them to be so?'. He is concerned to emphasize firstly that the judgement of the good man is true and secondly that that judgement is our only means of telling what is the case with regard to pleasantness etc. The further question 'What *makes* the good man's judgement true?' is one to which Aristotle's text seems to provide no definitive answer; a possible explanation of this silence is that the question itself had not occurred to Aristotle.

17.2.12. We see, then, that Aristotle's attempt to discriminate 'real' pleasures (i.e. unqualified pleasures, or, equivalently 'things pleasant by nature') from 'pleasures' which are so called only with some qualification (or, equivalently, 'things incidentally pleasant') though central to his ethical enterprise, leaves two major questions unanswered. These are, firstly, the metaphysical question 'Assuming it to be a fact that certain things are unqualifiedly pleasant, what is the nature of that fact?' and, secondly, the epistemological question 'How can we discover which things are unqualifiedly pleasant?'. The former question is literally unanswered; indeed, as we have seen, it is not even explicitly posed. To the latter Aristotle does supply an answer, viz. 'By observing what the *phronimos* enjoys', but the question yet remains unanswered in the sense that that answer is unsatisfactory, since in the *Nicomachean Ethics* Aristotle provides no directions on how to identify the *phronimos*.

17.2.13. It is worth remarking in conclusion that Aristotle appears to remedy that deficiency in the *Eudemian Ethics*, since in the last chapter of that work (1249a22 ff.) he does what he nowhere does in the *Nicomachean Ethics*, viz. specify the rule or standard (*horos*) by which the good man (*spoudaios* (= *phronimos*)) determines what is right in action and in the choice of such external goods as wealth and friendship. The standard is 'whatever choice and use of things good by nature, whether goods of the body or possessions or friends or other good things, will best promote the contemplation of God, that is best and that the finest standard; but if any choice and use impedes the service and contemplation of God, either through deficiency or excess, that is bad' (1249b17-21). It is indeed the consensus of commentators (Monan,[2] Cooper,[3] Rowe[4]) that Aristotle is not here specifying the norm for actions, but merely the norm for the choice of external goods; but that dichotomy seems quite artificial, in view not only of the explicit mention of actions together with choices of external goods at a25, but also of the fact that choice of external goods *is* action manifesting one's state of character. Thus excess in the acquisition of wealth is covetousness (part of *aneleutheria*), excess in the

[2] pp. 129-31.   [3] (2), pp. 137-41.   [4] (1), p. 110.

acquisition of pleasure (a bodily good) is intemperance (*akolasia*) and so on.[5] Thus it is no accident that Aristotle explicitly relates this specification of the standard of action and choice of goods to his general doctrine of excellence of character as a mean. This passage provides the missing identification of the *phronimos*; good actions are those which best promote the study of the divine nature,[6] and the *phronimos* is he who does and enjoys good actions. The same point might be put in terms of the function of human nature: it is appropriate to man above all to contemplate reality, and the man in perfect condition is he whose intellect and desires are so harmonized as to promote the achievement of that end. Yet this identification of the *phronimos* will be both useless and otiose as a means of identifying real pleasures. It will be useless because of the requirement that the *phronimos* enjoys good actions (see 17.2.6-7); that requirement makes it impossible to find out that e.g. a certain kind or amount of bodily pleasure is really pleasant by *observing* that that is what the *phronimos* enjoys. For, given the knowledge that that kind of pleasure, in that amount, best promotes *theologikē* anyone who doesn't enjoy it is not properly *phronimos*, but is at best *enkratēs* (self-controlled). And it is precisely that knowledge which makes the proposed criterion of reality in pleasures otiose. For if we know that a certain pleasure best promotes *theologikē* we know that it is best suited to the proper functioning of human nature, i.e. that it is something pleasant by nature, as opposed to something which is pleasant only when nature is in one way or another disorganized. Given independent knowledge of the purposes of nature, we have no need to rely on anyone's judgement as a test of what is naturally, i.e. really or unqualifiedly pleasant. It is, therefore, probably not accidental that, in contrast with the *Nicomachean Ethics*, the *Eudemian* are comparatively reticent on the role of the good man as a criterion of real pleasures: he is nowhere *described* as a standard or measure of what is really pleasant, and only one passage implies that role (1235b31 ff., see 17.2.1). On the other hand a number

---

[5] So Kenny (4), pp. 182-3.
[6] This is identified in *Met.* E 1. as the subject-matter of metaphysics, there called *theologikē*. See Kirwan's commentary on the chapter.

of passages (1237a1–10, a25, 1238a27, 1239b30 ff.) indicate that the unqualifiedly good and the unqualifiedly pleasant are determined by the proper functioning of human nature. It is a further question whether this difference of emphasis between the *Eudemian* and *Nicomachean Ethics* is better explained on the assumption of the priority of the former or of the latter.

Chapter 18

Epicurus

1. Introduction

18.1.1. The topic of pleasure continued to excite lively interest among philosophers contemporary with and following Aristotle, as is shown by the fact that most of the best-known writers of the period, including Theophrastus, Aristoxenus, and Strato among the Peripatetics and Xenocrates, Heracleides Ponticus, and Crantor among the Academics, are reported as having written on pleasure. The scanty surviving fragments of this literature provide no evidence of any development in the theoretical treatment of the topic, consisting as they do mostly of picturesque anecdotes illustrative either of sybaritic hedonism or of unqualified anti-hedonism. (The fact that some of these works were in dialogue form allows both attitudes to be found in the same work, as we see from the excerpts from Heracleides preserved by Athenaeus (frs. 55–9 and 61, Wehrli). The interest was not, of course, wholly moralistic: thus Theophrastus wrote in addition to treatises on pleasure a work *On False Pleasure* (DL V.44 and 46), apparently critical of Plato's treatment of that topic in the *Philebus*, but the evidence of its content is too scanty to allow any useful conclusions to be drawn.[1] For significant evidence of post-Aristotelian theoretical treatments of the subject we must turn to Epicurus.

18.1.2. Although he was one of the most voluminous writers of antiquity, very little of Epicurus' work has survived. In his life of him Diogenes Laertius has preserved three supposed letters and a collection of *Principal Doctrines*. Of the letters, the first, which gives the fundamentals of his

---

[1] The Neoplatonist commentator Olympiodorus mentions a single argument from this work (Theophr. fr. 85, Wimmer).

physical theory, and the third, which is on ethics, are probably genuine, and so too are the *Principal Doctrines*. The second letter is probably at least a reliable record of doctrines. There are also a good many isolated quotations in various authors as well as ascriptions of doctrines. The quotations can probably for the most part be taken as reliable, although one has of course no guarantee that they are being interpreted aright. This is particularly true where the quoters are hostile. When it comes to description of doctrines the risk with the hostile authors is obvious, but even a sympathetic commentator like Diogenes Laertius cannot be assumed to have caught every nuance. Finally there is a collection of dicta known as the *Vatican Sentences*.

18.1.3. While Epicurus almost certainly looked upon his philosophy as a unified whole, the astronomy and physics being needed to show that the ethical conclusions were right, we shall take the ethical remarks as a starting-point, only venturing into other areas in so far as is necessary to explicate these. With regard to the ethical remarks priority will of course be given to those which directly bear on the form of his hedonism. Here the easiest place to start will be with a sketch of the general doctrine and some apparent inconsistencies in it. The attempt to remove the inconsistencies will lead to a clearer articulation of the doctrines.

18.1.4. According to Diogenes, Epicurus used an argument reminiscent of Eudoxus (DL X.137), appealing to the fact that all living things are well pleased with pleasure and are by nature, without recourse to reasoning, hostile to pain, and so we automatically flee the latter. It does not, however, seem identical with Eudoxus'. To begin with (cf. 8.3) Eudoxus adduced various considerations that are quite absent from Epicurus. Secondly, Epicurus seems to insist on the fact that the recognition of the value of pleasure is pre-rational. This suggests that he is insisting on the relation of pleasure to perception. If Cicero reports him right, he seems to have thought that strictly no argument is necessary to show that pleasure is to be pursued, pain shunned, for we perceive it directly, as we do that fire is hot or honey sweet (*Fin*.I.ix.30).

In other words, the experience of pleasure is experience of its goodness. Indeed for consistency with his theory of knowledge Epicurus must be able to give a perceptual basis for judgments of value if he is to claim that they can be known. This is sometimes construed as though pleasure were a feeling attached to a perception. The word *'pathos'* which Epicurus uses to categorize pleasure and pain, means, rather, a way of being affected. Thus according to Diogenes (X.34), the Epicureans say that there are two *pathē* that occur with every living thing, pleasure and pain. One might be tempted to think that there are also others, e.g. a Platonic neutral state. But Epicurus allows of no midway between the two: pleasure is defined as the absence of pain. Not, of course, that any absence of pain (e.g. death) is pleasure, but any painless conscious life is a pleasure, where, we must remember, life would not consist simply in being alive, but in living the kind of life characteristic of the species. So with sentient beings there are just two ways in which in their sentient activity they can be affected: painfully or pleasurably, the first being aversive, the second appetitive. So every perception involves being affected in one or other of these ways and in such perception a sentient being grasps the value or disvalue of being so affected, a grasp that is, at a pre-logical level, constituted by acceptance or aversion. Clearly the whole bias of this way of thinking will be to make the goodness of each particular pleasure obvious in each perception. There will be no temptation to make the value of pleasure maximization over a life obvious to perception. Nor will any need be felt to appeal to Eudoxan observations as to how human beings argue about the worth of things, what questions they do or do not ask, still less to argue from premises that suppose that there are other goods than pleasure. If a judgment of worth can be known to be true then it must be possible to refer to some value given in perception to substantiate it, and the only answer can be that it contains pleasures, for anything else can only be judged good in so far as it yields this. If now we are to compare lives it can only be by some comparison of pleasantness, and anyone who makes a judgment about the worth of a life is making a judgment that can only be substantiated by reference to its pleasantness, which can only be judged in the last resort by the perception of those who live it. There is room for argument as to what form of life is pleasantest, but no room at all for discussion as to what makes something good. (For a fuller discussion see Ch. 20.)

18.1.5. When it comes to assessing various degrees of pleasantness, Epicurus seems to have thought that pleasures are of two sorts, those of change (kinetic) and those of stable condition (katastematic) and perhaps that either sort could be primarily bodily or mental. (DL X.136, 144). Those associated with motion seem to be those which accompany a change from pain to its removal, whereas those of a stable state are those of conditions where pain is absent, and with it any cause of change (DL X.128-9). Quite generally, pleasures cannot increase in degree beyond the point of removal of pain (*PD* 3; DL X.139). With bodily pleasures this limit is reached when the need that is causing pain is removed. Mental pain is largely caused by such things as grief and fear, and so is only to be removed by reflections on the sources of these emotions (*PD* 18; DL X.144). In either case there is no possibility of increase past the point of the removal of pain, only of variation. There is no need, therefore, to get into complexities of comparative intensities or other methods of assessing the comparative pleasantness of different activities. A life free from pain *ipso facto* wins over one not so free.

18.1.6. The main problem, then, is to discover whether a life of pleasure can in fact be attained and if so how. At the bodily level this is a question of whether we can live without bodily distress. Epicurus held that severe pain was generally short-lived, and long-lasting pain allowed of excess of pleasure over distress, so that properly viewed unavoidable pains of illness should not be given much weight (*PD* 4; DL X.140). For the rest, the meeting of bodily needs was a fairly easy matter (*PD* 15, 21; DL X.144, 146). When it comes to removing the distresses of the mind the matter is more complicated. To a large extent these are emotional, especially fears (*PD* 20; DL X.145 and also X.137). If we take fears, as the main trouble-makers, they are aroused by the prospects of future evil. In Epicurus' view they were to a large extent based on false views either of the nature of man and the universe or of the nature of pleasure. Thus one of the main fears is that of death. But if one understands the constitution of man and the soul properly one realizes that the soul is made up of very fine atoms that disperse when at death the enclosing sheath of the body fails to hold them together (DL X.63–9). With its dispersal sensations, and so both pleasure and pain, cease, and consequently death is not a condition to be feared since it contains no evil (pain) (DL X.81, 124–5), and indeed, it is not a state of ourselves. Other things such as illness will become less fearful when one gets a true view of their status as pains and the wise man's capacity to cope with them. Similar points will hold for other disturbing emotions, such as longing for honour: absorption of the correct view of things will diminish them, and something approaching true peace will be found to be obtainable. A simple life removed from public affairs and bolstered by reflection on the basic facts about the structure of the universe can be relied upon to yield a stable happiness.

2. Problems

18.2.1. So much for the outline. Now for some complications. These may be put under six headings:

18.2.2. (i) The above would suggest, and Epicurus states, (DL X.131–2), that he does not attach importance to the sensual pleasures, and yet he is quoted by Athenaeus (VII. 280a) as saying that he can conceive of no good if the pleasures of taste, love, hearing and sight are removed, and more dramatically (XII.546 ff.) as saying that the pleasure of the stomach is the source and root of all good, and clever or ingenious things are to be judged by reference to it. This remark was seized on by his opponents as a stick to beat him with.

18.2.3. (ii) This suggests that he thought bodily pleasures the greatest, but according to DL (X.137) he differed from the Cyrenaics in thinking that mental pains were worse than bodily ones and mental pleasures greater than bodily ones.

18.2.4.(iii) Yet *PD* 18 (DL X.144) implies that once distress is removed there is no difference of degrees among pleasures, but at most only of quality.

18.2.5.(iv) Epicurus also refuses to take extension in time as supplying a measure of pleasantness. This secures peace for the wise man, who will not discriminate between a life of two years, twenty years, or eternity so long as it is of pure pleasure, and so will not be gnawed by anxiety to secure extensions of life. Yet in the *Letter to Menoeceus* (DL X. 129-30) we are told to judge pleasures and pains by their effects, and here it seems very implausible to suggest that if course *X* leads to a year of pure pleasure followed by a month of pain, course *Y* to two years of pleasure followed by a month of pain, still there is nothing to choose between the two. Plausibility suggests that duration must be an important factor here.

18.2.6. (v) Epicurus talks as though pleasure were some positive feature in life, and yet (DL X.128-9, 131) he defines pleasure purely negatively as freedom from pain. This no doubt enables him to speak of pleasures of replenishment and of removed desire as equally pleasures, while giving preference to the latter, but it seems a simple fraud, nonetheless.

18.2.7.(vi) There seems to be some confusion over just what the good is. Usually it is pleasure, but also we are told that the greatest good is wisdom or prudence (DL X.132). Yet at best this could only be a useful piece of equipment for ensuring possession of the good.

18.2.8. It is inconsistencies such as these that have made people think that Epicurus is something of a patchwork moralist who did not thoroughly think through his position, but was prepared to be shocking or traditional to serve the need or whim of the moment. Some degree of obscurity or inconsistency is compatible with a serious attempt at thinking, but the above list would surely justify demotion to the second rank.

3. Response to problems

18.3.1.   (i)' To take the first first: an enemy of Epicurus, of course, could be expected to seize upon such remarks to show that Epicurus advocates a life of profligacy. Even the sympathetic Bailey seems to suppose ((1), pp. 487-8) that Epicurus would believe that the body yielded the most evident feelings of pleasure, and so the prime/greatest pleasures, so that he is only following his principles to their logical conclusions in giving pride of place to sensual pleasures. He saves himself from advocating profligacy only by calling in the hedonistic calculus which (cf. *PD* 10; DL X. 142) is the only reason for downgrading the pleasures of the flesh. It would seem, however, that Epicurus can be given a stronger defence than this. It is not, after all, obvious that he ought in consistency either to hold that sensual pleasures are the most evident, over mental ones, or, indeed, that they have any special claim to the title of pleasures of the body. So far as the latter point is concerned, one might expect Epicurus to say that the real pleasures of the body came with the removal of pain. Indeed he states (*VS* 33) that the voice of the body (flesh) is: not to hunger, not to thirst, not to feel cold. This suggests that what is perceived as obviously good to the body is not sensual pleasure as usually conceived. It might therefore, be worth reconsidering the passages from which we started. The first thing that strikes one is that the first passage does not say that the pleasures of taste etc. are either greater or more important than any others. That is sheer inference from general probabilities and the second passage. By itself it simply says that Epicurus cannot conceive of the good if these pleasures are removed. Of course it lays him open to hostile interpretation, but suppose one is a friend. In that case the remark at most claims that these pleasures are ones without which the good life is inconceivable. It does not entail that others are not also necessary nor does it suggest any ranking. There were, after all, those (e.g. the naturists of the *Philebus*, and cf. *EN* VII, 1154a8 ff.), who thought that no bodily pleasures had any part in the good life. To Epicurus this must have seemed to involve a very peculiar view of man, and one perhaps tenable only if one held some extreme dualism. But one also has to remember

Epicurus' views on real pleasure. The limit of pleasure is reached when pain is removed. It may be that the pleasures of sight and hearing are generally unmixed, but if those of taste are the pleasures of satisfying hunger, then with regard to taste and sex, the body will find unmixed pleasure only with removal of distress. Since there are only two *pathē*, pleasure and pain, then in Epicurean terms anyone who says that one should avoid these pleasures is (*a*) in the unmixed cases simply advocating avoiding an obvious good, and (*b*) in the other cases claiming that we should avoid the state of painless perception which is genuine pleasure, as well as the titillations of the pleasure of replenishment. But that is advocating distress. It will seem obvious to Epicurus that there is no good life without these pleasures properly conceived.

18.3.2. The second remark, however, viz. that the pleasure of the stomach is the source and root of all good, seems to give a definite primacy to the stomach and so, surely, to the body generally. The 'and so' of course does not strictly follow, and indeed the singling out of the stomach might suggest that other bodily pleasures do not occupy such an important position. For the rest, we still have to remember that the pleasure that the stomach desires is not, or not primarily, either that of being replenished or those of unnecessary titillation, but the condition of being without pain. Since desires for gustatory titillation are ones whose lack of gratification does not entail pain, they are due to illusory opinion (*PD* 30; DL X.149). Those of replenishment (i.e. being replenished) on the other hand, are not the body's object. The question is, then, why should Epicurus consider peace of stomach so important? To which the answer might simply be: experience. Hunger causes headache, inability to concentrate, short-temper; over-eating causes heaviness, dyspepsia, inability to appreciate things. Irregular or ill-managed diet results in constipation or other digestive upsets with their usual effect on one's capacity to appreciate other pleasures. It is a common view of sages that a well-regulated diet is the foundation of a well-regulated life. It would not be surprising if Epicurus thought that the pleasure (properly

understood) of the stomach is the starting-point and root of
all good. But this is not to say that the pleasures are greater,
still less that bodily ones generally are, nor to deny that there
are many other even more important ones.

18.3.3. It is however, true (cf. 19.2) that Epicurus thought
that bodily pleasure, i.e. a condition of painless sensory
pleasure, had a certain primacy, in that *ataraxia* consists in
confident expectation of bodily pleasure and pleasant memory
of it. Since such *ataraxia* will only be secured if the expectation and memory are well-based, pleasure of the mind is
clearly dependent on bodily pleasure. This, however, does
not make bodily ones greater. Further, since anxiety can ruin
one's bodily pleasure, and since *ataraxia* requires bodily
pleasure as a general rule, there is a sense in which *ataraxia*
constitutes the highest condition of pleasure, and so can be
said to be more important.

18.3.4. The above does not, of course, constitute a proof
that this is what Epicurus meant by the comments cited. But
the standard interpretation does seem to involve ascribing to
him an insistence on the primacy of sensual pleasures which
seems to be straightforwardly inconsistent with other remarks
that he makes, whereas the above interpretation makes these
remarks fully consistent with his other statements. So unless
there are general grounds for supposing Epicurus to be a
shoddy inconsistent thinker, it should be preferred.

18.3.5. (ii)' De Vogel (III, p. 33) takes it that the passages
dealt with in the first objection commit Epicurus to the view
that bodily pleasures are greater than mental ones. Yet
Diogenes states clearly that one thing that distinguished
Epicurus from the Cyrenaics (Aristippus and his followers
(see Ch. 2)) was that he considered that mental pains and
pleasures were greater than bodily ones. If the remarks in (i)'
are right, then this difficulty can be met by pointing out that
Epicurus is not in fact committed at all to saying that bodily
pleasures are greater than mental ones by the passages cited.
The most that can be claimed is that he thinks certain bodily
ones essential and that certain bodily ones are the beginning

and root of a good life. Not even the latter commits him to their being greater pleasures. So Diogenes could be right and Epicurus could have thought that mental pleasures were the greater.

18.3.6. (iii)' But this brings us to the third problem. For Epicurus should not be prepared to allow that one unmixed pleasure can be greater than another. The 'greater than' relation can only hold between pairs of pleasures at least one of which is mixed, it cannot hold between two unmixed ones. So this at least looks like a fairly blatant inconsistency.

18.3.7. The only hope here is to query the testimony of Diogenes, but it clearly will not do simply to dismiss it because it is awkward. Two things are, however, worth noting: first, although Diogenes (DL X.136, 137) sounds as though he is reporting an explicit set of disagreements with the Cyrenaics, he is probably only working out divergencies, and secondly, when the point at present under discussion is introduced the dispute is over whether physical or mental pains are worse; it is only after an explanation of why Epicurus thought mental ones were worse that Diogenes adds that for the same sort of reason he thought that mental pleasure were greater. Now the Cyrenaics dismissed the idea of calculating the effects of actions and advocated pursuing the immediately available pleasure. So far as immediately available pleasures were concerned they considered bodily ones to be the greater, presumably judging degrees of pleasure on a scale of intensity. Since pleasure is the only good, and this does not mean pleasure maximization over a life, they are obviously going to think that bodily pains are worst and bodily pleasures best just because most painful and pleasurable respectively. One would not, however, expect Epicurus to settle the question of which were better in these terms (DL X.129–30). He would not deny, perhaps, that some bodily pains are very intense, and even more intense than any mental ones, but he thought that intense bodily pain was always short-lived and that therefore one should not make much fuss about it (*PD* 4; DL X.140). For, in such pain the body has only to cope with the present disorder, which is only of brief duration. The mind, by contrast, dwells on not only present evils but past and future ones as well, and so its pain endures as long as the memory and expectation of evil. These are also typically fertile of pain. The memory of past failure leads to fear of future ones in turn aggravated by memories of past ones. So the body's limitation to its present condition in contrast to the mind's wandering over past, present, and future would make one, on Epicurean grounds, consider the pains of the mind to be worse, and this is precisely the ground cited by Diogenes in X.137. But this is, note, a ground for considering them worse, not in any ordinary sense as more painful. Epicurus' disagreement with the Cyrenaics would be precisely on the point of equating what is more painful with what is worse. It is only after his reports of the Epicurean grounds for thinking mental pains to be worse that Diogenes comments that 'so in this way he holds that the pleasures of the mind are also greater'. But 'this way' has given no grounds for supposing them greater in the sense of more intense, nor pleasanter in any sense found elsewhere in Epicurus. At most it gives grounds for supposing them more enduring and more productive of pleasure. It is simplest in fact, either to suppose that 'greater' does not mean 'more pleasant', or to suppose that this has slipped in because of carelessness on the part of Diogenes who was constructing a dispute in which Epicurus' 'opponents' were using 'greater' as equivalent of 'more pleasant' and taking greater pleasures as *ipso facto* better. Either way Epicurus is not committed to saying that mental pleasures are pleasanter than bodily ones, though he will doubtless say that unmixed mental ones are pleasanter than mixed bodily ones. So the probability is that the basis of Diogenes' report is quite consistent with Epicurus' remarks elsewhere on degrees of pleasure.

18.3.8. (iv)' One thing, however, that seems implicit in the idea of fertility used to explain Epicurus' disagreement with the Cyrenaics is the view that time is important, that a long period of pleasure is preferable to a short one, a long period of pain worse than a short one. Even if it is not implied, it certainly is the most natural and plausible way to take the calculation of pleasure, and Epicurus' remarks on the transitory nature of severe bodily pain at the very least suggests

that he thought this way. And yet in *PD* 19 (DL X.145) he
says that if by reason we measure the limits of pleasure, an
unlimited and a limited period provide the same amount of
pleasure. In other words, no extension of the period of a
pleasure will increase it. In the next doctrine the idea that
pleasure has no limits and so requires an unlimited period for
its acquisition is said to come from the flesh. This seems to
imply that a wise man will not take the duration of pleasure
or pain into account, not even presumably in operating the
calculus.

18.3.9. Now it is not difficult to see why Epicurus might
have wanted to deny the importance of duration. The need
to assess and review the likely durations of the pleasant and
painful effects of our actions would at once introduce an
un-Epicurean anxiety into our lives. It is the same as the
objection to certain forms of act utilitarianism, that with
most of us the burden of calculation would defeat its own
end. Further, one can see how Epicurus may have thought
that it is characteristic of the flesh to be concerned about
duration. As a matter of observation, those who pursue
bodily gratifications do put stress on differences of duration,
and show an anxiety of behaviour that suggests that they
think that pleasure is or can be increased indefinitely with time.

18.3.10. No doubt according to Epicurus all this shows
the error of the flesh. Rational reflection reveals that there is
a limit beyond which pleasure is not increased, but unfortunately one further essential point that rational reflection
must reveal is that time does not increase pleasure either. It
looks as though Epicurus thought that one can in practice
acquire an attitude to the standard pains and pleasures which
make one indifferent to duration, but the question at issue
is whether such an attitude, which is based on certain beliefs,
is rational. This in turn brings us back to the question
whether the view that duration does not effect the degree of
pleasure is true.

18.3.11. At this point it might help to put the question
from the other side and ask: how could more time yield more

pleasure? Suppose someone is enjoying a lamb chop. What does one have to suppose if one supposes that simply by extending the meal one increases the pleasure? What one probably thinks is that one's appreciation grows with time as one savours more of the subtleties of flavour. But this is not to put the increase at time's door, but either to claim that some other factor, such as further removal of pain, has come to explain the increase of pleasure, or to claim that other pleasures have been added, which is not to say that that one has been increased. Similarly, if we suppose someone to be contented with life, we may ask how time could add to the contentment? Once again it can only be that with time some element of discontent is removed, but then it is this removal that makes for the increase of pleasure. Whether we are thinking in terms of enjoyment or contentment (being pleased with life) mere extension of time plays no part in increasing pleasure. If the pleasure continues unchanged except in respect of duration then it is in no way increased. That Epicurus would have thought this way is suggested by his view of time. For he considered time to be an accident of accidents (SE *M* X.219; DL X.70-3). In his usage (see Bailey (1), pp. 304 ff.) an accident is a property which an object may acquire or lose without changing its nature. It is not one of those properties which constitute a thing as the thing it is. Time is an attribute of actions, events, and so on, which in turn happen to, but do not constitute the nature of various objects. The time at which Brutus killed Caesar does not constitute the nature of the killing, but is accidental to it. Nor does the duration of the murder constitute the nature of the murder. The same killing might have been prolonged for five minutes without becoming a different killing, and without becoming more of a killing. Since time is only an accident of actions and *pathē*, a change in time is not thereby a change in the nature of that which changes in time. This point is quite general and would apply to pleasure as to any other *pathos*. The mere fact of persisting over a long period could not alter the nature of a *pathos* or make it either more or less of such and such a sort.

18.3.12. While this view on time would incline Epicurus

to deny that duration could increase pleasure, it is not clear
that it entails this denial. For this we need another Epicurean
doctrine, that the good is *ataraxia*, and not prolonged *ataraxia*.
This is not at all obvious. Observation of both men and
animals, but perhaps especially the former, would on the
contrary, lead one to suppose that prolongation is important,
so that if one infers that pleasure is the good one will be
inclined to take increase of duration as one form of increase
of pleasure. It is at this point important to recall the perceptual basis of Epicurus' theory of knowledge and the difference between his obervations of animals and what might
have been Eudoxus'. For all that perception can hope to give
us knowledge of is the goodness of being affected in such and
such a way. One could not perceive the goodness of being
affected in this way indefinitely. Any belief that indefinite
extension is better will have to face the test of perception.
But no perception could show us the value of that. This is
not to deny that men and animals can be seen to pursue
indefinite extension, but this is where Epicurus parts company
with Aristotle and Eudoxus by not accepting indiscriminately
all observations of actual pursuits as evidence as to what the
good is. What is important is observation of the loved and
hated perception. But Epicurus simply thinks it is true that
most men have illusory objectives, and among other things
groundlessly suppose that pleasure is increased with time.

18.3.13. Yet while this may explain not only why Epicurus
might want to deny that extra time might increase the
pleasure units, but also how that denial fits in with other
independently held doctrines, it does not show how he can at
the same time declare that some pleasures are to be preferred
to others in that they lead to fewer distresses, for this must
surely in part mean that they result in a smaller proportion of
one's life being taken up with distress? But this is just
another way of saying that the wise man prefers the course
that leads to a longer stretch of pleasure over against pain.

18.3.14. At this stage two points need distinguishing:
first, we want to know whether there is any inconsistency
between asserting that one pleasure is better than another if

it leads to a longer period of pleasure over pain and denying that an activity is made pleasanter by being prolonged; and secondly we want to know whether Epicurus can save his wise man from the anxiety of daily calculations as to the likely extent of his pleasure under various options. As to the first, it seems clear that Epicurus must in some sense hold that one course is better than another if it leads to more pleasure, and so must make room for some notion of pleasantness that will attach to periods and in particular lives, such that· lives can be compared for pleasantness. Yet he could surely do this in some such way as follows: just as pleasures can be compared just so long as at least one is mixed, so periods can be compared just so long as at least one is mixed. As in the other case, one will be pleasanter than the other if the proportion of pleasure to pain is greater. But there will be no way of comparing two unmixed periods for pleasantness, whatever their differences in length. Comparison will only enter in if we can extend one or both periods until they become mixed. But if Theaetetus dies young while Plato lives on to old age, then so long as both have lived unmixed or equally mixed lives, neither life can be said to be either better or pleasanter than the other. Nor, since death is not to be feared, has either anything to gain by trying to prolong life. This is, however, to look on the lives from the outside as it were. In actual practice it will surely still be true that a wise man will always be concerned with increasing the proportion of pleasure in his life and reducing the amount of (unavoidable) pain. It is only in fanciful utopian conditions that he will not be concerned with duration.

18.3.15. The answer here lies in the answer to the second question above. We are so used to problems about utilitarianism that we are inclined to assume that anything that sounds like a hedonic calculus is meant for day to day use. But this does not seem to be true with Epicurus. He is not telling us that a wise man must go in for daily intricate calculations of the sort *perhaps* envisaged in Plato's *Protagoras*. Not at all. A wise man needs to know certain basic facts about man and nature, convince himself of them and acquire certain habits of life. These will ensure that pleasure predominates. The calculation is all at the stage of working out the facts, the effects of belief in them, and the proper regimen. One will have from time to time to rehearse one's knowledge and confirm one's attitudes and practices, but the latter will not include anxious logistics. Once one is convinced of the truth of Epicurus' doctrines and has incorporated his teachings into one's life, one ceases to worry and leads a life as near to *ataraxia* and *aponia* as is possible for one. One's mental equipment ensures that no future suffering will be such that one will not be able to cope with it with a balance in favour of pleasure, and there is going to be no benefit in seeking to extend one's life as though it would improve with length. To achieve the best life possible one does not need exceptional intellectual ability or mathematical competence either, like Plato's Socrates. Conviction and good habits are enough. The wise man then is relieved from the fruitless fuss of assessing the relative durations of pleasure in various activities. His wisdom shows in the acquisition and development of those characteristics that will keep his life as pleasant as it can be, and that being so he will not be deluded into thinking that it will improve if only it lasts a little longer. So he will be content with life from day to day and not disturb himself about the future. So although in a mixed life a longer spell of pleasure over pain is better than a shorter, and sense could be given to saying that that makes the life pleasanter, that is not because the longer pleasant episode is pleasanter; and the wise man neither concerns himself in day to day life with extending pleasant periods nor deceives himself into thinking that his life will be improved or made pleasanter by being made longer.

18.3.16. (v)′ Epicurus' eulogies of the good life make it clear that he thought of it in positive terms of contentment, and yet his terms *aponia*, *ataraxia* are purely negative, and he talks as though the mere removal of pain or disturbance were all one was after. Yet as Plato pointed out, in both the *Republic* and the *Philebus*, absence of pain is not a pleasure. This seems to be true in two senses (*a*) 'absence of pain' is not the name of a pleasure, nor does '*A* has no pain' entail that *A* has some pleasure; (*b*) in fact there are conditions where pain is absent and pleasure not present, and one such, death, was asserted by Epicurus to be of this sort. Yet if death is a state of perfect *aponia* an Epicurean should advocate immediate suicide. In fact, however, death is considered indifferent rather than desirable. The question arises, therefore, whether Epicurus is confused or just cheating, or whether he can be interpreted so as to escape the difficulty.

18.3.17. The first point to remember is that Epicurus is considering the question of what the good is that living things pursue in life, and this is the question what sort of life is their good. Death is not a form of life, and the good is not just absence of pain, but a life without pain or disturbance. Once again, living a life free of disturbance is not just a matter of staying alive and not being disturbed, as with a person under heavy sedation, but living the sort of life specific to the being in question. Epicurus could concede to Plato that there are states of living things which are neither pleasant nor painful, as for instance, states of unconsciousness, but he would not concede to the subtlers of the *Philebus* that once the process of coming-to-be had finished the pleasure was over. Faced with the problem which it was suggested faced Plato after the *Republic* (cf. 6.8) Epicurus refused to make a choice. Granted we have a conscious living thing, then he seems to have thought, if it is living its specific form of life that life will be pleasant except to the extent that the proper balance is disturbed. In pleasures of restoration the condition of the organism is not entirely disrupted. To the extent that it approximates to proper balance there will be pleasure, (for to that extent some of the imbalance will have been removed and some balance restored), but the pleasure will be perfect only when the balance is. Having a physicalist view of the constitution of man he will be very inclined to some view of the good state as consisting in a physical balance of the organism, but he has no inclination to follow Plato or Aristotle in their views of the exquisite pleasure of philosophy. There is nothing special about the mind in this respect and indeed, un-Platonically, its main value is not in the divine glory of the intellect, nor its special pleasantness, but in its contribution to the general stability of the system. In some ways this has an Aristotelian ring: if one is living according to one's nature then one is enjoying one's life, and failure of enjoyment is a function of disrupted nature. But Epicurus' physicalism makes him stick firmly by physical balance, and this in turn makes him less interested in individual activities and their enjoyments, which gets Aristotle embroiled with external goods (cf. 13.4.3-4), and more in a condition of the individual which ensures him balance independently of external circumstance.

18.3.18. (vi)' Yet this suggests that wisdom is to be seen merely as a means to producing pleasure in the way that it was suggested (cf. 7.2.2) remained a possibility in the *Philebus* after 20-3. It may be that if we are wondering what equipment would be desirable for someone starting out in life we should want to add in wisdom as a security, but surely (*a*) one could have a pleasant life without wisdom, although doubtless it would be sheer luck, and (*b*) the worth of that or any other life is judged quite independently of the presence of absence of wisdom. Of course, it must not have been lived unwisely in the sense of in a way that a wise man would not, but it could surely have been lived without the benefit of wisdom? Yet according to the *Letter to Menoeceus* (DL X.131-2) the virtues are necessary for a pleasant life, and wisdom is the source of all the virtues.

18.3.19. This last seems clearly to rule out the possibility of a pleasant life without wisdom, but the question remains how such ruling out can be justified. Here the first thing to note is that Epicurean wisdom (*phronēsis*) is more like Aristotle's practical wisdom than Plato's wisdom. In the passage just cited from the *Letter to Menoeceus* it is declared to be more important than philosophy and in the *Letter to Herodotus* (DL X.78-82) Epicurus is quite clear that the study of physics is of value primarily because it leads to the removal of various fears and troubles. Secondly, it consists not in the possession of high intellectual abilities but in a firm appreciation of the basic truths about the universe and human pleasure and pain. Part and parcel of this will be the possession of true beliefs about what is to be feared or not, and so a condition of relative fearlessness. Similarly it will involve freedom from illusory desires and their consequent disturbance. Now a human being has a mind willy-nilly and consequently will acquire beliefs about what is to be feared and what is pleasant. Freedom of disturbance in this area consists primarily in having the right convictions and acting on them, and this is precisely what wisdom is. A moron may live happily without wisdom, but has not a properly consti-tuted human nature. Consequently his cannot be an example of a good human life. Granted a normal constitution of human soul-atoms in a human frame, *ataraxia* consists in a condition of correct belief, *aponia* in a condition free of bodily lack. The distinction between wisdom and *ataraxia* is therefore verbal rather than real. So one could not have a pleasant human life without wisdom. Similarly, since its absence is equivalent to the absence of *ataraxia* and so of mental pleasure, and its presence to the presence of mental pleasure, using it or mental pleasure as a criterion of worth come to the same thing.

18.3.20. In short it seems that Epicurus can be acquitted of inconsistency on the points mentioned and emerges with a view that normal life is pleasant unless one's constitution is disturbed; that one's whole tendency is against disturbance (disruption) and towards a state as free of it as possible; since pleasure is only reduced by disturbance this means that the organism appreciates as good/best the pleasant/most pleasant, whose worth is recognized in perception; there is no going higher than the unmixed condition; but once one recognizes the nature of the good as given in perception one can see that many beings actually pursue illusory goods; the wise man recognizes that a relatively unmixed life is attainable, and to a large extent achieves it in that recognition; he thereby acquires an indifference to either death or the extension of life and a contentment with what he has. One may be sceptical about the possibility of achieving an Epicurean calm, especially about the Platonic remark that a good man will be happy on the rack; but one has to remember that he is himself reputed to have died in considerable pain and to have written during his last illness: 'My continual sufferings from strangury and dysentery are so great that nothing could augment them; but over against them all I set gladness of mind at the remembrance of our past conversations' (DL X.22). In all this we have largely assumed an account of the relation of katastematic and kinetic pleasure which is, to put it mildly, open to dispute. Since a good deal of the defence of Epicurus depends on it, we shall devote the next chapter to it.

Chapter 19

Katastematic and Kinetic Pleasures

19.0.1. Notoriously, Epicurus considered pleasure to be the good and by that primarily meant that *ataraxia/aponia* was the good. While he allowed of other, kinetic pleasures, these katastematic ones take pride of place. The highest pleasure and greatest good is to be without pain or disturbance, and it is this condition at which all living things naturally aim. It has usually been taken as fairly unproblematic which pleasures are kinetic. All sensory pleasures fall into this category and perhaps some mental ones such as learning. This determines Usener's selection of passages, and it tends to be a point of agreement among commentators who disagree about the nature of katastematic pleasure and its relation to kinetic. Thus Diano, and after him Rist,[1] argue that every kinetic pleasure presupposes the presence of a katastematic one, since any sensory pleasure requires the good, and therefore painless, condition of at least part of the organ in question, and that is another way of saying that there is prior katastematic pleasure in the organ. On the other side Merlan argues for a more positive view of katastematic pleasure, considering it the state of joy of a being free of pain and anxiety. But he agrees that all sensory pleasures are kinetic.

19.0.2. With the nature of kinetic pleasures thus agreed, the point of dispute becomes just how Epicurus thought of katastematic pleasures, and why he used the same word for both kinds. The Diano/Rist position makes katastematic pleasure in danger of being the negative condition of lacking pain or anxiety, and this makes one wonder why Epicurus was not content to join those mentioned by Aristotle (*EN* 1104b24) who thought the best condition one of *apatheia*. On the Merlan view it becomes slightly more intelligible why

---

[1] Diano (2), (3); Rist (2).

he should not take this route, but still a question why he did not make his point by reserving some word especially for his *summum bonum* and contrasting it with kinetic pleasure. Yet so far is he from doing this that he claims he doesn't know what he could conceive the good to consist in if one takes away sensory pleasure (fr. 10 = U 67), although the good is apparently katastematic pleasure. In general these interpreters feel the pull of the difficulty developed by Cicero, in *de Finibus* I and II, that Epicurus seems to be using the same word confusingly for significantly different and unrelated phenomena.

19.0.3. To begin with we shall try to bring out how any view which sees kinetic pleasures as comprising at least the sensory ones, and as constituting a distinct class from katastematic ones, involves attributing an awkward view to Epicurus. We shall then outline our own interpretation indicating how it meets this difficulty. Only then shall we systematically consider the evidence.

19.0.4. The kind of view we wish to oppose holds that it was an important feature of Epicureanism to insist on dividing pleasures into two sorts, sensory ones on the one hand, and katastematic ones, of which lack of disturbance of mind (*ataraxia*) and lack of pain (*aponia*) are the important examples, on the other. The distinction was important to Epicurus because it was the latter which he wished to put forward as the good in life, and he needed the contrast in order to defend himself against the charge that he was advocating a life of debauchery. He can be seen doing this in the *Letter to Menoeceus* (DL X.131-2) where he says that when we call pleasure the goal we do not mean the pleasures of profligates, but to be without pain of body or distress of mind. The pleasures of profligates are obviously the sensory pleasures, and Epicurus is making it clear that he is putting forward something else as our goal. There are four objections which such views have to meet (see 19.0.6-9).

19.0.5. There are various ways of construing the contrast. (i) The words might be taken at their face value. In that case, granted that sensory pleasures are all in the kinetic category it seems that katastematic pleasures are simply conditions of being without various forms of distress. This is certainly the line taken by Cicero, and the views of Diano and Rist at least teeter on the edge of it.

(ii) Epicurus could hardly have intended to use the word 'pleasure' to refer to so negative a condition as lacking distress. He must have been intending to refer to a state of joy achieved in a life from which pain and distress are absent, a joy which is distinct from and independent of any sensory pleasures which might or might not be experienced. This seems to be the view of Merlan.

(iii) Epicurus has not got any special notion of joy, but he is drawing our attention to the fact that it is possible to get pleasure, in fact the greatest pleasure, from realizing that we are without pain. This is suggested by two things: first, Plutarch refers directly (*Non Posse* 1091a–b) to remarks by both Epicurus and his follower Metrodorus to the effect that there is great pleasure in escape from evil (not, of course, death, as De Witt suggests, (p. 154), since for Epicurus death is not an evil): secondly, Cicero (*Fin.* I. xi.37), makes the Epicurean Torquatus insist on the pleasure we get from emancipation from pain. Both sources are supposed to clarify what pleasure Epicurus had in mind as the greatest good, and so should be giving the nature of katastematic pleasure. It seems to us that this would be building a lot on a little evidence. These remarks form a very small part of the accounts of katastematic pleasure and do not feature in any of the major passages on either *aponia* or *ataraxia*. In addition the view is open to the objections below.

19.0.6. As we have pointed out, all these views assume that the distinction between kinetic and katastematic pleasures was one on which Epicurus put a particular emphasis, and that they were different kinds of pleasure, the good in life consisting in some of the latter. It is this feature of all such views which creates the problems. These are as follows:

(i) It is agreed on all these views that the good is *ataraxia* and *aponia*, as distinct from sensory pleasures. But Epicurus is very insistent on the importance of sensory pleasures. This is most obvious in two quotations given by Cicero (*Tusc.* III. xviii.41-2):

> In that book which contains all your teachings [Epicurus,] . . . you say: 'For my part I cannot understand what that good is if one subtracts those pleasures perceived by taste, those from hearing and music, and those sweet movements, too, got from visual perception of shapes, or any of the other pleasures generated by any sense in the whole man. Nor can one hold that joy of mind is alone among the goods. For as I understand it the mind is in a state of joy when it has hope of all those things I have mentioned above, that nature may acquire them with complete absence of pain.' And these are his very words, so that anyone may understand what Epicurus recognizes as pleasure. Then a little lower down he says: 'I have often enquired of those who were called wise what they had left among the goods if they removed those ones, — unless they wanted to emit empty noises; I could learn nothing from them; if they want to boast about virtues and wisdom they will say nothing unless they mean the way by which those pleasures are achieved which I mentioned above.'

Here Epicurus is not just saying that sensory pleasures are a good thing, but that nothing is left to the good life if you subtract them. Indeed virtue and wisdom can only be praised if they are considered as a means to them and joy of mind is entirely dependent on them. Yet on any of the interpretations under consideration one would expect Epicurus to know perfectly well what would be left among the goods if sensory pleasures were subtracted: *ataraxia* and *aponia*. Since these are the good, the loss of the other pleasures would not be catastrophic: one would still have painlessness, joy, or the recognition of the absence of pain. Indeed, one would expect that virtue and wisdom would be shown valuable as productive as these, not of sensory pleasure. Yet these quotations are not isolated and all the ancient critics, admittedly hostile, got the impression that sensory pleasures loomed large in the ideal Epicurean life. So it looks as though at worst we have an inconsistency, at best a confusion into which Epicurus was perhaps led by polemical over-enthusiasm.

19.0.7. (ii) Epicurus is insistent that the senses are the criterion of truth, and in particular the criterion of goodness (DL X.124, 129, 137). This is confirmed by Cicero (*Fin.* I.

ix.30–1) who reports a dispute among Epicureans on the
point, Epicurus holding that the good is recognized in
perception 'as that fire is hot, snow white, honey sweet'.
What precise form this view took we shall discuss in detail in
the next chapter. For the moment it is enough to note that
the good is appreciated or grasped in perception. It is easy
enough to see how sensory pleasure might be grasped in
perception. It is not so easy to see how the various versions
of katastematic pleasure might be. If we turn to the first
version above we find Cicero (*Fin.* I.xi.39) defending the
Epicureans against the following objection: a hand that has
nothing wrong with it lacks nothing; but if pleasure were a
good, it would lack pleasure; therefore pleasure is not a good.
The obvious assumption is that the pain-free hand is without
any (felt) pleasure. Cicero's defence is that while this might
be an objection to a Cyrenaic it cannot tell against Epicurus
since for him the mere absence of pain is pleasure, indeed the
greatest pleasure. This objection and the defence against it
are used by Cicero to bring out the contrast between familiar
sensory pleasures and conditions of being without pain either
altogether or in particular organs. He is surely right to claim
that if the mere absence of pain is the greatest pleasure then
the greatest pleasures pass for the most part unnoticed, and
certainly could hardly be given in perception without
becoming sensory pleasures. In short, this interpretation
makes it hard for Epicurus consistently to hold that the good
is given in perception. Of course, Epicurus could say that
when we realize that we are without pain we experience the
greatest pleasure. This would be the third interpretation
above. It would, however, involve *reflection* on our state, a
state quite possibly lacking sensory pleasure, and no sensory
pleasure is necessary for the state to be seen as good. So this
would leave it obscure how Epicurus could hold that the
senses are the criterion of goodness. The end of *De Finibus*
I.xi does, indeed, provide some evidence that some Epicureans
did consider that it was reflection that convinced us that
katastematic pleasure is the good, but the same chapter is
also evidence that that was not the view of Epicurus himself.
The same objection holds with joy: if this is not a sensory
pleasure it is unclear how its goodness is given in perception.

19.0.8. (iii) The third objection is that Epicurus seems to be cheating. This is most obvious if we insist on a purely negative account of *aponia* and *ataraxia*. For in this case, as Cicero points out, many people would not agree to call these states pleasures simply in virtue of lacking pain, so that Epicurus would seem to be trading on using 'pleasure' in a new sense while relying on its old sense for part of his argument. But even if we take *aponia* and *ataraxia* to be joy, or the realization that pain is absent, if Epicurus is insisting on the difference between these and the kinetic pleasures of sense, then we have the following oddity: what the senses reveal as good is in fact something quite different from what really is good, for they give experience of kinetic pleasures whereas it is the quite different katastematic kind that is the good.

19.0.9. (iv) Finally, it would be somewhat surprising to find Epicurus allowing the existence of a state of a living thing lacking both pain and sensory pleasure. For according to *PD* 2 there is no life without perception, and, according to the *Letter to Menoeceus* (DL X.124) it is in perception that good and evil are to be found: 'Get used to the thought that death has no relation to us; because every good and evil is in perception; and death is the deprival of perception.' Good and evil are pleasure and pain respectively and these (DL X. 34) are the only *pathē*. One would expect every good state to be a mode of perception, and perception to be the form of life. This is reinforced by the *Letter to Herodotus* (DL X.64-6) where after asserting that the soul brings perception to a body he writes: 'this is why so long as the soul is present, even if some other part is lost, perception never ceases'. As the passage goes on it is clear that this life and perception is a function of motions of the soul-atoms made possible by the protective sheath of the body. The picture is of a living thing in a state of constant motion of its atoms in interaction with its environment, the congenial motions being pleasures (DL X.34), the uncongenial ones pains. There is no place for a static or non-perceptive condition of pleasure.

1. Suggested interpretation

19.1.1. We would not pretend that these objections are conclusive, but they do indicate that certain styles of interpretation involve attributing rather obvious awkwardness to Epicurus. An interpretation which does not attribute them is thus far preferable. We shall now expound such an interpretation, and then proceed to defend it against at least the more obvious objections.

19.1.2. The passages quoted by Cicero in *Tusculan Disputations* (cf. 19.0.6) suggest a different picture of *aponia* and *ataraxia* whereby *aponia* is a condition of having sensory pleasures but with no accompanying pain, and *ataraxia* is a state of confidence that one may acquire such sensory pleasures with complete absence of pain. This confidence is itself a positive state. However unadulterated by pain one's sensory pleasures may be, one's pleasure is all too likely to be spoiled by various misapprehensions. These will be false beliefs about death, about the gods, about fancy diet, about the limits of bodily pleasure, about the desirability of long life and so on. These erroneous beliefs disturb the mind (cf. *PD* 10-12, 18-22) and their removal is required for *ataraxia* (cf. passages just referred to and also DL X.81-2, 124-6, 130-2). But for *ataraxia* more than the absence of false beliefs is needed: they have to be replaced by true ones. It is these that give confident expectation of a pleasant life, and so constitute the removal of anxiety. In short, those ancient critics who complained that Epicurus laid great emphasis on bodily pleasures would on this view be right: what is important is to get a life of sensory pleasure untainted by pain; *ataraxia* is itself geared to *aponia*, and joy of mind generally is a matter of memory and expectation of unadulterated pleasure, based on true belief. The objection to the pleasures of profligates (DL X.131-2) and perhaps the only objection Epicurus has (cf. *PD* 10), is that they fail to remove anxiety. The point with profligates is, presumably, that they erroneously believe fine food to be necessary, fail to see when desire is satisfied, and so pursue their objectives to the point of consequent distress, and so foolishly fear, as threats to their good, things which should not be feared.

2. How this interpretation meets the earlier difficulties

19.2.1. If we look at the objections which we held that some styles of interpretation have to meet, it should be clear that this interpretation does not have to meet them. So far as the first objection is concerned it would be no oddity on our view that Epicurus insisted on the importance of sensory pleasure. On the contrary, that is just what he thinks we should be after, with the proviso that we also secure absence of pain.

19.2.2. As to the second objection, on our view *aponia* is not a non-sensory pleasure but a condition of sensory pleasure. What perception reveals to us directly is the goodness of pleasure and the badness of pain and thereby that the only unqualified good is pleasure without pain. Since any painless perception is pleasant, perception reveals the goodness, though not, of course, the achievability, of *aponia*[1]. The value of *ataraxia* is parasitic upon that of *aponia*, since the only *ataraxia* worth having on Epicurus' view is that which comes from pleasant memories and confident expectations of sensory pleasures of a painless kind. These extend, as it were, present pleasures or modify present pains by surrounding them with a pleasurable ambience. Thus the body's pleasures have pride of place.

19.2.3. As to the third objection, Epicurus is clearly not, on our view, using 'pleasure' in a strained sense in applying it to katastematic pleasure. The most that could be claimed is that he is inclined to use '*ataraxia*' and '*aponia*' of conditions of life rather than particular pleasures, but this sort of use had been familiar at least since Plato's *Protagoras*, and is derived from the application of the word to particular pleasures. Whether our view is altogether free from criticism along these lines depends on what account we can give of kinetic pleasure, but at least Epicurus is not straining language, or obviously cheating in calling katastematic pleasures pleasures.

---

[1] Nor does it reveal the choiceworthiness of individual pleasures (see 20.1.1).

19.2.4. Since, on our view, *aponia* just is a condition of painless perception it creates no expectation that Epicurus might envisage a non-perceiving state as pleasurable. The fourth objection, therefore, simply does not arise.

3. Kinetic pleasures

19.3.1. The most obvious objection to the view proposed is that it simply shifts the difficulty elsewhere. A problem with the kind of view discussed earlier was how Epicurus could plausibly put katastematic pleasures into the same class as kinetic ones. On the present view the problem is reversed. Since sensory pleasures have been transferred to the katastematic class, it is a good question what has been left over to count as kinetic. For the moment we shall content ourselves with expounding our answer to this, leaving till later in the chapter an objection to it. The reason for this is that while expounding the answer helps to fill out our picture of Epicurus, and so contributes to the development of the chapter, the treatment of the objection would be a distracting digression.

19.3.2. To begin with, it is important to note that we are not saying that all sensory pleasures are katastematic, although we are saying that *aponia* is a condition of having painless sensory pleasures. The question that one has to ask is what force Epicurus might have given to the terms 'katastematic' and 'kinetic'. The word 'katastematic' is an adjective from the noun '*katastēma*', and we know (cf. Plut. *Non Posse* 1089d = U 68) that one Epicurean expression for *aponia* was 'the well-established *katastēma* (condition) of the flesh'. One might therefore expect that katastematic pleasure is pleasure of the organism in proper condition. We also know (cf. 8.2, 15.1, Appendix B) that during the fourth century, and in many cases associated with the Academy, there had been various analyses of pleasure which had portrayed it as a *genesis*, a replenishment, a movement, or a *katastasis eis phusin* (restoration to the natural state). The purpose of many of these views had been to show that pleasure could not be the good since it was a movement aimed at an end term, and it is the end term that must be the good. Clearly anyone wishing, like Epicurus, to hold that pleasure is the good, might feel the need, against such views, still in evidence when the *Magna Moralia* was written, to assert that in addition to such kinetic pleasures (pleasures of movement) there are pleasures of the *katastēma*. Indeed, if our view is correct, Epicurus, perhaps taking a hint from Aristotle, seems to have held that when the organism is operating properly it will be in a state of pleasure, and pain is a matter of unnatural operation. This, note, is a view about the organism, not individual organs. At any time a properly functioning organism will be perceiving, but not, of course, with every organ. Many organs will be in good condition, but pleasure-less because not perceiving. There is no reason for Epicurus to hold, in Cicero's example (cf. 19.0.7) that a hand without pain experiences pleasure, only that an organism which is perceiving and without pain experiences pleasure.

19.3.3. If this is right two things follow: first, kinetic pleasures are not a different kind of pleasure from katastematic ones; they too are sensory and are a matter of some part of the organism operating properly. When one quenches one's thirst some parts of the organism are working naturally, some not, and there is a steady increase in the area of natural operation; but no different account of the nature of pleasure is needed. Secondly, one would not on this account expect Epicurus to lay great stress on kinetic pleasure in the exposition of his views, except in the polemical context suggested. Otherwise one would not look for any prime role for the distinction in Epicurean theory. This commits us to discounting in large measure the testimony of Cicero, and we shall aim to do that in due course.

19.3.4. It is perhaps worth emphasizing that any view on this subject owes us an account of Epicurus' choice of terminology. On the more traditional view one has to suppose that 'kinetic' is chosen because Epicurus has an account of perception in terms of the movement (*kinēsis*) of atoms. The trouble with this is that Epicurus' account of the organism quite generally is in terms of the movements of atoms, so that it is difficult to know what 'katastematic' is referring to. This might tempt one to Merlan's version of the contrast in terms of stable (katastematic) as against passing pleasures. There is no evidence that we can find for this version in the original context of Epicurus' writings, though it has to be admitted that perusal of Cicero, and acceptance of his translations, does give some colour to the view. On the other hand, there is evidence in the background to Epicurus for the kind of contrast which we are suggesting, and it fits well with a view which relieves Epicurus of the awkwardness mentioned earlier in this chapter.

4. The ancient evidence

19.4.1. So far we have contented ourselves with pointing out some oddities in certain current interpretations of the katastematic/kinetic distinction and describing an alternative interpretation together with a certain amount of evidence for it from the writings of Epicurus. Anyone familiar with the literature on Epicurus might be forgiven for feeling uneasily that the weight of the ancient evidence is nevertheless heavily against such an interpretation, and that one simply has to accept that Epicurus is in a state of some confusion on the subject. We shall now, therefore, turn to the examination of this evidence. For convenience we shall divide the relevant texts into three groups:

(i) There are passages such as Lucretius IV.627–9, and the passages cited in Usener (408–15) as giving Epicurus' position on kinetic pleasures.

(ii) There is the evidence of Cicero, mainly from the *De Finibus* but also from the *Tusculan Disputations*.

(iii) There is one passage (DL X.136) where Epicurus uses an expression which might be meant to refer to kinetic as distinct from katastematic pleasure.

These passages are usually taken to show between them that the Ciceronian view, that all sensory pleasures are kinetic and katastematic ones form a different class, correctly reflects the position of Epicurus.

19.4.2. (i) *Usener etc.* The passage of Lucretius does not

even seem to have anything to say about the nature of kinetic pleasure unless we already assume that pleasures of sense are kinetic. Lucretius is enquiring into the location of taste and arguing that it is in the palate. The ground for this is that when the food passes down to the stomach the pleasure ceases. Nothing is said as to whether the pleasure is kinetic or katastematic — understandably since he is concerned not with pleasure but the location of perception. The mention of pleasure is purely incidental. Granted that any perception is either pleasant or distressing, and that the taste in question is pleasant, the termination of the pleasure will signalize the termination of the perception. It is only if we know from elsewhere that sensory pleasures are kinetic ones that we can use this passage in discussing the relation between the two.

19.4.3. Other passages are on the face of it more difficult in that they refer to the sensory pleasures as *kinēmata*, or cite them as kinetic pleasures. Thus Plutarch (*Col.* 1122e = U 411) writes 'For they invite one themselves, without need of a teacher, these beautiful, smooth and gentle motions of the flesh, as they (the Epicureans) themselves say.' This certainly suggests that Epicureans, and so probably Epicurus, considered sensory pleasures to be motions. But then, as we have seen, Epicurus would have to think of all pleasures as motions, so that this sort of passage gives no ground for supposing these pleasures to belong to the special class of kinetic pleasures. The other sort of passage is more problematic. Thus Athenaeus (XII.546e = U 413) writes 'Epicurus and his followers were fond of kinetic pleasure. I need hardly mention the storms of passion and delicacies which Epicurus often proposes, the titillations, too, and solicitations of the senses.' Clearly Athenaeus considers these sensory pleasures to be kinetic. He does not, however, give us a quotation from any Epicurean declaring them to be kinetic rather than katastematic pleasures, and the question arises which will arise later with Cicero, whether Athenaeus is declaring them to be so because he has read Epicurean texts calling them kinetic, or because he himself believes these pleasures to be *kinēmata* and so assumes them to be kinetic for Epicurus; or perhaps because he is relying on Cicero. As our evidence stands only DL X.136 has any claim to give us words of Epicurus himself on the nature of kinetic pleasure and its relation to katastematic. While the *Letter to Menoeceus*, the *Principal Doctrines*, and the *Vatican Sentences* have a good deal to say about *ataraxia* and *aponia*, they are silent on the nature of kinetic pleasure. This might strike some as false, and *PD* 18 might be cited: 'Pleasure will not be increased in the flesh when once that which suffers because of lack is removed, but it is only varied.' This is often taken as saying that sensory pleasure only varies the katastematic pleasure achieved when pain is removed. The passage, however, has to be read with Cicero in hand to yield this result. As it stands it has nothing to say about kinetic pleasure. It simply states that there is no increase of pleasure once pain is removed, only variety. As to whether those varied pleasures are kinetic or katastematic, it is silent. It is quite consistent with the view that the process of removal of pain will be a process of extending the area of pleasure, so increasing pleasure, and this process is what has been called kinetic pleasure, but once that process is over there can be no increase of pleasure, only variation according to the perception operative in the painless condition. This variety, however, is variety in katastematic pleasure.

19.4.4. This would not, indeed, be possible if Epicurus thought there could be no variation in katastematic pleasure. This is a view attributed to him by Rist on the basis of *PD* 9. Before turning to that difficult *Doctrine* it is worth asking what reason Epicurus might have for denying diversity in katastematic pleasure. *PD* 18, already cited, makes it clear that he had no general thesis about lack of variety of pleasure. That *Doctrine* does, indeed, indicate that among katastematic pleasures there could be no difference of degree, but that is a different point. If katastematic pleasure simply consisted in the proper, painless, condition of the whole organism, then, of course, there would be but one; but clearly Epicurus distinguishes at least between *ataraxia* and *aponia*, and in claiming that a wise man will be 'happy' on the rack (DL X. 118 = U 601) implies that one could have the first without the second. On the Diano/Rist view, whereby every part of the organism is capable of katastematic pleasure in virtue of being in a good condition, it is utterly obscure why variety should be denied, since the good condition of one part of an organism will be different from that of another. The only reason for homogeneity that suggests itself here is that a katastematic pleasure is constituted as such simply by the absence of pain in a part of the organism. This entails a heavily negative view of katastematic pleasure, which would certainly leave Epicurus open to Cicero's complaint of equivocation with the word 'pleasure'.

19.4.5. It is not, then, clear why Epicurus would want to hold that katastematic pleasure is homogeneous, except on this negative thesis; and it is clear that he admits of variety among pleasures even if, to concede a point for the sake of argument, that is only in the case of kinetic pleasures. How, then, does *PD* 9 help? The first difficulty is that the text is very much disputed and almost all commentators have suggested emendations. The trouble now is that emendations will seem more or less plausible according to what one thinks Epicurus likely to say, and that weakens the independent evidential value of the *Doctrine*.

19.4.6. As they stand the manuscripts read as follows:

Ei katepuknou(to) pasa hēdonē (kai) tōi (kai) chronōi kai periodon (peri hodon) to athroisma hupērchen ē ta kuriōtata merē tēs phuseōs, ouk an pote diepheron allēlōn hai hēdonai.

The brackets contain alternatives. Thus some manuscripts have an active, some a middle or passive verb to start with, they vary in the placing of '*kai*' some having just a lacuna, and some separate '*periodon*' into two words. Most commentators have taken the middle or passive verb, giving various translations, e.g. 'if every sort of pleasure were added together' (Boyancé), 'if every pleasure were maximized' (Rist), — all of them slightly awkward; the verb means 'condense', but it is not clear what would be meant literally by 'if every pleasure were condensed'. There is then a tendency to keep the first '*kai*' (and), drop the second and emend '*periodon*', after Rossius, to *peri holon*. The whole

would then read: 'If every pleasure were condensed and
continued for a time and through the whole aggregate (i.e. of
atoms) or the most important part of the nature in question,
pleasures would never differ from one another.' This involves
a minimum of emendation. Others have further suggested
filling the lacuna of some manuscripts, to read either: 'If
every pleasure were condensed both spatially and temporally
and obtained through the whole organism' (Diano); or 'If
every pleasure were condensed in intensity and temporarily
and . . . ' (Bignone). The justifications of these further
additions lie in the general views on Epicurus held by their
proponents.

19.4.7. Rist thinks that a message can be.extracted even
though the precise form of the text is left uncertain. He
writes: 'According to Basic [= Principal] Doctrine 9, if every
pleasure were condensed (*katepuknouto*) and occurred
throughout the whole organism, or at least its most important
parts, pleasures would never differ from one another' (Rist
(2), p. 114). He cites two passages to illuminate 'condensed'.
First, a fragment from the comic poet Damoxenus reads,
'Epicurus thus condensed pleasure, he chewed carefully'
(Fr. 2, Kock); secondly, the second century AD sophist
Alciphron describes an Epicurean lasciviously embracing a
dancing girl. According to the Epicurean this is 'the undisturbed state of the flesh and the condensation of that which
enjoys'. Rist thinks it certain from these passages that 'condensing' implies squeezing out the maximum of pleasure. To
us the certainty is not apparent. First we have a contemporary
comic poet who has obviously come across an Epicurean use
of 'condense' and also, presumably, Epicurean statements in
favour of the stomach and sensory pleasure. Since chewing
can be presented as a form of pounding or condensing he
joins the two in a (not very good) joke. There is no reason to
suppose that he is offering an interpretation of 'condense',
or even that he understood what Epicurus meant. Much the
same holds with Alciphron. There is obvious irony in
describing the lecher as free of disturbance of the flesh, and
again the reference to condensation is either just picking on
an Epicurean phrase for ironic purposes for a situation when

a man's limbs are obviously loosed, and/or is suggesting erection of the penis. While Rist's interpretation may be right it is hardly made certain by these passages. After all *PD* 9 may be all these authors had to go on (an easily available source is the most likely), and why should we take them as experts?

19.4.8. Taking 'maximised' as the meaning of 'condensed' Rist argues as follows:

> He (Epicurus) says that (i) if all pleasures are condensed, that is, maximised and spread over the whole organism, then pleasures will not differ from one another. (ii) This means that in terms of quality there is no difference between the katastematic pleasure of touch and the katastematic pleasure of taste or sight. (iii) *Qua* pleasure they are equally pleasurable, insofar as they all equally consist in an absence of pain. (iv) Hence it follows that, if they could all affect all parts of the body, they would be indistinguishable one from another. (Rist (2), p.115 (our numbering)).

The argument here is obscure. Sentence (i) rightly preserves the original's generality in referring to *every* pleasure, but it is not clear what is meant by them spreading over the whole organism. If it only means that no part of the organism is without pleasure, it is not clear why there should be no differentiation. If it means that each pleasure is spread through the whole organism, then while this suggests a picture of general confusion, it is utterly obscure what Epicurus is supposed to have in mind. Sentence (ii) just gives a conclusion from a supposedly intelligible sentence (i). Sentence (iii) promises some help, but only doubtfully gives it. After all, absence of pain, for Epicurus, forbids difference of degree only; according to *PD* 18 it allows for variety. It might be, however, that he thought that katastematic pleasures, at least, simply consisted in the absence of pain and so were, *qua* katastematic, indistinguishable in quality as well as degree. But in that case we are left with no argument for the homogeneity of kinetic pleasures, and so the remark about *all* pleasures in sentence (i) remains unjustified. Certainly kinetic pleasures cannot consist simply in the absence of pain, and it is hard to think what the argument for their homogeneity with katastematic ones is going to be. Sentence (iv) contains all the obscurity of the second possibility for interpreting the latter half of sentence (i). It seems that nothing sensible is being attributed to Epicurus on Rist's interpretation, and nothing that supports a thesis of homogeneity.

19.4.9. Bollack (pp. 267-72) proposes to preserve the reading of some of the manuscripts, and the result would read as follows:

> If every pleasure produced condensation, and in a long time, too, and so the aggregate (of atoms) persisted for a period, or the main parts of the nature concerned, the pleasures would never differ from one another.

The result of preserving the text is awkward Greek, but that would be less surprising in Epicurus than elsewhere, and might even be an argument for preserving it. The protasis of the conditional is supposing that each pleasure produces a condensation of the atoms of the organism, thus excluding (so far as possible) the void. If this were the effect of each pleasure and the organism persisted so, or the chief parts of it, then each pleasure would produce a cessation of motion at least in the main parts of the organism, and so they would be indistinguishable. It is possible to interpret the thrust of the doctrine in one of two ways. First, one might take the conditional in the standard logician's way whereby the protasis presents a sufficient condition for the truth of the apodosis. But the condition is not one which Epicurus will want to countenance. Presumably, then, he is relying on the obvious falsity of the apodosis. But the logician's interpretation of the conditional is not the only one possible. Sometimes 'if . . . then' operates like 'if . . . then indeed', where the protasis serves to introduce an absurd condition which would be needed to secure the truth of the apodosis: 'if the optimists were right, then indeed it would be sensible to keep one's money in equities.' Here, the suggestion is commonly that the protasis introduces a necessary and sufficient condition which plainly does not hold. On this version (Bollack's, if we understand him), Epicurus would be drawing our attention to the obviously impossible condition which would have to hold if there were to be no variety of pleasures. As it is, the organism is always in motion and its patterns of motion vary from part to part, and time to time, and so there is variety of pleasure. On either version the *Doctrine* is hardly arguing for the homogeneity of pleasure.

19.4.10. The position then is that if we keep one manuscript version of the text we can extract a sense, but it gives no support to a thesis of homogeneity: quite the contrary. This version has an active form of the verb 'condense'. Some manuscripts have a passive form which must yield 'If every pleasure is condensed . . . ' Commentators have disputed the interpretation of that phrase, ('aggregated' 'maximized' and 'all pleasures' for 'every pleasure' have been proposed) and have suggested emendations elsewhere in the sentence to yield a sense. Doubtless changes can be made so as to produce an assertion of the homogeneity of pleasure, but the plausibility of such changes will in part rely on the independent plausibility of attributing such a doctrine to Epicurus.

19.4.11. There seem to us, then, no grounds for attributing this view to Epicurus, some grounds for expecting he would not hold it, and possible versions of *PD* 9 which would constitute rejection of it.

19.4.12. It seems, then, that we can interpret *PD* 18 in the way suggested so that once pain is removed we are in a state of katastematic, even if sensory, pleasure, and in that state there is a variety though no increase of pleasure. In fact the main evidence in favour of the view that it is kinetic pleasure which brings variety and that all sensory pleasure is kinetic comes not from the writings of Epicurus but from Cicero and DL X.136.

19.4.13. (ii) *Cicero*. In *de Finibus* Cicero is quite unequivocal. Thus in I.xi.37 he makes Torquatus, the Epicurean spokesman say,

For we do not only pursue that (pleasure) which moves our nature *itself with a certain gentleness and is perceived with a certain sweetness by the senses, but we also have that greatest of pleasures which is perceived when all pain is removed.*

Further evidence for the Diano/Rist view comes in *Fin.* I.xi. 39 (see 19.0.7) where Torquatus considers an objection relying on the supposition that a hand in good condition merely is not experiencing pleasure. He considers that the objection would touch the Cyrenaics, but not Epicurus. For Epicurus can admit that the hand wants nothing and claim that for that very reason it has pleasure.

19.4.14. Similar points emerge in Book II. Cicero is developing the objection that two such different things should not be called by the same name. He gets Torquatus to admit that the pleasure of quenching one's thirst is different from that of a thirst quenched, the latter being katastematic, the former kinetic (II.iii.9-10), and makes two complaints: first, that they deserve different names, and secondly that he is baffled as to what is meant by variation. He understands the idea of different pleasures from different sources, but

I cannot get an adequate grasp of the nature of that variety you mean when you say that we are at the peak of pleasure when we lack distress, but· when we enjoy those things which bring a sweet motion to the senses, then the pleasure is in motion (kinetic), which brings variation of pleasures, but that pleasure of not suffering is not increased, — though why you call it pleasure I do not know.

Cicero proceeds to press Torquatus to distinguish absence of pain from pleasure and not besmirch the name of virtue.

19.4.15. It seems abundantly clear that Cicero thinks that Epicurus

(*a*)   distinguishes sharply between katastematic and kinetic pleasures
(*b*)   holds that the former consist in the painless good condition of any part of the organism
(*c*)   holds that all pleasures of the senses are kinetic.
(*d*)   holds that in some way there can be variation of katastematic pleasure when pain is removed.

This supports all the Rist position except on the homogeneity of katastematic pleasure. The problem, of course, is to decide how reliable an interpreter Cicero is.

19.4.16. One might well hesitate to take Cicero as gospel. As Rist points out ((2), p. 105) he at least underestimates Epicurus on the subject of what small children desire (*Fin*. II.x.32–xi.39), and there are several points at which one starts to lose confidence. For instance in *Fin*. II.ii.4–iii.7 he argues that Epicurus is not using the word 'pleasure' in its ordinary sense. It becomes clear (cf. II.v.15–16) that the Epicureans generally felt their view misunderstood, and Cicero thinks this is because they perversely persist in using the same word both for the vivid pleasures of the senses and for mere absence of pain. 'Perversely' because 'everyone agrees that pleasure is that by the reception of which the sense is moved and imbued with a certain sweetness' (II.iii.6), and 'That sweet motion by which the sense is exhilarated everyone calls, in Greek *hēdonē*, in Latin *voluptas* (pleasure)' (II.iii.8). This is a doubtful statement, which at least requires forgetting some of the major Greek philosophers apart from Epicurus. Later the point is modified: 'Anyone in the world who knows Latin brings two things under this word (*voluptas*): joy of mind and the gentle arousal of delight in the body' (II.iv.13). No attempt is made to wonder whether this makes any difference nor is any notice taken of Epicurus' use of the word '*chara*' (= 'joy') in relation to katastematic pleasure (DL X.22, 66, 136), which might well correspond to 'joy of mind' to the ruin of Cicero's argument.

19.4.17. In the course of the discussion Cicero challenges Torquatus to say whether the pleasure of quenching one's thirst is the same as that of having quenched it (II.iii.9). The first is kinetic the second katastematic. The pleasure of tasting wine when not thirsty, however, is not considered, though it would be a pleasure of someone whose thirst is quenched and it would be sensory (cf. *Fin*. II.v.16 on the pleasure of eating a good dinner). For Cicero's failure to notice Epicurus' distinction between good and choiceworthy see Chapter 20. None of this shows careful attention to either the original texts or the refinements of argument. Further, Cicero is clearly unsympathetic to Epicurus, and while he obviously finds it difficult to make consistent sense of him, he is not predisposed to try too hard. The passage cited from II.iii.9–10 (19.4.14) on variation of pleasure shows either that Epicurus was very confused or Cicero has got him wrong: the passage does not suggest that Cicero understood much from his source.

19.4.18. These doubts arise from within Cicero's own text. Another source of doubt is authors other than Cicero. First we shall consider some remarks in Lucretius,[1] and secondly Plutarch's *Non Posse* where he argues that it is not possible to live happily by Epicurus' prescription. In neither does one find any sign that the distinction between katastematic and kinetic pleasure is of any importance in Epicureanism.

19.4.19. Lucretius is mainly concerned with Epicurus' natural philosophy and gives very little attention to the ethical side. At the beginning of Book II, however, we find a passage where he writes of the pleasure of being above the common hurly-burly where people pursue useless ends:

Do you not see that nature's only vehement demand is that pain be quite absent from the body, and that it enjoy with the mind sweet sense free of care and fear? So we see that altogether there are few things necessary for our bodily nature, just what will remove pain and be able to spread a picnic of many delights (16–22).

In the context 'sweet sense' must refer to sensory pleasure. There is no sign of an important contrast between this and katastematic pleasure, which is the good. On the contrary, what the body requires is pleasure-without-pain, where 'pleasure' refers to sensory pleasure. Lucretius shows just the lack of interest in any contrast between kinetic and katastematic pleasure, or between sensory pleasure and the good, which, on our interpretation, one would expect him to show, but which might be surprising if the distinction had the importance for Epicurus that Cicero's text suggests.

[1] We are indebted to Professor A. A. Long for making us realize the significance of this passage.

19.4.20. In his *Non Posse* Plutarch is arguing against the Epicureans to the effect that a life of constant bodily pleasure and tranquillity of mind is impossible. The sometimes sensible criticisms need not delay us. What is important for present purposes is the total lack of any sign that Plutarch saw in his Epicurean texts any stress on an important distinction between katastematic and kinetic pleasures. To begin with *ataraxia* and *chara* (joy) are treated as two names for the same thing, and they are geared simply to the body's pleasures, with no hint that this is some non-sensory absence of pain:

'they (the Epicureans) do well indeed,' said Theon, 'and take the way of nature [in passing from the pleasures of the body to the soul] if in their pursuit there they find something better and really more perfect as do men in academic or public life. But if you listen to them shouting in protest that the soul is only constituted to take joy and be calm with regard to present and expected pleasures of the body, and that this is its good, don't you think that they are using the soul as a decanter for the body . . . ?' (*Non Posse* 1088e)

The word translated 'be calm' is '*galēnizein*', which seems to have been a common Epicurean word for referring to *ataraxia*. The coupling of this word with one for to take joy in, and the insistence that tranquillity is directed to present and future pleasure and is not just an absence of distress, suggest that Plutarch saw these words as referring to the same condition, differing at most in that they draw attention to different aspects of it. As to the bodily pleasures, it has already been made clear (1087b–e) that his sources suggested that these were familiar sensory ones. It is true that at 1089d–e Plutarch suggests that the absurdity of their position when applied to bodily pleasure probably explains their retreat to talk of painlessness and established good condition of the flesh; but there is no suggestion that this reflects a distinction insisted on by his opponents; the point is rather that the terminology serves to conceal the otherwise patent absurdity. Plutarch (cf. 1095c, 1098b–d) is as clear as Cicero that Epicurus and his followers insisted on the primacy of sensory pleasure, but he seems not to have noticed any important role being given to the kinetic/katastematic contrast.

19.4.21. What we find in Lucretius and Plutarch is wholly consonant with the interpretation we have offered. It is, of course, unlikely that Cicero invented the distinction, but it is also unlikely that if it loomed large in Epicurean theory it would have been ignored by Lucretius and gone unrecorded by Plutarch. On our view one would expect the distinction to occur in a particular polemical context, so that it is perfectly possible that Cicero found it there and misconstrued the contrast. This would be made easier by two factors: first, that although not all sensory pleasures are kinetic, at least all the kinetic pleasures mentioned would be sensory (note that Cicero himself at *Fin*. II.iii.9–10 cites the replenishment pleasure of quenching as his example of kinetic pleasure) and secondly, Cicero is obviously convinced ·of an account of pleasures as sensory movements (*Fin*. II.iii.8) and so might understandably take Epicurean talk of kinetic pleasure as referring to just these. One might well complain that it ought to have seemed unlikely that Epicurus, living in the aftermath of Plato, and presumably knowing of those mentioned by Aristotle who thought the virtues to be states of *apatheia*, would have been insensitive to the difference between supposed states of lacking sensory pains or pleasures, and such pleasures. But then Cicero was not a friendly critic. We take it, then, that there is some reason for being suspicious both of Cicero's suggestion of the importance to Epicureans of the contrast between kinetic and katastematic pleasure, and of his interpretation of its nature.

19.4.22. It remains that Cicero is not ignorant of Epicurus. Often he more or less translates independently attested fragments (e.g. *Tusc*. III.xviii.41, *Fin*. I.xi.38; cf. DL X.6, *PD* 18 respectively). The passage on the role of perception, referred to at 19.0.7 shows acquaintance with the literature. At other points it is difficult to know whether Cicero has a source or is speculating. Thus in *Fin*. II.v.16 we find 'But if he thinks that pleasure in motion [kinetic] has to be included [in the good] (for he calls this sweet pleasure "in motion", the one of having no distress "in a stable state") what does he mean?' What we do not know is whether Cicero is quoting or inferring. If the former, the dispute is over, if the latter, it is alive, and general considerations would favour the kind of interpretation we have offered.

19.4.23. (iii) *DL X.136*. This brings us finally to the one passage of Epicurus where he seems to make a comment on the contrast of katastematic and kinetic pleasures, DL X.136. In this passage Diogenes is pointing to some contrasts between Epicurus and his followers and the Cyrenaics, followers of Aristippus. The latter do not recognize katastematic pleasures. According to DL II.89 they considered *aponia* the condition of someone asleep. But Epicurus recognizes both, and mental as well as physical (in contrast again with the Cyrenaics (cf. DL II.87)). Various sources are cited for Epicurus and also for Metrodorus and Diogenes of Tarsus. Most commentators at this point read as follows:

similarly Diogenes, too, in the seventeenth book of the *Epilecta* and Metrodorus in his *Timocrates* say as follows: 'but both kinetic and katastematic pleasure being considered pleasure'. And Epicurus in *Of Choices* says this: 'For *ataraxia* and *aponia* are katastematic pleasures; but joy and well-being are seen in actuality in motion (*kinēsis*).'

This makes Epicurus put joy and well-being down as kinetic pleasures, and would certainly entail that he is not just considering pleasures of restoration to a natural state as kinetic. Indeed, it would be hard to avoid a strongly negative view of katastematic pleasure. It seems that once a pleasure is experienced it becomes kinetic. As we have seen, such a view would raise severe difficulties for Epicurus' view that the good is given in unthinking perception, since it would seem that only kinetic pleasure is so given, while the position requires that katastematic pleasure be so known as the good. There are also certain awkwardnesses in taking the passage in the way proposed. To begin with, we get a single fragment apparently attributed to two authors, and the fragment is not a sentence, but a genitive absolute: 'but both kinetic and katastematic pleasure being considered (pleasure)'. Secondly, we are first given various works in which Epicurus asserts the distinction, then places where his followers do, and finally we return to Epicurus on the same point. Thirdly, we have to take '*chara*' ('joy') and '*euphrosunē*' ('sense of well-being') as referring to kinetic pleasures. There are two awkwardnesses here. First, Cicero regularly makes Torquatus use the word '*gaudium*' to talk of katastematic pleasure and this suggests (but does not prove) that Epicureans (*a*) used the natural Greek equivalent '*chara*' in this way and (*b*) did not have a totally 'negative condition' view of katastematic pleasure (cf. DL X.66). This is also borne out by Plutarch's use of '*chara*' and its associated verb '*chairein*' in *Non Posse*. Secondly, '*euphrosunē*' is an unusual word for sensory pleasures and would normally suggest a sense of well-being. In fact '*chara*' and '*euphrosunē*' seem to correspond to '*ataraxia*' and '*aponia*' in being their positive counterparts, whereas on the interpretation under consideration we have to take '*chara*' as a stand-in for an unspecified class of mental kinetic pleasure (as, perhaps, learning (cf. *VS* 27)), and '*euphrosunē*' as a stand-in for kinetic pleasures such as those of taste, smell, and sexual intercourse, instead of the state of well-being of one who has the pleasures painlessly.

19.4.24. These considerations might dispose one in favour of Bollack's view, though we can find no reason for accepting the contrast which he seems to espouse between *ataraxia* and positive happiness, which is the goal which makes *ataraxia* worthwhile (cf. Bollack, pp. 114–20, 182–6). For the rest his view is as follows: it is clear from DL II.87–9 that Aristippus and his followers thought that the good was bodily pleasure and that there was no other; and that they rejected the Epicurean idea of the good consisting in the removal of all painful areas, seeing that as being not pleasure but a state similar to that of a man asleep. Bodily pleasure they considered to be kinetic and they rejected the pleasure of the stable state. As we have seen there were at that period, apart from Aristippus, both philosophers who thought all pleasures to be *kinēseis* to some state and philosophers who thought the ideal to be a condition of being unaffected by pleasure or pain. In such a context Epicurus would want (*a*) to assert the existence of pleasures of the natural condition, (*b*) with his views on the disturbing power of superstition and the pleasures of memory, to assert the importance of mental pleasures, and (c) to make clear that his ideal was not one of *apatheia*. It seems clear in the first part of DL X.136 that the first two points are being made: that Epicurus insisted on katastematic pleasure as well as kinetic, and on mental as well as physical (though this sentence *might* be asserting that both are mental and physical in line with the *Letter to Herodotus* (DL X.63–6)). The rest might then read as follows

as he (Epicurus) says in *On Choice and Avoidance* and in *On the Goal* and in the first book *On Lives* and in the letter to his friends in Mytilene. And similarly Diogenes in the seventeenth book of *Epilecta* and Metrodorus in his *Timocrates* say the same; but with both kinetic and katastematic pleasure being apprehended by the mind. [Note that this is no longer a quotation, but a further attribution by Diogenes Laertius which is then going to be supported by the next fragment.] Epicurus in *On Choices* says as follows: 'While *ataraxia* and *aponia* are katastematic pleasures joy and well-being are seen in actuality by/in motion.'

19.4.25. On this reading there would be no attribution of one fragment to two authors: the genitive absolute gives Diogenes' attribution of a further point to Epicurus, that *both* kinds of pleasure (the Greek suggesting an emphasis on katastematic) have to be apprehended by the mind. This would be making the point that katastematic pleasures are not states of *apatheia*. This is backed up by a quotation from Epicurus which would then be read as saying that while these two negative sounding conditions are katastematic pleasures, joy and well-being are observed by motion. On this reading Epicurus would here be using '*chara*' and '*euphrosunē*' as terms giving the positive sides of the *ataraxia* and *aponia* coins, pointing out, therefore, that katastematic pleasures are experienced. Further, he would be pointing out that they are experienced in motion. This is what he certainly ought to hold in consistency with his general position on perception and is a point he ought at some stage to have made to distinguish himself from those who (like Speusippus?) thought the best state to be one of neither pleasure nor pain.

19.4.26. So far as we can see there is no proof from within the passage that one or other of these readings is right. Each has its awkwardnesses, and how great they appear will to a large extent be conditioned by one's prior views about Epicurus which will make the various points 'naturally' to be expected or surprising. With our own predilections we incline to Bollack's reading with the proviso, as we have said, that we see no ground for contrasting *ataraxia* and *chara*. To attribute such a contrast would leave Epicurus having something beyond *ataraxia* as the good, contrary to apparently clear statements. Bollack seems led to his contrast in part by a combination of a negative view of *ataraxia* with a laudable feeling that Epicurus could hardly have intended that his good should be indistinguishable from *apatheia*.

19.4.27. With the laudable feeling we are sympathetic, but consider that it can be satisfied without any contrast. *Ataraxia* is achieved by the removal of superstitious fear and false beliefs, the constant memory of the truth (cf. *Letter to Herodotus*, DL X.81-2), and attention to present experience and perception. Now the mind is freed of disturbance and so memory and expectation operate without anxiety. Similarly when physical pain is removed the body operates without pain and that will mean that always some pleasurable and painless perception is occurring, a condition of good cheer.

19.4.28. Bollack finds his contrast in the *Letter to Menoeceus* (DL X.127-9). Epicurus first says that some necessary desires are directed to *eudaimonia*, some to the undisturbed state of the body, some just to life.

For steady consideration of these things knows to refer all choice and avoidance to the health of the body and *ataraxia* of the mind because . . . * [at this point most commentators would read] this is the perfection of happy life. For we do everything for this reason: not to be in pain or fear; and once we achieve this all the soul's storm is done away with, since the animal has nothing to make for as something it lacks or anything else to seek with which the good of mind and body will be brought to fulfilment.

After the asterisk Bollack would read: 'this, the happy life, is the goal. It is for its sake that we do all we can to avoid pain and fear . . . ' and then as above. This introduces a distinction between *ataraxia* and happy life, the former being not the good, but a necessary means to the latter, which is the good.

19.4.29. While the translation 'this, the happy life, is the goal' is possible it is not mandatory. Nor, of itself, does it secure Bollack's point, since the happy life might consist in *ataraxia*. It is the next part that is important, since on Bollack's translation we try to secure *ataraxia* with a further goal, happiness, in mind. This, again, is possible but not mandatory. Bollack's complaint about the standard translation is that Epicurus is being repetitious; first he tells us that *ataraxia* is the goal, and then tells us (in effect) that *ataraxia* is what we do everything for. But in fact Epicurus seems in characteristic Greek fashion to be appealing to the fact that we do in fact pursue absence of pain and fear to show that it is the *telos* or goal. Further, if Bollack's contrast is at all important to Epicurus, then Epicurus is very bad at underlining it. A little later (DL X.131) he writes 'When we say pleasure is the goal we do not mean the pleasures of profligates . . . but not being in physical pain and not being disturbed in mind', yet according to Bollack he has just been saying that not these things, but the happy life is the goal.

19.4.30. The outcome of all this is that there is no conclusive evidence for the view that all sensory pleasures are kinetic. The only firm evidence is Cicero, and while his testimony is unequivocal we have tried to undermine its claim to reliability. Apart from that we either have passages which are no evidence at all, passages where the author might well be fathering his own conception of the kinetic on Epicurus, and a fragment of Epicurus on which the most favourable interpretation makes all experiences of pleasure kinetic, and so, by implication, sensory pleasures, but which might also be saying nothing about kinetic pleasure at all but rather making the point that *ataraxia* and *aponia* are not just negative states, but the experiences of *chara* and *euphrosunē*. In addition the evidence of both Lucretius and Plutarch supports our view that 'pure sensory pleasure' and '*aponia*' 'joy' and '*ataraxia*' are four names for two conditions. The main argument for doubting Cicero and one possible reading of DL X.136 is that both suppose a view of katastematic pleasure and the good which makes it hard to see how it could be appreciated in perception, since any perception-pleasure is kinetic. This is acknowledged by Rist ((2), p. 102) when he says that the experience of katastematic pleasure consists in gentle motions of atoms, so that the difference between the two pleasures comes down to a difference between the steadiness and endurance of the motions. The more one stresses this the less important the distinction comes to look, since any condition, however steady, of a living thing, must according to Epicurus, be a condition of perceiving: but there is no evidence of a special kind of perceiving or object of perception to constitute *ataraxia* and *aponia*. Consequently we should be left with steady long-lasting perceptions over against fleeting ones. It seems simplest just to suppose that when the organism is functioning harmoniously it is always having some form of perception; that since the operation is harmonious the perception is pleasant and without pain; and that is just what *aponia* is. *Ataraxia* is the condition when, because of correct views, our expectations are undisturbed by fear, our desires do not pursue empty objectives and our memories are pleasant: this leaves us to enjoy our pleasures unanxiously.

19.4.31. One advantage of this interpretation is that it fits Epicurus into the philosophical context of the time. It is hard to believe that he would have been unaware of claims about a neutral state, or the possible charge that his ideal was indistinguishable from *apatheia*. So he would probably have a positive account of katastematic pleasure. It is probable that 'kinetic' would at that period suggest a view of process towards a state, and he would need to claim other pleasures than that. The interpretation has him do this in a way readily available after Aristotle's defence of Eudoxus, but adapting that way to his own preferred account not in terms of the actualization of capacities, but of the balance of nature, adopting a Platonic, not Aristotelian, criterion of relative pleasantness. It is an interpretation which has the best chance of allowing him to make perception the criterion of the good, and of allowing him to make strong claims about sensory pleasure without playing fast and loose on the nature of pleasure. While it has to be acknowledged that it flies in the face of Cicero, it needs emphasizing once more that Cicero's

interpretation stands in need of defence: it is not supported
by extant writings of Epicurus, and attributes views to him
which ought to be surprising. Its main support comes from
equally unsympathetic and so suspect interpreters. All are
interestingly baffled by the apparent inconsistency between
eulogizing sensory pleasures and so, presumably, unbridled
sensuality, while advocating a life of simple asceticism and
lack of disturbance. Perhaps the Epicurean complaint of
persistent misunderstanding was justified (cf. Cicero *Fin*. II.
iv.12).

5. An objection: the Cyreniacs

19.5.1. The interpretation might be objected to on one or
both of the following grounds:

(i) Epicurus (Plut. *Col*. 1122e = U 411) used the expression
leia kinēmata of sensory pleasures (the *iucundi motus* of
Cicero *de Finibus* II.iii.8), and this expression is taken from
the Cyrenaics, who (DL II.85, 86) defined pleasure as *leia
kinēsis* and (DL II.87, 89) explicitly contrasted it with
ataraxia and *aponia*, which they rejected as not pleasures at
all. This makes it certain that in talking of kinetic pleasures
Epicurus must have had in mind these *kinēseis* and so sensory
pleasures.

(ii) Even if Epicurus did not get his expression '*leia kinēmata*'
from the Cyrenaics, it is clear from Diogenes Laertius that
they rejected *aponia* as the condition of a person asleep
(DL II.89). They obviously did not take it in the way we
have suggested, but on the contrary considered it quite
distinct from a waking condition packed with sensory
pleasure. It is one thing to suggest that Cicero, some centuries
later, misunderstood Epicurus, quite another to hold that he
was so grossly misconstrued by contemporaries in dispute
with him.

19.5.2. To take point (i) first: our sources provide no
evidence of when the Cyrenaics formulated their definition
of pleasure. Plato does not address himself to any such definition, and while Aristotle criticizes the view that pleasure
is a *kinēsis*, those criticized develop the view in order to

show that pleasure is not the good, and so can hardly be the Cyrenaics. This only shows, of course, that the view did not make much impact on those philosophers whose work has survived, but it also leaves us with no positive evidence. It is quite possible that the Cyrenaics devised the view later than Epicurus and even influenced by him. So to the first point we would merely say that ignorance forbids us to give it weight. Point (ii) might seem more weighty, but would only be really strong if we could assume three things: (*a*) that the Cyrenaics were familiar with Epicurus' work, (*b*) that they were reliable interpreters, and (*c*) that their rejection of *ataraxia* (DL II.87, 89) and *aponia* was aimed at Epicurus. Assumption (*c*) is certainly suggested by the way Diogenes Laertius conducts his discussion on the *Life of Aristippus* (II.86–93) and in the *Life of Epicurus* (X.136–8). In fact, however, the discussion is in terms of contrast rather than controversy, and it would be obviously of interest to Diogenes to spell out the points of contrast between two schools of thought apparently agreeing in their main tenet that pleasure is the good. The detailed listings readily give an impression of original controversial intent; but it has to be remembered that others besides Epicurus used negative expressions for their ideal or had negative ideals. Thus Antisthenes (see 1.1.1) and the naturists of the *Philebus* (see 8.1) both advocated freedom from both pleasure and pain, Pyrrhon of Elis possibly considered *ataraxia* the best state (cf. Cicero *Fin*. IV.xvi.43; SE *P* I.3–4, 12; Burnyeat (2)), Aristotle refers to those who considered the virtues *apatheiai* (*EN* 1104b24–5), Speusippus is said to have advocated *aochlēsia* (see 12.1.1) and similar views may well have been rife in the Academy, and a little after Epicurus Hieronymus of Rhodes (Cic. *Fin*. II. iii.8, v.16, xi.35) was advocating similar negative ideals. There were plenty of philosophers against whom the Cyrenaics would want to say (DL II.89) that a state of neither pleasure nor pain was one of no *kinēsis* and so like the condition of one asleep. A commentator like Diogenes might then well apply this view to produce a point of contrast with Epicurus, but we cannot be at all confident that the objection was originally directed at him. Even if we suppose it was, we have no evidence of their degree of familiarity with or sympathetic attention to the works of Epicurus. In a context where many different philosophers advocated aloofness from (bodily) pleasures and pains it would be easy to misconstrue the negative terms, especially as they were allied to a view that not all pleasures should be chosen and that a simple life was the ideal.

19.5.3. Finally, we have no grounds for supposing the Cyrenaics to be exceptionally sympathetic interpreters of Epicurus, or more gifted at understanding him than is general with philosophers of rival schools.

19.5.4. There is, indeed, one statement by the fourth-century AD writer Eusebius (*PE* XIV.xviii.31 = U 450) to the effect that Epicurus took his start from the Cyrenaics. There is also, however, evidence of the influence of the Democritean atomist Nausiphanes and of connections with the school founded by Eudoxus at Cyzicus. Either or both might have been a stimulus to hedonism. He may also have come under the influence of the Platonist Pamphilus, and later visited Athens when the Academy was still flourishing under Xenocrates (for evidence of these matters see Rist (2), Ch. 1). In short we have no strong evidence for supposing Cyrenaic influence on or connection with Epicurus; whereas we do have some evidence of Academic influence which would make it likely that he thought those views worth combating. The Academy seems to have been one of the homes for views to the effect that pleasure is a *kinēsis*, of the sort which Aristotle set out to refute, and after him the author of the *Magna Moralia*.

Chapter 20

Pleasure as a Criterion of Truth in Epicurus

20.0.1. In Chapter 17 we saw how both Plato and Aristotle appealed, in different ways, to the judgement of the good, i.e. rational man, as a criterion of discrimination between pleasures; that judgement was the test of which of the various possible lives was the pleasantest, or which of the many available pleasures were real pleasures, and hence necessary constituents of a fully worthwhile human life. In the thought of Epicurus, too, we find pleasure associated with the concept of a criterion, but here the nature of the association is apparently quite different. Instead of the good man's judgement being a criterion of reality for pleasures (or, equivalently, a criterion of truth for judgements to the effect that such and such activities are pleasant), we find pleasure itself described as a criterion of truth. In order to interpret this we shall have to consider in general the role of criteria of truth in Epicurus' thought and the way in which the criteria he recognized were thought to fulfil that role; in so doing we shall be able to place his treatment of pleasure in its epistemological context.

1. Epicurus' conception of a criterion

20.1.1. The considerably greater prominence given to the concept of a criterion of truth in Epicurean and Stoic thought than in that of Plato or Aristotle reflects the emergence of epistemology as a central philosophical concern, a feature characteristic of post-Aristotelian philosophy. While traces of sceptical thought can be found in fifth-century writers, notably Democritus (see in particular DK frs. 6–10, 117 and 125), it was the systematic development of sceptical arguments by Epicurus' contemporary Pyrrho which faced any 'dogmatic' system such as the Epicurean with the challenge to justify its claim to teach the truth about things, and, as part of that justification, to specify its tests (i.e. criteria) of truth.[1] Accordingly Epicurus prefaced the exposition of his physical and ethical system with a book entitled *The Standard* (*Kanōn*), which dealt with criteria and first principles, and contained the elements of the system (DL X.30). According to Diogenes Laertius (X.31) Epicurus recognized three criteria of truth, viz. perceptions, concepts, and feelings (*pathē*), understanding by 'feelings' pleasure and distress, which were the criteria of pursuit and avoidance (X.34). Perceptions and concepts naturally complement one another as criteria of truth; thus the belief e.g. that there is a cow in the field is tested for truth by appeal to the evidence of perception, but the recognition of particular sensory data as tending to confirm or refute that belief presupposes knowledge of the normal perceptible characteristics of cows and fields, which amounts to a grasp of the concepts of a cow and of a field (X.33). It would be natural to suppose that pleasure operates as a criterion of truth in much the same way as perception, the truth in question being the truth of the belief that such and such a thing is to be pursued, or is to be avoided. Just as in perception we apprehend something as having certain features which we know to be those of a certain kind of thing (e.g. we perceive this thing as having shape, colouring, and behaviour characteristic of cows), so in finding this glass of wine pleasant we apprehend it as something to be chosen, and in finding this wormwood unpleasant we apprehend it as something to be avoided. This is the picture which is presented, at least on a first reading, by Cicero. His Epicurean spokesman Torquatus says that Epicurus denied that there was any need for argument to support the thesis that pleasure is to be sought and pain avoided; rather we perceive this, just as we perceive that fire is hot, snow white and honey sweet (*Fin.* I. ix.30). He adds that some Epicureans differ from the master in holding that perception is insufficient to judge what is good and bad, and that the reason is capable of establishing that pleasure is to be pursued and pain avoided (ibid. 31). Yet, despite that evidence, Epicurus' own words show that that simple picture is altogether inadequate, for in his *Letter to Menoeceus* Epicurus points out that not every pleasure is to be pursued, nor every pain avoided; pleasures

---

[1] See Sedley.

which lead to an overall predominance of pain are to be avoided, and pains which lead to an overall predominance of pleasure are to be pursued (DL X.129–30). In this passage Epicurus makes a firm distinction between the concept of goodness and that of choiceworthiness, and a corresponding distinction for their respective opposites: every pleasure, since it has a nature akin to ours, is good, but not every pleasure is choiceworthy. Similarly, every pain is bad, but not every pain is to be avoided. This makes it clear that choiceworthiness and avoidance-worthiness are not perceptible features of any experience or activity; rather we judge experiences and activities choiceworthy or not by considering their likely effects, i.e. by an intellectual operation. On the other hand, this passage suggests, without explicitly asserting it, that goodness and badness are directly perceptible features of experiences or activities, perceptible in so far as those experiences or activities are found pleasant or unpleasant. The position thus articulated is subtler than that presented by Cicero, but not incompatible with it. According to Cicero, Epicurus says that we perceive that honey is sweet, snow white, pleasure to be pursued, etc. Yet these are universal propositions, whereas every instance of perception is the perception of some particular instance, this pleasant drink, this piece of honey, etc. Of course, our knowledge that honey tastes sweet depends upon our knowledge of how individual instances of honey taste; but it also depends on our knowledge that ordinary observers generally agree in their accounts of how those instances taste, which is a general truth concerning the application of the concept of honey. Hence that honey is sweet is not a truth which is guaranteed by any act of perception; in Epicurean terms it is a belief which is judged to be true by the evidence of how things seem and by our grasp of the conditions of the application of the concepts. Yet at the same time it is true that we know by perception, not by argument, that honey is sweet etc., in that we establish the truth of such propositions by tasting etc., not by inference from prior data. We can reconcile Cicero's evidence with that of Epicurus himself by assuming the latter to have grasped this point.[2]

[2] A major defect of Cicero's exposition is his failure to make any clear

2. *Phantasia* as a criterion

20.2.1. We now seem to have a problem in determining what it is that pleasure and pain are criteria of truth for. Are they criteria of truth of the belief that e.g. this drink is good, or that it is choiceworthy? Or are they criteria of truth for both? If the latter, do they operate differently in the two cases? And what about the belief that this drink is pleasant, and the universal beliefs (*a*) 'Pleasure is good' and (*b*) 'Pleasure is choiceworthy'. In order to answer these questions we must look in more detail at Epicurus' theory of the way in which perceptions functioned as criteria of truth, on the assumption that pleasure and pain function similarly to perceptions.[3] This is justified by the fact that, in accordance with his materialist theory of mental functioning, Epicurus regarded perception properly so called and such non-perceptual cognitive states as dreams and hallucinations as species of a single genus called *phantasia*, arising from physical stimulation of the atoms composing the soul by physical images (*eidōla*) of external objects (*Letter to Herodotus*, DL X.50–1). Later writers treat the perception of pleasure and pain as examples of *phantasia*; indeed Sextus takes them as paradigm instances of the Epicurean doctrine that all *phantasiai* are true (*M* VII. 203 ff. = U 247), while as we have just seen, Cicero differentiates Epicurus from some of his followers on the ground that the former treats the apprehension of pleasure as choiceworthy as an exercise of sense-perception.

20.2.2. In Epicurean theory *phantasiai* are the basic evidence on which all our beliefs about the world are founded, since the only way in which the world can act on us, and hence provide us with any knowledge of it, is by physical impact. They are treated as witnesses on the strength of whose testimony we form beliefs about the world; such

---

distinction between 'Pleasure is good' and 'Pleasure is choiceworthy', both of which he simply describes as shown to be true by the senses (cf. the passage referred to above with II.xii:36). While it is, in our opinion, true that both propositions are shown to be true by the evidence of the senses, it is important to recognize that they are shown in different ways, as is explained in this chapter. The conclusion of that discussion is summarized at 20.5.

[3] The treatment of criteria which follows is based on that by Taylor (4) which contains documentation in support of the views advanced here.

beliefs are shown to be true in so far as they are confirmed
by that evidence ('witnessed for' or 'not witnessed against'),
false in so far as they are disconfirmed ('witnessed against' or
'not witnessed for'). And just as the evidence of witnesses
must be true if a sound verdict is to be reached, so the
evidence of *phantasiai* must be true if we are to attain knowledge of the world. But here the forensic analogy breaks
down, for witnesses frequently say what is false, whereas it was
an Epicurean principle that all *phantasiai* are true. The reason
for this insistence was that, since *phantasiai* provide the basic
data for all judgements, we can have nothing more ultimate
to which to appeal. But if we were to judge one piece of
evidence true and another false, we should have to appeal to
some more ultimate principle in order to discriminate
between them. Hence we must either reject all *phantasiai* as
unreliable, or accept all as true; no third alternative is possible. Since the first alternative leads to total scepticism,
which Epicurus regarded as a self-refuting position,[4] the final
outcome is the acceptance of all *phantasiai* as true.

20.2.3. This position appears paradoxical in the extreme,
since it is notorious that appearances conflict; the same wind
feels cold to one man, warm to another, the same tower
looks small and round from a distance but large and square at
close quarters. In what sense then, can each of these conflicting appearances be true? The physical theory provides
the answer. Every instance of *phantasia* is a registering by the
conscious subject of a physical structure impinging on a sense
organ or otherwise reaching the physical seat of consciousness,
and in that process the physical properties of that structure
are registered precisely as they are in reality. The theory is at
its clearest when applied to geometrical properties such as
shape and size. When the distant tower looks small and
round, the observer's visual apparatus is stimulated by *eidōla*
which actually are small and round. The tower, being itself
large and square, emits *eidōla* which are similarly large and
square; these reach the eye of the nearby observer more or
less intact, but on their journey through the air to the eye of

---

[4] See Taylor (4), pp. 122–3, and Burnyeat (1).

the distant observer they are so worn down by impact with the innumerable atoms jostling in the intervening space that they reach the eye small and round. Thus both appearances are true, in the sense that each faithfully reproduces the physical stimulation which causes it. Epicurus was careful to distinguish the appearances themselves from the opinions which we come to by inference from them; the appearances are always true, the opinions may be true or false. Thus on the strength of how the tower looks from a distance one forms an opinion of what shape and size it actually is, an opinion which awaits confirmation by further evidence of appearances. Suppose that the opinion in question is that the tower actually is small and round; that opinion is witnessed against by the evidence of the appearances which one receives when one approaches the tower, and is thereby shown to be false; if on the other hand, one has the opinion that the tower is large and square, that is confirmed by the favourable witness of the subsequent appearances, and is thereby shown to be true.

20.2.4. Matters become somewhat more complicated when the theory is applied, as it certainly was in Epicurean theory, to secondary qualities, e.g. colour and taste. For, in the first place, while it is plausible to attribute objective size and shape to physical objects, and to postulate a process in which *eidōla* reproducing those properties are physically modified to such an extent that they present different properties to distant observers, variations in perceived secondary qualities cannot plausibly be explained in similar terms. For one thing, perceived secondary qualities do not vary systematically according to changes in distance and angle of vision, as perceived size and shape do; rather they are to a greater degree dependent on the condition of the observer and (in certain cases) on the environmental conditions. Accordingly, the Epicureans adopted an alternative pattern of explanation of differences in perceived secondary qualities. The perceived object was conceived as an atomic macro-structure containing countless micro-structures of different kinds; the atomic films which it emitted contained instances of all kinds of the constituent micro-structures, which were differentially registered by sense organs of the appropriate structure. Thus the same volume of wine might contain and emit structures of smooth and structures of spiky atoms; if the taste-buds of observer *A* were so shaped that the smooth atoms could penetrate them, but not the spiky ones, and the taste-buds of *B* so shaped as to admit the spiky but not the smooth, then the wine would taste sweet to *A* and sour to *B*, and both appearances would be true, in that both would represent the appropriate physical structure (Plut. *Col.* 1109a = U 250). This theory presupposes that secondary qualities can be theoretically identified via the description of physical structures in terms of primary qualities; thus the thesis that whatever tastes sweet actually is sweet becomes the substantial thesis that, whenever anything tastes sweet to a percipient, that percipient is being stimulated by an atomic structure of a specific type *S* (e.g. a structure of smooth atoms). This identification is necessary to save the theory from trivialization; for if any structure at all could give rise to an impression of sweetness, then the thesis that whatever tastes sweet actually is sweet would collapse into the triviality that, whenever anything tastes sweet, the percipient is stimulated by an atomic structure such as to cause him to have an impression of sweetness.

3. Pleasure as a criterion

20.3.1. The thesis that all appearances are true thus presupposes theoretical identifications of secondary qualities via physical structures, and we have independent evidence that the theory provided at least the materials for such identifications (especially in Lucretius' account of hearing, taste, and smell, IV.522–721). Since pleasure and pain share many of the features which distinguish secondary from primary qualities, it would be natural to expect the theory to offer such an identification in their case, and to show them operating as criteria of truth in much the same way as impressions of secondary qualities do. We suggest that such an identification is provided by Epicurus' description of pleasure as 'having a nature which belongs (or 'is akin') (sc. to us)' (*dia to phusin echein oikeian, Letter to Menoeceus,* DL X.129), which is complemented by Diogenes' report of the doctrine that pleasure belongs (sc. to us) while pain is alien (X.34).[5] On this view pleasure is consciousness that one's psycho-physical structure is operating as it should, or (equivalently) in a way appropriate to it, while pain is consciousness that it is being forced to operate in a way alien to it. This view helps to explain the distinction between kinetic and katastematic pleasure and the prima facie puzzling doctrine that the highest pleasure (i.e. katastematic pleasure) is simply absence of pain. The organism may be said to be functioning appropriately under two sets of conditions, firstly when it is in a state of total equilibrium, every part functioning perfectly, and secondly when, that state of equilibrium having been lost (e.g. by nutritional deficiency, of which the consciousness is the distress of hunger), those parts of the organism whose function is to remedy the deficiency do their job properly. In the first place we have katastematic pleasure, in the second kinetic. It is now clear why the former should be valued above the latter, and perhaps less surprising that the highest form of pleasure should be identified with freedom from bodily pain and distress of mind (*Letter to Menoeceus*, DL X.131). If, as we have suggested, for 'pain and distress' we have to read 'consciousness of improper functioning', the doctrine that the highest pleasure is freedom from pain and distress becomes the doctrine that the highest pleasure is freedom from consciousness of improper functioning. Given the assumptions (*a*) that there is no intermediate state between proper and improper functioning, (*b*) that the organism is always conscious of how it is functioning and (*c*) that all appearances are true, that doctrine is in turn equivalent to the doctrine that the highest form of pleasure is consciousness of proper functioning, which is very close to Aristotle's account.

20.3.2. Lucretius gives us some indication of how the physical basis of pleasure and pain may have been conceived: 'there is pain when the bodies of matter, disturbed by some force throughout the living flesh and limbs, tremble each in their abode within, and when they settle back into their

---

[5] Compare the doctrine of *VS* 37 that nature is saved (or preserved) by pleasures and destroyed by pains.

place, comforting pleasure comes to pass' (II.963-6, tr. Bailey (2), I. p. 287). Here pain is consciousness of the disruption of the organism, conceived spatially, in that some of the constituent atoms are forced out of their places in the structure, and the consciousness of the movement of the displaced atoms back to their proper places, which restores the functioning of the whole is a pleasure. The pleasure thus described is an instance of kinetic pleasure.

20.3.3. We can now construe the functioning of pleasure and pain as criteria of truth on the general model which describes the functioning of *phantasiai* in that role. When the oar in the water looks bent, that appearance is true, in that it faithfully represents the nature of the *eidōla* which are currently stimulating the observer's visual system. But if he believes on the strength of that appearance that the oar is bent, he will believe something false. To avoid that, he must subject this appearance to the test of further appearances, e.g. how the oar looks when out of the water, how it feels when he runs his hand along it, etc. The real nature of external objects is revealed, not by any single appearance, but by the appearances considered as a totality. Similarly, a particular feeling of pleasure is true, in that it faithfully represents the fact that a part of the organism is functioning properly. But just as one could not safely assume that something's looking bent under some particular condition adequately represented its real shape, so one cannot assume that what is recognized as appropriate to the functioning of some part of the organism under some special conditions will *ipso facto* be appropriate to the functioning of the whole organism under different conditions. So while the appearance of this as good, i.e. as appropriate e.g. to one's sexual functioning under these conditions, e.g. previous sexual deprivation, must be true, the belief that this is choiceworthy, i.e. such as to promote the proper long-term functioning of the organism, may be false, and must await confirmation by other appearances. These further appearances are of course other pleasures (both kinetic and katastematic) and pains; as in the perceptual case, it is by the totality of appearances that the truth of the belief is to be judged.

20.3.4. If this is correct, Epicurus' theory might be seen as offering a reconciliation, in Aristotelian fashion, of the views of pleasure which Aristotle opposes to one another in *EN* VII, viz. the thesis that pleasure is a perceived process towards the natural state and his own theory of pleasure as unimpeded actualization of the natural state.[6] The former amounts to a description of kinetic pleasure, the latter of katastematic. But at the same time kinetic pleasures can themselves be seen as satisfying the latter description also, since every process of restoration of the neutral state of the whole organism is itself an actualization of the natural state of that part of the organism which is contributing to the restoration of the whole.[7] Epicurus thus sees the psycho-physical organism as having a built-in nisus towards its proper functioning, and consequently sees the pursuit of pleasure, understood as consciousness of proper functioning, as the way of life dictated by man's nature and hence as the appropriate way of life for a man. Thus he says in *PD* 25, 'if on each occasion instead of referring your actions to the end of nature you turn to some other nearer standard when you are making a choice or an avoidance, your actions will not be consistent with your principles' (tr. Bailey). It is presumably not accidental that this maxim follows immediately after one where he distinguishes perceptual appearances from the 'judgements awaiting confirmation' which one forms on the basis of those appearances. In order to avoid error one must not affirm that things are precisely as they appear, but one must distinguish those judgements which are confirmed by further appearances and those which are not, taking the former as true and the latter as false. That is to say, one's judgement must be determined, not by the immediate appearance (i.e. of pleasure and pain), but by the goal which nature sets us, that is the life of unhindered, i.e. painless physical and mental functioning. The natural drive of the organism towards unhindered functioning is emphasized by Epicurus not only in the *Letter*

---

[6] This does not, of course, imply that Epicurus intended his theory to reconcile these two positions, but merely that it provides a way of doing so.

[7] cf. Aristotle's description of *kinēseis* as incomplete *energeiai*, discussed in Ch. 16.

to Menoeceus, especially 128 and 131, but in two other quotations, *VS* 33 and fragment 44 (= U 200): both contain the sentence 'The voice of the flesh is not to hunger, not to thirst, not to be cold.'

4. Difficulties in Epicurus' theory

20.4.1. As thus interpreted, the theory is open to a basic objection. We have argued that the physical reality which is truly represented by the feeling of pleasure is the proper functioning of that part of the organism where the pleasure is felt. But if that pleasure leads, not to the unhindered functioning of the whole organism, but to subsequent pains, i.e. malfunctions, then surely the original function which was felt as pleasure could not have been *proper* functioning, since the proper functioning of any part must be what contributes to the smooth functioning of the whole. While this is indeed a difficulty, it is rather a difficulty for the theory than for the interpretation. Nor is it peculiar to the Epicurean theory, since it applies, for example, to any theory which maintains both that pleasure is a restoration of the natural state and that certain pleasures result, not in the restoration of the natural state but in unnatural states accompanied by distress. In fact the difficulty can be met, given rather more precision in the formulation of the theory. Thus one might maintain that the proper functioning of the nutritive organs consists in the ingestion of food, and that this is constituted as their proper functioning in virtue of the fact that the ingestion of food enables the organism to function free of the distress of hunger. So animal organisms are so constituted as to feel pleasure when they eat. But in a particular instance someone may eat to excess, producing not the unhindered functioning which results from freedom from hunger, but instead the distress of nausea or indigestion. Here the defect does not lie in his nutritive organs, which are working properly and so produce pleasure, but in his lack of control over their functioning in that he does not recognize the limit to which that function should be exercised. In a series of maxims (*PD* 18–21) Epicurus emphasizes the importance of understanding the limits of pleasure. Nature sets a limit to pleasure in that once distress arising from deficiency (e.g. hunger) has been removed, pleasure cannot be increased, but can only be varied . (*PD* 18). Consequently, complete pleasure, once achieved, cannot be increased by being enjoyed for a longer time; hence infinite time contains equal pleasure with finite time (*PD* 19). At the same time the flesh has a tendency to look on pleasure as infinite and as requiring infinite time for its achievement; hence the task of philosophical wisdom is to curb this tendency to the immoderate pursuit of pleasure by recognizing the natural limits of pleasure and by moderating one's desires to meet those limits (*PD* 20-1). The atomic motions which are represented in consciousness by desires and pleasures have not only an inherent tendency to promote the natural goal of the organism, viz. unhindered functioning, which is in turn represented in consciousness by katastematic pleasure, but also a tendency to expand beyond their proper limits, thus frustrating their own nisus towards the natural goal. The theory is complex, but not inconsistent, and it has the merit of doing justice to the phenomena on the one hand of the biological utility of physical desires and on the other of their only too obvious tendency to get out of hand.

20.4.2. The theory can thus cope without too much trouble with the problem of how there can be bad forms of natural pleasures. It is less successful in dealing with the problem raised by the fact that, in addition to various kinds of natural desires, Epicurus classified certain desires, e.g. for public honours, as 'empty' in that their satisfaction does not contribute to any natural good (*Letter to Menoeceus*, DL X. 127; *PD* 29; *VS* 20). The task of wisdom was to eliminate these desires (and their concomitant pleasures) entirely; yet as long as they are felt, the theory is committed to counting the pleasure which is occasioned as good, i.e. as something appropriate (*Letter to Menoeceus*, DL X.129). But what are such pleasures appropriate to? Not to the proper functioning of either the organism as a whole, or any part of it. One might perhaps suggest that they are appropriate, not to human nature proper, but to the disordered nature of the man who likes that kind of thing. But in that case the notion of appropriateness is emptied of content, and with it the thesis that the perception of any atomic motion as pleasant is true. If any pleasure, even one which lacks any connection with the proper functioning of the organism, is *ipso facto* appropriate, then 'appropriate' means no more than 'pleasant'. This appears to be an instance of the trivialization which threatens the thesis that all appearances are true. Since it is an *a priori* thesis, maintained on epistemological grounds, it cannot be falsified however things turn out. Hence it places no restrictions on the nature of the physical states of affairs which are represented in appearances, and thus trivializes the thesis that appearances represent those states of affairs as they really are.[8] A possible line of defence for the general theory would be that it is sufficient for it to have determinate content that it should be possible to conceive of a situation which would falsify it, while the epistemological requirement provides an *a priori* guarantee that such a falsifying instance will not in fact occur. For example, supposing that sweetness has been identified empirically as a structure of smooth atoms, we know *a priori* that every instance of something's tasting sweet will be produced by a structure of smooth atoms, while being able to conceive of a falsifying instance, viz. a sweet taste in the absence of that structure. The theory would then face the problem of explaining the possibility of such *a priori* knowledge, which appears totally mysterious. In the case of pleasure, however, this escape route is not open, since unnecessary pleasures provide actual cases which either falsify the theory or trivialize it.

20.4.3. An alternative solution is suggested by Epicurus' reliance on the desires of children and animals as evidence of natural tendencies, in contrast with the perversions of those tendencies imposed by 'civilization'. At the outset of his exposition (*Fin.* I.ix.30) Torquatus says that as soon as it is born every living thing seeks to attain pleasure as its supreme good and to avoid pain as the worst evil, 'and does this so long as it is not yet corrupted, nature itself giving an unbiassed and honest judgement'. Hence there is no need of argument to prove that pleasure is choiceworthy. He repeats this claim in his conclusion (I.xxi.71): the thesis that there is

---

[8] See Taylor (4), p. 123.

nothing good except pleasure and nothing bad except pain is confirmed by the evidence, not only of the senses, which are uncorrupted and honest witnesses, but also by the testimony of animals and infants who, under the guidance of nature, give their judgements free from perversion and corruption. (For the characteristically Epicurean use of forensic terminology see 20.2.2). Epicurus might then be taken as holding that unnecessary pleasures are not good at all, on the ground that the criteria of truth concerning what is good and bad are the natural feelings. Feelings such as pleasures in public honours which are had only by those who have been corrupted by the bogus values of society, i.e. who have acquired various false beliefs, are no evidence of what is good, and hence of what is choiceworthy. If this is right, then Epicurus too will have made use of a criterion to discriminate between pleasures, a criterion, moreover, which is very similar to Aristotle's. For both, what is really pleasant is what is pleasant to the person in sound condition, i.e. to the person who conforms to the standards of functioning laid down by nature. The difference will be that while for Aristotle the paradigm of such functioning is the person who displays practical and theoretical rationality in as perfect a form as possible, for Epicurus the paradigm is the uninstructed (i.e. unspoiled) being who lives in harmony with the dictates of his physical constitution, i.e. the infant and the animal. On this view rationality of either kind is valuable, not as intrinsic perfection (as in Aristotle's thought), but only as a means of recapturing the simplicity of children and animals, free from unnecessary desires and the corrupting influence of false beliefs about the world and man's place in it (see *Letter to Herodotus*, DL X.78-83; *PD* 11-12, 26; *VS* 21; fr. 45 = U 202).

20.4.4. If Epicurus did take this way out (the evidence does not allow us to proceed beyond speculation on this point), he is still not free of difficulties. For, as we have seen, his criteria of truth are appearances (including feelings) and concepts; but now he is apparently appealing to a prior criterion in order to discount certain appearances, which is expressly declared impossible in *PD* 24. Justification might be claimed for this procedure on the ground that it is possible to identify certain feelings as dependent on false beliefs; e.g. pleasure at being accorded the freedom of the city presupposes the false belief that such honours are worth having. But those beliefs have to be judged false by the evidence of appearances; and in making *that* judgement Epicurus could not without circularity exclude any appearances. So for at least some purpose unnecessary pleasures have to be counted as good, which reinstates the original objection.

20.4.5. A further problem arises regarding the notion of proper functioning which we have used in this discussion. We have argued that Epicurus' physics and epistemology require that he regarded pleasure, whether kinetic or katastematic, as consciousness of proper functioning. If this account is to fit the general theory, proper functioning must be capable of being specified without the inclusion of pleasure as part of the description; otherwise the thesis that the appearance of pleasure is true becomes the triviality that pleasure is consciousness of the sort of functioning which produces pleasure. Yet what account of proper functioning could Epicurus give other than that it is the sort of functioning which nature bids every creature pursue (*VS* 21)? And since nature's bidding is to pursue pleasure (e.g. *Letter to Menoeceus*, DL X.129), it does not appear that his theory offers him the independent specification of proper functioning which he requires (cf. the formally similar objection to Aristotle's account of the criterion of real pleasure, Ch. 17). He might, of course, have maintained that nature bids every creature pursue its own survival and that of its kind, and hence that pleasure is consciousness of functioning which is such as to promote the survival of the individual or the species. But it seems unlikely that that was his thought, for in his classification of kinds of desires in the *Letter to Menoeceus* (DL X.127) he lists three sorts of necessary desires, those necessary for *eudaimonia*, those necessary for avoidance of bodily pain, and those necessary for survival, without any suggestion that the latter are in any way more fundamental, as the view under consideration would require. Other suggestions are equally implausible, e.g. the Aristotelian suggestion that appropriate functioning is functioning distinctive of the species, which seems incompatible with the choice of children and animals as paradigms of such functioning.

5. Recapitulation

20.5.1. We are now in a position to answer the questions raised at the outset of this chapter (20.2.1). Taking the example of a pleasant drink, the pleasure experienced is a criterion of truth of all three beliefs (*a*) that the drink is pleasant, (*b*) that it is good and (*c*) that it is choiceworthy. The way in which it is a criterion for the first two, however, differs from that in which it is a criterion for the third. Since pleasantness of the drink consists in its appropriateness to the functioning of the organism, which also constitutes its goodness, the perception of the drink as pleasant represents it as it is in reality; hence that perception immediately guarantees those beliefs as true. Since this is so in every case, it follows that the universal belief 'Pleasure is good' is true. The choiceworthiness of the drink, on the other hand, is determined not by its pleasantness here and now, but by its long-term effects. But since those effects are measured in terms of pleasantness and unpleasantness, its pleasantness here and now is part of the evidence which shows the belief that it is choiceworthy to be true or false. The position regarding 'Pleasure is choiceworthy' is therefore complex. Taken as equivalent to 'Every pleasure is choiceworthy' it is false. On the other hand, it can be construed on the model of 'Honey is sweet', as 'Every natural pleasure is choiceworthy'. Thus construed it is shown to be true by the evidence of particular instances.

20.5.2. The doctrine that pleasure and pain are among the criteria of truth seems, then, to be a special case of the general doctrine that appearances are criteria of truth. The identification of a physical basis for pleasure and pain allows consciousness of them to be assimilated to the perception of secondary qualities, and hence to fit the general physical account of appearances. The main objection to the account of pleasure, viz. that it cannot deal satisfactorily with unnecessary pleasures, is in fact an objection to the general theory. That theory is an impressively systematic attempt to revive the early physiological accounts of pleasure as a form of perception (see Ch. 1), and to apply to it the epistemological theory which fitted the general account of perception. In thus striving for generality it paid the usual price, viz. failure to deal with recalcitrant counter-instances. As always, the multi-coloured butterfly of pleasure eludes the net of necessary and sufficient conditions.

Chapter 21

The Stoics[1]

21.0.1. Our survey of ancient views on pleasure would not be complete without a glance at the theory of perhaps the most influential of all the post-Aristotelian schools, the Stoics. It is beyond the scope of this work to undertake any general survey of Stoic ethics or psychology, or to engage in the complex problems surrounding the attribution of positions to individual Stoics. We shall confine ourselves to a brief survey of the view of pleasure which appears to have been developed by the first three heads of the school, Zeno, Cleanthes, and Chrysippus, during the lifetime of Epicurus and the period of approximately seventy years after his death in 271 BC.

1. Stoic and Epicurean views on pleasure compared

21.1.1. Prima facie, Stoic and Epicurean views of pleasure stand in radical opposition. The latter, as we have seen, held that pleasure is the good and that all conscious beings naturally seek it. The Stoics, on the other hand, denied that there is any natural impulse towards pleasure, and ranked it on the evaluative scale among things which are indifferent, i.e. neither good nor bad. Hence for the Epicureans pleasure was a central concern, while for the Stoics it was at best peripheral. Yet while these points of contrast are all true, it should not be overlooked that the views of the two schools on the nature of pleasure had more in common than might be suggested by these differences, and that differences themselves sprang from a single fundamental disagreement between two closely similar views. The fundamental point of disagreement, moreover, is one of considerable philosophical interest.

[1] We wish to acknowledge our indebtedness to a paper by Professor W. Görler, to be published in the proceedings of the Seventh Congress of the International Federation of the Societies of Classical Studies. The collection of texts appended to that paper has been particularly helpful.

21.1.2. As we have seen, Epicurus held pleasure to be consciousness of proper functioning or, equivalently, consciousness of being in a good state. Given the thesis that all appearances are true, every state which is experienced as pleasant is in fact a good state; hence the universal impulse towards pleasure is an impulse on the part of every conscious being to achieve its good. Central to this position are the theses (a) that experiencing pleasure is having certain appearances, and (b) that those appearances necessarily give a true representation of reality. The reality which is thus experienced is the natural functioning, either in whole or part, of the conscious organism.

21.1.3. For the Stoics too the idea of functioning according to nature is central. In their theory the whole universe is a rational being, self-organized in such a way as to promote the harmonious interaction of all its constituents. For every kind of thing, the good of the members of that kind is to exhibit to a high degree those properties which are distinctive of the kind, and thus play as well as possible the role which nature has assigned it. Man being a rational creature, fitted by nature for a social existence, human good consists in the exercise of rationality directed towards the perfection of that kind of life, i.e. in the exercise of moral virtue. Everything else, including the traditional goods such as health, wealth and honour, and their opposed evils, is strictly speaking indifferent, since the possession or lack of any of these neither promotes the achievement of virtue nor hinders it. The theory did, however, take account of the fact that some 'indifferent' things e.g. health are universally pursued and others e.g. illness universally shunned, by distinguishing within the genus of indifferents a class of 'preferred' things (*proēgmena*, the traditional natural goods) from their opposites, which they called 'unpreferred' (*apoproēgmena*).[2]

21.1.4. Allowing for differences in emphasis, this general view does not yet seem to require an evaluation of pleasure

[2] For a fuller account see Long (2), Ch. 4, esp. Section V.

very remote from the Epicurean. For a start, we should recall Epicurus' assertion that a life of pleasure is impossible without the moral virtues and vice versa, since the two are naturally inseparable (*Letter to Menoeceus*, DL X.133). Reading the above summary of Stoic theory through Epicurean spectacles, we should expect the Stoics to hold that a certain sort of pleasure is at least a necessary accompaniment of the good life, and that pleasure is in general something 'preferred'. Some, including Chrysippus, did hold the latter view (DL VII.102 = *SVF* III.117). Others, however, apparently refused to ascribe any value whatever to pleasure, even to the extent of denying that it is 'preferred'. Sextus (*M.* XI.73 = *SVF* III.155) mentions various Stoic opinions, which all agree in denying pleasure even that modest status: Cleanthes held that it was neither natural nor had any value, Archedemus (third or second century BC) that it was natural but valueless, like hair in the armpit, and Panaetius (second century BC) that some pleasures were natural and others unnatural.

21.1.5. In order to maintain this position, the Stoics had to deny the existence of a universal impulse towards pleasure. A passage of Diogenes Laertius (VII.85–6 = *SVF* III.178) cites the view of Chrysippus: the primitive natural urge of every creature is not towards pleasure, but towards the preservation of its own nature.[3] To put the point in Stoic terminology 'to every living thing its own constitution and the consciousness of that is akin'; (hence it seeks that as its own goal, rather than looking on it as something alien to it). Pleasure is merely something additional (*epigennēma*) which occurs when each nature achieves that state which best fits its own constitution. In similar vein, Clement of Alexandria (*Stromateis* II. p. 491 = *SVF* III.405) records the Stoic view that the *pathos* of pleasure is an accompaniment (*epako-louthēma*) of such natural needs as hunger and thirst.

[3] One must, however, acknowledge the contrary testimony of DL VII.148 = *SVF* II.1132 'this (i.e nature) aims at what is advantageous and at pleasure, as is clear from human craftmanship'. Of this we can say only that it conflicts with the bulk of the evidence.

21.1.6. Here we come to the heart of the disagreement between Stoics and Epicureans on the nature and value of pleasure. Chrysippus counted not only the proper functioning of the organism but also consciousness of that functioning as a natural goal of every living thing. Now for the Epicureans, as we have seen, consciousness of proper functioning is precisely what pleasure is. Hence in maintaining that consciousness of proper functioning is a natural goal, while denying that pleasure is such, the Stoics were committed to rejecting that Epicurean account of pleasure. It is clear from the ancient evidence what the crucial issue was. In Epicurean thought, pleasure, pain and the various forms of sense-perception were different kinds of appearance (*phantasia*), distinguished only by their modes of production but epistemologically on a par, in virtue of the thesis that all appearances are true. The Stoics, on the other hand, distinguished perception (*aisthēsis*) from *phantasia*, not as co-ordinate species of a single genus, but as distinct stages in the cognitive process; perception was not *phantasia* itself, but assent (*sunkatathesis*) to *phantasia* produced by sensory mechanism (Porphyry *ap*. Stob.I.349.23 = *SVF* II.74, *aisthētikēi . . . phantasiai sunkatathesis estin hē aisthēsis*). They thus analysed perception as a voluntary act (Porphyry loc. cit.; Cic. *Acad.* I.xi.40 = *SVF* I.61, *Acad.* II.xii.37 = *SVF* II.115), the acceptance of an appearance as a true representation of the world. Perception thus entails belief; *phantasia* is seen as presenting a putative state of affairs for inspection 'It looks as if *p*', and perception is the mental act of accepting that things are as they appear, i.e. of coming to have the belief that *p* on the strength of how things appear. The Stoics seem thus to have assimilated all perception to perception *that* something is the case; for that sort of perception they were right to this extent at least, that '*A* perceives that *p*' entails '*A* believes that *p*, on the strength of sensorily presented information indicating that *p*'. (This condition is, of course, not sufficient.) As a general account of perception this will not work, since (among other reasons) one may e.g. see a cow without believing that one sees a cow, or that there is a cow in one's vicinity. Yet any perception seems to require that the perceptual situation causes the perceiver to have some

belief or other, and the Stoics may at least be given the credit
of having indicated the intimate, though obscure, connection
of perception with belief.

2. Pleasure and belief

22.2.1. The relevance of this to pleasure is that the Stoics
counted the *pathē* including pleasure as either themselves
judgements or beliefs (the term *krisis* 'judgement' and *doxa*
'belief' or 'opinion' are both used), or as effects of judgements. A passage of Andronicus (first century BC: *On the
Passions* 1 = *SVF* III.391) gives alternative definitions, first
of *pathos* in general, 'A *pathos* is an irrational and unnatural
movement of the soul, or an excessive impulse (*hormē*)', and
then of the four principal *pathē*, distress, fear, desire, and
pleasure. The definition of pleasure runs 'Pleasure is an
irrational elevation (*eparsis*, from the verb *epairō* 'lift up,
excite'); or a recent belief in the presence of a good, about
which they think one should be elevated'. The first disjunct
defines pleasure as the effect of a belief, a change brought
about by the belief that one possesses a good, the second
defines it as that belief itself. Various other sources attest one
or other of these definitions: the former is attested by
Stobaeus (II.90.7 = *SVF* III.394), the latter by Cicero (*Tusc.*
IV.vii.14 = *SVF* III.393), Galen (*On the Opinions of
Hippocrates and Plato* IV.2.(135) = *SVF* III.463), and Servius
(*Commentary on Aeneid*, on VI.733 = *SVF* II.387).
According to Galen (op. cit. V.1 (155) = *SVF* III.461) Zeno
held the view of the *pathē* as effects of beliefs ('contractions
and flowings-out, elevations and depressions of the soul'),
while Chrysippus regarded them as judgements. We shall
comment briefly on this disagreement below (21.4.1); for
the present the most significant point is a feature common to
these rival theories, viz. that on either view someone who
feels pleasure believes that he is in a good state. Plainly,
someone who accepts either view must deny first that
pleasure is the only good (for the belief that one is in a good
state is itself something good, one presumes, only if it is
true), and secondly that pleasure is the ultimate good (for, in
virtue of the point made in the preceding parenthesis, it is
absurd to maintain that certain states are good only because

they cause the belief that those states obtain; rather that belief is good only because those states are themselves independently good).[4] Further, this account of pleasure seriously undermines the thesis that the desire for pleasure is a universal motivation. Even leaving aside the difficulty of attributing to animals and infants the desire to have the belief that one is enjoying some good, it is totally implausible to suggest that rational creatures want anything whatever which they consider good because they want to believe that they possess that thing. To put it shortly, since that would be an irrational motivation (for the reason just given) it cannot be what universally motivates rational creatures. The Stoics' theory of pleasure thus gave them good reason to reject the Epicurean theses that pleasure is (*a*) the good and (*b*) the aim of all living things. But, for all that, could they not have acknowledged it as *a* good? In reply to this, we must recall that given the Stoic theory of goods, all pleasure except pleasure in the exercise of virtue either is or is caused by *false* belief, viz. the belief that the things whose possession gives rise to pleasure, e.g. bodily satisfactions or public honours, are themselves goods. Hence the pejorative descriptions of pleasure as an 'irrational elevation', 'unnatural movement', or 'excessive impulse'. Feelings such as pleasure make no contribution at all to the goodness of life; rather they indicate that the perfection of human nature, which consists in the supremacy of reason, unsullied by irrational impulses, has not been achieved. On this view, so far from its being surprising that some Stoics should have regarded pleasure as unnatural, it is rather surprising that some, like Archedemus and Panaetius, should have held it to be natural, and still more surprising that Chrysippus should have classed it among the 'preferred' things. A possible explanation may be that those Stoics regarded pleasure and the pursuit of pleasure, while indeed irrational and hence unnatural for the fully rational

---

[4] A similar argument is sufficient to refute those versions of hedonism according to which ultimate value is possessed by the state of being pleased that one has succeeded in one's projects, has lived up to one's standards, etc., and ultimate disvalue by the states of being displeased, ashamed, etc., that one has not done those things.

man, as natural for the mass of mankind, whose rationality was in an undeveloped state.[5]

21.2.2. This leaves us with pleasure in the exercise of virtue itself, which they do seem to have regarded as a sort of good. In order to highlight the difference between this form of pleasure and the 'irrational excitements' just discussed they introduced a terminological distinction, reserving the term *hēdonē* for the latter, while the wise man's pleasure was designated by the term *chara* (joy), and defined as rational elevation. Of the four principal *pathē*, three, viz. fear, desire, and pleasure, had their rational counterpart, or, in Stoic terminology 'opposite'. The wise man, instead of feeling the irrational excitement of fear, recognized vice as an evil, and hence showed rational caution in avoiding it. Similarly, instead of irrational desire he rationally wished for the good, and instead of irrational pleasure he experienced rational joy in achieving it (DL VII.115 = *SVF* III.431). There was no rational counterpart to distress, because distress is an unfavourable reaction to the presence of an evil, and the only evil is vice, which cannot be present in the soul of the rational man (Cic. *Tusc.* IV.vi.14 = *SVF* III.438). These reactions were 'opposite' to their irrational counterparts in that the former were or were caused by true beliefs, the latter were or were caused by false. Hence it was obviously impossible to treat pleasure and joy as basically the same in nature, and so even more absurd to suppose that pleasure is the good. It seems that these 'good conditions' (*eupatheiai*, DL loc. cit; the word is chosen to contrast with *pathos* which has connotations of suffering and constitutional disorder, cf. Cic. *Acad.* I.x.38 = *SVF* I.207) were not themselves the judgements e.g. that one was acting virtuously, but rather effects of these judgements. Thus Stobaeus says that every wise man always possesses virtue and rational perception (*phronimē aisthēsis*), but that joy etc. are not universal attributes of the wise (II.68.24 = *SVF* III.103). Yet if joy were itself the belief that one is virtuous, it is hard to see how that could fail to be a universal possession of the wise

[5] For evidence of Stoic belief in the gradual development of rationality, and of its incompleteness in all but a very few instances see Long (2), pp. 184-9.

(for how could a wise man be so lacking in insight as to fail to see that he was virtuous?), and indeed hard to see how that would not count as 'rational perception'. If, on the other hand, joy is some sort of response to that belief, it is easier to see how it might be thought that some wise men might on occasion lack it.

3. Pleasure and perception

21.3.1. The central position assigned to belief is perhaps the most interesting feature of the Stoic theory of pleasure, whether *hēdonē* or *chara*. There is a close affinity with their treatment of perception. Just as we found that their account of perception best fitted the case of perceiving that p, so we may say that they attempt to treat all pleasure as being pleased that p. The analogy extends to details: just as A's believing that p is a necessary but not sufficient condition for A's perceiving that p, so A's believing that p is a necessary but not sufficient condition for A's being pleased that p. And just as the 'perceiving that' account runs into difficulty in the case of perceiving an object, the 'being pleased that' account meets similar difficulties when dealing with cases of enjoying something. Just as one may see a cow without believing that what one sees is a cow, or even, in the case of subliminal perception, without believing that one has seen anything, so one may enjoy ϕ-ing without the belief that it is ϕ-ing that one is enjoying,[6] or even, in an extreme case of self-opacity, without the belief that one is enjoying anything. But just as one can't perceive x without thereby acquiring some relevant beliefs, so, it seems, one can't enjoy ϕ-ing without having some beliefs regarding the situation in which one ϕ-s. In fact belief is even more intimately connected with pleasure than with perception. Unlike perception, being pleased that p is a second-order attitude, a response not directly to how the world is, but to how one believes the world to be. This response presupposes certain values; one believes that p,

[6] This may be either through lack of belief that ϕ-ing is what one is doing, as in the case of Oedipus who, it may be presumed, enjoyed sleeping with his mother but didn't know *that* was what he was doing, or, more subtly, through lack of awareness that its being a case of ϕ-ing is what makes what one is doing enjoyable, as in the case of someone unaware that what he is enjoying in the bantering conversation is *flirting*.

judges that its being the case that p is in some way good or valuable, and responds favourably to this coincidence of the facts (as one believes them to be) with one's values.

4. Pleasure: belief or an effect of belief?

21.4.1. These considerations perhaps help us to understand why different Stoics should have taken opposite sides on the question of whether pleasure and the *pathē* generally are to be identified with beliefs, or judgements, or acts of assent on the one hand, or are rather to be considered as effects of those cognitive states. Our analysis of being pleased that p reveals it to be a complex propositional attitude, which pre-supposes the possession of a fair degree of conceptual equip-ment. In Greek terminology that point would naturally be made by ascribing that attitude to the *logistikon*, which is concerned with thoughts and judgements. Hence we find Chrysippus defining the *pathē* as judgements of the intellect (*kriseis . . . tou logistikou (SVF* III.461)) and with heroic consistency denying that they are felt by animals (Galen *On the Opinions of Hippocrates and Plato* IV.5 (144) = *SVF* III.462, IV.5 (143) = *SVF* III.476), while some Stoics went so far as to deny them to children (Galen op.cit. V.1. (156) = *SVF* III.476; Origen *Comm. on Matthew* III. p. 591 = *SVF* III.477). On the other hand, we have a strong inclination to say that being pleased that p is not identical with believing or accepting that it is a good thing that p, nor fearing that p with believing that it will be a bad thing that p. In either case, we are inclined to say, one might have the belief but be left entirely cold by it, and in that case one wouldn't have been really pleased, or afraid. So pleasure or fear must at least include something over and above the judgement, some kind of felt response to that intellectual act; or perhaps the *pathos* just is that response itself, as Zeno is reported to have held. Yet what is this response? It cannot plausibly be identified with any bodily sensation, or bodily movement, since we can recognize occurrences of the *pathos* where neither sensation nor movement occurs. One way of meeting, or seeming to meet, the pressure to say what the response is is to rely on the very spatial metaphors which the Stoics themselves used, and to talk of elation, uplifted feelings, depressions etc.

arising from judgements. But metaphors demand to be cashed, and when, in a reductive frame of mind, we try to say in turn what depression, elation, etc. *are*, we find ourselves driven once again to describing these attitudes as ways of looking at the world; that is we move back in the direction of analysing the *pathē* as some kind of thoughts. An obvious suggestion is that what is missing here is the element of desire; the response which we are trying to pin down is some desire caused by the judgement. There are two problems confronting this suggestion. Firstly, it is not always clear that some desire is present whenever one feels a *pathos*; thus if I am pleased that a friend has had some success it is not obvious that my belief that he has had that success must awaken in me any desire whatever. Secondly, the frame of mind which led us to ask what the response is will naturally lead us to ask the same question about desires themselves. Yet desires are not specifiable independently of thoughts. When we treat the occurrences of desires as mental events, as when we say that at precisely 12.35 John felt an intense desire for a pint of beer, we are saying that at that moment John thought of a pint of beer as something attractive, as something exercising a kind of force on him. And when we explain someone's conduct by reference to his beliefs and desires, the reference to desire does not introduce any element additional to the beliefs, but merely indicates that the beliefs were sufficient to motivate him.[7] Desire itself has thus a tendency to slip through the analyst's fingers, leaving him grasping nothing but thoughts.

5. The Stoic explanation of action

21.5.1. This modern view is strikingly anticipated by the Stoics. Voluntary action results from internal impulse or impetus (*hormē*), and, Stobaeus tells us (II.88.1 = *SVF* III. 171), all *hormai* are agreements or acts of assent (*sunkatatheseis*), and practical agreements contain motive force (*to kinētikon periechein*). In the same passage Stobaeus says that

---

[7] This view is maintained by some modern writers: see Nagel, Ch. 5; Locke; McDowell. It is disputed by Kenny (3), pp. 117–19.

the acts of assent are given to certain propositions, while the impulses are towards the predicates which are contained in the propositions assented to. This prima facie obscure doctrine is somewhat clarified by another passage of Stobaeus (II.86. 17 = *SVF* III.169), which tells us that what stimulates the impulse is 'an impulse-containing appearance of the immediately fitting' (*phantasian hormētikēn tou kathēkontos autothen*), and by a passage from a letter of Seneca (*Ep.* CIII.18 = *SVF* ibid.) which concisely states the Stoic theory of the genesis of action: the agent is first stimulated by the appearance of something, then receives an impetus, and then strengthens that impulse by assent, for example, as soon as one assents to the proposition 'I should walk', one thereupon walks. The sequence is clear; one has an appearance of something under some description showing it as an immediately appropriate object of action, e.g. it seems to one that this food is appropriate to eat. That appearance has itself a certain attractive force (cf. 21.4.1), but is insufficient to bring about action until the agent assents to the appearance, or, more strictly, as Stobaeus rightly indicates, assents to the proposition which the appearance represents, viz. *that* this food is appropriate to eat. That assent is then the impulse to action, which directs the agent towards the predicate contained in the proposition, i.e. he goes for *the wholesome food*. The resemblance to Aristotle's doctrine of the practical syllogism is striking and plainly not coincidental; compare *EN* 1147a26–31

when a single opinion results from the two (sc. premisses) . . . in the case of opinions concerned with production it must immediately act (e.g. if 'everything sweet ought to be tasted', and 'this is sweet', in the sense of being one of the particular sweet things, the man who can act and is not prevented must at the same time actually act accordingly). (tr. Ross, revised Ackrill)

Hence it is not surprising to find the Peripatetic Alexander of Aphrodisias presenting his explanation of action in Stoic terminology: 'the assent (*sunkatathesis*) to things not present as choiceworthy is impulse (*hormē*) which is the same thing as desire (*orexis*)' (*On the Soul*, p. 77.26; cf. Aristotle's definition of choice (*prohairesis*) as deliberative intellect or intellectual desire, *EN* 1139b4-5).[8]

6. A modern error of interpretation

21.6.1. Both desire and pleasure are then in Stoic theory kinds of belief, the former the action-determining belief that something not possessed, but presented in appearance as choiceworthy is in fact a good to be achieved by action, the latter the belief that something possessed and presented in appearance as a good is in fact so. The fact that pleasure is in this way a response to appearances has misled some modern commentators. Thus both Rist[9] and Sandbach[10] maintain that the Stoics recognized two kinds of pleasures, viz. on the one hand bodily satisfactions and on the other 'mental' pleasures occasioned by the recognition of the presence of goods, including the bodily pleasures themselves (which are, of course *falsely* believed to be goods). According to Rist they distinguished these two types of pleasures 'implicitly if not explicitly'; according to Sandbach they gave the name 'pleasure' to both kinds, but his statement that the 'mental' form of pleasure 'is to be distinguished from what may be called agreeable physical feelings' leaves it unclear whether he thinks that the Stoics themselves made that distinction or that they failed to do so. In our view, the texts which we have examined give no support to the view that the Stoics regarded agreeable bodily sensations as a form of *pleasure*. In their theory such sensations were appearances which might indeed give rise to pleasure, provided they were assented to, but which must always be distinguished from pleasure, which was the act of assent itself. To be more specific they were the appearance of bodily functioning, e.g. the ingestion of food, as good; such appearances are indeed counted as pleasures by Epicurean theory, but emphatically not by Stoic. In stating that the Stoics counted them as a form of pleasure Rist and Sandbach misrepresent the truth that they were an

---

[8] Long (1), p. 81 calls attention to the close analogy between Aristotle's account of *prohairesis* as deliberative desire (*bouleutikē orexis*) and the intellectual impulse (*logikē hormē*) of the Stoics.

[9] (1), p. 38.

[10] p. 62.

indispensible element in their theory of pleasurè, and thereby distort a central feature of Stoic thought.[11]

7. Conclusion

21.7.1. Like its Epicurean rival, the Stoic theory of pleasure succumbs to the dangers of over-generalization, but its defects are perhaps attributable in some measure to its virtues. It was a considerable merit of Stoic theory to recognize, following the lead of Plato, the close connection of pleasure with belief, and to see that at least some forms of pleasure are second-order attitudes, being evaluative responses to the contents of beliefs. Their main deficiency lies in taking this account as adequate for pleasure as a whole, with the consequence that they were unable to deal satisfactorily with enjoyment. A fully adequate theory of pleasure needs to combine the Stoic insights with elements drawn from other theories, in particular with something more like an Aristotelian/Epicurean theory of enjoyment; for students of the Stoics it is not without interest that at least one modern writer regards being pleased, rather than enjoyment, as the central concept in the elucidation of the complex phenomena of pleasure.[12]

---

[11] Haynes commits the same error: '. . . one can make a distinction between *pathē* of the body and mental *pathē*, between sensations and emotions. Pleasure as a bodily *pathos* is a sensation with which the animal is endowed by nature' (p. 414). He cites Aulus Gellius *Noctes Atticae* XII.v.7 (= *SVF* III.181); in fact the crucial passage is XII.v.8 (not in *SVF*) ' . . . the newly-born child is endowed with these first sensations of pain and pleasure before the appearance of judgement and reason, and is attracted to pleasure by nature . . . '. Gellius (second century AD) who cites no Stoic source in this passage cannot be accepted as evidence to the views of the Old Stoa in the face of the explicit contrary testimony of the views of Chrysippus cited above (21.1.5). Rist suggests (p. 41) that his view shows the influence of Posidonius (second century BC).

We find the same mistake in Long (1): referring to the same passage of Aulus Gellius, he asserts that 'it (i.e. *hēdonē*) often denotes a physical feeling, and as such it is a sensation common to all creatures' (p. 80). The malign influence of the empiricist view of pleasure as an internal impression is presumably to be discerned in this unanimity in error on the part of modern writers in English.

[12] Gosling (3), pp. 132–8.

Appendix A: False Pleasures

A.0.1. The topic of false pleasures has attracted more recent discussion than any other aspect of the *Philebus*, partly because of the obscurity of Plato's treatment and partly because it shows some interesting links with modern discussions of pleasure and its relation to belief. Since discussion of this latter point presupposes interpretation of the relevant passages, it will be postponed until the interpretation has been undertaken. But discussion of the first point can hardly be postponed, since a major source of obscurity about this topic is, precisely, what the topic is. Less oracularly, when Plato speaks of 'false pleasures', what does he mean by 'false', and what does he describe as being false? Does a pleasure's being false imply that it is in one way or another not a real pleasure (e.g. an illusory pleasure), or is its falsity like that of a belief, a defect which nevertheless does not disqualify whatever has the defect from counting as a genuine instance of its kind? Connected with that question is the question of what is said to be false: for example, is falsehood attributed to some enjoyments, or to a propositional attitude such as is picked out by the expression '. . . is pleased that p'? If the latter, then we can readily see how falsity of the sort attributed to beliefs could be attributed to such an attitude (see below). But that sort of falsity does not appear to be applicable to enjoyment. It is, indeed, quite problematic how 'false enjoyment' should be understood: one possibility is that it be taken as equivalent to 'illusory enjoyment'.

A.0.2. These problems present themselves as soon as one turns to the text. Even before the main discussion (36c–44a), the first mention at 32b–c of pleasure of anticipation (one of the types of false pleasure discussed), raises the question of what Plato thinks the pleasure of anticipation is. Socrates is listing the sorts of pleasure that there are, in order to decide which sorts contribute to making a life a good life. Having described bodily pleasures such as those of eating and drinking which arise, according to the physiological model, from the restoration of the proper balance of the bodily elements, he lists next pleasures which consist in or arise from (the terminology is deliberately vague, to avoid the begging of questions) the anticipation of such experiences as that of drinking when one is thirsty. This sort of pleasure is described at c1-2 as *to . . . pro tōn hēdeōn elpizomenon hēdu kai tharraleon*, literally 'the pleasant and confidence-inspiring thing which is hoped (for) before the pleasant things'. This can be taken as meaning either, 'that pleasant . . . thing which one hopes for before one actually has the pleasant experience of getting it', i.e. what one anticipates with pleasure, or 'that pleasant . . . hope which one has before one has the actual experiences', i.e. the pleasant anticipation of a future pleasure. Now if the pleasant thing in question is the thing that is hoped *for*, that is of course nothing other than the future pleasure itself: hence if pleasure of anticipation consists in having that, it would amount to enjoyment, by some sort of precognition, of a pleasure which doesn't yet exist and may never in fact do so (for the significance of this point for false pleasures, see below). The other alternative, viz. the pleasant anticipation of a future pleasure, might itself be understood in either of two ways, firstly (and more plausibly) as the 'present enjoyment of the anticipation of a future pleasure', or, secondly as 'being pleased that one will experience a certain pleasure'. Given the first reading we have a genuine episode of enjoyment, viz. enjoyment of the anticipation of a further enjoyment, while given the second we have the occurrence of a propositional attitude. One might reasonably think the precognition account extremely implausible, and incline to the view that Plato must have had in mind one version (or both) of the 'pleasant anticipation' account. The immediate context, however, provides no further evidence, while it is of considerable significance for the later . discussion of false pleasures of anticipation that Plato's language admits the precognition account as a possible interpretation. Having noticed the alternatives, we cannot at this stage rule out the possibility that Plato's thought was undetermined between them.

A.0.3. The main discussion of false pleasures divides into three sections:

1.   36c6–41a6: false pleasures of anticipation
2.   41a7–42c4: over-estimation of future pleasures by comparison with present distress
3.   42c5–44a11: mistaking a neutral state for pleasure.

We shall consider these in turn, the first fairly fully, the second and third considerably more briefly.

1. 36c6–41a6: False pleasures of anticipation

A.1.1. Our other main question, viz. what it means to say that a pleasure is false, is raised right at the outset of the discussion. Having distinguished pleasures of anticipation from pleasures in the making-good of bodily lacks (31d–32c, see above), and given a lengthy account of the role of memory in both kinds (33c–36c), Socrates now asks (36c6–7) whether 'we shall say that these pains and pleasures are true or false; or are some of them true and some not'. ('These pains and pleasures' refers specifically to pleasant and unpleasant anticipations, which have been discussed immediately before (36a–b)). Protarchus asks how pleasures and pains could be false, to which Socrates replies 'How then could fears, expectations, or opinions be true or false?' (c10–11). In reply Protarchus says that he would admit that opinions can be true or false, but not any of the others (d1–2). At this point it is not clear whether Protarchus holds (*a*) that the pair of predicates 'true' and 'false' applies only to opinions or judgements (*doxai*), but not to fears, expectations, pleasures, or pains, or (*b*) that while opinions may be true *or false*, pleasures (and presumably, therefore, fears, expectations, and pains) may be true, but not false. The former position would represent the fairly straightforward view that of the items under consideration only opinions have propositional content, and are hence open to assessment as true or false. By contrast the other items would be thought of as non-propositional (i.e. not involving the thought or judgement that anything is the case), perhaps as something like sensations. The obvious objection would be that fear and expectation manifestly have propositional content — (I expect that John will ring up, and am afraid that all the tickets may be sold before I get to the box office); and that some sorts of pleasures and distress also seem to — (I am pleased (or distressed) that (or because) the Conservatives have a lead in the opinion polls). So that position, though plainly wrong, is at least fairly clear. The other position, however, viz. that while opinions may be true or false, pleasures etc. may be true *but not false*, is extremely obscure, since once the contrast with falsehood is eliminated, it is not clear what content attaches to the description 'true'. That this is in fact Protarchus' position is unequivocally established at 37b5–9; we have therefore still to find the senses of 'true' and 'false' according to which Protarchus thinks the former applicable to pleasures and the latter inapplicable. The lack of the 'true-false' polarity would suggest that the senses must be different from those of the terms as they apply to opinions. One possibility could be that Protarchus wants to apply the term 'true' to pleasures in the sense of 'genuine', and that in denying that there are any false pleasures he means to deny that there are any non-genuine pleasures. But this thesis in turn is not unambiguous. It might merely amount to the triviality that non-genuine pleasures are not *pleasures*, just as false friends are not *friends* and forged banknotes are not *banknotes*. Alternatively, it might be the substantial thesis that every putative case of non-genuine pleasure is in fact a case of genuine pleasure, which would imply that it is impossible to believe that one is enjoying oneself when one is not in fact doing so.

A.1.2. Socrates in fact begins (apparently) by understanding Protarchus' position in this way, for at 36e5–8 he responds to Protarchus' denial that there are true and false pleasures as follows:

So according to you no one, either dreaming or awake, in a fit of madness or some delusion, ever thinks that he is enjoying himself, but is not enjoying himself at all, or thinks that he is suffering some distress, when he is not.

Gosling ((5), pp. 106–7) points out a difficulty, viz. that whereas Protarchus was asked whether any pleasures *of anticipation* were false, Socrates is now attributing to him a view as to the impossibility of mistakes about *present* enjoyments. It is perhaps simplest to suppose that Plato represents Protarchus as holding the specific view that no pleasures of anticipation are false on the strength of the general view that no pleasures of any sort can be false, and that Socrates is bringing out a further implication of that general view. A more serious difficulty arises from the fact that, while at 36e 'false pleasures' is equivalent to 'unreal pleasures' or 'illusory pleasures' at 37b5–9 Socrates emphasizes, with Protarchus' agreement, that just as true and false judgements are genuine judgements, so, on the view to be examined, true pleasures are genuine pleasures, though there are no such things as false pleasures. The course of the argument (see below) consists in pressing the analogy between pleasure and judgement, to the point where it is admitted (40b7–c2) that some pleasures which some people actually have are false (just as some judgements which some people actually make are false). That is to say, the sense of 'false' with which the first argument is concerned appears to have shifted from that in 36e to a sense (as yet unexplained) in which a false pleasure is not an unreal pleasure.

A.1.3. A possible explanation is that at 36e Socrates is getting out of the way an *ir*relevant sense of 'false pleasure'. Protarchus sets out by denying, in a vague fashion, that pleasures can be false, to which Socrates responds, 'You don't mean, of course, that there are no such things as illusions · of pleasure?' and Protarchus immediately replies 'Of course I don't mean that' (e9–10). Having cleared up that possible misunderstanding Socrates then goes on to investigate what Protarchus does mean. This suggestion will be the more attractive the more clearly the discussion of false pleasures of anticipation can be seen to be free of any signs of the assimilation of false pleasures to illusory pleasures. In so far as that assimilation does affect the argument, it will be more plausible to suggest that Plato is unclear as to how far false pleasures can be distinguished from illusory pleasures. In investigating this question it will be helpful to summarize the argument.

A.1.4. Beginning at 37a2 Socrates cites a number of points in which being pleased or experiencing pleasure (*hēdesthai*) resembles thinking or having an opinion (*doxazein*). Both have objects: there is something which one thinks, and something one is pleased about, takes pleasure in, etc. Opinion, whether right or not right (*orthē ē ouk orthē*) is genuine opinion: similarly pleasure, whether right or not right, is genuine pleasure. (Protarchus' agreement to describing pleasure as 'right or not right' must be merely conditional: see below.) Moreover, opinion, whether true or false, is genuine opinion: so what has to be examined is the putative assymetry between genuine opinion, which may be true or false, and genuine pleasure, which can only be true.

A.1.5. Socrates now recapitulates: first (37c) pleasure is properly qualified by some predicates, then (d2-e9) pleasure and opinion may be qualified by a certain range of common predicates, viz. both may be wicked, both may be right or not right, and both may be said to go wrong or be mistaken (*hamartanein*). Protarchus remains, however, unconvinced; he agrees merely that pleasure may be called 'not right' *if* it can properly be said to be mistaken (e8-9) and when Socrates tries to clinch the argument by pointing out that many pleasures arise 'not with right opinion, but with false' (e10-11) he makes the obvious objection that in that case it is the opinion that is false, not the pleasure (e12-38a2). Socrates replies to this with a brief sketch of the role of imagination or mental imagery (the two not being clearly distinguished in his mind) in the formation of judgements. Its role is as follows: through the operation of memory, perception, and their accompanying conditions we form judgements. These are spoken of as *logoi* which memory etc. write in our souls as in a book (39a); the use of the term suggests strongly that what is thought of here is the formation of judgements which either are or at least can be expressed in words; that is also suggested by the example given at 38c11-e7, where someone is represented as forming the judgement 'What I see in the distance is a man', which he communicates verbally to his companion, or which, if he is alone, he thinks to himself. There follows this writing in the book another process, that of illustrating the *logoi*, which is the work of the imagination (39b3–c3); now according to whether or not any particular *logos* is true or false, the picture illustrating that *logos* will represent the facts accurately or inaccurately, and hence may itself be called a true or a false picture (c4–5). Socrates now makes his final move: having established that the pictures painted in the book may as readily be pictures of the future as of the past or present (c10–12) he recalls the agreement of 32b9–c5 that pleasures and pains 'of the soul itself' may arise by anticipation of 'bodily' pleasures and pains, 'so that it happens to us that we experience pleasure and pain in advance about the future' (39d1–5). It is then said (e4–6) that *logoi* plus pictures referring to the future are hopes, and that all men, good and bad alike, are full of such hopes; an example of such a hope is given (40a9–12), that of a man who entertains in his imagination a picture of himself acquiring a vast fortune, and living in a transport of delight at all the pleasures which he enjoys as a result. The crucial difference between good men and bad is that the expectations of the latter turn out to be false (b2–4), and hence the pictures of pleasures which they had painted for themselves turn out to be false pictures (b6–7); hence it is generally the case that the pleasures of the wicked are false pleasures, which are described as 'somewhat ludicrous imitations of true pleasures' (c4–6). Hence the concept of false pleasures has been shown not only to have application, but to be of some importance from the moral point of view, since most if not all of those pleasures whose attraction leads men to wickedness turn out to fall within that classification.

A.1.6. The crucial point in this argument is the relation between pleasures of anticipation and the imaginative picturing of future pleasures. For it will be readily conceded that such picturing consists in the production of pictures which, having a propositional content, can be straighforwardly true or false, while it may seem an easy and unobjectionable extension to apply these terms to the activity of picturing. Hence if pleasures of anticipation can properly be assimilated either to imaginative pictures or to acts of picturing, it will be defensible to describe them as true or false. Most commentators have agreed that something is wrong with Plato's argument at this point, but there has been much disagreement as to the precise diagnosis.

A.1.7. It will be convenient to take a typical case of a pleasure of anticipation. I am looking forward to my Mediterranean holiday; I picture myself enjoying a long drink under a beach umbrella, and I enjoy the picture. We may distinguish four aspects of the situation:

(i) My enjoying the drink. This is the anticipated (pictured) pleasure. It has not occurred at the time when I picture it, nor need it ever occur, though I must, at the time when I picture it, believe that it will occur, if my pleasure is to be one of *anticipation*. Otherwise, what I am here and now enjoying is not anticipating, but day-dreaming.

(ii) The picture of myself enjoying the drink (see under (iii) below).

(iii) My picturing myself enjoying the drink. (iii) is an episode in my mental history, which occurs at a certain time. (ii) is related to it as object to act, as a belief is to a state of believing, or an assertion to an act of asserting. (ii) is not an episode in my mental history, but is the content of such an episode, as an assertion (i.e. something asserted) is the content of an act of asserting. (ii) and (iii) are liable to be confused because the noun 'picture' may be used indiscriminately for either 'act of picturing' or 'content of an act of picturing' (the same holds true of 'assertion', 'belief', 'thought', etc.). But their conditions of individuation are different. Acts of picturing are individuated by their temporal location and by their belonging to particular mental histories. Two acts of picturing occurring at distinct times, or in the histories of distinct persons, are distinct acts, but such distinct acts may have identical content.

(iv) My enjoying picturing myself enjoying the drink. (iv) is also an episode in my mental history. We shall not discuss whether it is the same episode as (iii), under a different description, or a distinct episode.

A.1.8. To which of these aspects are the predicates 'true' and 'false' applicable? Plainly, not to (i), my enjoying the drink: 'I falsely enjoyed a glass of beer' is simply nonsensical. Of course, I may think that I shall enjoy a drink, when in fact I shall not, but in that case it is my belief which is false, not any enjoyment. The same holds of 'true'.

A.1.9. 'True' and 'false' are equally inapplicable to (iii) and (iv). Episodes in a mental history may be, *qua* episodes, brief or lengthy, inspiring or embarrassing, precedent or subsequent to other episodes, etc., but they cannot *qua* episodes be true or false. The sentence 'His assertion was ill-mannered but true' conceals equivocation on 'assertion'; what it means is that he performed the ill-mannered act of asserting something true.

A.1.10. 'True' and 'false' are, on the other hand, applicable to (ii). Since the picture of myself enjoying the drink is the content of an act of thought (viz. the thought that I enjoy a drink), expressed in a particular form of mental presentation (viz. mental picturing), it can, like any content of thought, be true or false. Whether the thought contains a belief is irrelevant to its truth or falsity, though not to its status as e.g. anticipation or day-dream. A picture of myself making love to Cleopatra is a false picture, whether or not I believe that I did or shall; it is false because it is a representation of the thought that I (at some time) make love to Cleopatra, which is false.

A.1.11. The only aspect of a pleasure of anticipation which can properly be called true or false is, then, the content of the anticipation, i.e. the thought (in this case the belief) that I shall enjoy a drink. It makes no sense to describe either the anticipated enjoyment or the enjoyment of anticipating that enjoyment as true or false. I may indeed say, in the situation where I anticipate some enjoyment which does not in fact accrue to me, that my anticipated enjoyment proved unreal. But that too is merely a misleading way of saying that I believed that I should enjoy something, but that the belief was false. For in that situation there *was* no enjoyment which was unreal, nor anything which was unreal enjoyment. All that happened was that I believed, falsely, that I should enjoy something. Protarchus was therefore right to insist that, in a case where pleasure is accompanied by false belief, it is the belief which is false, not the pleasure (37e10–38a2).[1] Socrates, however, rejects that position, maintaining that in pleasures of anticipation it is literally the pleasure which is true or false, not just the belief. How is that to be understood?

A.1.12. Most commentators on the passage agree that Plato is trying to show that the enjoyment of imaginative picturing (our number (iv)) can be false, while disagreeing on the account of the moves by which he reaches that conclusion. The differences turn on the interpretation of the description of the bad man's imaginative picturing at 40a–b. Gosling ((1), (2) and (5) pp. 215–19) suggests that two stages are involved. Firstly, in the light of his general tendency to think of pleasures as activities which are enjoyed, Plato takes it for granted that the enjoyment of imaginative picturing is identical with the act of picturing (i.e. (iv) = (iii)). Secondly, he makes the natural error of identifying the content of the picturing (ii) with the act of picturing (iii) and hence (by transitivity of identity) with the enjoyment of the act of picturing (iv). The second assimilation is embodied in the statement (40b6–7) that bad men have *hēdonai . . . ezō-graphēmenai*, which are false. On Gosling's views the Greek phrase, literally translated 'pictured pleasures' is to be read as covering both 'pictures of pleasures' and 'picturings of pleasures', a reading of which the Greek is certainly susceptible. The next sentence (c1–2) contains the first assimilation: from the premiss that the bad man's pictures/picturings are for the most part false it is inferred that bad men for the most part enjoy false pleasures (*pseudesin . . . hēdonais . . . chairousin*). Since the identification of pleasure with enjoyed activities is defensible (it is in fact a possible sense of the plural *hēdonai*, as it is the most natural sense of the English 'pleasures') on this interpretation the crucial error lies in the identification of the content of a picture with the act of picturing.[2]

---

[1] Cf. Williams

[2] McLaughlin, while accepting the main outlines of Gosling's view, defends the

A.1.13. Kenny's account (Kenny (1)) is essentially similar, since he too sees the crux of the argument as the move from 'Bad men take pleasure in false pictures of pleasures' to 'Bad men take false pleasures in pictures of pleasures'. The main difference between his account and Gosling's is that, instead of seeing this move as embodying the conflation of pictures and picturing and the identification of picturing with pleasure in picturing, Kenny sees it as depending on the suppressed premiss 'Pleasure in false pictures is false pleasure'. But since this premiss *is* suppressed, and since it is open to the objection that it depends on the very conflation which Gosling has identified, it is unclear how this interpretation differs from Gosling's other than verbally.

A.1.14. Dybikowski (2) locates Plato's error in a different place, viz. in a conflation of the pleasure which is anticipated (i) with the pleasure of anticipating it (iv). In his view the crucial phrase *hēdonai ezōgraphēmenai* is to be read not as in the Gosling/Kenny view as 'pictures of pleasures' but literally as 'pictured pleasures', i.e. the pleasures (in Socrates example, the pleasures of enjoying a vast fortune) which the bad man anticipates. Socrates is attempting to show that the pleasure of anticipation is false, but confuses this with the claim that the anticipated pleasure is false, which Protarchus readily grants 'since he has agreed that for the bad man what is pictured is false' (p. 164). We saw earlier that Plato describes pleasures of anticipation in language which allows this confusion, at 32c1–2 where he uses the ambiguous expression *to . . . pro tōn hēdeōn elpizomenon hēdu*, and again at 39d1–5, where the expressions 'experience pleasure and pain in advance' (*prochairein te kai prolupeisthai*) might suggest that anticipatory pleasure is thought of as a sort of shadowy precognition of full-blooded bodily pleasure. (Compare the description of anticipatory pleasures and pains as 'pre-enjoyments and pre-distresses' (*proēstheseis te kai prolupeseis*) at *Rep.* 584e.) The confusion which Dybikowski

---

identification of the anticipatory pleasure with the content of the imaginative picture (p. 60). Against this philosophical thesis see above A.1.7–9. McLaughlin is criticized (on other grounds) by Dybikowski (1).

attributes to Plato is, therefore, certainly one which he could have committed. But it is not clear why *this* confusion should make it easier for Socrates to convince Protarchus that the bad man's pleasures are *false*. Dybikowski rightly emphasizes that Socrates' argument turns on the assimilation of anticipatory pleasure to belief via the account of that pleasure as picturing: but that argument leads Protarchus to accept that those *pictures* (*eikones* 39c4, *zōgraphēmata* d7, *phantasmata ezōgraphēmena* 40a9) are false. If, as is plainly the case, Socrates is appealing to that argument to convince Protarchus that the bad man's *pleasures* are false, then the confusion of anticipated pleasure with pleasure of anticipation will not be sufficient to explain the mistake. Dybikowski's interpretation must be supplemented by the postulation of confusion between the representation and something else; this supplementation has the effect of bringing it closer to the views of Gosling and Kenny. While Gosling and Kenny see the argument as turning on a conflation of (or a suppressed move between) picture and picturing, Dybikowski makes it depend on a conflation of picture and object depicted, together with a further conflation of the object depicted (a pleasure) with the pleasure of depicting that object.

A.1.15. All these interpretations share the view that in maintaining that there are false pleasures of anticipation Socrates is arguing that some kinds of anticipatory enjoyment are false enjoyments. The differences between them are differences of detail, between which the text does not seem to offer any definitive decision. Penner (1) following the suggestion of Thalberg, proposes a different interpretation, according to which what is shown to be false is not any enjoyment which the wicked man has, but rather his state of mind of being pleased *that* he will have certain pleasures, when, *ex hypothesi*, he will not in fact have those pleasures. Plato's main concern is to stress that 'being pleased that ... ' shares with belief, hope, and fear the fundamental feature that all have propositional content, which therefore qualifies them for assessment as true or false. Now the thesis that 'being pleased that . . . ' and various other similar attitudes invoke belief, not as an accompaniment or cause but as an essential component (for some details, see Penner's article and those cited in his footnotes) is a most important contribution to the understanding of the concept of pleasure, and one to which reflection on Plato's discussion of false pleasures of anticipation has undoubtedly contributed. But if Penner's thesis is to come to more than that he has to show that Plato distinguishes between, or at least writes in a way best explained by postulating a grasp of the distinction between being pleased that p on the one hand and enjoying the thought of p on the other. But not only does Plato's language nowhere suggest a grasp of this very subtle distinction; even more damaging to Penner's thesis is the fact that the example on whose description the argument turns is clearly seen as that of someone enjoying the picturing of future pleasures, gloating over the picture in Gosling's phrase ((5), pp. 216–18). The vocabulary of 'experiencing pleasures in advance' etc., noticed above is appropriate to the description of anticipatory enjoyment, but inappropriate to the description of simply being pleased that one will have some future enjoyment, which may come to no more than this, that one believes that one will have the enjoyment and regards the fact that one will have it as something to be welcomed. This is not, of course, to deny that *one* way of manifesting the state of being pleased that one will have enjoyment E is enjoying anticipating E; what is maintained is that 'A is pleased that he will enjoy E' and 'A enjoys anticipating E' are logically independent descriptions, in that neither implies the other. Since Plato takes as his central case a case of enjoying anticipating E, nothing justifies the contention that he is really concerned with being pleased that one will have E, *rather than* enjoying anticipating E.

A.1.16. As a footnote to this discussion of false pleasures of anticipation, it is worth asking why we should suppose that the wicked man's anticipations of pleasures will be for the most part false. Plato does not explain, presumably taking the point as obvious, as is suggested by Protarchus' unhesitating acceptance (40b2–5). Of the commentators cited above, only Kenny gives a clear answer. In the example, what is false is not the wicked man's belief that he will acquire a fortune, nor the belief that he will spend it in self-indulgence. 'What is false . . . is the belief *that he will enjoy these activities*' (p. 51). Kenny's example is that of a man who takes pleasure in anticipating spending £70,000 on beer, but who is mistaken in thinking that he will enjoy drinking that amount of beer. If this is correct then Plato is maintaining that it is characteristic of the wicked man to find his expectations of pleasure disappointed, and in consequence to find his life subjectively miserable. This is certainly the picture of the wicked man which he paints in the first argument in *Rep.* IX to show that the just life is the pleasantest life (576c–580c): the thought which Kenny attributes to him here is, therefore, certainly Platonic.

A.1.17. But other possibilities cannot be excluded. Firstly, despite Kenny's claim that it would be odd for Plato to attribute to Socrates the view 'that material prosperity is in direct proportion to piety' (ibid.) it would not be in the least odd for Socrates to suggest, and Protarchus to accept, the traditional view that the wicked, carried away by unrealistic expectations of worldly success, are likely to find these expectations shattered by divine vengeance, whereas the good, who have curbed their expectations within the proper bounds, find those more modest expectations fulfilled by divine favour. (NB. 40b2–4; good men have the truth written in their souls 'because they are dear to the gods': cf. *Rep.* 560b7–10. For evidence of the traditional view in e.g. Herodotus and Aeschylus see Lloyd-Jones index s.v. '*atē*'.) Secondly, it is surely rather unconvincing to suggest that wicked expectations *of pleasure* are *characteristically* disappointed: that must surely depend on the expectation. Kenny is no doubt correct to assume that the pleasure of beer-swilling would pall long before one got through £70,000 worth, but it is not so clear that Don Juan's expectations of pleasure must have been similarly disappointed. The other arguments of *Rep.* IX do not require that inferior pleasures be disappointing to the person who experiences them, but rather that they are less real or complete by an objective standard, either because they involve confusion of pleasure with a neutral state, or because the lacks to which they answer are such that they cannot be completely satisfied. The description of the bad man's false pleasures as 'somewhat ludicrous imitations of true pleasures' (40c4–6) perhaps suggests this sort of criticism, recalling as it does the description of bodily pleasures in the third argument of *Rep.* IX as illusions and images (583b, 586b). On this view, the bad man pictures, say, unstinted bodily indulgence as pleasure; but even if he gets it, *and enjoys it*, so that he wouldn't change it for anything (cf. *Rep.* 581c8–d3), what he gets is not the real thing, and so not what he really wanted (for this notion of 'really wanting', cf. the argument with Polus (*Gorg.* 461b–481b), where Socrates argues that even successful criminals do not get what they really want, viz. the best life). While we do not think that Kenny's suggestion can be rejected, it seems to us at least as likely that Plato may have had in mind the point just mentioned; since we find both in successive arguments in *Rep.* IX it is possible that both are intended in this passage. Plato might, for instance, have in mind a view which combines both lines of thought; while the bad man is condemned by his insatiable thirst for pleasure to a life of continual frustration (cf. the image of the leaky pitchers at *Gorg.* 493d–494a), nevertheless he is so lacking in insight into his own condition that he still maintains that the life is the most desirable of all. Hence his life is both a succession of disappointments and, from the objective standpoint, a ludicrous counterfeit of a life of real pleasure.[3]

A.1.18. We may attempt to sum up Plato's first discussion of false anticipatory pleasures as follows. While he emphasizes the intimate link between pleasure and belief, in such a way as to foreshadow modern discussions of propositional attitudes invoking pleasure, he does not distinguish such attitudes from enjoyment. Rather, he attempts to show that some anticipatory enjoyments are false, by assimilating such enjoyments either to what is anticipated or to the anticipation of it: the test appears indeterminate between a number of detailed variants. If the suggestion made in the preceding

---

[3] For an alternative view see Brandt.

paragraph is correct, then the sense of 'false' in which some anticipatory pleasures are said to be false is not firmly distinguished from 'unreal', since on that suggestion the wicked man's anticipations are defective in so far as the pleasures which he anticipates are unreal. That point *could* indeed be coupled with a clear distinction between falsehood and unreality; one needs simply to state explicitly that, if one anticipates enjoyment E as an instance of real enjoyment, then, if E is an unreal enjoyment, one's anticipation of E as an instance of real enjoyment is false anticipation. But that distinction is not in fact made.

2. 41a7–42e4: overestimation of future pleasures by comparison with present distress

A.2.1. The treatment of the second sort of false pleasures is brief and schematic. Socrates recalls the earlier discussion of pleasures arising from bodily conditions (31b–36c) and in particular the state of pleasantly anticipating relief from present bodily distress (36a–b), which involves the simultaneous occurrence of pleasure and pain. This association makes it difficult to make reliable estimates of the relative amounts and intensities of different pleasures and pains (41e2–6), just as variations in distance make it difficult to make reliable estimates of the size of perceived objects (e9–42a4). Whereas in the previous section it was true and false opinions which infected pleasures and pains with truth and falsity, it is emphasized that the difficulty in this class of cases is a function of the temporal proximity of distance of pleasures and pains to the agent and of their comparison to one another, without any influence of opinion (a5–b6). But the difficulty is not described in terms of truth and falsity at all: rather 'pleasures seem greater and more intense by comparison with what is unpleasant, and pains seem the opposite of those by comparison with pleasures'. The error which this situation leads to is over- or under-estimation of the amount and intensity of pleasures and pains: it should be dealt with by subtracting the amount by which the over-estimated phenomenon exceeds the reality, and classifying that amount as something unreal (*ouk on*) and pleasure in it as something 'not right and true (or genuine)', (*orthon te kai alēthes*) (b7–c3). Nothing is said about how under-estimates are to be dealt with.

A.2.2. It is clear that in this passage Plato is telling us that we make mistakes in our assessments of future pleasures and pains because of the distorting influence of present pleasures and pains. Thus the man parched with thirst imagines that the brackish water at the water-hole will be delicious, while the reveller plays down the unpleasantness of tomorrow's hangover: these judgements are mistaken in that they are refuted by the actual experiences, the foul-tasting water, the splitting headache. In these cases it is plausible to suggest that one's error consisted in over- or under-estimating something whose true extent is revealed by closer inspection. But the simple perceptual model is itself unable to stand closer scrutiny. For cases which involve comparison of pleasures and/or pains at different times do not present a simple contrast of forecast with present perception. Thus if I am dis-satisfied with my job I may think that another job *will be* more satisfying than this one *is*; having made the change I discover to my chagrin that the new job *is* not more satis-fying than the old one *was*. My forecast of the relative satisfactoriness of the two jobs is shown to be mistaken, but not by the correct present viewing of what I mistakenly forecast.

A.2.3. Since we have no independent criterion either of how unpleasant my present job is in fact, or of how pleasant the alternative is in fact, we have no ground for the judge-ment that I exaggerate either the one or the other. Nor will it do to say that I exaggerate the difference between the situations, since we have equally no independent criterion of how much worse the present situation really is. What we can say is that a certain anticipation, viz. of how one *will* view the relative pleasantness of the two jobs, is falsified by the event, and hence that the pleasure in that anticipation was ill-founded. But that is precisely the first case of false pleasure of anticipation, where the falsity of an anticipation infects the pleasure in that anticipation with its falsity. Plato seems here to be trying to describe a special case of false pleasure of anticipation, where the error springs, not from the falsity of the anticipation, but rather from misperception of future pleasure through the distortion produced by temporal distance and comparison with present discomfort. But this attempt fails, because pleasures and pains, whether future, present, or past, are not public objects, and hence are not such that they can be perceived or misperceived. One can indeed be mistaken about one's future pleasures, as a result of one's present discomfort; but the mistake does not lie in any failure of fit between how the pleasures really are or will be and how they seem, but in the failure of fit between one's anticipation of how they will seem and the truth of how they will seem. It does not appear, then, that Plato has succeeded in diagnosing a different kind of error from that which he discussed in 36c–41a. He has merely singled out one sort of erroneous anticipation.

A.2.4. The failure of Plato's account of this sort of mis-anticipation as a kind of misperception is shown by the fact that if that were the correct model it ought to apply to present pleasures and pains rather than to future ones. Thus if there were a distinction to be made between how pleasant something really is and how pleasant it seems when associated with distress in the immediate perceptual vicinity, it ought to apply to the case of the desert traveller who, parched with thirst, actually does find foul, brackish water delicious, rather than to the man who mistakenly expects to find it so. For it is the former, rather than the latter, who is actually experiencing something, and if misexperience is supposed to provide the diagnosis of what goes wrong in this type of situation, then that should be the paradigm case.

A.2.5. Since Plato does talk (41d1–3) of 'pleasures and pains and peceptions of them', we should expect him to describe this type of case as a case of false pleasure deriving from false perception, to contrast with the former type, where false pleasure supposedly derives from false belief. In fact he does not say specifically what is false in this case, which has misled some commentators into supposing that he means that that part of the exaggerated pleasure which exceeds the reality (described at 42b9–c1) as 'apparent but not real' is false. But Gosling ((5), p. 220) points out that at c1–3 he distinguishes from the 'apparent' future pleasure (or pain) the part of the (actual) pleasure (or pain) which is taken 'in' the apparent future pleasure. As the former is unreal, so the latter cannot be called right and true. It seems fairly clear that in denying it the description 'true', Plato implies that it merits the description 'false'. If this is correct, then the move from 'what one takes pleasure in is unreal' to 'the pleasure that one takes in it is false' is once again undefended (see above, A.1.18).

A.2.6. But there is a further complication, in that at 41e9–42a4 it is agreed that, just as variations in the distance of perceived objects give rise to false *judgements* about relative sizes, the same thing happens in cases of pleasure and pain. Hence, whereas in the previous section false opinions gave rise to false pleasures, here we have the opposite situation (a5–9); that is, in this case false pleasures give rise to false opinions (this conclusion is not explicitly drawn, but is implicit in the structure of the argument). Plato must then suppose that anticipatory pleasure arising from over-estimation of anticipated pleasure does not already involve the judgement that the pleasure will be greater than it will be in fact; otherwise the pleasure could not cause that false judgement. But this is incoherent, since the over-estimation of the pleasure is itself the false judgement of the size of the pleasure: hence pleasure in that over-estimation cannot give rise to the false judgement. Plato perhaps means to say that, as in the case of actual perception, viewing some future pleasures in non-ideal conditions produces false anticipations, i.e. false pleasures (which re-introduces the difficulties encountered in section (1) on how he sees the relation between false anticipations and false pleasures). But he seems to confuse that with the incoherent view that in these cases non-ideal perceptual conditions produce false pleasures, which in turn produce false judgements. He may perhaps at this point be thinking of false pleasures as pictures *lacking* propositional content, which then cause propositional judgements. But this is not only difficult to understand (since the sort of representational pictures of which Plato is thinking must have propositional content, in so far as they are representational), but inconsistent with the treatment of imaginative pictures in the first section, where the argument turned on the attribution to those pictures of truth and falsehood, which presuppose propositional content.

A.2.7. Consistency would be preserved if he thought of the pictures as having propositional content, but not as involving judgement, in that the content is not affirmed, i.e. one first of all imagines oneself having some pleasure, without yet believing that one will have it, and is then seduced by the attractiveness of the picture into believing that one will have precisely that pleasure. This is not indeed incoherent, but merely psychologically implausible as a general account of the over-estimation of future pleasures.

3. 42c5–44a11: Mistaking a neutral state for pleasure

A.3.1. This third class is said (c5–7) to contain pleasures and pains which 'seem and are false even more than these (others)'. In terms of the previously accepted theory of distress as arising from upsetting of the natural balance of the organism and pleasure from the restoration of the balance, it is agreed that a state in which neither process is taking place is a state which is neutral as to pleasure or pain (c8–e12). Further, the occurrence of these processes themselves is not sufficient for the organism in which they are occurring to feel pleasure or pain; for that to happen the organism must be aware of the processes, but many physical processes occur of which the organism is unaware, e.g. growth. Large changes (i.e. sufficiently large to be perceived) cause pleasure and pains, small and moderate changes cause neither (43a1–c7; cf. 33d). So for both these reasons we must admit the existence of a neutral state (42c8–d6). But people very often say that the pleasantest of all things is to pass one's whole life without distress (d7–8), and say that they believe they are experiencing pleasure (*chairein*) when in fact they are in a neutral state (d10–44a8). But since the neutral state is distinct alike from pleasure and from distress, such people judge falsely about their pleasure (*pseudē . . . doxazousi peri tou chairein*, a9–10). At this point Socrates raises the question whether there are in fact these three distinct states, or merely two. viz. pain and release from pain, of which the latter, being a good, should be called pleasant. The discussion shifts to the details of this question (see 8.1), and the topic of false pleasures is not further pursued, though at 51a3–6 Socrates says that he will accept the view of those who think that some apparent pleasures are not pleasures at all.

A.3.2. The first question about this passage is whether Plato is still dealing just with pleasures of anticipation, or whether he is broadening the discussion to include some cases of mistakenly identifying a present state as one of pleasure. If the former, then this type of false pleasures is simply a limiting case of the second type; having described cases of over-estimation of pleasures, he now describes the limiting case where, having anticipated a certain amount of pleasure, one actually experiences, not a lesser amount, but no pleasure at all. Examples would be the sorts of case mentioned at *Rep.* 583d, of people in various kinds of distress (e.g. sickness) who think that nothing could be pleasanter than being free of their distress. But immediately it is clear that the anticipation model, as described in 41a–42c, fits those cases very awkwardly: for on that model the mistaken anticipation of pleasure, instead of a neutral state, being an extreme case of misanticipation, ought to produce extreme disappointment. One hasn't just got less pleasure than one anticipated, one has no pleasure at all. But it is clear, not merely that the experience of people who recover from illness etc. is not (or at least not always) like that, but that Plato sees that it is not. At *Rep.* 583c10–d1, he observes that sick people say that nothing is pleasanter than being well, but that they did not appreciate before they were ill, how pleasant it is. He is plainly not implying that, as soon as they recover, they will once again recognize that being healthy is not in fact pleasant, but neutral; their point is that you don't appreciate good health properly until you've been ill. That is to say, we must suppose that, when they are back in health, they will go on saying how pleasant it is to be well:

that is, on Plato's view they will mistake the neutral state for pleasure not just in anticipation but when they are actually in it. In two places in *Republic* IX Plato says explicitly that this mistake is made, whether by people who find it unpleasant when a pleasure stops (583e1–2), or by people who find it pleasant when distress stops (585a2–3), e.g. the man who banged his head against the wall because it was so nice when he stopped. It seems plausible, then, that this wider range of cases is referred to in the *Philebus* passage also. Kenny ((1), p. 45) suggests that this conclusion is clearly established by 44a4–5 'Don't they (i.e. people) also think that they are experiencing pleasure at that time when they are not in distress' (*poteron . . . kai chairein oiontai tote hotan mē lupōntai*). But that particular sentence is ambiguous, due to the ambiguous scope of 'at that time': it could mean either 'At the time when they are not in distress, at that time they think they are experiencing pleasure' (specifically a mistake about *present* pleasure) or 'They think that they experience pleasure at a certain time, when in fact they are merely not distressed at that time', a formula which applies alike to anticipation and to judgements about present pleasure. It seems best to say that the fact that this sentence is ambiguous, together with the resemblance to the passages in *Rep.* IX, indicates that Plato is not making a further point specifically about anticipatory pleasures, but is now describing what he regards as an error common to anticipation and to assessment of one's present condition.

A.3.3. In fact the only error which is involved in the description of the situation is one committed by Plato himself, rather than by those whom he is describing. For Plato overlooks the fact that it is possible to be pleased that one is no longer suffering distress, and even to enjoy freedom from distress. The man who banged his head against the wall because it was so nice when he stopped may have been imprudent, but he did not in any way misdescribe the aim of his activity. It is indeed a mistake to describe as pleasant a state which is neither pleasant or unpleasant, but the invalids and others whom Plato describes do not make that mistake; they expect to find, and do find, a certain state enjoyable *just because* it is a state of freedom from distress. There is no misidentification involved here, any more than there is a mistake involved in finding a cool shady room pleasant just by contrast with the heat and glare outside.

A.3.4. This account of the invalid's enjoyments is indeed inconsistent with any general account of pleasure as consisting in the (perceived) filling-up of deficiencies. For what the invalids enjoy is not any (perceived) process of restoration, but the state of having been restored, i.e. of not having some deficiencies any longer. Thus they provide further evidence of the inadequacy of the general account, to add to the others (pleasures of anticipation, pleasure in colours, smells, etc.) which Plato cites in this dialogue (cf. 7.3). Plato has used a type of case to support the false thesis that certain pleasures are false, when in fact that type of case supports the true thesis that a certain account of pleasure is false.

A.3.5. In this passage, too, it is unclear just what Plato thinks he shows to be false. At the outset (42c5–7) he says that he will describe another kind of false pleasures and pains, while in conclusion (44a9–10) he says that those who mistake the neutral state for pleasure judge falsely about pleasures. The distinction between false judgement and false pleasure, so strongly emphasized in the first argument, is not mentioned, and we are left to speculate on the justification of the move from '*A* judges falsely about pleasure' to '*A* has false pleasures'. Once again, the notion of unreal pleasure may be used to bridge the gap. We saw that at 51a Plato appeals to the experts, who believe that all pleasures (or all bodily pleasures) are flights from or cessation of pain, as showing that some pleasures seem to be such, but are not really so at all (*hēdonas einai dokousas, ousas d' oudamōs*). This fits well Plato's description of the invalids etc., to whom states which are not pleasures, but states of relief from pain, seem to be pleasures. So the pleasures in question are unreal, and, as at the end of our discussion of the first section (A.1.18), we are left wondering how clear Plato was as to the distinction between the unreality (as a pleasure) of a bogus pleasure, and the falsity of the judgement that the bogus pleasure is a real pleasure.

4. Conclusion

A.4.1. Plato's treatment of false pleasures is, then, a failure. The types of error which he singles out in his first two sections are adequately accounted for as cases of false anticipation, while the third section does not describe any error at all. Nowhere does he provide an adequate justification of the attribution of falsehood to pleasure, as distinct from its attribution to belief. This failure arises partly from his failure to clarify the relation between anticipatory pleasure and belief, and partly from his failure to make a clear distinction between truth and reality. Nonetheless, his discussion, especially that of the first section, has great value in providing a starting-point for the investigation of the role which belief plays in enjoyment and in other aspects of pleasure.

A.4.2. There is, finally, the question of what importance Plato attached to the thesis that pleasures can be false. Here it seems that Plato's tendency to conflate the notions of truth and reality, referred to at several points in this discussion, affects the direction of his treatment of the topic as a whole. For the whole long discussion of false pleasure is part of a classification of kinds of pleasure, whose ultimate aim is to isolate, as sole candidates for inclusion in the good life, a class of unqualified or totally genuine pleasures (52d–53c, 61d ff.). To quote Gosling ((5), p. 212)

The basic interest would be in isolating examples of things called pleasure or knowledge to which the descriptions could be applied without demur, i.e. of which they were strictly true. Demur is justified either by clear absence of pleasure/knowledge, or by the presence of their opposites: distress/ignorance. Thus, all 'mixed' pleasures, as well as neutral states, are 'false'.

But while false pleasures of the third type are ruled out by the first criterion, as not really pleasures at all, and those of the second type are a sort of mixed pleasures, since they are pleasures in anticipation exaggerated by current distress, and therefore not really pleasures by the second criterion, neither criterion rules out the first type of false pleasures. For the bad man does not mistake any neutral state for the state of anticipatory pleasure, nor does present distress in any way contribute to that pleasure, at least as the case is described at 40a–b. Plato then needs independent grounds for denying such pleasures a place in the good life; he could argue that any sort of involvement with falsehood is a debasement of the highest and most divine part of the soul, or, alternatively or in addition, that it can be no part of a sensible ideal of life to indulge oneself in groundless expectations. But he does not provide these arguments. Rather the treatment of the first type of false pleasure is, like that of the second and third types, subordinated to the quest for genuine pleasures in such a way as to suggest that Plato did not fully appreciate the significance of his own distinction between truth, as opposed to falsity, and reality, as opposed to unreality.

Appendix B: The *Magna Moralia*

B.0.1. Some remarks should be made about the treatment of pleasure in a strange ethical work, traditionally included in the Aristotelian corpus, called the *Magna Moralia*. The general problems of this work are beyond the scope of this book.[1] It roughly follows the development of the *Nicomachean Ethics* as regards topics treated, so long as we take the disputed books V–VII to belong to the *Nicomachean Ethics*, but it stops after the discussion of friendship. Alternatively, if the disputed books are allotted to the *Eudemian Ethics*, it roughly follows that book. It was almost certainly composed in the third century BC. What concerns us here is the treatment of pleasure and its likely relationship to the treatments in Books VII and X of the *Ethics*. Clearly some of what we say will have to be provisional on wider theses about the work as a whole.

1. Sketch and comparison with the *Nicomachean Ethics*

B.1.1. As in Book VII of the *Ethics* the treatment of pleasure follows that of self-control and develops as follows:

1204a19–30   Pleasure is to be discussed because
     (i) all think either
     (*a*) that pleasure is related to 'happiness' or, if disgusted by pleasure
     (*b*) that at least absence of pain is necessary, which is close to pleasure;
     (ii) 'happiness' is the exercise of virtue, which is concerned with pleasure and pain.

a31–b3   Some think pleasure is no part of the good because
     (i) pleasure is a becoming;

---

[1] See Allan; Dirlmeier; Cooper (1); Rowe (2); Kenny (4), Ch. 9.

(ii) there are some bad pleasures and the good is never to be found in badness;

(iii) pleasure is found alike in the good and the bad, in wild beasts and tame, but good is unmixed with bad;

(iv) pleasure is not the best thing, but the good is;

(v) pleasure is a hindrance to right action.

1204b4–1205a7	(A) Pleasure and becoming (Objection (i)).
1204b4–20	(i) Not all pleasures are becomings, e.g. thought, smell, for these are not the effects of want or excess, which are pains. So these pleasures may be good.
b21–37	(ii) No pleasure is a becoming. Pleasure ensues on the righting of a defect, but there is a part of the soul with which we experience pleasure and it is the motion or actualization of this, concomitant with the remedy, that is pleasure. Since the righting is visible, but the part of the soul not, people take the first to be the pleasure.
b38–1205a7	(iii) Pleasure is not a perceived restoration to a normal state, for there are pleasures without such restoration. *Therefore*: pleasure may be a good.
1205a8–b12	(B) Some pleasures are not good (Objection (ii).
1205a8–16	(i) 'Good' is predicated in all the categories; every actualization of good is attended with pleasure, so pleasure will also be good — indeed every pleasure will be good.
a16–25	(ii) Pleasures differ in kind: those of drunkenness and sex do not dispose one in the same way. [So that all are bad does not follow?]
a26–b12	(iii) That some pleasures are bad shows nothing: so are some natures (beetles) and

sciences (mechanical), but one judges the quality of *X* from its successes, not its failures. Similarly pleasure is good in kind, though some are bad since creatures differ (man is good, wolves are bad), and since, if pleasure is a restoration of nature, bad natures will have bad pleasures.

b13–27   Summing up. The opposition view is based on ignorance. They only know bodily pleasures and seeing these to be processes of coming-to-be and/or not good they infer to all pleasures. Pleasures of a normal state are superior to those of restoration.

1205b28–37.   (C) That pleasure is common to all (Objection (iii)).
This might be an objection in the eyes of an ambitious person; but that all pursue pleasure shows it to be good.

1206a1–25   (D) Pleasure is a hindrance (Objection (v)).
Pleasure intensifies the activity enjoyed, and stimulates the virtuous to virtue. The virtuous do not act in distress — that is a proof of compulsion. *But* virtuous acts must be done with either distress or pleasure, since there is no middle condition. (So: since not with distress, with pleasure.)

1206a26–30   (E) That there is no skill of pleasure.
Cookery is one, and sciences which do not have pleasure as an end still have pleasure in the end.

1206a31–5   (F) That pleasure is not the best thing (Objection (iv)).
Parity of argument would show the virtues not to be good. So pleasure may still be good.

B.1.2. It is instructive to compare this outline with those of Books VII and X of the *Ethics*. There is a general similarity of structure; an introduction giving reasons for discussing; an outline of objections to the thesis to be held; and a refutation of the objections. The main difference at the general level is that there is no account of the nature of pleasure to establish the thesis and underpin the refutations. For the rest, the dissimilarities are most noticeable, as can be brought out by the comparison set out in Table I on p. 460.

B.1.3. There is clearly more overlap with Book VII than with Book X, but still, three Book VII objections are ignored (as against seven from Book X), and there are two objections peculiar to the *Magna Moralia*. One would expect counters to its special objections to be peculiar to the *Magna Moralia*, but there are also interesting differences in the counters to the common objections (see Table II, p. 461).

B.1.4. Here the rejection of the view that pleasure is a *genesis* shows overlap with both books of the *Nicomachean Ethics*, but for the rest it is the lack of relationship with either that is more noticeable. Of course the whole has an Aristotelian air to it; there is talk of 'good' being predicated in all the categories, and there is the terminology of *energeia*. Yet it would be hard to hold that the treatment of pleasure is based on either of the other works. It could certainly hardly be following Book X: there is no trace of a Plato/Eudoxus opposition, and most of the Book X objections to saying pleasure is a/the good are missing. As to Book VII, not only are three of the Book VII objections missing, the main thesis seems noticeably different: the *Magna Moralia* aims no higher than to show that pleasures may be good. Finally not only are some counters to objections peculiar to the *Magna Moralia*, so also are some of the objections countered. At the risk of some slight repetition we shall now consider in more detail first some of the objections shared with the *Nicomachean Ethics* and the treatment of them, and then the objections found only in the *Magna Moralia*. This will help bring out the special features of this work.

2. Objections common to
the *Magna Moralia* and the *Nicomachean Ethics*

B.2.1. *Objection* (i): *Pleasure is a genesis*. The treatment of this objection is curious. It falls into three sections. In the first the counter is made that not every pleasure is a *genesis*; in the second that none is, since the *genesis* is only the occasion for the soul to take pleasure; in the third that pleasure is not a perceived restoration since there are pleasures where there is no restoration because no lack. Except for the intrusion of the word 'perceived' there is an air of repetition about the first and third points. On close inspection, however, the first and second points recall Book X, the third Book VII. In Book X (1173b13 ff.) Aristotle explains the view as arising from pleasure and pains related to nourishment; lacking it, and so being distressed, we take pleasure in the replenishment, but pleasures of learning, smell, hearing, vision, as well as memories and hopes involve no lack or distress. In the *Magna Moralia* too we get (1204b4 ff.) the same explanation of why pleasures of eating and drinking are held to be becomings, with a similar list of counter-examples: hearing, sight, and smell, with thought (doing duty for learning, memory, and hope), are all said not to be becomings because not preceded by distress.

B.2.2. The second counter also recalls Book X. There (1173b4–13) Aristotle argues that if pleasure were a *genesis*, since it is a *physical genesis* or restoration, the body would do the enjoying, whereas the fact is simply that when the restoration occurs someone takes pleasure. In the *Magna Moralia* we get a similar point, differently made. It is simply asserted that the opposition make their mistake because pleasure accompanies the observable restoration. In fact, however, the actualization of a part of the soul on the occasion of the restoration is that whereby we take pleasure. Now this is not so close to Book X as the previous point. There is no attempted reduction of the opposition. On the other hand some play is made of the opposition mistaking the restoration, which they can observe, for the unobservable reality — a point of which there is no sign in Book X. So the point might simply be elaborated from elsewhere, e.g. the *Philebus*, which might explain the soul coming in for

Table I

	Book VII	Book X	Magna Moralia
Introduction:	The philosopher must discuss pleasure, because he constructs the end.	Pleasure is important because of its role in education.	—
Thesis	Some pleasure is the good.	Either pleasure is the good, or pleasure is hard to distinguish from the good.	Pleasure (some pleasure) is *a* good
Objections:	Pleasure is a perceived *genesis*. The temperate flee pleasure. The wise pursue absence of pain. Pleasure hinders thought.	Pleasure hinders 'activity'.	Pleasure is a perceived restoration. Pleasure is a hindrance to right action.
	There is no skill of pleasure. Children and animals pursue pleasure. Some pleasures are base.	Some pleasures are shameful.	There is no skill of pleasure.
	Pleasure is a *genesis*. (Pain has two opposites)	Pleasure is a *genesis*/movement Pain has two opposites. Intelligence, added to pleasure, makes it better. It is false that what all desire is the good. Pleasure is not a quality. Pleasure is indeterminate. Friends differ from flatterers in aiming at good, not pleasure. Some things we should want even without pleasure.	Some pleasures are disreputable/inferior Pleasure is a *genesis*.

461

Table II

Counters:

Pleasure not a perceived *genesis* since some pleasures related to no *genesis*. Explanation of perceived *genesis* view.	Pleasure not a *genesis*: (i) *genesis* only the occasion for someone to have pleasure; (ii) not all pleasures becomings e.g. thought, smell where there is no prior lack.	Pleasure not a perceived *genesis* for Book VII reasons. The soul experiences pleasure on the righting of a defect; some pleasures (thought, smell) occur without prior lack.
		'Good' is predicated in all the categories, and every actualization of good accompanied by pleasure. Therefore pleasure also good. Different pleasures dispose in different ways. Some species are bad, and so their pleasures will be bad.
Bad pleasures are only inci-dentally, not naturally, pleasant. Pleasure aids its own activity.	Bad pleasures are only pleasant to things in a bad condition and so are not pleasant *tout court*. Pleasure aids its own activity.	Pleasure aids its own activity. Further: the virtuous do not act in distress, because they act freely; and if not in distress then with pleasure. Therefore pleasure cannot be a hindrance.

Aristotle's 'someone'. The general point, however, that replenishments are physical, whereas pleasure is taken by a person or soul, is shared with Book X, and is at least not a point made in this context in Book VII.

B.2.3. The third counter, on the other hand, addresses itself to the Book VII opposition, that pleasure is a perceived restoration. The account of the relation of restoration to lack and pain is recalled (it is also in Book VII 1152b33 ff.) and the Book VII point made that there are pleasures without restoration. This suggests that perhaps the author had both the Book VII and the Book X treatments in mind and either realized that there were two different *genesis* views, or was uneasily unsure that there were not. The precise degree of relation to these two books is, however, hard to determine. This is most obvious with regard to the second point. For here there are two oddities. First, there is the claim that for any restoration there is a part of the soul that is actualized on the occasion of a (pleasant) restoration. There is no source for this in Book X, but it might be an echo of Book VII 1152b33–1153a2. There Aristotle has an obscure explanation of pleasures of restoration. He says either (*a*) that in the case of desires the actualization is of the defective state of nature, or (*b*) that in this case (of restoration) the actualization is of the desires of the defective state or nature. In either case the claim could be glossed as saying that for any instance of enjoyed restoration there is some element of the *psuchē* that is actualized, and it is this (unobserved) actualization, not the (observed) restoration, that constitutes the pleasure. But if the view is an echo of Book VII, it remains that there the point is made as part of an argument that the pleasures of restoration are only 'accidentally' pleasures, whereas in the *Magna Moralia* it is part of an argument against identifying the pleasure with the restoration, and this *aim* more directly recalls Book X. Clearly there is no direct 'copying' of either book.

B.2.4. The second oddity is the charge that the opposition are concentrating on what is observable, and fail to realize the role of the relevant part of the soul because they cannot see it. It is like supposing that a man can be equated with his body because that is visible, while the soul is not — but souls exist. This is not a point which has any ancestry in either of the *Nicomachean Ethics* passages.

B.2.5. These two oddities, together with the point that both Book VII and Book X arguments seem to have some influence, make it clear that the connection is not in either case as close either as copying or as note-taking.

B.2.6. *Objection* (ii): *Some pleasures are bad.* (*a*) The first counter to this objection is peculiar to the *Magna Moralia*, and is, indeed, simply peculiar. The other counters argue that it does not follow from the premiss that some pleasures are bad that none is good. Since they are rejections of a hypothetical, they would be quite consistent with the position that all pleasures are good, but in fact the third counter commits the author to the view that some natures/species (e.g. wolves, beetles) are bad, and that the actualizations (=? pleasures) of bad natures will similarly be bad. This first counter seems just to contradict this by claiming that all pleasures will be good. So the first oddity is that this counter introduces an inconsistency with other points made.

B.2.7. The second oddity is that this inconsistency-producing conclusion is not only stronger than what is required, it also fails to follow from the premises. The argument is as follows: 'good' is predicated in all the categories; every actualization of good is attended with pleasure; therefore since pleasure is in all the categories, pleasure is good; since goods and pleasures are in these, and the pleasure that comes from goods is pleasure, every pleasure is good. The most that seems to follow from the given premises is that pleasure will accompany goods — but not that it will only accompany goods; and it is not at all clear why it is supposed that every pleasure is good. The only way to save the argument is to interpret the sentence that the pleasure that comes from the goods is pleasure as saying that they constitute the set of pleasures. Given that what accompanies a good is good (perhaps that the actualization is the pleasure) then the conclusion will follow, but only via a strained interpretation.

B.2.8. The third oddity is the irrelevance of the assertion that 'good' is predicated in all the categories. All that it seems to contribute, in conjunction with the unqualified assertion that every actualization of a good is accompanied by pleasure, is the absurd implication that the e.g. occurrence of good weather for germination must be, or be accompanied by, pleasure. There is no parent for this confused hotchpotch in the *Nicomachean Ethics* and it is hard to imagine what the author thought he was up to. If we take the assertion about actualizations seriously we must conclude that he was quite at sea on the Aristotelian thesis about pleasure as an actualization.

B.2.9. (*b*) The second counter also seems peculiar to the *Magna Moralia*. The argument is that different pleasures dispose one in a different way (contrast those of drink and sex). The point presumably is that while those that dispose one to bad acts will be bad, those that dispose to good acts will be good, and so the existence of bad pleasures will not stop some being good. The *Nicomachean Ethics*' view, that we tend to do what we enjoy and that enjoyment improves and lengthens our indulgence in the activities enjoyed (cf. 1153a 20-3, 1175b13-16), doubtless implies that different pleasures dispose differently. The point is there made, however, in the context of the objection that pleasure is a hindrance to activity. It is not developed or applied, in the manner of the *Magna Moralia*, to the objection that pleasure cannot be a good since some are bad.

B.2.10. (*c*) The third counter is to the effect that nothing follows, from the fact that some pleasures are disreputable, about pleasures in general. After all, some natures and some sciences are bad (disreputable), but one judges the quality of X by reference to successful Xs. There *are* bad pleasures, since there are bad natures, but pleasure is good in kind.

B.2.11. This might seem to be drawing together two points from Book VII of the *Nicomachean Ethics*, 1153b7-9 and 1154a31-4. But there are differences. The *Magna Moralia* seems to argue that some species are inferior and consequently their pleasures are inferior, but then some species are good and so their pleasures are good. In other words, what seems to be meant by the claim that there are inferior natures is that there are inferior species — and so we get examples such as beetles and wolves. The argument then is that pleasures of inferior species may be inferior, but there are superior species such as man, and their pleasures will be good. As it stands the argument only tells against someone who infers the worthlessness of pleasure from the fact that worthless species indulge in it. This idea seems barely to be suggested by the second passage from Book VII, but the thought might be that some of the pleasures indulged in by humans are activities indulged in by inferior species and so must be inferior pleasures. If so, it is not clearly brought out, though it may be a part of the point of Book VII. Both Book VII and Book X, however, are mainly concerned not with saying that certain pleasures are inferior (*phaulos*) as characterizing inferior species, but with pleasures that are blameworthy, shameful, harmful, and so on (cf. 1152b20-2, 1173b20-30, 1176a10 ff.), and when (e.g. 1148b15 ff.) there is talk of bad (*mochthēros*) natures, it is beastly humans, not normal beasts, that the author had in mind. Further, there is no tendency to suppose that because a pleasure is characteristic of an inferior species, therefore it is blameworthy (the view at *EN* 1154a30 ff. is attributed to others — it is not Aristotle's); after all, eating and drinking are such, but are perfectly reputable. The pleasures which are base or blameworthy are disposed of as either, in Book VII terminology, not naturally but only 'accidentally' pleasant, or, in the Book X terminology as only pleasant to someone in a bad condition and not pleasant *tout court*. 'Bad natures' are corrupt members of species, not inferior species, and what is pleasant to them is not (really) pleasant. Interestingly, this style of reaction is totally absent from the *Magna Moralia* passage. At 1205b21 ff. we are told that pleasures of the natural state are *better* than those of restoration, but there is no hint that the latter are not really pleasures. This may be an improvement, but the point is that it is a difference.

B.2.12. *Objection* (v): *Pleasure is a hindrance.* While the answer to this has something in common with the *Nicomachean Ethics* treatments, it has a strange added argument: that the virtuous do not act with distress — which is a proof of compulsion (and, presumably, good acts are not done under compulsion) — and therefore must act with pleasure since there is no third possibility. There are two strange features of this argument: first, the idea that a person who acts in distress acts under compulsion, and secondly the idea that there is no third option between pleasure and pain.

B.2.13. As to the first, there is, in the *Nicomachean Ethics*, a view that 'involuntary' acts done through ignorance are accompanied by distress (1110b18–22), but nowhere is the view expressed that distress shows compulsion. Indeed, it is explicitly recognized of a brave man (1117b9 ff. and cf. *EE* 1229b30 ff.) that he will be distressed at the prospect of death but will still (freely) choose the noble course, and this will, if anything, underline his courage. It is true that Aristotle is here trying to defend his thesis that nevertheless the virtuous man takes pleasure in his virtue, but he does not defend it at the cost of claiming that he enjoys the performance of the deed which shows him brave (for further discussion cf. 14.9.10–15).

B.2.14. As to the second, the *Magna Moralia* argument is as follows: it is impossible to act virtuously without either pleasure or distress as there is nothing in between. For virtue occurs in passion, and passion in pleasure or distress, and there is no state between. But a good man cannot act in distress, and therefore must act with pleasure.

B.2.15. In *EN* 1106b13 ff. (and cf. *EE* 1221b33 ff.) Aristotle certainly says that virtue (that is, in context, behavioural virtue) is concerned with pleasure and pain. The argument is: the virtues are concerned with actions and passions, and pleasure and distress follow every passion and every action, therefore the vitues are concerned with pleasure and distress. If we take the statement strictly as that every individual action or passion is followed by pleasure or distress, then clearly in the practical field there is no option but one or other. But two points should be made: first the remark need only mean that there is pleasure or pain related to every *type* of action or passion, and allow that with actions, at least, while there are, say, both pleasant and painful instances of walking there are also others which are neither pleasant nor painful. This would allow the possibility that the actions of a virtuous man are neither pleasant nor painful, and require special argument for the thesis that in fact a good man takes pleasure in his virtue. In fact Aristotle never uses a version of the 'no middle state' argument, but relies rather on the thesis that what people love is pleasant to them. Not only would this be a more sensible position, but one would expect Aristotle's view to yield a spectrum from distress through neutrality to pleasure, without any sudden break. The height of pleasure is achieved by a perfect subject operating in relation to a perfect object. This suggests that a humdrum eye looking at a humdrum picture might not yield either distress or pleasure. On the other hand, seeing, as a type of activity, can be either pleasurable or painful, and has its specific pleasures and distresses.

B.2.16. Secondly, Aristotle's remark only covers the subject matter of behavioural virtue. It is quite possible that most acts of thought, which are not concerned with action (*praxis*) or passion (*pathos*), are neutral with regard to pleasure or pain. In particular, they will not be concerned with passion (*pathos*), but the *Magna Moralia* argument baldly asserts that all virtue is concerned with *pathos*. The options are as follows:

(i) When the *Magna Moralia* talks of virtue, only behavioural virtue (*ēthikē aretē*) is meant. But since (1197b3 ff.) philosophy is not only a virtue, but one superior to practical virtues, the position will be too weak for the conclusion. We should have no proof that the highest virtue was pleasant, nor that the pleasures of the inferior virtues did not interfere with its exercise.

(ii) By virtue, the whole of virtue is meant. In this case we should have the very un-Aristotelian view that philosophy, along with the rest, was concerned with passions, since virtue's involvement with passion is one of the grounds for the conclusion that it involves pleasure.

B.2.17. This does not, of course show that the *Nicomachean Ethics* is not an influence, only that the argument used is not simply taken over from that work, but is at best a confused adaptation of points made there. It is of interest, however, in that it sounds like some relation of the Epicurean equation of pleasure with absence of pain.

3. Two objections peculiar to the *Magna Moralia*

B.3.1. We now turn to the two objections found in the *Magna Moralia* but not in the *Nicomachean Ethics*.

B.3.2. *Objection* (iii): This objection is that pleasure is shared by inferior and superior alike, but the good is not a common possession and has no commerce with the disreputable. As presented at 1204a38 ff. this objection recalls *Gorg.* 496-8, but nothing in the *Nicomachean Ethics*. The response to it at 1205b29 ff., however, suggests that it is not precisely the *Gorgias* point. For there Socrates argues that the vicious experience pleasure equally with the virtuous, so if a good life is one whose subject is in posession of the good, and pleasure is the good, a vicious life will be as good as a virtuous one. In the *Magna Moralia* the opposition seems rather to be holding that if pleasure is the good, then the good will not be anything exceptional. They would seem to be viewing virtue and the good life as something only attained by outstanding people and perhaps having to be worked for. The objection to pleasure is not that the wicked enjoy it, but that any mediocre Tom, Dick, or Harry enjoys it. This recalls a tradition going back at least to Prodicus' story about Heracles (cf. 1.1.3, 1.1.5). It is, however, difficult to show what precisely the background to the objection is. After all, anyone reading Plato or Aristotle would get the impression that a good life is hard to come by, and so might well think pleasure an odd candidate.

B.3.3. The response to the objection is itself slightly surprising, in that it just appeals to the Eudoxan thesis used by Aristotle, that if everything desires pleasure then pleasure is good. It is surprising in that it would be so obviously unconvincing to the opposition. Aristotle, of course, could have replied that the pleasures which are good are 'real' pleasures, that these just are the pleasures of a person in a good condition, that the condition is not shared by many, and so neither are the pleasures that are good. But as has been remarked, the author of the *Magna Moralia* either has not grasped or does not accept the thesis on real pleasures, and so cannot make that move to 'accept the truth' in his opponents' position.

B.3.4. *Objection* (iv). This objection claims that pleasure is not good because it is not the best. The reply is that by parity of argument courage would not be good, because it is not the best thing.

B.3.5. The obvious puzzle about this objection is how anyone could be so crass as to make it; and a closer look at the text raises the suspicion that we have here a case of *ignoratio elenchi*. For when the objection is introduced at 1204b1–2 it reads: 'fourthly, that pleasure is not the best, but the good is the best.' A possible, but unlikely translation, 'but what is good is best of all things' is sometimes adopted, presumably in order to make the reply relevant; and it might, perhaps, reflect the way the author takes the objection. One suspects, however, that the thesis was in fact that pleasure cannot be the good and was perhaps relying on the argument found in the *Philebus* that since if knowledge is added to pleasure the result is better, pleasure cannot be *the* good. Aristotle is, of course, aware of this position, but one could only refute it by rejecting the premiss and so showing that pleasure is the best thing of all. This the *Magna Moralia* never attempts.

B.3.6. In short, it is difficult to be sure whether we have here a report of a position found in Aristotle and misunderstood by the author of the *Magna Moralia*, or an accurate report of a quite inept objection.

4. Conclusion

B.4.1. To sum up: the *Magna Moralia* sets up the disputes differently; shows no sign of closely following the order of either book of the *Nicomachean Ethics*; shows some influence of each, but especially Book VII; omits many of the arguments and objections of those books; contains objections and arguments peculiar to itself; and contains some remarks quite out of tune with, if not inconsistent with, the Aristotelian works. It also argues for a different conclusion, and contains no explicit account of what pleasure is.

B.4.2. In view of all this it is intriguing to speculate on the provenance of the *Magna Moralia* (or at least this section). If, as some have thought, it was written by Aristotle, he was either very young or very old indeed. For Aristotelian doctrine would have to be either hardly developed or no longer grasped. If young, then he had failed to appreciate the arguments against Eudoxus, and only came to appreciate them in the *Nicomachean Ethics* X era; but then one wonders why at that stage he ignored those who thought pleasure was a perceived process. If old, then it is odd that his enemies left no rumour of such debilitating senescence.

B.4.3. Yet clearly there is Aristotelian influence. The argument that 'good' is predicated in all the categories, that the actualization of a good is accompanied by pleasure, and in general the terminology of 'actualization' in relation to pleasure, all smell of Aristotle and not of the earliest Aristotle (see 11.1). Then there are the elements shared with Books VII and X. Such connections are even more obvious if we consider the whole work. As noted above, however, there are some un-Aristotelian features, and an apparent inability to grasp Aristotelian ones, an omission of some characteristic Aristotelian positions and the adoption of arguments not found elsewhere. None of this, of course, would stop it being an emanation from Aristotelian circles. It is quite unrealistic to suppose that (even?) philosophers in the same department either read all each other's writings, hear all each other's lectures, understand or agree with all they read or hear, or share the same assessment of the importance of different points. There are always those who fail to understand the current jargon or to see the importance of various distinctions or arguments, but still produce work festooned with reminders of better intellects. So it is quite possible that the author was a follower of Aristotle.

B.4.4. The fact remains that the work is disappointing for present purposes. One might perhaps hold that at least the author of the *Magna Moralia* held the positions expounded there, but the state of confusion is such as to leave one in doubt, where they depart from Aristotle, whether even he had any clear idea what those views were. For the rest we have evidence for the existence of a set of objectors who thought the good should be a rare attainment, without any precise indication of the form or provenance of the view; and just possibly for the existence of some incompetents who argued that if pleasure is not the best thing it cannot be good. The author himself also seems to accept in effect that a good life without distress must be pleasant. One point of interest in considering Epicurus is that the author still thinks it is worthwhile to refute those who hold that pleasure is a form of motion or *genesis*.

Bibliography

Ackrill, J. L., (1) 'Aristotle's Distinction between *Energeia* and *Kinesis*', in *New Essays on Plato and Aristotle*, ed. Renford Bambrough, London, 1963, 121–41.

—— (2) *Aristotle's Ethics*, London, 1973.

Adam, J. and Adam, A. M., *Platonis Protagoras*, 2nd. ed., Cambridge, 1905.

Allan, D. J., '*Magna Moralia* and *Nicomachean Ethics*', *JHS* lxxvii (1957), 7–11.

Annas, Julia, 'Aristotle on Pleasure and Goodness', in *Essays on Aristotle's Ethics*, ed. A. O. Rorty, Berkeley, Los Angeles and London, 1980, 285–99.

Bailey, Cyril, (1) *The Greek Atomists and Epicurus*, Oxford, 1928.

—— (2) *Titi Lucreti Cari De Rerum Natura Libri Sex*, edited with Prolegomena etc., Oxford, 1947.

Bennett, Jonathan, 'Substance, Reality and Primary Qualities', *APQ* ii (1965), 1–18.

Bignone, E., *L'Aristotele perduto e la formazione filosofica di Epicuro*, Florence, 1936.

Bollack, Jean, *Epicure, La Pensée du Plaisir*, Paris, 1975.

Boyancé, P., *Lucrèce et l'épicurisme*, Paris, 1963.

Brandt, Reinhard, 'Wahre and Falsche Affekte im platonischen Philebus', *AGPh* lix (1977), 1–18.

Burnyeat, M. F., (1) 'The Upside-down Back-to-front Sceptic of Lucretius IV 472', *Philologus* cii (1978), 197–206.

—— (2) 'Tranquillity without a Stop: Timon Frag. 68', *CQ* xxx (1980), 86–93.

Bury, R. G., *The Philebus of Plato*, Cambridge, 1897.

Cahn, Stephen M., 'A Puzzle Concerning the *Meno* and the *Protagoras*', *JHP* xi (1973), 535–7.

Cooper, John M., (1) 'The *Magna Moralia* and Aristotle's Moral Philosophy', *AJP* xciv (1973), 327–49.

—— (2) *Reason and Human Good in Aristotle*, Cambridge, Mass. and London, 1975.

Cross, R. C. and Woozley, A. D., *Plato's Republic: A Philosophical Commentary*, London, 1964.

de Vogel, C. J., *Greek Philosophy* (3 vols.), Leiden, 1957.

De Witt, N. W., *Epicurus and his Philosophy*, Minneapolis, 1954.

Diano, C., (1) 'Note epicuree', *Sitzungsberichte der Kön. Akad. zu Berlin* xii (1935), 61–86, 237–89.

—— (2) 'Questioni epicuree', *Rendiconti dell' Accad. dei Lincei* xii (1936), 819–95.

—— (3) 'La psicologia d'Epicuro e la teoria delle passioni', *Giornale*

Critico della Filosofia Italiana xx (1939), 105–45; xxi (1940), 151–65; xxii (1941), 5–34; xxiii (1942), 5–49, 121–50.

Dirlmeier, F., *Aristoteles, Magna Moralia*, Berlin, 1968.

Duncan, Roger, 'Courage in Plato's Protagoras', *Phron.* xxiii (1978), 216–28.

Düring, Ingemar, (1) *Aristotle's Protrepticus, An Attempt at Reconstruction*, Goteborg, 1961.

—— (2) *Aristoteles, Darstellung und Interpretation seines Denkens*, Heidelberg, 1966.

Dybikowski, James C., (1) 'Mixed and False Pleasures in the *Philebus*: A Reply', *PQ* xx (1970), 244–7.

—— (2) 'False Pleasure and the *Philebus*', *Phron.* xv (1970), 147–65.

—— (3) Review of Gosling (5), *Mind* lxxxvi (1977), 446–8.

Dyson, M., 'Knowledge and Hedonism in Plato's *Protagoras*', *JHS* xcvi (1976), 32–45.

Festugière, A. -J., *Aristote, Le Plaisir*, Paris, 1946.

Gallop, David, *Plato, Phaedo*, Oxford, 1975.

Gauthier, R. A. and Jolif, J. Y., *L'Éthique à Nicomaque* (2 vols. in 3 parts), Louvain and Paris, 1958 and 1959.

Gooch, Paul W., 'The Relation between Wisdom and Virtue in *Phaedo* 69a–c3', *JHP* xii (1974), 153–9.

Gosling, J. C. B., (1) 'False Pleasures: *Philebus* 35c–41b', *Phron.* iv (1959), 44–54.

—— (2) 'Father Kenny on False Pleasures', *Phron.* vi (1961), 41–5.

—— (3) *Pleasure and Desire: The Case for Hedonism Reviewed*, Oxford, 1969.

—— (4) 'More Aristotelian Pleasures', *PAS* lxxiv (1973–4), 15–34.

—— (5) *Plato, Philebus*, Oxford 1975.

Graham, Daniel W., 'States and Performances: Aristotle's Test', *PQ* xxx (1980), 117–30.

Grant, Sir Alexander, *The Ethics of Aristotle illustrated with Essays and Notes* (2 vols.), 4th. (revised) ed., London, 1885.

Guthrie, W. K. C., *A History of Greek Philosophy*, (6 vols.), Cambridge, 1962–81.

Hamlyn, D. M., *Sensation and Perception*, London, 1961.

Hardie, W. F. R., *Aristotle's Ethical Theory*, 2nd (enlarged) ed., Oxford, 1980.

Haynes, R. P., 'The Theory of Pleasure of the Old Stoa', *AJP* lxxxiii (1962), 412–19.

Irwin, Terence, (1) *Plato's Moral Theory: The Early and Middle Dialogues*, Oxford, 1977.

—— (2) *Plato, Gorgias*, Oxford, 1979.

Joachim, H. H., *Aristotle, The Nicomachean Ethics*, ed. D. A. Rees, 2nd. impression, Oxford, 1955.

Kenny, Anthony, (1) 'False Pleasures in the *Philebus*: A reply to Mr Gosling', *Phron.* v (1960), 45–52.

—— (2) *Action, Emotion and Will*, London, 1963.

—— (3) *Will, Freedom and Power*, Oxford, 1975.

—— (4) *The Aristotelian Ethics*, Oxford, 1978.

Kirk, G. S. and Raven, J. E., *The Presocratic Philosophers*, Cambridge, 1957.

Kirwan, Christopher, *Aristotle's Metaphysics, Books* Γ, Δ, E, Oxford, 1971.

Lieberg, Godo, *Die Lehre von der Lust in den Ethiken des Aristoteles*, Munich, 1958.

Lloyd, G. E. R., 'Who is attacked in *On Ancient Medicine?*', *Phron.* viii (1963), 108–26.

Lloyd-Jones, Hugh, *The Justice of Zeus*, Berkeley, Los Angeles, and London, 1971.

Locke, D., 'Reasons, Wants and Causes', *APQ* xi (1974), 169–79.

Long, A. A., (1) 'Aristotle's Legacy to Stoic Ethics', *Bulletin of the Institute of Classical Studies, London University* xv (1968), 72–85.

—— (2) *Hellenistic Philosophy*, London, 1974.

Luce, J. V., '*Phaedo* 69a6–c2', *CQ* xxxviii (1944), 60–4.

Manuwald, Bernd, 'Lust und Tapferkeit: Zum gedanklichen Verhältnis zweier Abschnitte in Platons "Protagoras"', *Phron.* xx (1975), 22–50.

McDowell, John, 'Are Moral Requirements Hypothetical Imperatives?', *PASS* lii (1978), 13–29.

McLaughlin, Andrew, 'A Note on False Pleasures in the *Philebus*', *PQ* xix (1969), 57–61.

Merlan, Philip, *Studies in Epicurus and Aristotle*, Wiesbaden, 1960.

Monan, J. Donald, *Moral Knowledge and its Methodology in Aristotle*, Oxford, 1968.

Murphy, N. R., *The Interpretation of Plato's Republic*, 2nd. impression, Oxford, 1960.

Nagel, Thomas, *The Possibility of Altruism*, Oxford, 1970.

Owen, G. E. L., 'Aristotelian Pleasures, *PAS* lxxii (1971–2), 135–52. Reprinted in *Articles on Aristotle*, eds., Jonathan Barnes, Malcolm Schofield and Richard Sorabji vol. II, London, 1965.

Penner, T. M. I., (1) 'False anticipatory Pleasures: *Philebus* 36a3–41a6', *Phron.* xv (1970), 166–78.

—— (2) 'Verbs and the Identity of Actions', in *Ryle*, eds., Oscar P. Wood and George Pitcher, London and Basingstoke, 1971, 393–460.

Pickering, F. R., 'Aristotle on Walking', *AGPh* lix (1977), 37–43.

Poste, E., *The Philebus of Plato*, Oxford, 1860.

Potts, Timothy C. and Taylor, C. C. W., 'States, Activities and Performances', *PASS* xxxix (1965), 65–102.

Ricken, Friedo, *Der Lustbegriff in der Nikomachischen Ethik des Aristoteles*, Gottingen, 1976.

Rist, J. M., (1) *Stoic Philosophy*, Cambridge, 1969.

—— (2) *Epicurus: An Introduction*, Cambridge, 1972.

—— (3) 'Pleasure 360–300 BC', *Phoenix* xxviii (1974), 167–79.

Ross, Sir David, *Aristotle*, 5th. (revised) ed., London, 1953.

Rowe, C. J., (1) *The Eudemian and Nicomachean Ethics: A study in the Development of Aristotle's Thought*, Cambridge, 1971.

—— (2) 'Reply to John Cooper on the *Magna Moralia*', *AJP* xcvi (1975), 160–72.

Sandbach, F. H., *The Stoics*, London, 1975.

Schofield, Malcolm, 'Who were οἱ δυσχερεῖς in Plato, *Philebus* 44a ff.?', *Museum Helveticum* xxviii (1971), 2–20.

—— Burnyeat, Miles and Barnes, Jonathan, eds., *Doubt and Dogmatism: Studies in Hellenistic Epistemology*, Oxford, 1980.

Sedley, David, 'The Protagonists', in Schofield, Burnyeat and Barnes eds., 1–19.

Spengel, L., 'Uber die unter den Namen des Aristoteles erhaltenen ethischen Schriften', *Abhandlungen der Bayerischen Akad., München*, iii.2 (1841); iii.3 (1843).

Stewart, J.A., *Notes on the Nicomachean Ethics of Aristotle*, Oxford, 1892.

Sullivan, J. P., 'The Hedonism in Plato's *Protagoras*', *Phron.* vi (1961), 10–28.

Taylor, C. C. W., (1) see Potts, T. C. and Taylor, C. C. W.

—— (2) 'Pleasure, Knowledge and Sensation in Democritus', *Phron.* xii (1967), 6–27.

—— (3) *Plato, Protagoras*, Oxford, 1976.

—— (4) '"All Perceptions are True"', in Schofield, Burnyeat and Barnes eds., 105–24.

Tenkku, Jussi, *The Evaluation of Pleasure in Plato's Ethics* (*Acta Philosophica Fennica* xi), Helsinki, 1956.

Thalberg, I., 'False Pleasures', *Journal of Philosophy* lix (1962), 65–74.

Urmson, J. O., 'Aristotle on Pleasure', in *Aristotle: A Collection of Critical Essays*, ed. J. M. E. Moravcsik, Garden City, N. Y., 1967 and London, 1968.

Vlastos, Gregory, (1) 'Ethics and Physics in Democritus', *PR* liv (1945), 578–92; lv (1946), 53–64. Reprinted in *Studies in Presocratic Philosophy*, eds. D. J. Furley and R. E. Allen, London, 1970, vol. II.

—— (2) Socrates on Akrasia', *Phoenix* xxiii (1969), 71–88.

Voigtländer, Hanns-Dieter, *Die Lust und das Gute bei Platon*, Würzburg, 1960.

Webb, Philip, 'The Relative Dating of the Accounts of Pleasure in Aristotle's Ethics', *Phron.* xxii (1977), 235–62.

White, N., *A Companion to Plato's Republic*, Oxford, 1979.

Williams, C. J. F., 'False Pleasures', *Philosophical Studies* xxvi (1974), 295–7.

Zeyl, Donald J., 'Socrates and Hedonism — *Protagoras* 351b–358d', *Phron.* xxv (1980), 250–69.

Index Locorum

References following the semi-colon are to chapter, section, and paragraph number in this book. Chapter numbers are given in **bold** type.

General Index

(For ancient authors not cited here see Index Locorum)

relation to *Phaedo* 5.1.1-3;
'replenishment' and ambiguity
6.8.3-5; skill 4.0.1, 4.2.5, 15.2.
3-4; theory of pleasure 4.2.1-3,
4.3.7, 10.3
hedonism, propounded in *Protagoras* 3.1-2; not refuted in
Gorgias or *Phaedo* 4.2, 5.2; rejected in *Republic* 6.3, 6.4.1-3;
attitude to in *Philebus* 7.3.7;
in *Laws* 9.0.2-4
Hippias Major 'pleasure' idioms in
10.1.1
insatiability and bodily desire/
mixed pleasure, 6.7, 7.4.1
Laches, definition of fear 5.2.2;
early dialogue 3.2.10; expertise
and courage 3.1.6; virtue and
state of personality 4.3.8
Laws, definition of fear 5.2.2;
good life pleasantest 9.0.2;
good man as criterion of pleasure
9.0.2, 9.0.4; pleasure and
thinking one is doing well 9.0.5-
9
Meno, acting against the good 3.1.9;
desire for *eudaimonia* 3.1.11,
3.2.8; distinction of knowledge
and belief 3.2.10; teachability
of virtue 3.2.10
Phaedo, and hedonistic calculation
5.2; and hedonism of *Protagoras*
5.1.2, 5.2; and pleasures of the
soul 5.1.3; being brave through
fear 5.2.1-2, 5.2.4; in Plato's
development 6.1; 'pleasure'
idioms in 10.1.1; pleasure nailing
soul to body 5.1.2; relation to
Gorgias 5.1.1-3
Philebus, anticipatory pleasures a
different class from restorative
7.3.3; degrees of pleasure 7.3.2,
7.7; desire and lack 7.3.5;
developments *vis-à-vis Republic*
7.3-7; falsity A.1; insatiability
and mixed pleasures 7.4.1; kinds
of pleasure 7.2.1. 7.3.2, 8.3.7-9;
lack and desire 7.3.5; life of
pleasure or intellect: false
choice 14.4.1; mixed pleasure
and insatiability 7.4.1; neutral
state 8.1.3-4, 8.2-6, A.3; outline 7.2; 'pleasant'/'good' and

synonymy 10.7.3; pleasure and
perception 10.5; pleasure and
wanting 10.7.4-5; 'pleasure'
idioms in 10.1.1, 10.8.1; pleasure
and the indeterminate (*apeiron*)
category 7.2.1-2, 7.3.2, 11.3.
21-3, 14.3; pleasures of 'spirit'
(*thumos*) 7.3.4, 7.5.1; pure
pleasures (bodily) 7.4.2, (intellectual) 7.5.2; pure pleasures,
no degrees of 7.7.1; replenishment 7.3.3; similarity and
pleasure 7.3, 15.4.1; theory of
pleasure 7.3
pleasure, and perception 10.5;
anticipatory 6.5-7, 7.3.3, A
passim; degrees of 6.3.1, 6.4.3-5,
6.5, 6.7, 6.8.9, 7.3.2, 7.7, 9.0.2;
desire and lack 4.1.1, 4.2.1-3,
6.7.3-8, 6.9.1, 7.3.5; immediate/
long term 3.1.10-12, 3.2.12,
4.2.1-4, 4.3.1; insatiability and
mixed pleasure 6.7, 7.4.1; kinds
of 7.2.1, 7.3.2, 8.3.7-9; physiological model 4.2.1-3, 4.3.7,
6.4.3-7, 6.7.3-9, 6.8-9, 10.3;
'pleasure' idioms 10.1.1; pure
pleasures 7.4.2, 7.5.2, 7.7.1;
real/true pleasure (*see also* pure
pleasures) 6.3.1, 6.4-8, 6.10,
17.1, A.1; 'spirit' (*thumos*)
6.7.8, 6.9.2, 7.3.4, 7.5.1, 17.1.
5-12
Protagoras see also Hedonism, in
Protagoras; a problem in Plato's
development 3.0.3; and apparent
anti-hedonism of earlier dialogues 3.2.5-9; and courage
3.1.9; and justice 3.2.8; and
weakness of will 3.1.6-9; earlier
than *Gorgias* 3.2.5; hedonist
thesis propounded by Socrates
3.1; accepted by Plato 3.2,
consistent with Xenophon 3.2.
3-4; hints of non-seriousness
3.1.6, 3.2.2
Republic, and *Laws* 9.0.6-7; ambiguity of 'replenishment' 6.8;
apparent hedonism 6.3; avoids
need of *Protagoras* calculation
6.4.5-6; cowardice and error
5.2.2; degrees of pleasure and
reality 6.3.1, 6.4.3-5, 6.5, 6.7,
6.8.9, 17.1; extension of